LONG AGO GOD SPOKE

❧ LONG AGO GOD SPOKE TO OUR ANCESTORS
IN MANY AND VARIOUS WAYS BY THE PROPHETS.

HEBREWS 1: 1

Long Ago God Spoke

How Christians May Hear the Old Testament Today

∽

William L. Holladay

FORTRESS PRESS   MINNEAPOLIS

LONG AGO GOD SPOKE
How Christians May Hear the Old Testament Today

Cover design: Cindy Olson
Cover art: Sandra Bowden, *Light from Darkness,* used by permission of the artist.

Library of Congress Cataloging-in-Publication Data

Holladay, William Lee.
    Long ago God spoke : how Christians may hear the Old Testament today / William L. Holladay.
        p.   cm.
    Includes bibliographical references and indexes.
    ISBN 0-8006-2932-9 (cloth : alk. paper). — ISBN 0-8006-2884-5 (paper : alk. paper)
    1. Bible.   O.T.—Introductions.
    BS1140.2.H65   1995   95-11848
    221.6′1—dc20   CIP

Manufactured in the U.S.A.   AF 1-2932 (cloth)/1-2884 (paper)

99   98   97   96   95   1   2   3   4   5   6   7   8   9   10

Contents

Abbreviations

AB	*Anchor Bible*
ABD	David Noel Freedman and others (eds.), *Anchor Bible Dictionary* (New York: Doubleday, 1992).
ANET	James B. Pritchard (ed.), *Ancient Near Eastern Texts Relating to the Old Testament* (Princeton: Princeton University Press, 1955).
BCP	*The Book of Common Prayer* (New York: The Church Hymnal Corporation, 1979).
BKAT	Biblischer Kommentar—Altes Testament
BZAW	Beihefte zur *Zeitschrift für die alttestamentliche Wissenschaft*
ed(s).	editor(s)
esp.	especially
HSM	Harvard Semitic Monographs
IB	*Interpreter's Bible*
ICC	International Critical Commentary
IDB	G. A. Buttrick (ed.), *Interpreter's Dictionary of the Bible*
IDBSup	*Interpreter's Dictionary of the Bible,* Supplementary Volume
JBL	*Journal of Biblical Literature*
JSOTSup	*Journal for the Study of the Old Testament*—Supplement Series
KAT	Kommentar zum Alten Testament
KJV	King James Version
NJB	H. Wansworth (ed.), *New Jerusalem Bible*
no.	number
NRSV	New Revised Standard Version
OTL	Old Testament Library
p.	page
REB	Revised English Bible
repr.	reprinted
RSV	Revised Standard Version
SBT	Studies in Biblical Theology
sect.	section

TDNT   Gerhard Kittel and Gerhard Friedrich (eds.), *Theological Dictio-
           nary of the New Testament* (Grand Rapids, Mich.: Eerdmans,
           1964–74).
TDOT   G. Johannes Botterweck and Helmer Ringgren (eds.), *Theological
           Dictionary of the Old Testament* (Grand Rapids, Mich.: Eerdmans,
           1974–   ).
tr.   translator
v.   verse
VTSup   Vetus Testamentum Supplements
vv.   verses

Short Titles

Boling and Wright, *Joshua*   Robert G. Boling and G. Ernest Wright, *Joshua* (AB 6; Garden City, NY: Doubleday, 1982)

Bright, *History of Israel*   John Bright, *A History of Israel* (Philadelphia: Westminster, 1981)

Childs, *Exodus*   Brevard S. Childs, *The Book of Exodus* (OTL; Philadelphia: Westminster, 1974)

Crenshaw, *Ecclesiastes*   James L. Crenshaw, *Ecclesiastes* (OTL; Philadelphia: Westminster, 1987)

Cross, *Canaanite Myth and Hebrew Epic*   Frank M. Cross, Jr., *Canaanite Myth and Hebrew Epic* (Cambridge, Mass.: Harvard University, 1973)

Good, *Irony*   Edwin M. Good, *Irony in the Old Testament* (London: Society for the Propagation of Christian Knowledge, 1965)

Habel, *Job*   Norman C. Habel, *The Book of Job* (OTL; Philadelphia: Westminster, 1985)

Hanson, *Dawn of Apocalyptic*   Paul D. Hanson, *The Dawn of Apocalyptic* (Philadelphia: Fortress Press, 1975)

Hillers, *Treaty-Curses*   Delbert R. Hillers, *Treaty-Curses and the Old Testament Prophets* (Biblica et Orientalia 16; Rome: Pontifical Biblical Institute, 1964)

Holladay, *Jeremiah 1*   William L. Holladay, *Jeremiah 1* (Hermeneia; Philadelphia: Fortress Press, 1986)

Holladay, *Jeremiah 2*   William L. Holladay, *Jeremiah 2* (Hermeneia; Minneapolis: Fortress Press, 1989)

Holladay, *Psalms through Three Thousand Years*   William L. Holladay, *The Psalms through Three Thousand Years* (Minneapolis: Fortress Press, 1993)

Mayes, *Deuteronomy*   Arthur D. H. Mayes, *Deuteronomy* (The New Century Bible Commentary; Grand Rapids, Mich.: Eerdmans, 1979)

McCarter, *II Samuel*   P. Kyle McCarter, Jr., *II Samuel* (AB 9; Garden City, NY: Doubleday, 1984)

McKane, *Proverbs*   William McKane, *Proverbs* (OTL; Philadelphia: Westminster, 1970)

Meyers, *Eve*   Carol Meyers, *Discovering Eve: Ancient Israelite Women in Context* (New York and Oxford: Oxford University, 1988)

New Jerome   Raymond E. Brown, Joseph A. Fitzmyer, and Roland E. Murphy (eds.), *The New Jerome Biblical Commentary* (Englewood Cliffs, N.J.: Prentice Hall, 1990)

Trible, *God and the Rhetoric of Sexuality*   Phyllis Trible, *God and the Rhetoric of Sexuality* (Philadelphia: Fortress Press, 1978)

Women's Bible Commentary   Carol A. Newsom and Sharon H. Ringe (eds.), *The Women's Bible Commentary* (Louisville: Westminster/John Knox, 1992)

Introduction

∾

The Christian churches have rarely been comfortable with the Old Testament. The good news of God is plain in the New Testament, but the word from God seems much more muffled in the Old—and this in spite of a torrent of books about the Old Testament that pour from our presses.

A young pastor in my office admitted recently, "Frankly, I'm scared of the Old Testament." It is to try to relieve this fear that the present book has been written, for I am convinced of the crucial importance of the Old Testament for Christians.

Let me mention here two works that have influenced my own thinking, one a quarter-century old, one just published. The first is John Bright's *The Authority of the Old Testament*,[1] a book that began as lectures to pastors at the divinity school of Duke University in 1959. This work helped me to ponder how even the narratives of the battles in the book of Joshua might be preached.[2] The second is Brevard Childs's *Biblical Theology of the Old and New Testaments*.[3] I do not share Childs's perspectives at every point, but his work is a magisterial analysis of the ways the Old Testament and New Testament inform each other.

This book is more modest. In comparison with Bright's work, I take it for granted that the Old Testament is authoritative for Christians in some sense; in comparison with Childs's work, I do not try to rethink a whole array of biblical questions theologically. On the other hand, I am not simply issuing a collection of sermon ideas from the Old Testament. I aim instead for a middle ground, offering a manual of theological considerations that can stimulate a reading of the Old Testament for *listening*—an expectant listening that heightens the possibilities for hearing God. I want to suggest some paths from the *then* of ancient Israel to our *now*, paths that can help preachers and teachers, Protestants and Roman Catholics, clergy and laypeople alike, to find their way with more grace within that looming long first section of the Bible. But readers must not expect an airtight set of proposals: I offer one set of suggestions for thinking about Edom and Babylon in Chapter 9, and another set of suggestions in Chapter 13. My suggestions are intended simply as stimuli to elicit responsible theological responses to the material in the Old Testament.

The first chapter lays out the issues—a preliminary consideration of the nature of God and of how God is understood to work; the question of the scope of the Old Testament; a catalog of some of the barriers to hearing God that the Old Testament manifests for us; the helps and hindrances brought by the emergence of the historical-critical method; and the nature of God-language. In subsequent chapters, beginning with the notions of covenant and law, I try to build up an understanding of how God is understood to speak in the Old Testament, so that the barriers may even be transformed into channels. I have made no attempt to be rigorous in separating the topics in various chapters; there is some overlap. For example, I deal with the deliverance of the Israelites from Pharaoh's army at the Sea in three chapters: in Chapter 5, with respect to the relation between a given historical event and its interpretation in the light of the Old Testament view of God; in Chapter 6, with respect to the way God is understood as a warrior fighting for the Israelites; and in Chapter 7, with respect to the implausible details of that deliverance over which we stumble in our reading. I deal with the issue of the fertility gods, Baal and Astarte, when I discuss the notion of the wrath of God (Chapter 4), the notion that God sponsors battles (Chapter 6), and the utterances of the prophets (Chapter 9).

I have assumed that readers have some awareness of the course of events narrated in the Old Testament, so that there is no need to review everything. They are reminded that Moses probably lived about 1250 B.C.; that David came to the throne about 1000 B.C.; that after Solomon's death (about 922 B.C.) the kingdom of Israel split into two, the northern portion (also called Israel) continuing until it fell to Assyria in 721 B.C., the southern portion (called Judah) continuing until it fell to Babylon in 587 B.C.; and that the leaders of Judah underwent exile in Babylon until 538 B.C.

From page to page, I have tried to indicate my indebtedness to many works of my colleagues, past and present, but I must confess that some ideas I have held for so long that I have forgotten whence they came. My greatest indebtedness, in any event, is to my students over the past thirty and more years, and to fellow church members over a longer span than that. By their questions and their answers, their hurts and their hopes, they have spurred me on to find ways to open the Scriptures. It is they whom I have always in mind. I want to express particular appreciation to my wife, Patricia F. Appelbaum, who has helped me at so many points to clarify my thinking and sharpen my wording, most particularly in Chapter 12.

Citations from the Bible use the New Revised Standard Version unless otherwise stated, and the verse numbers are those normally used in English Protestant Bibles when these differ from the verse numbers in the Hebrew text.

Notes

1. John Bright, *The Authority of the Old Testament* (Nashville and New York: Abingdon, 1967).
2. *Ibid.*, 241–51.
3. Brevard S. Childs, *Biblical Theology of the Old and New Testaments, Theological Reflection on the Christian Bible* (Minneapolis: Fortress Press, 1993).

1

The Issues

~

The Boston Globe for September 24, 1992, carried an Associated Press story from Brooklyn Center, Minnesota; the headline read: "Minnesota man says Bible lewd, wants it out of schools." A certain Gene Kasmar, a self-proclaimed atheist, stated in a petition of July 19, 1992, to the Brooklyn Center School District, "The lewd, indecent and violent content of that book are [*sic*] hardly suitable for young students. . . . The Bible quickly reveals its unsuitability in a school and learning environment." He went on to state that there are frequent biblical references to concubines, explicit sex, child abuse, incest, scatology, wine, nakedness, and mistreatment of women, and he cited twenty pages of examples. The assistant superintendent, Dennis Morrow, said in a two-page response that the Bible does indeed portray some "poor human decisions and some rather archaic social practices."[1]

A moment's thought will bring us to the realization that most of this description fits the Old Testament more than the New. So here, in the lurid and oversimplified approach of a nonbeliever and of the public press, one has some indicators of the barriers confronting current readers of the Old Testament. But our problems with the Old Testament are even more severe than a listing of instances of incest and child abuse.

The New Testament Letter to the Hebrews begins, "Long ago God spoke to our ancestors in many and various ways by the prophets, but in these last days he has spoken to us by a Son." The good news of God is plain in the New Testament, so that we might accept at least symbolically the statement that God has spoken to us by a Son. But what about the prior statement that long ago God spoke to our ancestors, the Israelites, through the utterances of the prophets and the rest of the speakers and writers of the Old Testament? A whole host of issues struggles for our attention.

One is the very *nature of God:* How do we make sense of the notion of God's "speaking" to us and of our "hearing" God? Another is severe, and does not necessarily come to mind quickly: What do we take to be the *extent of the Old Testament*—are we talking about the Old Testament that is found in

5

Protestant Bibles or the longer Old Testament found in Roman Catholic Bibles? Then there are indeed questions of the *content of the Old Testament,* such as were raised by the Minnesota atheist; the very nature of the material appears to put up many barriers to our listening. And there are at least two more crucial issues. One is the *emergence of the historical-critical method* in the past century, a method which, if accepted, makes our hearing even more complicated, and the other is the body of questions regarding the very *nature of language* and especially the *metaphoric nature of much religious language.* In the balance of this chapter, I discuss these one-by-one, at least in a preliminary way.

God Spoke

Consider the phrasing I use in the title: long ago God spoke. What might it mean that "God spoke," and what might it mean that we should "hear God"?

Those who do not believe in the existence of God will pass the expression by: if God does not exist, then the whole notion is simply an exercise in delusion.

Those who are not sure of the existence of God but have laid the question aside in order to get on with the more certain issues of life will likewise pass the expression by: without being sure that God exists, they most emphatically will not take seriously the notion that God has spoken, or take the trouble to listen to God: the matter will not be a serious expectation in their lives.

But what of those who do believe in God but who still are uneasy about the matter of God's speaking or of believers' hearing God? The great God "who fashioned the remotest bounds of earth is God eternally";[2] and if that God not only fashioned the remotest bounds of earth but the remotest bounds of the universe, then how could we expect any communication from God to dwellers on a minor speck called Earth, orbiting around a minor star? How could we ourselves expect to be singled out in our day; we who are part of the vast procession of human beings who have peopled the planet for tens of thousands of years; we who are among the teeming billions of human beings now alive? The whole notion seems self-indulgent past belief.

Even if we are able to accept the idea that God communicates with human beings, we may wonder about the exclusive claims of the Christian faith. Men and women have lived out so many religious convictions through the ages: surely all the non-Christians cannot have been altogether wrong! Are we excluded from hearing God in the Qur'ān? we wonder. Why are we so sure that Christian claims about the Bible are valid?

Yet the claim of the Old Testament is precisely that—that God has so spoken and that thus we can hear. Isa. 1:2a says it: "Hear, O heavens, and listen,

O earth; for the Lord has spoken." Deut. 8:3 says it: "[God] humbled you . . . in order to make you understand that one does not live by bread alone, but by every word that comes from the mouth of the Lord." Suppose we accept in some sense the claim that God has spoken: how might we conceive God's "speaking" and our "hearing" anyway? God has no physical mouth. When Isaiah made the claim that God had spoken, what was it, precisely, that he was convinced he had heard? How could he be so sure he heard rightly? Why were his followers so sure? Our questions come tumbling. Why do we confine ourselves to some specific texts that were written down hundreds of years ago? Could God not continue to speak in fresh ways to people in our own time?

Central to our faith as Christians is a notion of "word" that stretches our normal notions to embrace the notion that Jesus Christ is the incarnate Word of God (the beginning of the Letter to the Hebrews once more). This conviction is set forth most concisely in the prologue to the Gospel of John: "In the beginning was the Word, and the Word was with God, and the Word was God. . . . And the Word became flesh and lived among us. . . . No one has ever seen God. It is God the only Son, who is close to the Father's heart, who has made him known" (John 1:1, 14a, 18a). These passages of the New Testament affirm that God has always been communicating in a variety of ways through those who speak for God (the prophets and others in the Old Testament), but that finally, in a crucial self-revelation, God spoke through Jesus Christ.

For Christians, then, God's Word is not a vocable, not an utterance, not ultimately a text, but a human being. What might this mean?

This idea that a "word" is more than an utterance is not an innovation of the New Testament. In the Old Testament, the Hebrew for "word" (*dābār*) always means more than an utterance: a Hebrew dictionary will show that *dābār*, depending on the context, may be translated "word," "affair," "thing." In Judges 18:7, "they had no *dābār* with" does not mean simply "they had no conversation with" but "they had no dealings with." Planning, talking, and carrying out action, for the Israelites, were all parts of a single continuum. In Hebrew, that is to say, "word" implies "self-expression in action."

God's word is the supreme self-expression. Look at the elaborate comparison in Isa. 55:10-11; God is understood to be speaking. "For as the rain and the snow come down from heaven, and do not return there until they have watered the earth, making it bring forth and sprout, giving seed to the sower and bread to the eater, so shall my word be that goes out from my mouth; it shall not return to me empty, but it shall accomplish that which I purpose, and succeed in the thing for which I sent it." These verses affirm that God's word is not an empty echo but stays with its recipients to get things done.

This Old Testament notion of "word" then informs the New Testament affirmation of Jesus Christ as God's ultimate Word: Jesus Christ, by this understanding, is God's ultimate self-expression.[3]

To continue pondering in this direction, "hearing God," for Christians, does not so much mean "hearing a voice," whether understood as an outer or an inner voice, as it means being the recipient of this self-communication of God, apprehending Jesus Christ, allowing Christ to do his work in us so that we may be transformed by God's will. The ways in which that apprehension of Jesus Christ takes place are doubtless as various as the range of temperament of human beings and the sets of expectations in our churchly communities.

For Christians, the text of the New Testament is central for the enterprise of apprehending Christ: the four Gospels, in various ways, recount the memories of the first and second generations of the Church about Jesus; the Acts of the Apostles recount narratives of the spread of the new faith; Paul testifies to the faith in his letters to various new churches, and so on. But, ideally, what the hearers and readers of the New Testament expect is not simply the impact of the *wording* of the text itself but the impact of the *person* to whom the text testifies, Jesus Christ. This distinction between the words of the text and God's word, which is Jesus Christ, is crucial. This is what Paul meant in Col. 3:16 when he wrote, "Let the word of Christ dwell in you richly."

So far so good. But where does this leave the Old Testament? The Old Testament took shape before the coming of Jesus Christ, and much of it seems alien to the spirit of Jesus. How could one hope to hear God in the Old Testament? Christians may know some well-loved passages—psalms like Psalm 23, the narrative of creation in Genesis 1, sections of Isaiah that appear to predict the coming of Christ. But a few well-marked passages do not add up to the whole Old Testament.

I am convinced that the Old Testament, properly used, can be a channel for hearing God. How this can be done is the work of this book. First, we must face the difficulties of the Old Testament fair and square.

The Extent of the Old Testament

I must touch here on a problem that is not usually a prime issue for those troubled by the Old Testament but one that needs to be faced nevertheless: the question of the extent of the Old Testament. Protestants are accustomed to Bibles with thirty-nine books in the Old Testament. Roman Catholics use Bibles with the Protestant thirty-nine along with seven more: Tobit and Judith after the book of Nehemiah; (the) Wisdom (of Solomon) and Eccesiasticus (or Sirach) after the Song of Songs; Baruch after Lamentations; and 1 and

2 Maccabees at the end of the Old Testament. And Roman Catholic Bibles have a longer book of Esther, expanded by various prayers, and a longer book of Daniel—the third chapter of Daniel is expanded by a prayer and a hymn, and two extra chapters of the book contain the story of Susanna (chapter 13) and the stories of Bel and the Dragon (chapter 14). The question of what is included in the Old Testament arises for Protestants not only in connection with Roman Catholic Bibles: those accustomed to the Protestant list may well be puzzled by the occasional reading from the books of Ecclesiasticus or Wisdom in an Episcopal Church.[4]

And there is more: if one ventures to examine the Bibles of the Eastern Orthodox, one will find not only these additions but books like 1 Esdras, the Prayer of Manasseh, and 3 Maccabees. And even more still: the book of Enoch, part of the Old Testament only for the Ethiopic Church, is nevertheless cited as Scripture in the New Testament (see Jude 6 and 14). As one might suspect, there are historical reasons for each of these inclusions and exclusions. The details are intricate and confusing, but we need to offer at least a simple account of the whole matter in order to face the problem of what Old Testament we are talking about.

The question is what scholars call "canonicity": the "canon" is the list of biblical books that are deemed to be "canonical," that is, there is agreement that they make up authoritative Scripture. In the last few centuries B.C., there was no rigorous notion of canonicity among various Jewish communities. The "law," that is, the first five books of the Old Testament, held pride of place, and what the Jewish authorities call the "prophets," that is, the books of Joshua, Judges, 1 and 2 Samuel, 1 and 2 Kings, Isaiah, Jeremiah, Ezekiel, and the twelve minor prophets (Hosea through Malachi) were accepted as authoritative as well. (This is what Jesus means when he refers to "the law and the prophets," as in Matt. 5:17 and 7:12.) But many other books were understood by various groups of Jews to be authoritative, and the lists of these books differed from community to community. The Jewish community in Alexandria, Egypt, that had translated many biblical books out of Hebrew into Greek and used them in their synagogues (the so-called "Septuagint" translation), favored a longer list than Jewish communities in Palestine. It is fair to say, then, that familiarity and usage over a period of centuries, rather than the decrees of one council or another, have shaped these lists.

Ultimately, the Jewish authorities in Palestine settled on the thirty-nine books in Hebrew that much later would become the Old Testament in Protestant Bibles, rejecting the longer lists of the Greek-speaking Jews in Alexandria. But the New Testament Christian communities, which at the time the New Testament books were written were Greek-speaking, took over the Septuagint (the Greek Old Testament) and therefore the longer list of books from the Greek-speaking Jewish communities in Alexandria. When the Bible was translated into Latin, the Old Testament was again made up of that longer list: this became the Old Testament for Roman Catholics. When Martin Luther, however, translated the Old Testament into German, he rejected those books which had not come down from ancient times in Hebrew—that is, those books that were in the (Greek) list from Alexandria but not in the (Hebrew) list from Palestine. The result, as I have indicated, is that Protestants, following Luther's lead, have stayed with the thirty-nine books of what finally became the traditional Jewish Scriptures in Hebrew and have laid aside the extra books that are part of the Roman Catholic Old Testament.[5]

The question for us is, however, a practical one: in which Old Testament shall we try to hear God? It is obvious from the discussion thus far that our answer will depend to a large degree on the convictions of the Christian community to which we belong. Roman Catholics will not perceive any problem with the "extra" books; Protestants, on the other hand, while they may appreciate many passages from these books, such as the passage beginning "Let us now sing the praises of famous men" at the beginning of Ecclesiasticus (Sirach) 44, may still be uneasy when these books are assumed to be Scripture alongside the thirty-nine on which everyone is agreed. In this book, I shall stay with the thirty-nine books of the Protestant Bible for a simple, practical reason: these thirty-nine books offer challenges enough! I could well have discussed the books of Ecclesiasticus and Wisdom in the course of Chapter 11, in which we explore wisdom literature, but I have chosen not to do so. Readers who wish to explore the extra books, and ways to hear God in them, will not find it difficult to do so once we have explored some of the patterns of the thirty-nine together.

The Barriers of the Old Testament

The Old Testament, taken as a whole, has always raised formidable barriers for Christians—so much that Christian churches more than once have been tempted to abandon it.

At the very beginning of the Christian movement, there was no question about the Old Testament. Jesus was reared in a Jewish community, and the Old Testament, Scripture for the Jews, was his Scripture, as it was for his immediate followers. But as the new faith moved out into the Gentile world, voices were raised against the Old Testament, notably that of Marcion, a deacon in the church of Rome in the middle of the second century, who insisted that the God of the Old Testament had nothing to do with the Father of Jesus

Christ and that Christians should therefore reject the Old Testament as Scripture. Marcion was declared heretical, but the issues he raised could not easily
be disregarded.[6]

In more recent times, the Old Testament has not been so much rejected as
neglected. Over a half-century ago, when the Christian faith was spreading in
China, a thoughtful Chinese pastor wrote, "Intending missionaries or evangelists waste their time if they spend a lot of it studying the Old Testament. It
would be better for them to spend the time on Sociology or Psychology. They
need nothing more than a General Introduction, so as to be able to use the
Old Testament for reference. The Old Testament teaching given in theological
colleges in China is, in the experience of most students, devoid of interest or
value for their after work. Reading the Old Testament is like eating a large
crab; it turns out to be mostly shell, with very little meat in it."[7]

It is noteworthy that one can purchase Scripture editions containing simply the New Testament and Psalms,[8] as if to affirm that the Psalms are good as
prayers for the Christian but one may dispense with the remainder of the Old
Testament. What factors have led to the neglect of the Old Testament on the
part of so many Christians? I have implied several in the first few pages of this
book; let us name ten of them and examine them briefly.

1. Why do we need to know about what happened before Jesus? This is a
variation on Marcion's outlook and on the Chinese pastor's advice. Many
years ago, when I was a campus minister to students of both the United
Church of Christ and of the Christian Church (Disciples of Christ) at a state
university, I organized a Sunday morning Bible study group for students at
the Christian church. I suggested it might be good to take an Old Testament
topic—the prophets, perhaps. The suggestion was sturdily rejected: "We're
New Testament Christians," they maintained. If Jesus is the full revelation of
God, why bother with what has come before?

2. The Old Testament is so long. This objection is closely related to the
previous one. At a session on the Bible that I was leading in a rural church in
Massachusetts some years ago, I had made an initial presentation and then invited questions. None was forthcoming: people were shy. I made some passing
remarks about how it was all right to sit and ponder matters a bit, and that
any kinds of questions were welcome, any at all, but the silence of the group
began to get heavy. Finally, to my relief, a junior-high student in the back row
raised her hand hesitantly. "Yes?" I said. She asked, "Has anyone ever read the
Bible all the way through?"

She was asking a legitimate question. The New Testament is formidable
enough; it is roughly as long as the whole Muslim Qur'ān. But the Old

Testament is over three times the bulk of the New Testament! Long ago, the prophet Habakkuk understood himself to be instructed by God to write a particular vision "so that a runner may read it" (Hab. 2:2), but the Old Testament as it now stands is far too long for any runners to read. We lead busy lives; we are bombarded by words from our radios and televisions. How can we be expected to attend with any care to so long a text?

The problem looms large for those who resolve to read the Bible straight through. In most instances, such an enterprise is successful only under extraordinary circumstances. Some years ago, students beginning their first year of seminary studies at the Pacific School of Religion in Berkeley, California, had the option of coming ten days early to participate, as a group, in reading the Bible from beginning to end. They took turns, under the guidance of a professor, and found the ten days to be a transforming experience. Again, I knew a man in federal prison who pondered the months ahead of him, undertook to read the Bible cover-to-cover, and did it. But I suspect that most people who begin get bogged down, if not in the genealogies of Genesis, then in the laws governing burnt offerings in Leviticus.

3. Much of the Old Testament is only of antiquarian interest. The problem of the genealogies of Genesis and the laws of Leviticus leads to a related issue: how can one possibly gain anything from so much of this material, let alone hear God in it? Chapter 36 of Genesis is largely given over to the names of the descendants of Esau, understood to be the ancestor of the Edomites. Since the Old Testament story is of the descendants of Jacob, who was renamed "Israel" (Gen. 32:28), since Esau was the brother of Jacob, and since the Edomites, centered in the area southeast of the Dead Sea, were more often than not the enemies of Israel—they turn up in later history as the Idumeans (Herod the Great was an Idumean, and Idumea is mentioned in Mark 3:8)—of what possible good can this material in Genesis 36 be for Christians, except as a curious exercise in pronouncing exotic names? We have never met an Edomite: no group of people call themselves Edomites any more (nor Idumeans, for that matter). Surely God has more useful things for us to do than to meditate on a text like this.

Beyond the sense we have that the Old Testament is long and full of stuff that has no relevance to us, there are more substantial objections.

4. There is so much in the Old Testament that requires us to suspend our disbelief. What are we to do with the age of Methuselah at his death (969 years: Gen. 5:27)? or with the time the sun stood still for a whole day (Josh. 10:13), or with the axe-head that floated at the behest of the prophet Elisha (2 Kings 6:6), or with the shadow of the royal sundial that went backward for King Hezekiah at the behest of the prophet Isaiah (2 Kings 20:11), or with the

great fish that swallowed the prophet Jonah and then spewed him out more or less intact (Jonah 1:17; 2:10)? Many of us who would like to listen for God in the Old Testament find that the details of narratives like these leave us puzzled and dubious.

5. The world of the Old Testament is so distant from us and alien to us. Most of us have not undergone the experience of slavery, and we no longer throw people into prison for debt. Of course the world of the New Testament is distant and alien too, but the winsome figure of Jesus pulls us into the material in spite of its alienness, and we are able, one way or another, to accommodate ourselves to its distance from us.

The world of the Old Testament, being even older, and being bereft of Jesus, really is an alien landscape. The narrative of Abraham has it that at two points in his life he told his wife Sarah to pass as his sister (Gen. 12:13; 20:2). Jacob was polygamous (Gen. 29:23, 30). King Ahaz of Judah "made his son pass through fire" (2 Kings 16:3)—this was evidently a euphemism for child sacrifice. Where in all this is any guidance for us in living our lives?

Even when we can be sympathetic to the material, we sometimes have a feeling that "there must be more here than meets the eye." In a narrative in which God makes a covenant with Abraham, he was told to procure several animals—a heifer three years old, a female goat three years old, a ram three years old, a turtledove, and a young pigeon—and to cut the three animals in two; then, after dark, evidently in a vision, a smoking fire pot and a flaming torch passed between the animal pieces (Gen. 15:9-10, 17). What in the world, we wonder, is going on here? Again, when Isaiah understands God to say, "Your appointed feasts my soul hates" (Isa. 1:14), we may well ask ourselves, does God have a soul? Indeed, why is the Old Testament so hard to understand?

6. There are so many battles and so many instances of cruelty in the Old Testament. One of the greatest barriers in the minds of people who try to read the Old Testament is the sense that it consists basically of a long narrative of cruel kings and barbarous battles, and the worst of it is that God seems to sponsor these battles. What kind of God is this? And indeed one can begin with the annihilation of the Egyptian forces as the Israelites escaped from slavery in Egypt (Exod. 14:28) and continue with the Israelites' annihilation of the forces of King Og of Bashan in the wilderness (Num. 21:35), their annihilation of the population of Jericho (and their animals as well), saving only Rahab the prostitute and her family (Josh. 6:17, 21), their annihilation of the inhabitants of Ai (Josh. 8:22), the slaughter by the judge Ehud of the Moabites (Judg. 3:29), Saul's battles with the Philistines (1 Samuel 14): the dreary list goes on and on. King Menahem of Israel ripped open all the pregnant women of the village of Tiphsah (2 Kings 15:16). Do we not have enough cruelty displayed

on the evening news? Why, we wonder, must we be subjected to more of the same in the Old Testament, and under the sponsorship of God?

7. How can we believe that God chose one people, Israel? The question of the chosen people is, of course, closely related to the problem of the God of battles. The Christian churches have within them folk from every race and nation, and for Christians that is as it should be, given Jesus' post-resurrection commission to his disciples (Matt. 28:19). If God has created all humankind and loves the whole of creation, how can we take seriously the Old Testament claim that God chose a single nation, Israel? The idea reminds us of the belt-buckles on the German uniforms in the First World War: their inscription read *Gott mit uns*—"God with us." It reminds us of all kinds of racism and of conflict among peoples, each assuming they are somehow privileged under heaven. Even in the noblest of Old Testament passages, such as Deut. 7:7-8, we find this conviction that God chose Israel. How can we make sense of this notion?

Other issues come into the minds of those who read the Old Testament intensively; I note three here.

8. Some of the Psalms are so self-righteous. Probably most of us assume we lead acceptable lives, so that we usually have the seeds of self-righteousness within us, but we are certainly irritated by self-righteousness in others. And then we stumble on expressions of self-righteousness in the Psalms. For example, we may appreciate the words of Psalm 139, with its affirmations that God protects us and knows us through and through, and that there is nowhere where God is not present. But then we find, in vv. 21 and 23-24, "Do I not hate those who hate you, O Lord? . . . Search me, O God, and know my heart, . . . See if there is any wicked way in me, and lead me in the way everlasting." Or Ps. 107:7, "No one who practices deceit shall remain in my house; no one who utters lies shall continue in my presence." The Psalms are presumably a prayerbook for our use, yet again and again they urge on us this holier-than-thou attitude.

And this holier-than-thou attitude is often linked to prayers against one's enemies. Psalm 17 begins as a prayer that God will hear the speaker's woe, continues with an insistence of the speaker's innocence (vv. 3-5), offers a vivid description of the speaker's enemies (v. 10, "they close their hearts to pity"), and ends with a prayer that God will destroy these enemies (v. 13: "Rise up, O Lord, confront them, overthrow them! By your sword deliver my life from the wicked"). Some of these prayers are really curses (Ps. 55:15: "Let death come upon them; let them go down alive to Sheol"). If we pay any attention at all to Jesus' command that we love our enemies, then we will shrink from these prayers.

9. From time to time, we notice real contradictions between given passages in the Old Testament. One of the most famous, and notable, is the

contrast between the first narrative of creation (Gen. 1:1—2:4a) and the second (Gen. 2:4b-25). In the first, the animals are created before human beings, and human beings are created male and female (Gen. 1:20-25, 26-27); in the second, the male is created, then the animals, and finally the female (Gen. 2:7, 19-20, 21-25).

There are other contradictions, some of them quite severe. Thus, we read in 2 Kings 10 of the slaughter by Jehu of the house of Ahab, about the year 850 B.C. King Ahab of Israel, with his wife Jezebel, had sponsored the worship of the god Baal. Jehu, a military officer, wiped out the ruling house at the town of Jezreel, where there was a royal residence. In v. 30 of that chapter, God expresses his approval to Jehu: "The Lord said to Jehu, 'Because you have done well in carrying out what I consider right, and in accordance with all that was in my heart have dealt with the house of Ahab, your sons of the fourth generation shall sit on the throne of Israel.'" But then, in Hos. 1:4, the prophet Hosea, in about the year 735 B.C., understands God to instruct him to name his firstborn son "Jezreel," "for in a little while I will punish the house of Jehu for the blood of Jezreel, and I will put an end to the kingdom of the house of Israel." So what is God's judgment on Jehu's slaughter? Was it a good thing or a bad thing?

In the famous prophetic oracle in Isa. 2:4, repeated in Mic. 4:3, we are told that nations "shall beat their swords into plowshares, and their spears into pruning hooks." Yet, in Joel 3:10, we hear the opposite instruction to the nations: "Beat your plowshares into swords, and your pruning hooks into spears." Which is it to be? Are both visions valid, depending on the occasion? How are we to know?

In Jer. 2:2, the prophet records the word from God that the Israelites were faithful to God during the forty years they were wandering in the wilderness: "I remember the devotion of your youth, your love as a bride, how you followed me in the wilderness, in a land not sown." On the other hand, in Ezek. 20:13, the prophet records the word from God that Israel rebelled against God in the wilderness: "But the house of Israel rebelled against me in the wilderness; they did not observe my statutes but rejected my ordinances, by whose observance everyone shall live; and my sabbaths they greatly profaned." Which is it?

10. In the Old Testament women are subordinate in a world dominated by men. This is a painful reality: with few exceptions, it is the norm from the beginning to the end of the Old Testament. The value of women lay in the hope that they would become mothers of sons (even the song of Hannah, the mother of Samuel, reflects this perspective: 1 Sam. 2:5), but one has the impression that women are often thought of as little more than property. Thus,

in Exodus, the commandment against "coveting" lists someone's wife after his house and before his male and female slaves and animals (Exod. 20:17). The law in Deuteronomy governing divorce is completely one-sided (Deut. 24:1-4): only the husband may initiate divorce. A woman suspected of adultery must undergo an ordeal (Num. 5:11-31), but not a man. Genealogies list men, rarely women.

It is true that this imbalance of the sexes is found in the New Testament as well: the Gospel of Mark records the names of Jesus' brothers but not the names of his sisters (Mark 6:3), and many people remember Paul's warning to the church at Corinth that women should be silent in the churches (1 Cor. 14:34). But Jesus befriended and healed women as well as men and is remembered as telling not only a story about a shepherd who found his lost sheep but another about a housewife who found her lost coin (Luke 15:3-10). In the first account of creation in the Old Testament, the male and the female are created side by side (Gen. 1:27), but, in general, the Old Testament offers little guidance to those men and women who are struggling today to shape communities in which both sexes are in parity.

Here, then, is an array of barriers to our hearing God in the Old Testament. I shall not attempt to answer each in the form in which I have posed it, but I shall discuss most of them, or at least put most of them into perspective. In the course of this work, I will deal with a basic question: Are these barriers, and others like them, too formidable to make the task worthwhile, or can they be overcome—indeed, can they be clues to a richer understanding of God's communication to us than we had expected?

The Emergence of the Historical-Critical Method

I turn now to a development in Old Testament studies that makes our task even more complicated. For hundreds of years, the Christian churches read the Bible as a unique authority of the faith, written under the inspiration of the Holy Spirit. The Bible—the Old as well as the New Testament—was used as a source of doctrine for Christians. Various books were traditionally attributed to various authors—the first five books of the Old Testament to Moses, the Psalms to David, and so on. Careful readers noticed from time to time that different books of the Bible were written in different styles, but those differences were attributed to personal differences among the inspired writers. Whatever the contrasts within the Bible, however, all these writings were understood to testify in parallel ways to the glory and majesty and love of God.

In contrast to this traditional approach, however, scholars working on the Bible in the past two centuries have gradually evolved a different approach to the material, which has come to be called the "historical-critical" method. They have examined the Bible as they would any other ancient document, analyzing the various sections and books for stylistic traits, analyzing the literary steps by which various books might have come to be, attempting to date the material and to fit it within the historical circumstances of the time and the parallel findings of archeology, and comparing the biblical material with inscriptions and texts from Egypt, Babylon, and elsewhere.

As one might imagine, this approach is based on two related presuppositions. The first is that the theological affirmation of the authorship of the Holy Spirit plays no part *in the analysis*. This does not mean that scholars must cease to believe in God's participation in the writing of the books of the Bible—it simply means that such a theological affirmation does not play a direct part in the historical analysis of the books. (I shall return to the question of God's involvement later; for now, we must understand the assumptions of the historical-critical method.) The second, related presupposition is that the biblical books are the product of human beings, comparable to other products of human beings. The Bible may be unique in the claims that Christians make about it, it may even be unique in the claims it makes about itself, but it is still open to comparison with other literary works.

Thus, careful analysis of the Gospels of Matthew, Mark, and Luke have led to the so-called "Four Document Hypothesis," that is, that Mark was the earliest of these Gospels, that there was another early source (conventionally called "Q") consisting of sayings of Jesus, and that the writers of Matthew and of Luke drew on both Mark and "Q" in different ways, supplementing these two sources with special material unique to each ("special Matthew," "special Luke"). Given these literary relationships among the Gospels (that is, relationships based on the use of more than one source), it becomes difficult to maintain the conviction that the Gospels of Matthew and of Luke are eyewitness accounts.

In the Old Testament, by the same token, there are indications that Genesis is a work based on three sources (whether these be written sources or oral tradition), conventionally called "J," "E," and "P." In the hypothesis held by many scholars, the "Yahwistic Source" ("J") took shape in Jerusalem at the time of King David or King Solomon (about 950 B.C.), the "Elohistic Source" ("E") was an alternative tradition that took shape in the northern kingdom perhaps a century later, and the "Priestly Source" ("P") was a supplement by priestly writers two hundred or three hundred years after *that*. The implications are that the book of Genesis took shape over a period of several centuries, and that its author was not Moses, who probably lived much earlier, about 1250 B.C. This is the scholars' explanation for the existence of the two creation narratives: the first creation narrative (Gen. 1:1—2:4a) is to be attributed to the (late) Priestly Source, and the second creation narrative (Gen. 2:4b-25) is to be attributed to the (early) Yahwistic Source from David's or Solomon's time.

In the nineteenth and early twentieth centuries, the historical-critical method was often known as "higher criticism," in contrast to "lower criticism," a discipline that dealt with the determination of the most accurate possible Hebrew text of the Old Testament and the most accurate possible Greek text of the New. Grudgingly, the churches began to understand the need for "lower criticism" (one needs the most original texts possible of the biblical books from which to translate), but both Roman Catholic and Protestant churches struggled against the approaches and the claims of "higher criticism."

The details of the theological understanding of the nature of the Bible in the teaching of the Roman Catholic church and various Protestant churches are intricate, and I shall not review them here; suffice it to say that Roman Catholic teaching has understood the Christian faith to be based on twin authorities, Scripture and tradition (the latter being the teaching of the Church that has been defined in the course of centuries), while Protestants have based their authority on the Bible alone. But both Roman Catholic and Protestant authorities had assumed that only a certain few men (and perhaps women) were inspired by the Holy Spirit to write Scripture. Moses, clearly, was called by God and spoke for God. How, then, can the notion of several sources in Genesis be countenanced? Similarly, Isaiah was a prophet inspired by God, so all 66 chapters of the book that is called by his name are to be attributed to him: so went the argumentation. The famous text "All scripture is inspired by God and is useful for teaching" (2 Tim. 3:16) was frequently cited to this end. (The author of 2 Timothy had only the Old Testament in mind: this was the "Scripture" of his day. The logical question— How can a biblical verse be used to prove the Bible?—evidently did not loom large.) Protestants, to insist on the authority of the Bible, have sometimes resorted to the doctrine of biblical inerrancy: by this teaching, the Bible cannot err or contradict itself.

Protestants who have experienced the claim and counterclaim of these arguments[9] are sometimes surprised to learn of a parallel struggle in the Roman Catholic church, especially in the period from 1900 to the Second Vatican Council in the 1960s.[10] If Charles Augustus Briggs underwent a series of heresy trials in the Presbyterian Church in 1891 to 1893 for his views on the Bible, and was found guilty;[11] if several professors at Concordia Seminary in St. Louis (a seminary of the Lutheran Church, Missouri Synod) were forced to withdraw from the seminary in the 1970s over the question of biblical interpretation, then, by the same token, the Dutch Roman Catholic biblical professor Henry Poels was forced out of his professorship at the Catholic University in Washington, D.C., in 1909 over similar issues.[12]

If many Christians have looked on the historical-critical method as a bane, then is there a way to cut through the arguments and the emotions on this issue?

I would suggest that one of the issues that gets in the way of accepting the historical-critical method and, at the same time, understanding how God can be heard in the Old Testament is what I would call the "it's-just-a" reaction. When I present the Old Testament using the historical-critical method, people often react with, "But if the Bible is just a human book, then. . . ." And I have to reply that I never say that the Bible is *just* a human book, but rather that the Bible is a human book through which God has chosen to speak. That is to say, we are dealing here with both–and, not with either–or.

I would suggest that the traditional testimony about the person of Jesus Christ is a clue here: according to the definition of the Council of Chalcedon (A.D. 451), Jesus Christ was "truly God and truly man."[13] Jesus then was not half God and half human but rather fully God and fully human. By the same token, I would insist that the Bible is a *fully* human work of literature in which God's self-expression is to be *fully* discerned; and, in our instance, this understanding pertains to the Old Testament as much as to the New. Such an understanding clearly raises many problems, but then the Chalcedonian affirmation about Jesus Christ has raised problems too, over which the Christian churches continue to struggle. We shall have to see how to deal with the problems this approach raises for the Old Testament. But just as scholars who struggle to clarify the historical Jesus may help Christians to understand the self-revelation of God in Jesus, so scholars who struggle to clarify the historical situation of Old Testament texts may help Christians to understand the self-revelation of God in the Old Testament.

Central in the enterprise is an understanding of human history and God's involvement in human history. Paul affirms in the Letter to the Galatians that "when the fullness of time had come, God sent his Son, born of a woman, born under the law." The phrase "the fullness of time" conjures up for us the long succession of the years of humankind. "Born of a woman" suggests Christ's humanity; "born under the law" suggests the specificity of his coming in the Jewish community, subject to the Jewish law expressed in the Old Testament. And, as I pointed out earlier, the beginning of the Letter to the Hebrews suggests the parallel between God's speaking in Jesus Christ and God's speaking in the prophets—"Long ago God spoke to our ancestors in many and various ways by the prophets, but in these last days he has spoken to us by a Son." God has entered history definitively in Jesus Christ, but then God has steadily been entering history, and the Old Testament is the testimony to that entering in earlier times.

It follows that the more history we know, the more clearly we can hear God in that history—specifically, the history that bounds the Old Testament. This means that we must try to grasp not only the events that are directly related in the Old Testament, but the events of Canaan, of Egypt, of Assyria and Babylonia and Persia, that bear on the Old Testament. We must try to grasp the daily life of people in Old Testament times as that life is revealed in the constantly increasing findings of archeology. This attempt of ours to reconceive the history of Old Testament times prevents us from seeing Moses and Isaiah and the rest of the men and women of the Old Testament simply as figures in a stained-glass window.

Morever, we need to try to understand the conventional views of those to whom Moses and Isaiah and the others spoke. If Moses and Isaiah spoke to teach and to persuade, what were the views of the audience who needed to be taught and persuaded? We cannot assume that their views in their day were similar to our own in our day, nor that the views of people in Isaiah's day, in 735 B.C., were the same as those in Moses' day, in 1250 B.C., any more than the views of people in our day are the same as those 515 years ago, when Columbus had not yet planned his first voyage.

All of this leads us to try to date the books of the Old Testament, and the subsections of books: in short, it leads us to the historical-critical method. I would even affirm that the development of the historical-critical method is part of the providence of God in our day: God has allowed us to hear the material with a clarity it has not had since the years when it was first written. This is the steady testimony of people who hear the Old Testament proclaimed by a scholar who uses the method: "You make it come alive." The material is always open to being made alive, but, without such an aid, people find it hard to sense its aliveness. The historical-critical method, in short, can be a real blessing from God rather than a bane.

But questions still crowd into our minds. Here are a few.

1. With the skill of a scholar, any ancient literature can be brought to life. A specialist in archaic Greek can bring Homer's Iliad to life and move its readers, but that does not mean that God is directly involved in the Iliad. The Iliad and the Old Testament both narrate battles; in what ways is the Old Testament different from the Iliad?

2. The historical-critical method offers hypotheses by which to understand how the books of the Bible came to be. But if the theory of the Yahwistic Source, the Elohistic Source, and the Priestly Source to explain Genesis is simply a hypothesis rather than subject to strict proof, how can we trust it to help us discern what God is saying?

3. If our understanding of the process by which the Old Testament came to be is one of diversity, of multiplicity, of a great variety of voices within the books of the Bible, where again is the dependable voice of God?

The remaining chapters of this book are devoted to an attempt to shape some answers to these and related questions.

I close this discussion with an affirmation and a caution. The affirmation is this. The Old Testament was Jesus' Scripture; his own understanding of God was shaped by it. And countless folk in the centuries that followed have been able to hear God in the Old Testament. The challenge for us in our day, equipped with the tools that the historical-critical method has supplied, is to hear God in the Old Testament with all possible clarity.

In regard to the caution, I need to offer a bit of background. Some biblical scholars in the past two or three decades, having been nurtured by the historical-critical method, have turned to reject its purpose—these scholars in general go by the name of "deconstructionists." Deconstructionists have become convinced that, by definition, one cannot recover the background of an ancient text: for biblical texts, we cannot specify the authors or the circumstances in which they were written, or what the assumptions and purposes of the authors of these texts might have been. By these assumptions, indeed, there is no *objective* meaning to texts at all: the only meanings that may be associated with texts are the various meanings that readers, whether in ancient times or today, may bring to the texts. By the assumptions of the deconstructionists, then, one can make no claims about "hearing God in the Old Testament": the most that one can do is to say, "The Old Testament has functioned as a set of texts in which, in various ways, Jewish and Christian communities understood themselves to be hearing God."[14]

The caution then is this: We are reminded that, for all our historical investigation, we can never have one-hundred-percent certainty as to whether David or Isaiah wrote a particular text, never have one-hundred-percent certainty what the mindset was or the assumptions were that governed the author of any biblical text. But at the same time, I am convinced, for reasons I have already indicated, that the pursuit is worth making, even though all we can achieve is probabilities and possibilities. History can never be fully reconstructed, but the history into which, we are convinced, God has entered is worth pursuing with all the tools at our disposal.

Language and Metaphor

Because we are dealing with a written text, the Old Testament, in which we hope to hear God, we must pause to think about the nature of language. Too seldom are we moved to think about the nature of language—not only English, but any human language. Just as fish live and move and have their being in water, so, most of the time, we simply use the language into which we are born, without giving any particular thought to its nature, its glories, and its pitfalls.

Language is an intricate and arbitrary set of signs shared by a community and related to the experience of that community. How language is related to experience is controverted: some authorities believe that perceived experience is a given, to which language then refers; while others wonder whether the structure of language itself does not shape our understanding of experience.[15]

In any event, it is one thing when language refers to what can be videotaped, and another thing when language refers to what can only be testified to. Indeed, the very word "is" is slippery. If I say, "The call of the macaw is a squawk," the word "squawk" is imitative, so the word "is" here betokens an identity. But if I say, "This is a table," the word "table" is an arbitrary set of sounds. The word for the same object in Hebrew is *šulḥān;* either of these words, or any of hundreds of other sets of sounds having that meaning, will conjure up the idea of "table," depending on the speech-community that agrees on the meaning of the given set of sounds, a meaning corresponding to a photographable object. If I say, "This rose is a red one," the word "red" conjures up a set of impressions in my brain that match the color red, produced on the electromagnetic spectrum by wavelengths of roughly 750 nanometers (billionths of a meter). But such a statement conjures up nothing special to someone who is color-blind. The rose, however, is photographable, even if the characteristic "red" only communicates to those sensitive to particular variations on the visible spectrum. Now suppose I say, "God is love" (1 John 4:8). The word "is" produces a statement about "God," who is not photographable, and "love," a word that conjures up a set of real perceptions but perceptions compounded of social solidarity and affection, none of which is photographable either. The word "is" links many different though related kinds of statements. The philosophy of language thus turns out to be an intricate and brain-splitting enterprise, into which I shall not enter systematically: it is enough to point in the direction of some of the booby traps in our use of language. For example, when someone says, "Time flies like an arrow," we feel reasonably certain we understand the statement, in spite of the fact that "time" is hard to define, and "flies," normally used of a bird or an airplane, is here used figuratively. But if that statement is followed with another, "Fruit flies like a banana," our minds struggle with linguistic paradox. How do we *know* that "flies" is no longer a verb but a noun, and that "like" is no longer a preposition but a verb? How would we tell this to a computer that is being programmed to do machine translation?

Having gestured in the direction of the complications of language structure, I want to turn more specifically now to discuss *metaphor,* a matter that bears directly on God-language. The dictionary definition of "metaphor" is "A figure of speech in which a word or phrase literally denoting one kind of object or idea is used in place of another to suggest a likeness or analogy between them (as in *drowning in money*)."[16] By this definition, "Time flies" is a metaphor.

In my illustrations of the various uses of "is," we moved from more literal to less literal uses; we could say, using Paul Van Buren's phrase, that we moved from the center of language to its edge.[17] "God is love" or any other statement about *God* must be taken as metaphorical, because no language system is ever adequate to talk about God.[18]

It would not be too extreme to say that studying theology is learning how to say the least wrong thing about God. All God-language is wrong to some degree; the trick is to reduce the wrongness to a minimum.

The Bible understands this. In 1 John, just after the statement "God is love," we read, "No one has seen God; if we love one another, God lives in us, and his love is perfected in us" (1 John 4:12). This appears to mean, "Since God is not photographable, God's nature and God's presence with us are known in our experience in the community."

Rarely is the metaphorical nature of God-language more apparent than in the first chapter of Ezekiel, in which the prophet is attempting to describe his call and the vision he experiences of God at his call. Ezekiel strains to employ every visual and auditory detail he can, to communicate the vividness of the experience: the wheels of the throne-chariot of God had an appearance "like the gleaming of beryl" (v. 16), and the sound of the wings of the living creatures that were associated with God's chariot had a sound "like the sound of mighty waters, like the thunder of the Almighty, a sound of tumult like the sound of an army" (v. 24). And yet his description is hedged about with the repetition of expressions like "appearance" and "something like." This is especially the case when he describes the figure of God: "seated above the likeness of a throne was something that seemed like a human form" (v. 26). And when he has completed his description, he says, "This was the appearance of the likeness of the glory of the Lord" (v. 28): No matter how specific I try to be in my description of God, he seems to imply, I know I am four steps removed from reality. All God-language is metaphorical.

Our age finds it hard to recognize this; our age is saturated with scientific description and with mountains of prose. In our recognition of the metaphorical nature of God-language, then, we must struggle against this temper of our times, which tends to reduce all language to a dead level of provable "facts." The scholar Walter Brueggemann, in a recent book on poetry, speaks sadly of our "prose-flattened world." "By prose," he writes, "I refer to a world that is organized in settled formulae, so that even pastoral prayers and love letters sound like memos. By poetry, I do not mean rhyme, rhythm, or meter, but language that moves like Bob Gibson's fast ball, that jumps at the right moment, that breaks open old worlds with surprise, abrasion, and pace."[19]

It follows that whenever we hear that God is king (Ps. 47:8), God is judge (Ps. 7:11), God is a warrior (Zeph. 3:17), God is father (Ps. 89:26), God made a covenant with Israel (Deut. 5:2), we must always phrase it as Ezekiel did: "God is king, as it seems; God is judge, as it seems; God is a warrior, as it seems; God is father, as it seems; God made a covenant with Israel, as it seems." Indeed, every reference to God as "he" must be "God, he, as it seems." There are at least hints in the Old Testament that one could say, "God, she, as it seems" (Deut. 32:18b). With this understanding of the vividness, the poetry, the allusiveness of words about God, we approach the task of hearing God in the Old Testament: the matter may not be quite so simple as we had thought.

Notes

1. *The Boston Globe,* 24 September 1992, 12.

2. Isa. 40:28, translated by Ronald Knox, *The Holy Bible* (New York: Sheed & Ward, 1956).

3. Compare the rendering by J. B. Phillips of the first sentence of John 1:1: "At the beginning God expressed Himself." *The Gospels Translated into Modern English* (London: Bles, 1952).

4. For example, Ecclus. 15:11-20 is the Old Testament reading appointed for the Sunday closest to May 11 in Year A; Wisd. 12:13, 16-19 is the Old Testament reading appointed for the Sunday closest to July 20 in Year A.

5. The details of all this may be found in many handbooks about the Bible. Useful are: "Introduction to the Apocryphal/Deuterocanonical Books," in Bruce M. Metzger and Roland E. Murphy (eds.), *The New Oxford Annotated Bible, with the Apocryphal/Deuterocanonical Books, New Revised Standard Version* (New York: Oxford University, 1991), Apocrypha, v–viii; Charles T. Fritsch, "Apocrypha," *IDB* 1:161-66; David N. Freedman, "Canon of the OT," *IDBSup* 130-36; Raymond E.

Brown, "Canonicity," *The New Jerome Biblical Commentary* (Englewood Cliffs, N.J.: Prentice Hall, 1990), 1037-43.

6. See E. C. Blackman, *Marcion and His Influence* (London: Society for the Propagation of Christian Knowledge, 1948), esp. chapter 7, "Marcion and the Old Testament."

7. Cited in Godfrey E. Phillips, *The Old Testament in the World Church* (Lutterworth Library 13; London: Lutterworth, 1942), 23.

8. For example, *The New Revised Standard Version, New Testament and Psalms* (Iowa Falls, Iowa: World Bible Publishers, 1989).

9. For a vivid work against "higher criticism," see Harold Lindsell, *The Battle for the Bible* (Grand Rapids, Mich.: Zondervan, 1976).

10. A readable account of the struggle, from the American point of view, may be found in Gerald P. Fogarty, *American Catholic Biblical Scholarship* (San Francisco: Harper & Row, 1989).

11. Mark S. Massa, *Charles Augustus Briggs and the Crisis of Historical Criticism* (Harvard Dissertations in Religion 25; Minneapolis: Fortress Press, 1990).

12. Fogarty, *American Catholic Biblical Scholarship,* chapters 5 and 6.

13. See conveniently Henry Bettenson, *Documents of the Christian Church* (New York & London: Oxford University, 1947), 72.

14. See briefly Sandra M. Schneiders, I.H.M., "Hermeneutics," *New Jerome,* 1159. For a helpful presentation of this point of view, see David J. A. Clines, "Possibilities and Priorities of Biblical Interpretation in an International Perspective," *Biblical Interpretation, A Journal of Contemporary Approaches,* 1:67–87.

15. See the recent work by Steven Pinker, *The Language Instinct, How the Mind Creates Language* (New York: Morrow, 1994), especially chapter 3.

16. *Mirriam-Webster's Collegiate Dictionary,* Tenth Edition (Springfield, Mass.: Merriam-Webster, Inc., 1994).

17. Paul M. Van Buren, *The Edges of Language, An Essay in the Logic of a Religion* (New York: Macmillan, 1972).

18. This is the burden of Sallie McFague, *Metaphorical Theology, Models of God in Religious Language* (Philadelphia: Fortress Press, 1982).

19. Walter Brueggemann, *Finally Comes the Poet, Daring Speech for Proclamation* (Minneapolis: Fortress Press, 1989), 3.

2

Covenant God and Covenant People

~

I begin with the notion of *covenant*, which is perhaps the ruling metaphor of the Old and New Testaments.[1] Indeed, *testament* was originally the Latin word referring to either of the two covenants of the Bible: the old covenant between God and Israel (Exod. 19:5), and the new covenant anticipated in Jer. 31:31-34 and mediated, so the Letter to the Hebrews affirms, by Jesus Christ with the Church (Heb. 8:1-13).

The Hebrew word for "covenant," *běrît,* is heard today in the name of the Jewish organization B'nai B'rith ("Sons [or Children] of the Covenant") and gave rise to the Yiddish word *bris,* "circumcision." In the Old Testament, *běrît* is used in various ways. It may refer to a relationship on a human level, between two unrelated individuals or communities. In that usage, it may refer to a close friendship and permanent loyalty between two individuals, probably sealed by an oath, such as the covenant between David and Jonathan (1 Sam. 18:1-4); it may refer to a political–military pact between factions, as when David made a covenant with the military leader Abner, who had defected from the house of Saul and was ready to give his loyalty to David instead (2 Sam. 3:12); it may refer to a public agreement between king and people, as in the instance of Zedekiah's promulgation of the freeing of slaves (Jer. 34:8); it may refer to a treaty between kings, such as that between the victorious Ahab of Israel and the defeated Ben-Hadad of Syria (1 Kings 20:34—in this instance, the word is translated "treaty" in the NRSV).

Most of the time, however, the word is descriptive of God's covenanting, and here we must introduce the distinction between a conditional covenant and an unconditional one. The covenant between God and Israel mediated by Moses at Sinai is the conditional covenant par excellence in the Old Testament. (I shall indicate below what the conditions are.) Beyond this conditional covenant, there are various unconditional covenants depicted in the Old Testament, especially with King David, but because the conditional covenant mediated by Moses is by far the most crucial one, I shall deal with it first.

At the beginning, let us remind ourselves that the Old Testament people used the name "Yahweh" for their God. The history of this name is a complicated one;[2] suffice it to say that the tradition recalls that God revealed this name to Moses at the burning bush (Exodus 3), and it was used freely in Israel until the building of the Second Temple at the end of the sixth century B.C., when the conviction arose that it was too holy to be pronounced freely. The NRSV signals the presence of the name "Yahweh" in the Hebrew text by the expression "the Lord" in small capital letters (see the introduction "To the reader" in the NRSV). The covenant at Sinai was understood to bind Yahweh and Israel together, giving rise to the oft-repeated formula, "I will be your God, and you shall be my people" (phrased in various ways: see Exod. 6:7; Lev. 26:12; Deut. 29:13; Jer. 7:23; 11:4; 30:22; 31:33).

We lack any complete idea of how the notion of covenant first entered the thinking of the ancestors of the Israelites; there is some evidence that clan leaders among the Amorites (west Semitic peoples at the time before Moses) understood their special relationship to a given god to be covenantal,[3] but the extent to which the narratives of Abraham, Isaac, and Jacob in Genesis directly represent these early beliefs is difficult to say.

The Background of the Covenant with Yahweh: The Suzerainty Treaties

Most helpful for our grasp of the earliest understanding of religious covenant are not religious sources at all but rather the form of *political* treaties that were made in the ancient Near East by a king with a subordinate ruler of a nation that owed allegiance to the king. Typical of these treaties (which scholars call "suzerainty treaties") are those of the Late Hittite empire (an empire centered in what is now east-central Turkey in the years 1400–1200 B.C.), but the form of these treaties evidently became standard for hundreds of years across the ancient Near East, for we find it not only among the Hittites but among the Assyrians in later centuries as well. The form of such a treaty, made by the suzerain (king) with the vassal on whom he was imposing loyalty, offers many analogies to the Old Testament covenant understood to have been made by Yahweh with Israel.

The typical political treaty contained six sections. It began with (1) a preamble, "These are the words of X," naming the suzerain. It continued with (2) a historical prologue, listing the gracious acts of the suzerain on behalf of the vassal. Then there followed (3) a set of stipulations, that is, the obligations to which the vassal binds himself. For example, the vassal must maintain his sole loyalty to the suzerain and not enter into a treaty with any other king, he must answer the suzerain's summons to arms, he must divide with the suzerain a given proportion of booty at the end of a war, he must send yearly tribute to the suzerain. There was then (4) provision for a deposit and public reading of the treaty at stipulated intervals; (5) a list of witnesses to the treaty, typically the gods of both states, the features of the natural world such as the heavens and the earth, and the like; and finally (6) a set of blessings and curses—the consequences on the vassal for his obedience, and for any disobedience on his part.

Yahweh's Conditional Covenant with Israel

This form of political treaty, as I have said, turns out to be strikingly like the form of covenant in the Old Testament. The Ten Commandments offer analogies to the first three parts of the suzerainty treaty: (1) the preamble is reduced to "I am Yahweh your God"; (2) the historical prologue is the phrase "who brought you out of the land of Egypt, out of the house of slavery" (for both of these, see Exod. 20:2; Deut. 5:6); and (3) the stipulations are the various laws of the Ten Commandments: no relations with any other god; respect for the covenant God; justice and harmony within the covenant community. There are no analogies to the last three parts of the suzerainty treaty in the Ten Commandments, but these are found elsewhere in the legal material. Thus, for (4) the deposit and public reading of covenant law, one may compare the narrative of the preservation of the tablets of stone in the ark of the covenant (Exod. 40:20) and the provision for the public reading of the law (Deut. 31:9-13). For (5) the mention of witnesses, one may compare the mention of heaven and earth at the conclusion of Moses' address in Deut. 30:19-20 and the summoning of heaven and earth when God, through the prophets, challenges Israel for breaking the terms of the covenant (Isa. 1:2; Mic. 6:1-2). For (6) the blessings and curses, one need only read Deuteronomy 27 and 28. That is to say, one may well conclude that Moses himself used the form of the current political treaties of his day as the model for his understanding of Yahweh's covenant with Israel at Sinai.[4]

Theological Consequences of the Metaphor of Covenant

Let us pause here. If the suzerainty treaties were a model for Yahweh's covenant mediated by Moses with Israel, then there are several theological consequences, both for Israel and for us. I will offer ten of these consequences.

1. If a covenant is made, then each party enters consciously into a *personal* relationship. Therefore, Yahweh is not conceived of simply as some

kind of impersonal ultimate reality. Israel understands that Yahweh speaks (Exod. 20:1) and Israel is therefore to listen, and Israel presumes to speak to Yahweh in prayer with the expectation that Yahweh will listen and perhaps shift intentions (Amos 7:1-6; see the discussion of worship in Chapter 13).

2. The personal relationship between Yahweh and Israel is one of mutual *claims*. Neither party can coerce the other; both parties have expectations from the other. On the one hand, Israel is not a puppet in the hands of Yahweh: Yahweh can set forth expectations, but Israel must take responsibility to obey. On the other hand, Israel obviously cannot coerce Yahweh, though Israel has the right to have expectations from Yahweh, for support and for blessing.

3. This noncoercive relation in its turn suggested further metaphors, drawn from family life, for the relation between Yahweh and Israel. Israel is called Yahweh's firstborn son (Exod. 4:22), and in Deut. 32:6, where Israel is addressed, God is called "your father," where the possessive pronoun is masculine singular. Above all, there is the metaphor of husband and wife, a metaphor drawn by the prophet Hosea out of his own marriage experience (Hos. 1–3) and developed by the prophets Jeremiah (Jer. 2:1—4:4; 31:32) and Ezekiel (Ezekiel 16; 23), a metaphor that, in turn, lay in the background of the inclusion of the Song of Songs within the Old Testament (see Chapter 12).

4. Yahweh has entered into relation with the *people* Israel, that is to say, with a community rather than with a single person or a single family unit. Therefore, the Old Testament faith has little to do with the spirituality of individuals and much to do with the destiny of communities of people.

5. Yahweh is understood to have taken the *initiative* in making the covenant with Israel: Israel did not choose Yahweh, but rather Yahweh chose Israel (Deut. 10:15 and often). When the prophets spoke of Israel's faithlessness in going after false gods, such as the fertility god Baal, they understood that that faithlessness was at Israel's initiative (Jer. 2:5, 23, 25), but Israel was never portrayed as taking the initiative in choosing Yahweh.

6. At least one source in the Old Testament pondered the question of why Yahweh should have chosen Israel, of all peoples—Israel certainly did not deserve to be chosen. The only answer forthcoming was based on the mystery of love and the fidelity of promises that Yahweh was understood to have made with the ancestors (Deut. 7:7-8). Many passages in the books of the prophets warn Israel not to assume that her chosenness is her due or a matter of privilege (Amos 3:1-2; 9:7).

7. If Yahweh made a covenant with Israel, then Yahweh and Israel are separate parties; that is to say, Yahweh is not simply some kind of projection of Israel's ideas or national goals. The gods that other peoples worshiped might

well be projections of their national goals (compare the prophet's mockery of the gods of Babylon, being hauled off on the backs of weary animals after the defeat of Babylon [Isa. 46:1-2]), but not Yahweh. Yahweh is separate from the created world (Genesis 1) and could outlast the created world (Jer. 4:23-26); by the same token, it is hinted that Yahweh would be capable of choosing some nation other than Israel to be a covenant partner (Amos 9:7).

8. Not everything Israel does is pleasing to Yahweh: though Yahweh may support and bless Israel, Yahweh may also judge Israel for wrongdoing. Israel cannot afford to take Yahweh's support for granted: the covenant bond depends on whether Israel meets its stipulations.

9. If the blessings and curses represent the array of Yahweh's responses toward Israel, the stipulations represent the array of Yahweh's expectations for Israel. They clarify the nature of the relation. In our day, relations between two people or two groups are often clarified by a resort to the vocabulary of psychology. In the Old Testament, on the other hand, the relation between Yahweh and Israel is clarified by a resort to the language of *obligation,* that is to say, to the language of law—the Hebrew word is *tôrâ,* usually spelled "Torah" in English. Christians, shaped by Paul's contrast between law and gospel, view with ambivalence the Old Testament emphasis on law; in the next chapter, I shall offer a more intensive treatment of the matter. For now, I must simply stress that the Old Testament assumes without question that Yahweh's giving of the law to Israel was an act of grace (Pss. 1; 19:7-14).

10. The fact that Yahweh's covenant with Israel was modeled on the form of the suzerainty treaty implies that the metaphor of Yahweh as *king* was paramount. That is to say, in Moses' understanding, Yahweh functioned as king over Israel: Israel was to withdraw her support from any human king and to give her loyalty instead to Yahweh. At the beginning at least, Yahweh was understood to function as a human king would, to guarantee the prosperity of the people (Deut. 28:3-5) and to protect the people militarily (Deut. 28:7). Thus, when the judge Gideon is urged to set up a hereditary monarchy in which he would be the monarch, he refuses: only Yahweh is to rule the people (Judg. 8:22-23). (I shall discuss in a moment the complication that arose when Israel later moved to set up the institution of human kingship.) It follows then that if Yahweh takes on the role of king, Yahweh is intensely concerned with all the issues of Israel's well-being that are today governmental concerns—political and economic matters. This is why the prophets speak out so passionately on issues of politics and economics, and why biblical religion is so specifically this-worldly. I indicated in the previous chapter that God has entered history, by which I meant that God has become manifest in the experienced common life of humankind. But now we see the testimony of

the Old Testament to be that God has not only entered history but participated in that history and woven a plan within that history.

Yahweh's Unconditional Covenant with David

The time came in Old Testament history when the notion of covenant shifted from a conditional to an unconditional one: this shift appears to have taken place during the reign of King David. I cannot pause here to detail how, in the face of the idea of the sole kingship of Yahweh, affirmed by Gideon, the institution of human kingship came to lodge so centrally in Israel, but one factor certainly was the notion of God's unconditional covenant with David.

The notion began, evidently, with a divine word that came to the prophet Nathan (2 Sam. 7:4-17), that Yahweh would guarantee the dynasty of David forever: "I [Yahweh] will not take my steadfast love from him. . . . Your house and your kingdom shall be made sure forever before me; your throne shall be established forever" (vv. 15-16). Admittedly, the word "covenant" (*bĕrît*) does not occur here, but a covenant is certainly implied, and other passages referring to this promise to David do use the word "covenant"; for example, in the "last words of David" we read, "He has made with me an everlasting covenant, ordered in all things and secure" (2 Sam. 23:5), and again, in Ps. 89:3-4, we read, "You said, 'I have made a covenant with my chosen one, I have sworn to my servant David: "I will establish your descendants forever, and build your throne for all generations."'" Here, the notion of covenant becomes something new, without conditions, a "sure promise."

So now we have two contrasting sets of assumptions about God. When Moses mediated the covenant, he is remembered as presenting to the Israelites the choice of life or death (Deut. 30:19), just as, if a vassal should break the suzerain's stipulations, the curses will be invoked and the vassal destroyed. In the covenant of Moses, God's treatment of Israel is conditional on Israel's behavior. But in the covenant of David, God is committed unconditionally to the support of this particular royal dynasty, and therefore, by extension, to the welfare of the nation ruled by that dynasty.

Narratives of other unconditional covenants begin to appear very early in the story of the Old Testament people. We hear of a covenant with Noah (Gen. 9:9-17), in which God promised "never again" to unleash the waters to destroy all flesh, an "everlasting covenant" (v. 16), the sign of which is the rainbow (v. 13). And we hear of a covenant with Abraham (Gen. 17:1-13), again an "everlasting covenant" (v. 7); in this narrative, however, there is the expectation that Abraham and his offspring would respond by keeping the rite of circumcision (vv. 9-10). It is not clear whether keeping circumcision is a limiting condition of the covenant with Abraham or simply a description of the human response that was taken for granted.

The Davidic line did, as a matter of fact, continue for more than four hundred years, a very long span of time for a single ruling house, so that the very continuity of the Davidic line reinforced a sense of confidence, even complacency, that Yahweh would support the Davidic line forever. Ruling political establishments are always prone to complacency about their own status, and certainly a religious outlook that assumes that God will always continue to support the royal house is an outlook that does not encourage any critical scrutiny of royal behavior.

Conditional or Unconditional Covenant?
The Prophetic Proclamations

The religious history of the Old Testament from David's time onward is marked by the tension between the newer notion of God's covenant with Israel as unconditional and the older notion of God's covenant with Israel as conditional. Will Yahweh support Israel no matter what Israel does, or can Yahweh choose to break off the covenant with Israel?

One hears a variety of voices on the matter during the period of the monarchy. For example, two psalms extol Yahweh's covenant with David, but on the question of whether the covenant is conditional or unconditional they come down on contrasting sides. Psalm 89 is a psalm I have already cited: vv. 3-4 use the word "covenant" to refer to Yahweh's relation with David, and in later verses that psalm becomes even more explicit on the unconditional nature of that relation: "If his [David's] children forsake my law and do not walk according to my ordinances, . . . then I will punish their transgression with the rod and their iniquity with scourges; but I will not remove from him my steadfast love, or be false to my faithfulness. I will not violate my covenant, or alter the word that went forth from my lips" (vv. 30, 32-34). But another psalmist sees the covenant with David as a conditional one: "The Lord swore to David a sure oath from which he will not turn back: 'One of the sons of your body I will set on your throne. If your sons keep my covenant and my decrees that I shall teach them, their sons also, forevermore, shall sit on your throne'" (Ps. 132:11-12).

The prophet Isaiah, in the eighth century B.C., was part of the palace circle serving the kings in Jerusalem, and he was thus committed both to the Davidic monarchy and to the inviolability of Jerusalem. One recalls the glorious visions he had of future kings in the line of David (Isa. 9:2-7; 11:1-9), and one may read, too, of his assurance to King Hezekiah during the Assyrian siege of

Jerusalem that "for the sake of my servant David" the city would not fall (2 Kings 19:32-34). Yet Isaiah constantly voiced Yahweh's judgment on the conduct of both king and commoner. In scathing fashion (Isa. 1:10), he called the ruling class "rulers of Sodom" and the people "people of Gomorrah," and called them to listen to the "teaching of our God," where the Hebrew word translated "teaching" is *tôrâ*, the word which, as we have seen, is usually translated "law." So, in a way, Isaiah was able to combine both covenantal motifs— to say, in effect, "Yahweh supports kings in the line of David, but Yahweh expects both king and people to adhere to Yahweh's stipulations" (compare Isa. 1:21-28).

One of the crucial turns in the recovery of the notion of the conditional nature of the covenant was the discovery, in the seventh century B.C., of the lawbook that became the core of the book of Deuteronomy, the circulation of that lawbook by King Josiah, and the consequent reforms he undertook (2 Kings 22–23). In a sense, the recovery of the lawbook of Deuteronomy was the rediscovery by king and people alike of the covenant mediated by Moses. Not only does Deuteronomy set forth the covenant after the model of the suzerainty treaty, as we have seen; Deuteronomy most particularly sets forth a strong image of the king as one who studies Torah (Deut. 17:18). The king's adherence to the covenant stipulations is the guarantee that "he and his descendants may reign long over his kingdom in Israel" (Deut. 17:20).

This rediscovery of Moses caught the attention of the prophet Jeremiah (end of the seventh century B.C.); in his preaching, one hears almost nothing about promises to David and everything about the kind of covenant presupposed by Moses. Jeremiah became convinced that Yahweh was determined to judge Israel for having broken the covenant, so that Jerusalem would be destroyed (see, for example, Jer. 7:16-20). Indeed, he understood himself to be called by Yahweh to abstain from marriage as a sign of the end of the covenant people (Jer. 16:1-4).

Jeremiah's Word on the New Covenant

Jeremiah's word on a "new covenant" (Jer. 31:31-34) is a fresh attempt to solve the dilemma between the conditional and the unconditional understandings of covenant. "I will make a new covenant with the house of Israel and the house of Judah. It will not be like the covenant that I made with their ancestors when I took them by the hand to bring them out of the land of Egypt—a covenant that they broke, though I was their husband" (vv. 31-32). The implication here is that the covenant concluded under Moses is a dead letter because it has been broken by Israel—Yahweh has annulled it because Israel has annulled it. Yet Yahweh has further resources, drawing up a new covenant that is not like the old one. "This is the covenant that I will make with the house of Israel after those days, . . . I will put my law within them, and I will write it on their hearts; and I will be their God, and they shall be my people. No longer shall they teach one another, or say to each other, 'Know the Lord,' for they shall all know me, from the least of them to the greatest . . . ; for I will forgive their iniquity, and remember their sin no more" (vv. 33-34).

For Yahweh's law to lodge in the heart of the people is for the people to obey Yahweh not out of obligation at all but out of their glad free will. In this way, Jeremiah manages to affirm both the responsibility of the people to obey Yahweh (they failed, so the covenant is to be replaced) and the ultimate ability of Yahweh to fulfill the divine will for the covenant people in spite of their erstwhile defiance. But the conundrum is only postponed to the future: if Yahweh has lodged the law in the people's heart, are the people not reduced from being free agents to the status of puppets? We shall return to this question later.

Even Jeremiah's notion of a new covenant was unwelcome to his fellows: the anonymous prophet of the exile whose words we find in Isaiah 40–55 affirmed, "The word of our God will stand forever" (Isa. 40:8), an affirmation that sounds like a rejection of Jeremiah's notion of a new covenant. And, most assuredly, Jer. 31:35-37 gives voice within the tradition of Jeremiah to an anonymous protest, probably from the postexilic period, against Jeremiah's vision of a new covenant: "Thus says the Lord, who gives the sun for light by day and the fixed order of the moon and the stars for light by night, who stirs up the sea so that its waves roar—the Lord of hosts is his name: If this fixed order were ever to cease from my presence, says the Lord, then also the offspring of Israel would cease to be a nation before me forever. Thus says the Lord: If the heavens above can be measured, and the foundations of the earth below can be explored, then I will reject all the offspring of Israel because of all they have done, says the Lord." That is to say, the heavens cannot be measured and the foundations of the earth cannot be explored—similarly, I [God] will never reject Israel in spite of all they have done: the covenant with Israel is as firm as the fixed order of the sun, moon, and stars. Here, finally, against all the wildness of Jeremiah, is the affirmation that Yahweh's covenant is for keeps.

The Question of Monotheism

We shall come back to think further about how to hear God in the metaphor of covenant, but first I must turn to a different question, one that steadily arises in our minds. If the ruling metaphor of the Old Testament is the covenant between Yahweh and Israel, to what extent did Israel believe that Yahweh was the *only* God? For us, monotheism is an important issue. Those who believe in God take it for granted that there is one God only; polytheism strikes us as primitive, a belief system of the early Greeks and Romans that has long since been outgrown by the human race.

There is no way, of course, to establish a full answer to the question; what the average person in Israel's population really believed is long past recovery. As a matter of fact, scattered evidence from archeology and from inscriptional material from Israelite times indicates that many Israelites did believe in more than one god. For example, "Asherah" was a goddess that was evidently understood by some to be a consort of Yahweh; King Manasseh is said to have erected a carved image of Asherah in the temple (2 Kings 21:7), and an inscription recently uncovered at a remote desert way station in the extreme south of Israel (Kuntillat Ajrud) refers to "Yahweh and his Asherah."[5]

But our basic resource remains the Old Testament itself, and so the question arises: To what extent does the Old Testament reflect general beliefs, or, to the contrary, to what extent is the Old Testament a *normative* document, the testimony of a tradition of religious leaders as to what Israelites *should* believe? The Old Testament offers many of the characteristics of the latter. Indeed, I wonder sometimes whether the Old Testament is not the manifesto of the five percent of Israelites who cared: this is no doubt an exaggeration, but it underlines an important point. On the other hand, it is not the practice of the Israelites that is authoritative for us but rather the biblical text, and so we turn to that text.

Even in the Old Testament, however, we find passages that suggest the possibility of a belief in other gods. For example, there is Ps. 77:13: "Your way, O Lord, is holy. What god is so great as our God?" And even more urgently, there is Psalm 82, which begins, "God has taken his place in the divine council; in the midst of the gods he holds judgment." What, we wonder, is really being affirmed here?

The question may trouble us, but it evidently did not trouble the Israelites unduly, because the texts are not consistent. On the one hand, given the notion of Yahweh's covenanting with Israel, many early texts assume that other gods are the gods of their respective nations just as Yahweh is the God of Israel. Given the assumption the Yahweh gave Israel the land of Canaan (see Chapter 6), it was natural to assume that other gods gave their nations their territories. For example, Deut. 32:8-9, part of an early poem, states, "When the Most High apportioned the nations, when he divided humankind, he fixed the boundaries of the peoples according to the number of the gods; the Lord's own portion was his people, Jacob his allotted share."[6]

Again, in Judg. 11:24, the Israelite Jephthah is trying to arbitrate a territorial dispute between Israel and the Ammonites, and he says, "Should you not possess what your god Chemosh gives you to possess? And should we not be the ones to possess everything that the Lord our God has conquered for our benefit?"

A further example of the same notion is in 1 Sam. 26:19. David is pleading with King Saul to cease pursuing him as an outlaw. "Now therefore let my lord the king [= Saul] hear the words of his servant [= David]. If it is the Lord who has stirred you up against me, may he accept an offering; but if it is mortals, may they be cursed before the Lord, for they have driven me out today from my share in the heritage of the Lord, saying, 'Go serve other gods.'" David, in this speech, presumes that Yahweh may be worshiped only within Israelite territory, and he pleads that he not be exiled and forced to serve other gods in whom he has no interest. (Ironically, the next chapter tells of David's seeking sanctuary from Saul among the enemy Philistines, but no notice is taken there of his being forced to worship any Philistine deity.)

On the other hand, Deut. 32:8-9, which I have already cited, indicates that Yahweh was in charge of delegating various territories to various gods, so that Yahweh is thought of here as chief of the gods. Psalm 82 points in a similar direction: Yahweh is accusing the pagan gods of lack of concern for the weak and needy, with the result that they will die like mere mortals (vv. 3, 7). In Amos 1:3—2:3, we hear a series of judgments uttered by Yahweh against foreign nations for their cruelty in warfare (I shall examine this passage in more detail in Chapter 9). Amos therefore assumes that Yahweh is the only God, and that when foreign nations are to be judged, it is Yahweh who will do the judging. The insistence that Yahweh is the only God is pressed again and again in the words of the anonymous prophet of the exile (Isaiah 40–55), whose prophetic material is addressed to the Jews in Babylon. Yahweh confronts the gods of the nations and mocks them for their inability to do anything. "Tell us what is to come hereafter, that we may know that you are gods; do good, or do harm, that we may be afraid and terrified. You, indeed, are nothing and your work is nothing at all; whoever chooses you is an abomination" (Isa. 41:23-24). This testimony was a powerful tonic to Jews who might be tempted to believe that, because Babylon had won the war with Judah, the Babylonian gods were stronger than Yahweh.

We may conclude that, for early Israel, the belief in the covenant said nothing directly about the existence of other gods; what was crucial was that

Yahweh was the only God *for Israel*. Only later, as Israel pondered Yahweh's will for foreign nations, were the Isrealites moved to insist on the unique existence of the God to whom they owed allegiance.

New Testament Perspectives on Covenant

We have seen that the metaphor of covenant directed Israel's faith in quite specific directions. Now we must ask: Can Christians hear God through the expressions of this metaphor, and if so, how? At the beginning of this chapter, I pointed out that covenant was the ruling metaphor for the Bible, uniting the Old "Testament" (covenant) with the New "Testament" (covenant). There are all kinds of pointers from the Old Testament to the New on this matter; let me rather unsystematically suggest just a few.

One must first affirm that the metaphor is congruent with Jesus' teaching. Jesus was reared within the context of the covenant, as the Jewish community understood it in his day; he is remembered as saying, "I was sent only to the lost sheep of the house of Israel" (Matt. 15:24), the implication being that God sent him to gather together the covenant community that had been scattered.

The New Testament knows Jesus as "son of David"; that lineage is affirmed in the genealogies of Matthew and Luke (Matt. 1:1-17; Luke 3:23-38), in placing Jesus' birth in Bethlehem, the city of David (Matt. 2:5-6; Luke 2:11), and in many scattered notices (for example, Mark 10:47-48; Rom. 1:3). This is one of the ways the New Testament testifies that Jesus is ultimately the one with whom God has covenanted.

Through Jesus Christ, God has covenanted with the Church. We ponder the metaphor employed in Rom. 11:17-21, that God has engrafted the Gentiles onto the olive tree of Israel, so that the Gentiles have become part of the covenant people by faith in Jesus Christ. It is important, by the way, to grasp the message of the whole of Romans 11: God has not rejected the Jews in favor of the Christians—the new covenant passage in Jeremiah must never be understood that way. The new covenant in that passage is a covenant implicating the same Torah of God just as much as the covenant mediated by Moses did. We might then understand the new covenant as being not so much a replacement of an old covenant as a renewal of the covenant with Moses.[7] In any event, God has not rejected the Jews (Rom. 11:1). The tree of Christians has not replaced the old olive tree; rather, Christians are engrafted onto the old tree.

It is useful to ponder Jesus' prayer in the Garden of Gethsemane, "Abba, Father, for you all things are possible; remove this cup from me; yet, not what I want, but what you want" (Mark 14:36). This memory of Christian tradition, that Jesus did God's will utterly, led finally to the affirmation in the Letter to the Hebrews, where Jesus is understood to be the high priest "who in every respect has been tested as we are, yet without sin" (Heb. 4:15). That is to say, Jesus is one who really fits Jeremiah's description of the people of the new covenant: in Jesus' heart, God planted the Torah, the stipulations of obedience, without rendering him a puppet. Jesus obeyed God not simply because he was obligated to, certainly not because he was forced to, but more profoundly because he wanted to. This understanding then leads the writer of Hebrews to quote the whole new covenant passage from Jeremiah (8:8-12), to set forth what God has now done in the Church through the sacrifice of Jesus Christ.

The New Testament then can affirm that the Church is the "Israel of God" (Gal. 6:16), that the action of God testified to in the Old Testament has been reaffirmed and completed in the "new covenant" with the Church. This new covenant is thus not with a specific community bound by common ties of tradition and kinship, as Israel was, but with a new community of faith gathered from all the world, from every race and nation.

The theological consequences of the metaphor of covenant that I set forth earlier in this chapter are then valid for the New Testament faith as well, as I have indicated. The New Testament offers in both summary and climactic fashion that to which the testimony of the Old Testament has been pointing: God's initiative to call us into community, God's personal interaction with us in community, God's intention for that community expressed in norms of righteousness and devotion and love. The New Testament likewise offers in summary and climactic fashion the perception in the whole Old Testament, of the seriousness with which God judges us in our sin and the steadfastness with which God wills to save us. We hear God in the testimony of the people of the Old Testament, and that testimony emboldens us to respond ourselves to the covenanting God.

Notes

1. The literature on the topic is immense. A good introduction for "covenant" as a metaphor is Delbert R. Hillers, *Covenant, The History of a Biblical Idea* (Baltimore: Johns Hopkins, 1969), 4–5. For further reading, see George E. Mendenhall, "Covenant," *IDB* 714–23; Paul A. Riemann, "Covenant, Mosaic," *IDBSup* 192–97; Moshe Weinfeld, "Covenant, Davidic," *IDBSup* 188–92; William L. Holladay, "New covenant, the," *IDBSup* 623–25, and the bibliographies in these articles; or George E. Mendenhall and Gary A. Herion, "Covenant," *ABD* 1:1179–1202 and the bibliography there.

2. See conveniently Bernhard W. Anderson, "God, names of," *IDB* 2:409–11; Henry O. Thompson, "Yahweh," *ABD* 6:1011–12; David Noel Freedman, Michael Patrick O'Connor, and Helmer Ringgren, "YHWH," *TDOT* 5:500–21.

3. On this, see John Bright, *A History of Israel* (Philadelphia: Westminster, 1981), 98–99.

4. For the structure of suzerainty treaties and Old Testament analogies, see conveniently George E. Mendenhall, "Covenant."

5. For the inscription, see Michael Coogan, "Canaanite Origins and Lineage: Reflections on the Religion of Ancient Israel," in Patrick Miller, Jr., Paul D. Hanson, and S. Dean McBride (eds.), *Ancient Israelite Religion, Essays in Honor of Frank Moore Cross* (Philadelphia: Fortress Press, 1987), 115–24; for the whole matter of polytheism in early Israel, see Mark S. Smith, *The Early History of God, Yahweh and the Other Deities in Ancient Israel* (San Francisco: Harper & Row, 1990).

6. There is a text problem here: the standard Hebrew text reads "the Israelites" rather than "the gods" (compare the KJV), but that reading is probably the result of later editing. Other early texts of the passage, such as one among the Dead Sea Scrolls and the Greek Septuagint translation, evidently more original, do read "the gods."

7. For a careful examination of this whole matter see Norbert Lohfink, *The Covenant Never Revoked, Biblical Reflections on Christian–Jewish Dialogue* (New York: Paulist Press, 1991).

3

The Texture of the Covenant: Law

It was suggested in Chapter 2 that the Old Testament law embodies the stipulations of God's covenant with Israel, and so we must turn to ponder the ways in which we might hear God in the Old Testament law.[1]

What the Christians call the "Pentateuch"—the first five books of the Old Testament (Genesis through Deuteronomy)—the Jews call "Torah," that is, "Law" in the extended sense. As we know, the story of Moses begins in Exodus, and the laws that tradition maintains were given through Moses are found in Exodus, Leviticus, Numbers, and Deuteronomy. Genesis offers the traditions of Israel about what happened before Moses, but even in Genesis there are passages of law: the sabbath is in place on the seventh day of creation (Gen. 2:2-3); Noah is allowed to eat meat without blood (Gen. 9:3-6) in anticipation of the laws on kosher meat; and Abraham is given the commandment of circumcision (Gen. 17:9-14).

But the massive legal material is found in Exodus, Leviticus, Numbers, and Deuteronomy. These four books span the narrative of Moses' life: he is born in Egypt in Exodus 2 and dies in Deuteronomy 34, having brought the Israelites out of Egypt and through the wilderness and to the plains of Moab, east of the Jordan river, as he looks west to the Promised Land. Some of the content of these four books is thus narrative: the call of Moses, his confrontations with Pharaoh, and his taking the people out of Egypt and to the mountain called Sinai (all of this in Exodus 3–19). The notice of the departure of Moses and the Israelites *from* Sinai is found in Num. 10:11. Between Exodus 19 and Numbers 10, several incidents are narrated: the episode of the golden calf and Moses' breaking of the tablets of the commandments, the preparation of new tablets, and the making of the furnishings of the tabernacle (all of this in Exodus 32–40). A few incidents are narrated in Numbers 1–10, notably the taking of a census. But all of Exodus 20–31 (beginning with the Ten Commandments in chapter 20), the whole of the book of Leviticus, and much of Numbers 1–10 consist of laws and instructions from Moses. The narrative of the wanderings in the wilderness commences in

Numbers 10, but that narrative is interspersed with more laws and instructions, notably in Numbers 15; 18–19; and 28–30. The book of Deuteronomy purports to be Moses' farewell addresses to his people, offering sermonic material in chapters 1–11 (but including a review of the Ten Commandments in chapter 5) and laws in chapters 12–26, and closing with various miscellaneous matters in chapters 27–34.

In summary, roughly 64 percent of the four books, Exodus through Deuteronomy, consists of laws and other instruction of Moses (the proportion is 47 percent of the Pentateuch as a whole, when one counts Genesis).

Historically, the Jews have always understood the law to be God's primary mode of self-revelation. They have constantly discussed and refined the law. If we examine Jewish tradition past the period of the Old Testament, we find the Mishnah, a compilation of rabbinic opinions about the law that was collected by the end of the second century A.D., and then the Babylonian Talmud, an extended commentary on the Mishnah, upward of 30 volumes of text, compiled by the fifth century A.D.,[2] a veritable ocean of material for the guidance of Jewish lives. When we look back at the New Testament from this perspective, we realize how important the issue of the law was to the early church, to Paul, and to Jesus himself. When we look back from the New Testament to the Old Testament outside the Pentateuch, we are continually made aware of the centrality of the law for Jews: righteous people ideally meditate on the law day and night (Ps. 1:2), and the statutes and ordinances given to Israel are understood to be on a par with God's giving of peace and sending of snow and rain to the earth (Ps. 147:12–20). In other words, God's giving of the law is understood as grace (see Chapter 2).

Yet, for Christians, this bulk of law in the Pentateuch represents a kind of huge indigestible lump at the beginning of the Bible. I noted in Chapter 1 the barrier that the laws of Leviticus pose to those who want to read the Bible from cover to cover. Indeed, my experience with Christian theological students is that they often cannot develop any active perception of the presence of the laws of the Old Testament. Sometimes, for a final examination essay, I will ask them to summarize the Pentateuch, and what I get is a mention of Creation and the Flood; of Abraham, Isaac, Jacob, and Joseph; of Moses and his liberation of Israel from Egypt—but rarely do I read in their essays anything about the *law*. It is as if these students not only do not read the laws but come close to overlooking their very existence—as if that 64 percent of Exodus through Deuteronomy were simply invisible. We distort the Old Testament when we bypass material that bulks so large. If we are to try to hear God in the Old Testament, then we must inevitably take seriously this collection of laws that the Old Testament itself takes so seriously.

Any discussion of Old Testament laws will be complex, for they represent a complex phenomenon. I shall organize my discussion in five sections. First, I shall describe several kinds of classifications of the law. Second, I shall indicate some evidences for the historical elaboration of the law and the social setting of the law. Third, I shall briefly describe the New Testament attitudes toward the law. Fourth, I shall try to discern a theology of the law. Fifth, I shall work through a chapter of laws in Leviticus (Leviticus 19) to try to discern the intention of God and the understanding of Israel in these laws, especially the ethical laws.

Classifications of the Laws

The laws of the Pentateuch can be classified in several different ways. One basic way is the contrast made by scholars between "apodictic" and "casuistic" laws. Apodictic (or policy or categorical) laws are of the "you shall" and "you shall not" variety, typified by the Ten Commandments; these laws are normally quite short in form. In these laws, no punishment is prescribed if the law should be broken; indeed, with a law like "you shall not covet" (Exod. 20:17; Deut. 5:21), it is hard to imagine how it could be enforced. Casuistic laws, by contrast, are case (or procedural) laws, laws that begin in a form like "if someone" or "when someone." One reads, for example, "When an ox gores a man or a woman to death, the ox shall be stoned, and its flesh shall not be eaten; but the owner of the ox shall not be liable" (Exod. 21:28). This law continues for another four verses. Scholars suspect that apodictic law is old: some of it could plausibly be attributed to the historical Moses. Some casuistic law may be very old too, but a good deal of it, particularly laws concerning property—fields, vineyards, and the like, such as are found in Exod. 21:33—22:17—is likely to have been developed later, after Israel settled in Canaan.

Another way to classify the laws is to try to identify the various collections of laws—for it is clear that there are several such collections. For one thing, some of the same stipulations are often repeated within different collections. As an example, the prohibition against taking interest from a fellow-Israelite is found in Exod. 22:25, part of what scholars call the "Covenant Code"; in Lev. 25:36-37, part of the so-called "Holiness Code"; and in Deut. 23:19-20, part of the "Deuteronomic Code."

What is the extent of these various codes?

There is the set of laws we call the Ten Commandments, which, as is well known, exist in two almost identical recensions, Exod. 20:1-17 and Deut. 5:6-21.

There is the so-called "Covenant Code," evidently one of the oldest of the legal collections; it begins in Exod. 20:22 after the Exodus version of the Ten Commandments and continues until Exod. 23:19, after which there is a sermonic conclusion, Exod. 23:20-33.[3]

Exodus 34, a narrative embodying a renewal of the covenant, contains in vv. 14-26 a fresh set of laws which, to some degree, overlap those of the Ten Commandments and of the Covenant Code.

There is the "Deuteronomic Code," the legal material in Deuteronomy, that is, Deuteronomy 12–26 (plus, perhaps, 28:1-6, 16-19); we saw in Chapter 2 how the discovery and publication of an early form of Deuteronomy represented for the seventh century a kind of rediscovery of Moses. This material seems to have been influenced by the early prophets, particularly Hosea in the eighth century B.C.; it perhaps embodies the tradition of the Levites in northern Israel, brought south to Jerusalem after the fall of the north to Assyria in 722 B.C.[4]

To the Deuteronomic Code has been appended a collection of "Twelve Curses" (Deut. 27:14-26); scholars now think that this collection might be a quite late one, from the sixth or fifth century B.C.[5]

There is the "Holiness Code," Leviticus 17–26, so called because of its dominant theme: Israel must be holy as God is holy (compare Lev. 19:2). It is a presentation of old laws in a very distinctive style close to the style found in Ezekiel, so, like Ezekiel, it may have taken shape in the exilic period (sixth century B.C.), but the traditions it embodies are very old.

Finally, there is the so-called "Priestly Code," which includes Leviticus 1–16 and scattered material in Exodus and Numbers; indeed, one can envisage the Priestly Code as the latest of the collections to be completed and, in a sense, the amplification and integration of the rest—though, again, the oral tradition behind much of it may be very old.

It is noteworthy that several of these codes mix apodictic and casuistic law. Thus, the Covenant Code begins with apodictic laws prohibiting idols and prescribing how an altar is to be built (Exod. 20:22-26), continues with casuistic laws (called "ordinances") from Exod. 21:1 to 22:17, and then reverts to apodictic law for the balance of the collection (Exod. 22:18—23:19).

We may go on to note that many of these law codes have themselves undergone expansions and additions. For example, again in the Covenant Code, in Exod. 23:1-3 and 6-9, each of the verses is in a prohibition style ("you shall not"), and all the prohibitions deal with court procedure. This sequence is interrupted by vv. 4-5, where each verse begins with "when" and is concerned not with court procedure but with treatment of the animals of one's enemy.

One must conclude that, from a literary point of view, these legal collections have a very complicated history.

Within the laws, another twofold distinction has traditionally been made between ritual laws and ethical laws: ritual laws are concerned with the relation of human beings to God, and ethical laws are concerned with the relation of human beings with each other. The former include laws prohibiting idols and various ritual commands relating to offerings, sacrifices, and the like; the latter include what we would call both civil and criminal law. But alongside ritual laws and ethical laws one must introduce a third category that falls into neither of these classifications—what might be called laws prohibiting any break with the perceived perfection of creation. These would include dietary laws forbidding the eating of pork (Lev. 11:7; Deut. 14:8) and of shrimp (Lev. 11:10; Deut. 14:10).

The various law codes stress sometimes one category, sometimes another. Thus, the collection of laws in Exodus 34 concerns ritual matters, while the Covenant Code is almost entirely concerned with ethical matters but does contain some ritual laws (Exod. 22:18-20; 23:10-19). In some sequences of the law, ritual, ethical, and creational laws are inextricably interwoven, for example, in Leviticus 19, a chapter I shall analyze in detail below. It is as if Israel was hardly conscious of any distinction among one's obligations to God, to creation, and to one's fellows.

As we have already noted, the word that covers "law" in the Old Testament is "Torah." The Hebrew word *tôrâ* does mean what we mean by "law," particularly in later portions of the Old Testament, but in earlier times it might be more adequately translated "guidance," "teaching," "instruction." As we noted in Chapter 2, the word *tôrâ* appears in Isa. 1:10. In the KJV, it is translated "law"; in the RSV and the NRSV, it is perhaps more accurately translated "teaching." In Jer. 18:18, *tôrâ* is the responsibility of the priests: the word is again translated "law" in the KJV but "instruction" in the RSV and the NRSV. This verse reminds us that it was in priestly circles that Torah was preserved, taught, and elaborated.

Historical Elaboration and Social Setting of the Law

At this point, one can raise a whole series of questions. (1) How elaborate was the law at various stages of Israel's history? (2) How thoroughly did the population of the covenant community actually know the details of the law? (3) Did both leaders and the common people expect the law to be carried out and enforced, or was the law set forth as an ideal, a kind of gesture of public relations? (4) How did the law function in shaping the self-awareness of the community? (5) What was the attitude toward the law on the part of those who kept it, and on the part of those who broke it? These are crucial questions, but unfortunately they are very difficult to answer.

There are some clues, though indirect; one is the array of passages that appear to reject the sacrificial system in favor of justice and righteousness. A whole series of these can be found, mostly in the prophets. One of the earliest is Amos 5:21-24: v. 21 understands God to say, "I hate, I despise your festivals, and I take no delight in your solemn assemblies," and v. 24 reads, "But let justice roll down like waters, and righteousness like an everflowing stream." Other such passages are: Isa. 1:10-17; 65:1-4; Jer. 6:20; Mic. 6:6-8; and, outside of the prophets, Pss. 50:8-14; 51:16-17. Though in these passages God seems to reject sacrifice altogether, they more likely do not imply so much the rejection of the sacrificial system as that the priority must be given to justice and righteousness.

But two prophetic passages do imply that God never legislated concerning sacrifices at all: (1) Jer. 7:21-23, where v. 22 suggests that burnt offerings and sacrifices were not part of God's commandments at Sinai, and (2) Amos 5:25, which offers a rhetorical question that points in the same direction. These passages throw into question the legitimacy of the whole set of sacrificial laws.

In Isa. 29:13, there is another sort of critique: the prophet understands God to be offering judgment on those who worship. "These people draw near with their mouths and honor me with their lips, while their hearts are far from me, and their worship of me [literally, their fear of me] is a human commandment learned by rote [*miṣwat ʾănāšîm mĕlummādâ*]." The Hebrew of this final phrase means literally "a taught commandment of men"; the NJB translates "nothing but human commandment, a lesson memorised." The verse then suggests that (at least some of) the laws concerning worship in Isaiah's day were perceived by him to be of human origin.

Two more passages from Jeremiah throw some light on the questions I have raised. The first is Jer. 5:4-5. The verse is in the midst of a passage in which God accuses the people in Jerusalem of rejecting the norms of the covenant. But then the prophet himself interjects, "Then I said, 'These are only the poor, they have no sense; for they do not know the way of the Lord, the law of their God. Let me go to the rich and speak to them; surely they know the way of the Lord, the law of their God.' But they all alike had broken the yoke, they had burst the bonds." Here one has the impression that the details of the law were something that only the elite could be expected to know.

In Jer. 8:8, God accuses the elite with these words, "How can you say, 'We are wise, and the law of the Lord is with us,' when, in fact, the false pen of the scribes has made it into a lie?" It is important to stress, in other words, that it is not only the New Testament that has leveled a critique against aspects of the system of law understood to be of divine origin: such critique can be found within the Old Testament itself.

From such scattered verses, we must try to discern the social place of the law at various points in Old Testament history.

Who heard the law and pondered it—the male heads of families? The leading citizens of villages and towns? To what extent did females know and learn the law? How carefully was the law passed on to the next generation?

One can surmise that the earliest legal collections were short, easily repeated, and easily memorized. There are the Ten Commandments, and doubtless each was originally short: the elaborations that are now a part of the commandment against idol worship and of the commandment to keep the sabbath would be expansions from later times.

When one looks at the "Twelve Curses" in Deuteronomy 27, one notices two things. First, most of them are short; again, they could be easily memorized. Second, the form of the first and the last curses in Hebrew is different from the form of the intervening ten. The intervening ten all have a participle after the initial word "cursed" (v. 16, for example, begins literally "Cursed [anyone] dishonoring"), but the first and the last curses have instead a dependent clause with a finite verb—"Cursed who will make . . ." (v. 15); "Cursed who will not uphold . . ." (v. 26). One may conclude that the first and last curses, which do not conform to the participial pattern, were added later,[6] so again the central ones would have made up an original ten. People can be expected to be able to count to ten, and sequences like these must have been the backbone of what was understood as God's "instruction"—Torah—to the covenant people.

Both the Ten Commandments and the Twelve (or ten) Curses of Deuteronomy 27 are apodictic, as we have seen. Here are the parameters of behavior for the covenant people: these are the basics, the prime examples of how the covenant people are to live.

But always, in any community of people, troublesome specific cases come up: the Ten Commandments may forbid murder or adultery, but then what is one to do when one has a specific murderer or adulterer on one's hands? Case law (a body of casuistic laws) is always necessary in real communities, and Israel clearly took over much of its case law from other cultures in the ancient Near East: for example, the Covenant Code bears a remarkable resemblance to the Code of Hammurabi (promulgated in Mesopotamia in the eighteenth century B.C.).[7] But, as we have seen, case law too was understood in Israel to be part of the covenant stipulations imposed by God. And so case law evolved, through cases dealing not only with murderers and adulterers but with the liability of the owner of a goring ox and all the rest.

I wish to make one more point regarding the steady elaboration of the ritual law. In spite of Jer. 7:22, we must surely conclude that the Israelites offered some kind of sacrifices while they were in the wilderness: the narrative of the exodus from Egypt offers some very primitive details in the procedure of Passover sacrifice (Exodus 12). The verse in Jeremiah then would reflect the prophet's irritation at the elaboration of the sacrificial system in his day, an irritation that produced his denial of its antiquity. The complicated system of sacrifices set forth in Leviticus 1–7 reflects the procedure in the postexilic Temple in Jerusalem in the sixth century B.C. and thereafter, and that growing elaboration was doubtless the target of the judgments of the prophets to which I have pointed.

Our tentative conclusions at this point must be that some apodictic law (like the Ten Commandments) was early, and that some case law was an elaboration during later times; that the law was something that was known more to the elite in the community than to the poor; that there was a tendency for ritual law to become more elaborate as time went on, and at the expense of ethical law; and that there was a human tendency for elaborations of the law to reflect greed as well as compassion.

For many laws, a question becomes acute: To what extent were they intended to be enforced, and if so, how? I should like to analyze two such laws, the prohibition against taking interest and the provision for the execution of a rebellious son.

Regarding the prohibition against taking interest, three passages deal with the taking of *nešek* from a fellow-Israelite: Exod. 22:25; Lev. 25:36-37; and Deut. 23:19. (The verse that follows in Deuteronomy does, however, allow *nešek* to be taken from a foreigner.) The literal meaning of the word *nešek* is evidently "bite," and it is therefore assumed by many that the term refers to the *deduction* of what we would call interest from the amount loaned, repayment being for the full amount. In the Leviticus passage, not only is the taking of *nešek* forbidden but the taking of *tarbît* as well: this word seems to mean "increase" and therefore is assumed to refer to an extra payment in addition to the full amount of the loan, more like the interest to which we are accustomed.

Interest rates could be high: in Babylonian texts from Jeremiah's time, the rate was 20 percent per year.[8] If one assumed that fellow-Israelites were part of one's extended "family," and that one did not expect interest to be paid on loans within the family, then the prohibition made sense. But the discussions of these laws in the later Mishnah[9] suggest how complicated it could get. Rabbi Gamaliel taught that if a man purposed to borrow from another and made him a present and said, "That thou mayest lend me money," that is *nešek* paid in advance.[10] What then is legitimate profit in a transaction? "A tenant may offer increased rent in exchange for a loan to improve his field, without fearing that this is of the nature of *nešek*."[11]

When, to these later rabbinic comments, one adds two passages from Jeremiah in which another term appears—*beṣaʿ*, literally "cut," translated "unjust gain" in the NRSV—we begin to form a picture of the nature of the problem. In Jer. 6:13, one hears God's judgment against the whole covenant people: "For from the least of them to the greatest, each is [literally] 'cutting a cut,' and from prophet to priest each of them is dealing falsely." Jer. 22:17 is an indictment addressed to King Jehoiakim, "For your eye and your heart are on nothing but your 'cut,' on the shedding of innocent blood and practicing deceit and violence." It is a world in which the less powerful try to please the more powerful, in which favors are sought and palms are greased.

Let us look at one more passage, Neh. 13:4-9, from the fifth century B.C., in the postexilic period. The priest Eliashib had allowed a relative of his, a man named Tobiah, private use of one of the storage rooms in the temple, doubtless for some advantageous commercial purpose.[12] Eventually, Nehemiah, the governor, got wind of the abuse and put a stop to it. So one asks: How can a law against interest catch up with all of the ways farmers and merchants can devise both to help each other out, profiting from each other's situations, and to exploit each other's disadvantages?

I turn more briefly to another law whose application we could wonder about: Deut. 21:18-21, a law in which parents who have a refractory son ("stubborn and rebellious") are to bring him before the elders of the city and so state ("He will not obey us: he is a glutton and a drunkard"), after which the men of the city shall stone the son to death. This is doubtless part of old family law;[13] the closing comment speaks of the effect of carrying out such a sentence ("all Israel will hear, and be afraid").

It is noteworthy that the discussion in the Mishnah hedges this law about with all kinds of provisions:[14] the son cannot be condemned if only one parent wishes it, or if either parent is maimed in the hand or lame or dumb or blind or deaf, and so on. One may conclude that the law, at least in later times, was rarely enforced, and one could hope that, at times when this law might have been invoked, various elders in the city held quiet discussions, made discreet interventions, and did their best to avoid the ultimate punishment. But there *was* such a law, and we must reluctantly conclude that it must have been enforced from time to time in the course of the history of Israel. And we can imagine the circumstances, for, in our own day, there are, in some of our schools, a few young men who seem, as far as the principals and the teachers can judge, to be incorrigible, and there are in our courts today a few young men who seem, as far as the police and the judges can discern, to be steadily violent. No one knows why, completely, today, any more than anyone knew in ancient times. And, if the ancient Israelites lacked prisons, death would appear to have been the only solution. But again, the existence of the law, as much as its occasional enforcement, must have kept the number of cases of delinquency to a minimum.

New Testament Attitudes toward the Law

Now let us turn to the New Testament attitudes toward the law: Christians are more familiar with these attitudes, and we must at least touch on them here. The background to the New Testament is the steadily continuing elaboration of details of both the ritual law and the ethical law, particularly among the Pharisees. We tend to be impatient with this impulse to legal elaboration among the Pharisees, but we must bear in mind that it represented a genuine effort to keep the law relevant and current. Always, for Jews, fresh questions kept emerging. Rabbi Tarfon, who taught in the generation after A.D. 70, maintained that the oil for sabbath lamps must be olive oil (a ruling that is practical in Palestine); but then the question arose, is the ruling binding on Jews living in Babylon, where the only oil available is sesame oil?[15]

The texts of the New Testament are concerned through and through with questions about the Jewish law. Even though the Gospel tradition took final shape forty or fifty years after Jesus' earthly career, it is clear from its testimony that Jesus broke with the Pharisaic tradition of steady elaboration of the law. It is true that he assumed that the law was given by Moses and was normally valid, both the ritual law (Mark 1:44) and the ethical law (Mark 7:10); indeed, Matthew preserves the tradition that Jesus declared that "until heaven and earth pass away, not one letter, not one stroke of a letter, will pass from the law until all is accomplished" (Matt. 5:18). On the other hand, Jesus replaced the Old Testament divorce law (Deut. 24:1-4) with his own pronouncement (Mark 10:2-9), stating that Moses gave the divorce law "for your hardness of heart" and that the intention of God in creation is something altogether different. Jesus set his own judgment above the strictures about the sabbath, since "The sabbath was made for humankind, and not humankind for the sabbath" (Mark 2:27). The Gospel of Mark asserts that Jesus, by implication, declared all foods clean (Mark 7:19). Jesus accused the Pharisees of laying heavy burdens on people's shoulders, that is to say, minute interpretations of the law (Matt. 23:4—note that the parallel in Luke 11:46 is applied to the "lawyers"); and he accused them of fussing about tithes on small portions of herbs while forgetting larger questions of justice (Matt. 23:23, parallel in

Luke 11:42). He is remembered as having summed up the law in a double form by citing Deut. 6:4-5 ("Hear, O Israel: the Lord our God, the Lord is one; you shall love the Lord your God, with all your heart, and with all your soul, and with all your mind, and with all your strength") and Lev. 19:18 ("You shall love your neighbor as yourself").

But Jesus dealt almost exclusively with his fellow Jews, who took the law for granted. Paul, by contrast, addressed himself to Gentiles, who were thus outside Jewish law, and he understood the danger of antinomianism—the notion that in behavior, anything goes (compare Rom. 6:1). The law, Paul maintains, has been our "disciplinarian" until Christ came (Gal. 3:24; the New American Bible translates the word as "monitor"). It guides us and shows us where we have gone wrong, but it cannot bring about the kind of joyful obedience to God that Christ brings.

The New Testament sees the law as both a channel to God's intention and a barrier to it. Indeed, the New Testament appears to look at the law in somewhat the same way as the scattered prophetic critiques did. Finding our theological way in the Old Testament law, then, will not be simple.

A Theology of the Law

As we seek to sketch a Christian theology of the law, let us begin with the seriousness of God. The existence of covenant stipulations for Israel indicates that God is serious—serious in expecting fidelity and devotion from the covenant people, and serious about the behavior and attitudes of the covenant people. To say that God is "serious" does not imply that God has no sense of humor, nor that God is not profoundly loving, nor that God is unapproachable, nor that the people of the covenant do not experience profound joy in God's service—by no means; it is to suggest that it is not enough to assume (as the Deists have done) that God has simply set creation going and that it runs thereafter of itself; nor is it enough to assume (as some people casually do today) that since God understands all, God will forgive all, and that "anything goes."

Let us look at Jesus. Jesus clearly had a sense of humor: he suggested that the prospect of a rich man's getting into heaven had less chance of success than the attempt to squeeze a camel through a needle's eye. Jesus was profoundly loving. Jesus was utterly approachable. Those who followed Jesus knew great joy. But at the same time, Jesus was utterly serious: he understood his enemy to be the arch-enemy of God, Satan himself, and he worked tirelessly to rid those he met of Satan's touch (we shall return to this matter in Chapter 13). He expected people to turn their backs on their old ways, and he warned people of the cost of discipleship: Jesus was serious. In the same way, the existence of the Jewish law reminds us that God is serious.

There is no way to talk about the existence of the Old Testament law as expressive of God's seriousness without at the same time talking about the impact of the law on Israel. Perhaps the best human analogy we have is that of an effective parent with growing children: the parent is serious about child-rearing, but that seriousness includes humor, tact, love, approachability—all with a view to shaping a small community of supple and ultimately joyous human beings. In that process, parents will lay down rules: no harming each other; no damage to anyone's possessions; and so on. So it is with God.

The Old Testament law cannot force a sincere response from the covenant people, but it can serve as a framework of behavior in the community. Again, the behavior is the same as in a family. The rules in a family do not automatically bring about affection among its members, but the rules do offer a minimum framework for common life. Parents know this: if a parent tells a child to apologize—"Tell Mary you're sorry"—and if the child's "I'm sorry" is said with a sneer, the parent realizes that sincerity cannot be forced. Yet it must be acknowledged that the words "I'm sorry" have at least been said, and the parent can hope that a habit of saying "I'm sorry" at the appropriate time may encourage the development of sincerity in the growing child. Similarly, even if the Old Testament law cannot engender sincerity in one's devotion to God or neighbor, it does offer norms of behavior that may help to keep insensitive, willful, or antisocial people in line. This is at least part of what Paul meant in Galatians: the law cannot make people righteous, but it certainly revealed God's will so that people could recognize their transgressions (Gal. 3:19-25).

But the law has more than a negative function: it has a positive function as well, for it can encourage sensitivity among people who are willing to become sensitive. A discipline like the Old Testament law moves people to fidelity and compassion when they do not feel like it, when their impulses pull them toward self-will and forgetfulness. It integrates them into a community of obligation. Roman Catholics who abstain from meat on the Fridays of Lent understand: they may obey the rule reluctantly or resentfully, or indeed they may break it. But if they obey it dutifully or even gladly, then there is an opportunity for them to be strengthened in their identity in a community of faith. In Christian communities in which participation in Sunday worship is an obligation rather than simply an elective activity, that participation has the same positive function: an opportunity to be strengthened in the community of faith.

Let us turn then to laws concerned with devotion to God. A good guide is provided by the first four of the Ten Commandments. (I number the commandments in the way most Protestants do; it should be noted that Roman Catholics and Lutherans combine the laws about "one God" and "no images" into the First Commandment, and they divide the law about "no coveting" into two commandments.)

There is, first of all, an insistence that Israel must wholeheartedly worship God alone. This is the Old Testament analogy of the expectation in the suzerainty treaties that a vassal will make no arrangement with some other overlord (see Chapter 2). In the pre-exilic community, the most obvious rival to Yahweh, the God of Israel, was Baal, the fertility god of the Canaanites (see the narrative of the prophet Elijah in 1 Kings 18, or see Hosea 2 or Jer. 2:23-25).

Gods other than Yahweh were represented by images, so the prohibition against images (the second commandment) reinforced the worship of the true God, who cannot be represented by a static image. Idols are foolish because they represent the do-nothing gods of the pagans (Ps. 115:3-8; Isa. 41:23). The true God creates and redeems. Isa. 44:9-20 offers a fine mockery of those who build idols and take them seriously: during the time of the exile in Babylon, the context in which the passage in Isaiah 44 was written, the Jews must have been tempted to worship Marduk, the god of Babylon, called "Bel" in Isa. 46:1. After all, Babylon had been stronger militarily than Judah, so it would have been natural to assume that Marduk, the sponsor of the Babylonian way of life, was stronger than Yahweh.

How might that law regarding the exclusive claim of God be heard among us today? From one perspective, it would be easy to think that the problem is solved: Christians rarely believe they need to be reminded to worship the true God and to stay away from idol-worship. On the other hand, the theologian Paul Tillich insisted that *our ultimate concern* is the real deity we worship,[16] and thoughtful Christians need constantly to ask themselves whether the God whom they hear in the Bible is their ultimate concern. A multitude of lesser goods are part of our world—the search for self-fulfillment, for family harmony, for social stability, for economic security, for military supremacy can easily take up the lion's share of our attention. Being faithful to the true God might involve a more overwhelming reordering of our priorities than we had thought.

The third commandment is against misusing God's name, whether for magical purposes or simply in a casual or insincere use of God's name. As I said before, God is serious, and God is therefore not to be trifled with.

Beyond laws pointing to the exclusive claims of the true God are laws in the Old Testament that prescribe regular attention to worship. Preeminent among these is the fourth commandment, to observe the sabbath, the seventh day of the week, Saturday, by abstaining from work. In a striking omission, the law nowhere sets forth what to *do* on the Sabbath, but the implication is that it is for the worship of God.

Christians (except for groups like Seventh-Day Adventists and Seventh-Day Baptists) have replaced the seventh day with the first day, Sunday, in order to celebrate the resurrection of Christ on the first day of the week; but the fact that the phrase "breaking the Sabbath" among Christians refers to activity on Sunday other than worship indicates that Christians recognize the way they have taken over the Old Testament observance of the seventh day.

The sabbath law then reminds Christians of the importance of weekly worship in community. Churches that schedule church school at the same time as the adult worship service hinder church school teachers from such worship. They and the children they teach surely should share in at least part of the worship of the whole community; some remedy from this scheduling overlap should be sought! Others, by reason of secular work schedules, may be hindered from participation in the usual Sunday morning worship: for such folk, a service for worship in the evening on Sunday or Wednesday or Friday may be the answer.

The sabbath law also reminds "workaholics" of the importance of recurrent abstention from work: not only for one day a week but doubtless for longer stretches every year: for retreat, for recollection, for restoration of the spirit.

The designation of the sabbath as a "holy" day, that is, as a day that is special, that is set apart, leads us to consider festivals. Sabbath was linked in the Old Testament with the observance of the new moon (Num. 29:6; compare Isa. 1:13), and there were three great yearly festivals as well—Passover (unleavened bread), harvest (weeks, Pentecost), and ingathering (booths) (for these three, see Exod. 23:14-17). For Christians, Passover has been swallowed up by Easter, Pentecost has been reinterpreted (Acts 2), and the festival of booths has no analogue. But the liturgical calendar observed by Christians carries on the yearly rhythm experienced by Jews.

A consideration of holy days leads to a consideration of holy places and holy equipment, and here again similar considerations hold. The Deuteronomic law assumed that God would be worshiped at the one place that God would designate (Deut. 12:5), a place that the reformers under Josiah were quick to conclude was Jerusalem (compare 2 Kings 23:4-14), and Jerusalem became more than ever the "holy city" (Neh. 11:1). Christians may share that sense of the holiness of Jerusalem with Jews, given the association of Jerusalem with events in the New Testament as well, but since the destruction of the

Herodian temple in Jerusalem in A.D. 70, Jews have been led to the necessity of worshiping God in any locality, and Christians, spurred on by John 4:21, have done the same: but neither Jews nor Christians can forget the power of special places in the worship of God. And though Christians have no need for the details of building an altar or of the priests' vestments (Exodus 38–39), special "holy" things have always fed Christian worship—one thinks of the paten and chalice consecrated for Holy Communion, or the various colors appropriate for the seasons of the liturgical year, or a simple cross in the chancel, or an unadorned room for the silent meeting of the Society of Friends.

When we turn to the sacrificial system of the Old Testament, we find that the issues are more complex. Whatever the details of sacrifice in the earliest days of Israel, the system prevailing in the postexilic period, set forth in Leviticus, takes the attention of the reader. Though various nonanimal offerings—flour, oil, or wine (see, for example, Leviticus 2)—were prescribed for certain occasions, the sacrifices that loom largest for us are animal sacrifices.

Various animals were slaughtered and offered on the altar. On some occasions, as for what is traditionally called the "peace offering" (NRSV "sacrifice of well-being," Leviticus 3), only certain parts of the animal were burned (the suet and kidneys). The rest of the meat was consumed by the priests and people who made the offering. On other occasions (the so-called "burnt offering," Leviticus 1, and the "sin offering" and "guilt offering," Leviticus 5–6), the whole of the animal was burned; nothing was left for the people who offered the sacrifice.

We in our day cannot help thinking about the animals involved. The United States Supreme Court determined in 1993 the illegality of a local ordinance in Hialeah, Florida, forbidding animal sacrifice by the devotees of Santeria, the half-Christian half-pagan cult of many Cuban refugees in Florida.

We realize immediately that any thought of "animal rights" was alien to ancient sensibilities. Still, a little voice keeps saying, how could all this slaughter of animals have been pleasing to God? We can be fairly sure that the prophet who compared the slaughterer of an ox to a murderer (Isa. 66:3) was not concerned for animal rights but rather was condemning the slide into pagan ways that the sacrificial system in his day appeared to encourage.

Even when we lay aside any thought of animal rights, we cannot help pondering the total burning of perfectly good animals; "What a waste!" we cannot help thinking. And all of this offering up of animals leads us to ask what people understood to be happening through such offerings. On this question, the texts do not give us many clues; the texts set forth these laws as the will of

God, and if God makes these demands, who are we to question them? Yet we do wonder: From Israel's side, what was going on?

We must understand that Israel was not alone in offering sacrifice: everybody did it. Look at the narrative in Acts 14:8-18: when Paul and Barnabas preached at Lystra, in Asia Minor, they were mistaken for Hermes and Zeus, and the priest of Zeus, and the crowds, wanted to sacrifice oxen to them on the spot.

As for the pagans, the devotees of the various religious systems in the ancient Near East, they believed that their gods needed food: pre-Israelite Canaanite texts hint at this when they speak of a sacrifice as food for the gods.[17] But the Old Testament rejects the notion that God *needs* the sacrifice for sustenance (Ps. 50:9-15).

So, again, what did sacrifice accomplish? Evidently, three mingled motivations were present in various degrees when the Israelites offered sacrifices:

1. *Communion.* God is our covenant partner, and as God has given life to us, so we give life to God in return. When we are allowed to share in the meat of the offering, we share something of the divine life already given to us.

2. *Tribute.* God is our overlord, and we therefore bring to God the tribute that we owe. Whether we have been good or bad, we belong to God, and our allegiance to God is sealed by our offerings, whether we understand them to be "dues" or whether we understand them to be spontaneous gifts.

3. *Expiation.* God is our judge, and when we have erred and sinned, we can expect our sin to be purged and our broken relation to be restored by our offering.

About communion, little more need be said here. The intimacy of a meal taken together is obvious, and a meal shared with God offers the opportunity to practice the presence of God. The psalmist asks it: "When shall I come and behold the face of God?" (Ps. 42:2).

About tribute and expiation, more needs to be said. Here the emphasis is not on our intimacy with God but on our distance from God, whether that distance be measured by awe or by guilt. The sense of awe before God, the sense of our littleness in the face of God's greatness, the sense that we are not at all the masters of our fate and the captains of our souls but instead are God's creatures, moves us to want to give to God. The sense of guilt before God that comes over us, the sense that we have offended the majesty and the justice of God in one way or another, moves us to offer up something as expiation for our sins. God is so awesome that the gift we are impelled to offer, whether for tribute or for expiation, is that which we prize the most.

Doubtless lying far behind the practice of the Israelite system of animal sacrifice was the impulse to sacrifice children. We recall the story of Abraham's attempted sacrifice of Isaac (Gen. 22:1-14), a narrative that we shall examine in detail in Chapter 5. The rhetorical question in Mic. 6:7b, "Shall I give my firstborn for my transgression, the fruit of my body for the sin of my soul?" suggests the real possibility of child sacrifice. And, as we saw in Chapter 1, various kings in the history of Israel and Judah are recorded as having sacrificed their children.

Animals, then, were substitutes for children—but animals, too, were precious, and not simply economically. People in the Near East live close to their animals, and if one is sacrificing a beast one has raised, then the beast is virtually a part of the family circle: perhaps it even has a name.

One must think, too, of the awesomeness of shed blood. Even at such a secular event as a bullfight, one is aware of the ritual awesomeness of shed blood. In sacrificing an animal, one is sacrificing of one's precious substance; one is giving one's best to God.

I mentioned a moment ago the seeming waste, the lavishness, of animal sacrifice. It *is* a waste, but if God is a God of grace, then God's gifts to us are far more lavish than we expect or deserve. Israel did not deserve to be chosen by God in the first place—we saw that in Chapter 2. So the very covenant is grace. The land of Canaan is grace (Ps. 44:1-3 and often). The Old Testament is full of evidences of God's lavishness. Jonah is sent off to Nineveh to preach repentance to the cruel Ninevites, and Jonah complains because he knows God is more gracious than a God really should be (Jonah 4:2)—again, see Chapter 5. And Jesus, in the New Testament, catches that note of extravagance: he praises the generosity of the woman who poured ointment over his head (Mark 14:3-9). Given the God of extravagance, what can we do but be extravagant to God in return?

Deep down, we are aware that God wants our total selves. This is what Paul means when he asks his fellow Christians to "present your bodies as a living sacrifice, holy and acceptable to God, which is your spiritual worship" (Rom. 12:1). We are to devote our total selves to God, and the sacrificial system points in that direction.

But the New Testament takes a further, crucial step. In the Christian proclamation, God himself offers Jesus Christ as a sacrifice of atonement (Rom. 3:25). In Chapter 2, we touched on the understanding, in the Letter to the Hebrews, of Jesus' obedience. In particular, the author sees Jesus' offering of himself as both the culmination and the replacement of the sacrificial system of the Old Testament. Jesus was himself the victim on the altar, the once-for-all sacrifice (Heb. 9:11—10:18); his sacrifice has removed sin (Heb. 9:26). And the author of the Letter to the Ephesians affirms that this act brought both Jews and Gentiles near to God (Eph. 2:16). Jesus' self-sacrifice obviates our need to offer up a young bull without blemish as a burnt offering (Lev. 1:1-10), but his self-sacrifice urges on us both our gratitude for what he did and our calling to follow in his steps.

The language of sacrifice is renewed for us each time we participate in the liturgy of Holy Communion, as we hear the words regarding the Body and the Blood of Christ. "He stretched out his arms upon the cross, and offered himself, in obedience to your will, a perfect sacrifice for the whole world."[18]

What is our answer then to the question: Can we hear God in the sacrificial laws of the Old Testament? The critique of the sacrificial system by the Old Testament prophets, which we have already cited, suggests that one can entertain a negative answer to the question. The answer for Christians is clearly no, not if we understand these laws as commands for us to obey. But the answer for Christians must be yes, if we understand the sacrificial laws to be pointers to Jesus' sacrifice for our sake, if we understand them as urgent reminders of the cost of discipleship for Christians, reminders of our own calling to give ourselves totally to God.

Let us turn now from the sacrificial law to the ethical law, the laws concerned with our relations with our fellows; in the Ten Commandments, we look to the fifth through the tenth commandments. Indeed, there are hints in both the Old Testament and in Jesus' words that the Ten Commandments occupied pride of place as the basis of the Old Testament law, as the core of the law. Both the prophets Hosea and Jeremiah cited in sequence the breaking of several of the ethical laws of the Ten Commandments, as if these are the laws that above all should be known and obeyed: Hos. 4:2 mentions the sins of "swearing, lying, and murder, and stealing and adultery," and Jer. 7:9 mentions stealing, murder, and adultery, as well as swearing falsely, making offerings to Baal, and going after other gods. Jesus, in speaking to the rich young man (Mark 10:19), mentioned in sequence several of these ethical laws of the Ten Commandments: "You shall not murder; You shall not commit adultery; You shall not steal; You shall not bear false witness; You shall not defraud; Honor your father and mother." There is warrant then, in both the Old and the New Testaments, for giving central attention to the ethical commands in the Ten Commandments.

The seventh of the Thirty-nine Articles of Religion, the statement of faith of the Church of England (1563), reads in part, "Although the Law given from God by Moses, as touching Ceremonies and Rites, do not bind Christian men, nor the Civil precepts thereof ought of necessity to be received in any commonwealth; yet notwithstanding, no Christian man whatsoever is free from the obedience of the Commandments which are called Moral."[19]

A whole essay could be written about the use made of the Ten Commandments by Christians throughout history.[20] Augustine taught that the Decalogue becomes the Christian's charter of freedom. Luther embodied the Ten Commandments in both his larger and smaller catechism. Calvin understood the law as instruction for Christian life.[21] And the Ten Commandments continue to play an active part in Christian life. The Quaker scholar Elton Trueblood suggested their use as a basis for a new world order after World War II.[22] Their recitation is urged as part of the Penitential Order in the Liturgy for Holy Eucharist in the revision of *The Book of Common Prayer* for 1979.[23]

As we look at these commandments, we find them unassailable. What Christian could object to prohibitions against dishonoring one's parents, against murder, against adultery, against stealing, against bearing false witness, indeed against coveting? Surely these must be the bare minimum for any coherent society! Christians, in fact, are aware that adherence to these is only the bare beginning; "unless your righteousness exceeds that of the scribes and Pharisees, you will never enter the kingdom of heaven" (Matt. 5:20).

A minimum they may be, but they are a beginning. And present-day communities, whether civil or ecclesial, are always in danger of falling below that minimum—not just in the matter of adultery but in the matter of other prohibitions as well.

The Baptist biblical scholar Walter Harrelson has reconceived these commands for Christians in terms of prohibitions against *contempt*. The commandment to honor one's parents is reconceived as "no contempt for the family," the prohibition against murder to "no contempt for human life," the prohibition against adultery to "no contempt for sex," the prohibition against stealing to "no contempt for the goods of the community," the prohibition against false witness to "no contempt for the community's institutions," and the prohibition against coveting to "no lusting after the life or goods of others."[24] So stated, these commands continue to speak to our condition. Again the question: Do we hear God in these ethical commandments? The answer is clearly yes.

But then what about the large body of law in the Old Testament beyond the Ten Commandments, the laws concerned with regulating relations between persons? Much of this body of law is case law, and the cases deal with situations of an ancient culture that are not directly pertinent to us today. Few of those who read this book will be owners of a goring ox (Exod. 21:28-32), and none, I trust, will sell a daughter as a slave (Exod. 21:7). Yet all these laws

were the efforts of the Israelites in their day to legislate for a humane community, and inasmuch as Christians are called to help create a humane world,
these efforts cannot be ignored.

Leviticus 19

As we seek to answer the question whether we can hear God in the laws of the
Old Testament, it is appropriate to select a chapter of laws and work through
them one by one. I choose Leviticus 19, a chapter that offers both apodictic
and case laws. It mingles laws that pertain to relations with God, those that
regulate relations between human beings, and those that seek to preserve the
perceived perfection of creation. Let us try to grasp the impulse behind the
laws in this chapter. The first eight verses deal mostly with relations with God
and with "sacrifices of well-being," but within those verses is v. 3, "You shall
each revere your mother and father, and you shall keep my sabbaths; I am the
Lord your God." Then, in vv. 9-10, one is bidden at harvest time to leave grain
and grapes for gleaners, that is to say, those of the poor who come to gather
what is left in fields and vineyards. Martin Niemöller, a German Christian
leader in the middle of this century, once said that when he returned to his
home after being released from prison at the end of the Second World War, he
found that Christian households had made a covenant to save one slice of
bread from each loaf to share with the refugees streaming westward through
the cities of Germany.

Verse 11 reflects the wording of the Ten Commandments: "You shall not
steal; you shall not deal falsely; and you shall not lie to one another." Verse 12
similarly forbids swearing falsely by God's name.

Verse 13 states, "You shall not defraud your neighbor; you shall not steal [a
different verb than in v. 11, perhaps better translated "rob"]; and you shall not
keep for yourself the wages of a laborer until the morning": this last law suggests a situation in which day-laborers did not have the wherewithal to eat
until they had been paid.

Verse 14 is a sudden surprise. In the first half of the verse, the law assumes
the objective power of the spoken word (for which, see Chapter 1); thus, both
reviling a deaf person and tripping a blind person are equally wrong—one is
not to tease or take advantage of handicapped people, doubtless particularly
in business transactions.

Verses 15-18 all deal evidently with matters that come up in legal cases,[25]
though, as we ourselves read the passage, only a few of the phrases seem to
conjure up court procedure. Verse 15 deals with unjust judgments in court,
particularly in cases where participants can be open to bribery. Verse 16a

insists on the damage done by talebearing and slander, not simply idle gossip but testimony prejudicial to a legal case. The meaning of v. 16b is not altogether clear; the Hebrew says literally, "You shall not stand against the blood of your neighbor." The half-verse evidently reinforces the first part of the verse and seems to forbid casual testimony in a capital case (REB: "Do not take sides against your neighbour on a capital charge"). In v. 17, we must understand the word "heart" in the Old Testament sense, not so much the center of the emotions as of the character and the will. The law prohibits the steady hatred, the outgrowth, for example, of previous quarrels, that poisons judicial decisions (the REB translates: "You are not to nurse hatred toward your brother"). The last half of the verse is again not clear; if it reinforces the first part of the verse, then, word by word, it seems to mean that rather than nursing hatred one should "reprove" or "argue it out" with one's neighbor so as not to—what? to carry a burden of offense (against God) because of enmity against one's neighbor? to impose a burden of transgression onto one's neighbor? In any event, it urges the clearing of the air in decision making in a tight community where grudges easily continue their damage. Verse 18 sums up the passage: do not take vengeance, do not bear a grudge, and then the clause that is the most famous one in Leviticus, "You shall love your neighbor as yourself."

From this sublimity, we suddenly hear a prohibition in v. 19 that reflects an old taboo: no crossing of categories, whether it be the mating of two sorts of animals, or the sowing of two different crops in the same field, or mixed weaves (by which any ancient equivalent of cotton-polyester weaves would be outlawed!). These prohibitions fall into the category of laws prohibiting a break with the perceived perfection of creation. We may note in passing that this prohibition would outlaw the breeding of mules, but the existence of mules is certainly taken for granted in 2 Sam. 13:29, and it is noteworthy that when Deut. 22:9-11 replicates the same sort of law, the prohibiting against cross-breeding of animals is omitted. We can only conclude that laws like these reflect the mentality of a conservative people for whom the boundaries of categories are God-given—compare the prohibition against cross-dressing in Deut. 22:5.

In vv. 20-22, we suddenly come on case law, what to do in a complicated situation involving sexual relations. The background of this law is that when a young woman is betrothed (engaged), if a man (other than her fiancé) has sexual relations with her, it is a case of adultery and both are to be executed (compare Deut. 22:23-25). But the question arises, does this law apply to a slave girl? The answer given here is no; though she is betrothed (evidently the meaning of the term translated "designated for another man," NRSV), she has not yet been ransomed (presumably by her fiancé) nor given her freedom (by her owner), so her status is still a slave, and she thus belongs to her owner, not to her fiancé. The word translated "inquiry" is doubtful; it may well mean "compensation for damage." If that is the case, who is compensated? The ram that is mentioned in vv. 21-22 is compensation to God, but what about the owner of the slave girl? If the term in v. 20 does mean compensation, and if that compensation is to the owner, then it is curious that the amount of the compensation is not stated. And, we notice, in all of this the question is never raised whether the sexual intercourse was consensual. There is barely the discernment that the slave girl might not be responsible in the sexual episode, or at least not completely so, and the law stays within the assumption of slavery and patriarchy: a slave girl is not so "valuable" as a free woman, a slave girl is the property of her master, and, in any event, in sexual matters it is the honor of the male, not of the female, that is at stake. This law, like so many of the laws in the Old Testament, takes no account of the humiliation, and the shock, and the pain of the woman in the case (compare Chapter 12).

Verses 23-25 deal with fruit trees, of all things: the fruit of the first three years is not to be touched, and the fruit of the fourth year shall be an offering to God; only in the fifth year can the fruit be eaten. Like the law in v. 19 against mixing categories, this law doubtless had its origin in a taboo: the fruit of the first three years was an offering to placate the spirits of the soil, but the taboo persisted and was understood as God's will ("I am the Lord your God," v. 25).

Verses 26-31 are a miscellany. The first half of v. 26, as the Hebrew text now reads, forbids eating meat with its blood since, as 17:10-11 affirms, the blood belongs to God (compare Gen. 9:4-6). But the ancient Greek translation (the Septuagint) here reads, "You shall not eat *on the mountains,*" which, as a matter of fact, is a plausible reading: the Hebrew words for "the blood" and for "mountains" look similar. A prohibition against eating on the mountains is referred to several times in Ezekiel, for example, in Ezek. 18:6, and it evidently refers to sharing in fertility rites (compare Hos. 4:13; Jer. 2:20). If that is the correct reading, it brings the law into the orbit of other prohibitions in vv. 26-31 connected with pagan practices, particularly those of the Canaanites. The second half of v. 26 forbids augury and witchcraft: any attempt to discern the future in order to control it (as those who believe in astrology today understand it to be) is ruled out by Old Testament law, for the future belongs to God and is shaped by God's decisions and ours. Verse 27 evidently refers to cutting the hair or beard as a rite of mourning; the first prohibition in v. 28, against the gashing of flesh, is specifically related to mourning. (But Jer. 16:6 suggests that such practices were common and not understood as forbidden.) Tattooing is likewise forbidden, perhaps because it was associated with pagan cults. The prohibition against making one's daughter a prostitute in v. 29 is probably not a reference to secular prostitution but to fertility cult worship (Hos. 4:13-14 hints at this background). Verse 30 repeats the law to respect the sabbath (see v. 3); the mention of reverencing the sanctuary here might be made because sacred prostitution (v. 29) would defile it. The prohibition against resorting to mediums and wizards in v. 31 reflects v. 26.

At the end of the chapter, we come to a really random set of laws. Verse 32 enjoins respect for the elderly, perhaps as an extension beyond the family circle of the commandment to honor one's father and mother. Here the law is coupled with the command to "fear God": elders are to be respected because of the divine ordering of society. Verses 33-34 match "you shall love your neighbor as yourself" in v. 18: here we have "you shall love the alien as yourself." The Hebrew word translated "alien" (*gēr*) was translated "stranger" in the KJV and the RSV. It refers to those who, because of famine or battle in the territory where their kinfolk could protect them, have sought to live as protected persons elsewhere.[26] Unfortunately, people whose ancestors were refugees do not automatically show compassion to others who are now refugees in their midst, and this law reminds them to show compassion to others as God showed them compassion in Egypt. Verses 35-36 insists on honest weights and measures, and v. 37 is a summary.

The repeated closing phrase "I am the Lord (your God)" (vv. 3, 4, 10, 12, 14, 16, 18, 25, 28, 30, 31, 32, 34, 37) reminds the Israelites that the personal identity of God is all the reason one needs for these laws: it sounds like the commonly heard answer to a child today, "Because I'm your Mommy, that's why."

In the ethical laws here, the variety of the concerns is striking, and many of them have the power to reinforce our ethical sensitivity. Leave some grain and grapes for the poor (v. 10); do not take advantage of the handicapped (v. 14) or show contempt for the elderly (v. 32), and love the alien as yourself (v. 34). Pay your day-laborer promptly (v. 13b). Be honorable in your relations with your neighbor (v. 13a). Make sure that both your legal and your business dealings are fair (vv. 15-18, 35-36). On the other hand, one of these ethical laws reflects a male-dominated world (vv. 20-22), and in this way it may repel those of us who understand male and female to be intended for parity in God's world.

There are laws here that prohibit a break with the perceived perfection of creation; these laws reflect a world whose scruples and taboos appear to us simply irrelevant (vv. 19, 23-25), and so to the question, Do we hear God in such laws as these? the answer will have to be no.

If I pose now the summary question, Do we hear God in the ethical laws? our answer, as with the laws on sacrifice, will have to be both yes and no. As we have already seen, some laws have the power to deepen our sensitivity, when they are appropriately adapted to our world. Thus, we may ask, Who are the aliens in our midst today whom we are to love as we love ourselves? And how is that love to be manifested? But just as clearly there are laws reflecting a male-dominated world that in the view of many Christians do not reflect God's will.

I close this chapter by raising a question to which I can offer no definitive answer. Are the laws prohibiting homosexual relations (Lev. 18:22; 20:13) a reflection of the God-given order of creation and therefore incumbent on us, or are they of the same sort as the laws against eating pork or shrimp (Lev. 11:7, 10) and against mixing two different materials in the weave of a garment (Lev. 19:19), laws in which we do not hear God? I can offer no definitive answer to the question, but I think it needs to be posed in these terms. Christians who cite the laws against homosexual relations in Leviticus as binding on us without further ado need to be reminded of the existence of laws in Leviticus that simply reflect the taboos of a past society. One might argue that the creation of male and female at creation and the injunction to be fruitful and multiply (Gen. 1:27-28) are so foundational as to render heterosexual relations normative, and one might also argue that sexual relations between two human beings have a more profound effect on them than does the wearing of a cotton-polyester shirt. But the existence of these laws in Leviticus does not render them in and of themselves binding on Christians.

I have tried in this chapter to indicate that (1) the Old Testament law on many occasions can be a glorious revelation to us from God and on some occasions can be a barrier to God's revelation, and (2) the fact that some of these laws are a barrier to us should not exempt us from listening for God in the laws that are revelatory for us.

In this chapter, I have touched only lightly on the function of the law to discipline and to encourage our obedience to God. This function of the law leads us to consider two related themes in the Old Testament—our fear of God and the wrath of God. For most Christians today, who center their attention on our love for God and God's love for us, these themes are a problem, and it is to these themes that I now turn.

Notes

1. For helpful surveys, see Walter J. Harrelson, "Law in the OT," *IDB* 3:77–89; Samuel Greengus, "Biblical and ANE Law," *ABD* 4:242–52; Rifat Sonsino, "Forms of Biblical Law," *ABD* 4:252–54.

2. See conveniently Isidore Epstein, "Mishna," *IDB* 3:404, and "Talmud," *IDB* 4:511–15, or Roger Brooks, "Mishnah," *ABD* 4:871–73, and Gary G. Porton, "Talmud," *ABD* 6:310–15.

3. Brevard S. Childs, *The Book of Exodus* (OTL; Philadelphia: Westminster, 1974), 458.

4. On this matter, see Gerhard von Rad, "Deuteronomy," *IDB* 1:835–37; Norbert Lohfink, "Deuteronomy," *IDBSup* 229.

5. Arthur D. H. Mayes, *Deuteronomy* (The New Century Bible Commentary; Grand Rapids, Mich.: Eerdmans, 1979), 34–46; Joseph Blenkinsopp, "Deuteronomy," *New Jerome*, 106.

6. Mayes, *Deuteronomy*, 344, 346, 348.

7. Harrelson, "Law in the Old Testament," 82–83.

8. Georges A. Barrois, "Debt," *IDB* 1:809.

9. *Baba Metzia*, sect. 5; see conveniently Herbert Danby, *The Mishnah* (Oxford: Oxford University, 1933), 355–57.

10. *Baba Metzia* 5.10.

11. *Baba Metzia* 5.5.

12. Joseph Blenkinsopp, *Ezra-Nehemiah* (OTL; Philadelphia: Westminster, 1988), 354.

13. Mayes, *Deuteronomy*, 302.

14. *Sanhedrin* 8: see Danby, *Mishnah*, 394–95.

15. Mishnah, *Shabbath* 2.1-2: see Danby, *Mishnah*, 101.

16. Paul Tillich, *Systematic Theology* I (Chicago: University of Chicago, 1951), 12.

17. Hans-Joachim Kraus, *Worship in Israel* (Richmond, Va.: John Knox, 1966), 114.

18. Holy Eucharist II in the revision of The Book of Common Prayer for 1979: *The Book of Common Prayer* (New York: Church Hymnal Corp., 1979), 362.

19. See Edward J. Bicknell, *A Theological Introduction to the Thirty-nine Articles of the Church of England* (3rd ed., rev. by H. J. Carpenter; London, New York: Longmans, 1955), 127.

20. See, for example, Childs, *Exodus*, 431–39.

21. For Luther and Calvin, see Emil G. Kraeling, *The Old Testament Since the Reformation* (New York: Harper, 1955), 15, 26.

22. Elton Trueblood, *Foundations for Reconstruction* (New York: Harper, 1946).

23. *BCP*, 317–18, 350.

24. Walter J. Harrelson, *The Ten Commandments and Human Rights* (Overtures to Biblical Theology; Philadelphia: Fortress Press, 1980).

25. Martin Noth, *Leviticus* (OTL; Philadelphia: Westminster, 1965), 141–42.

26. Theodor M. Mauch, "Sojourner," *IDB* 4:397–99; Diether Kellermann, *gûr*, *TDOT* 2:443.

4

Our Fear of God, and the Wrath of God

⟨⟨⟩⟩

There is a recurrent reference to the "fear of God" in the book of Proverbs; there are several variations, but typical is Prov. 9:10a, "The fear of Yahweh is the beginning of wisdom." This sentiment is echoed several times in the Old Testament (I shall take it up again in Chapter 11). "Fear God": the phrase conjures up for us visions of dour Puritans and sermons of hell-fire, which many of us have consigned to the dustbin of history. And the phrase turns up not only in urgings to keep the law but in the tenderest contexts, such as the verse from the Psalms, "As a father has compassion for his children, so the Lord has compassion for those who fear him."

Matching the notion of our fearing God are expressions for the wrath of God. Psalm 90 begins, "Lord, you have been our dwelling place in all generations. Before the mountains were brought forth, or ever you had formed the earth and the world, from everlasting to everlasting you are God." It is a psalm much used for funeral services. But the psalmist then refers repeatedly to God's wrath: "For we are consumed by your anger; by your wrath we are overwhelmed" (v. 7; see also vv. 9 and 11). Is this psalm then suitable for a funeral service?

Two psalms voiced by those in illness begin, "O Lord, do not rebuke me in your anger, or discipline me in your wrath" (Psalms 6 and 38). And the notion of God's wrath is not confined to the Psalms, but appears steadily in the Old Testament (172 times in the NRSV).

These expressions are found in the New Testament as well: in the Letter to the Romans, the Greek word *orgē*, translated "wrath," pertaining to God, appears nine times; for example, Rom. 9:22-24 reads, "What if God, desiring to show his wrath and to make known his power, has endured with much patience the objects of wrath that are made for destruction; and what if he has done so in order to make known the riches of his glory for the objects of mercy, which he has prepared beforehand for glory—including us whom he has called, not from the Jews only but also from the Gentiles?" And as for the fear of God, Acts 9:31 states, "Meanwhile the church throughout Judea,

Galilee, and Samaria had peace and was built up. Living in the fear of the Lord and in the comfort of the Holy Spirit, it increased in numbers."

The New Testament stresses the possibility of punishment in hell, something the Old Testament does not do. These issues present a problem. Rarely have they been more succinctly expressed than by the southern novelist Lillian Smith, as she recalls her early childhood: "Our first lesson about God made the deepest impression on us. We were told that He loved us, and then we were told that He would burn us in everlasting flames of hell if we displeased Him. We were told that we should love Him for He gives us everything good that we have, and then we were told that we should fear Him because He has the power to do evil to us whenever He cares to. We learned from this part of the lesson another: that 'people,' like God and parents, can love you and hate you at the same time; and though they may love you, yet if you displease them they may do you great injury; hence being loved by them does not give you protection from being harmed by them. We learn that They (parents) have a 'right' to act in this way because God does, and that They in a sense represent God, in the family."[1]

Fear, and a First Look at Our Fear of God

Let us ponder the matter of fear. The capacity for fear, a capacity that leads to the avoidance of pain, is built into human beings (indeed, into higher animals as well). Every parent notices the moment when a baby begins to distinguish between family members on the one hand and strangers on the other and to fear the latter: it is a sign of growth. And though, as children grow older, we may view some of their fears as inappropriate from time to time—fear of dogs, fear at the seashore of going too near the water—still, we are glad to draw on their capacity to fear in order to teach them the real danger of pots on the stove and of cars in the street.

The reaction of fear to the risks and threats of everyday life is universal. The prophet Amos was a shepherd, and there were real lions in Palestine in his day. To hear him then say, "The lion has roared, who will not fear?" (Amos 3:8), is to share the same emotion across 2,750 years.

But if the capacity to fear has survival value, we also recognize how paralyzing an existence is that is dominated by fear. That recognition helped to give rise to the fourth of the Four Freedoms announced as goals in the course of World War II by Winston Churchill and Franklin Roosevelt: after freedom of speech, freedom of religion, and freedom from want, there was freedom from fear.

For those who read this book, freedom from fear might seem a realistic goal. But for a majority of men and women and children in the world today, the occasions for fear in daily life are far greater, and this certainly would have been the case for men and women and children in Old Testament times.

First we must ponder the infant mortality of those days, the omnipresence of parasites and insect pests, and the general lack of health care for everyone. There were doubtless recurrent plagues: the description in 1 Sam. 5:9, 12 of the tumors that struck the Philistines is evidently of bubonic plague. Then we must ponder recurrent famines and the difficulties of storing grain during the years of good harvests. The recurrence in the narratives of the Old Testament of drought (1 Kings 17:1; Jer. 14:1-6) and famine (Gen. 12:10; 42:5; Ruth 1:1) is a reminder of their power to induce fear. Beyond these daily threats were the more occasional threats to life and limb—from battle or from earthquake (for the latter, see Amos 1:1), or, for that matter, from locust plague (Joel 1:1—2:27). The situation in Jerusalem after the fall of the city in 587 B.C. was appalling: "Happier were those pierced by the sword than those pierced by hunger, whose life drains away, deprived of the produce of the field" (Lam. 4:9). The mention of cannibalism in this circumstance (Lam. 2:20; 4:10) is not surprising, since this was not the first time it had occurred (2 Kings 6:28-29). And beyond these horrors, who can reckon the terror in the hearts of children beaten by well-meaning parents (compare Prov. 13:24), or of lonely women violated in open country (compare Deut. 22:25-27)? In such circumstances, it is a profound act of faith to affirm, "God is our refuge and strength, a very present help in trouble. Therefore we will not fear, though the earth should change, though the mountains shake in the heart of the sea; though its waters roar and foam, though the mountains tremble with its tumult" (Ps. 46:1-3).

Though I postpone for the moment the matter of the wrath of God, it is important to note here that in the Old Testament the coming of disasters was attributed again and again to the work of God. For example, the prophet Amos lists a whole series of disasters—famine, drought, blight and mildew, locusts, pestilence, sword, and the sudden overthrow, perhaps by earthquake, of whole cities—that he understands God to have sent on Israel in the expectation that these disasters would lead to repentance (Amos 4:6-11). We remind ourselves that such disasters would be understood as covenant curses, part of the form of the covenant between God and Israel (see Chapter 2).

Preeminent among the objects of fear for the Old Testament, as we know, is the fear of God. The notion appears so often that it is important to understand its range.[2] In the first place, the kind of experience that human beings perceived to be God's sudden intervention and presence in their lives elicited the response of fear. For example, in response to God's appearance to Moses at the burning bush, Moses "hid his face, for he was afraid to look at God"

(Exod. 3:1-6). Indeed, it was thought that the experience of God's presence could be deadly: we recall God's word to Moses, "You cannot see my face, for no one shall see me and live" (Exod. 33:20).

The result, paradoxically, is that there are narratives in which God calls men and women to specific tasks and then offers the assurance "Fear not" (the Israelites at Sinai, Exod. 20:20; Gideon, Judg. 6:22-23; compare Lam. 3:57). This assurance is particularly voiced in narratives where the people are in godly combat (compare Ps. 118:6).

Most important for our purposes is the fact that there are passages that bring the fearing of God together with joy in God's presence (Pss. 40:3; 52:6), and there are passages that bring together fearing God and loving God. For example, Deut. 5:29 states that the people should "fear" God with their mind (literally, "heart"), and the injunction to fear God is repeated in 6:2; then, in 6:5, it is said that the people should "love" God with all their heart, soul, and might. This association of fearing God and loving God does not seem to have been a problem for Christians in past generations. Luther, in his *Short Catechism*, introduces his explanation of each of the Ten Commandments in the same way, with "We should fear and love God": for example, for "You shall not kill" he says, "We should fear and love God, and so we should not endanger our neighbor's life, nor cause him any harm, but help and befriend him in every necessity of life." Lutherans have been able to continue that tradition today; a current Lutheran prayer reads, "God, begin your work today. Through the mysteries of Word and Sacrament, prepare us to meet you with gladness and holy fear."[3] But if, for a modern reader, "fear" and "love" are perceived as opposites, as in the quotation from Lillian Smith above, then we need to tread carefully.

It is clear from the context in Deuteronomy that both "fearing" God and "loving" God are expressions of the appropriate stance of loyalty to the God of the covenant. Since the covenant is based on the political model of suzerain with vassal (see Chapter 2), the notion of fearing and loving one's overlord seemed plausible to those in earlier generations who lived within a stratified society.

Fearing and Loving an Overlord: Analogies Today

We in our day, however, lack that sense of how a stratified society works: what we need, to bring the matter to life, is the analogy of a community with a leader who is both authoritarian and benevolent, and such an analogy is not easy to locate. One thinks of military units in which soldiers are obligated to obey their officer in battle, but too many officers are something other than benevolent (Captain Queeg in Herman Wouk's novel *The Caine Mutiny* comes to mind),[4] and the fact that the purpose of military units is to kill and destroy may render the analogy unhelpful to our sensibilities. One thinks then of other quasi-military situations: prison camps, polar expeditions, survival in a lifeboat.

A more useful analogy in our day might be athletic teams under the direction of a coach. Players are chosen or hired by the coach. They are expected to respond, to obey, to cooperate, to function as members of their team. They may be taken off the team or fired for incompetence or misbehavior. In such a community, both fear and love may find a place.

The analogy I should like to explore at length is a musical organization under its conductor. Anyone who has sung in a chorus or played in a symphony orchestra understands the nature of the relation between the musicians and the conductor and the way in which "fear" and "love" approach each other.

The organization I have in mind is a boys' choir associated with the Roman Catholic diocese where I live: I myself sing with a small group of men attached to the boys' choir for the singing of high mass on Sundays. (The group is completely male, but the relationships I am describing are not dependent on the single gender of the group.)

The boys, about fifty in number, are chosen by the director in auditions. They attend a private choir school; as well as the lessons expected in grades five through eight, the boys take French, music theory, piano performance, and recorder playing; some of them also participate in a handbell choir. Before the school sessions of the day, they sing daily mass at eight o'clock; they are rehearsed with the men for an hour and a half Wednesday evenings and for an hour Sunday mornings before mass. In short, it is a rigorous, demanding program.

The music that the boys produce, it need hardly be said, is first-rate: they sing everything from Gregorian Chant and Palestrina to Zoltán Kodály. They prepare two concerts a year, are in demand for weddings, and have sung with major symphony orchestras. Many of the boys will continue their musical studies and activities when they leave the choir school and go on to high school and university.

But the boys, being boys, need frequent scolding and discipline. During rehearsal, the director often rebukes them, or rebukes particular boys, for not watching him; occasionally, a boy who is talking or not paying attention will be told to stand up for a stretch of time. Of a given class that begins grade five, perhaps two-thirds will graduate from grade eight; boys drop out if they move away or lose interest or stamina. Once in a while, a boy who is a behavior problem will be eased out.

Some years ago, during Holy Week, in response to the flagging responses and the whispering of the boys, the director gave them an awesome tongue-lashing, telling them how they had fallen down on the job when the whole congregation was depending on them to help in the leading of worship at this high point in the church year. Afterward, I was speaking with the director and remarked that I could sum up his speech with "Shut up and rejoice!" He ruefully admitted it was true and has reminisced with me about the remark a time or two since. Here it is, the blend of fearing and loving: shut up and rejoice!

The analogies with the relation between God and Israel in the Old Testament are plain. The director has chosen the boys, as God has chosen Israel. The director has a high purpose for the choir, as God has a high purpose for Israel. The director has the musical knowledge to direct the choir, and he knows in his mind the sound that he wants from the choir. He is a perfectionist and will not accept less than the best. Month by month, the boys learn what good music is, and what good sound is, and they experience a profound satisfaction when things go well. They know, too, when the director frowns or rebukes them, that the frowns or rebukes are not arbitrary or capricious: they know, from their own experience, that they have not done well. The word of God to Israel through Amos, "You only have I known of all the families of the earth; therefore I will punish you for all your iniquities" (Amos 3:2), makes sense in the light of the analogy of the boys' choir.

The analogy is not perfect: the director is human, not God, and the boys of course do not *worship* him. But the boys do respect him, they want to please him, they want to serve him, all in an effort to fulfill their calling as choirboys, and to that degree the analogy is helpful.

Still, for all this, "fear" is not fully helpful: if a boy thinks the director is being unfair or arbitrary, his parents can intervene, or he can leave the choir; the director does not have *absolute* power over the boys, as God is understood to have absolute power over Israel. (The issue of God's absolute power, and the inability of a human being to opt out of the arrangement, is part of the problem with which the book of Job wrestles; we shall ponder the matter in Chapter 10.) If God is presumed to have absolute power over Israel, then the notion of "fear" is appropriate.

Our Fear of God, Further Thoughts

"Fearing" God, then, implies the worship of God: this is the context of Deuteronomy 6, already cited for the collocation of "fearing" and "loving" God. "Take care that you do not forget the Lord" (v. 12); "the Lord your God you shall fear; him you shall serve, and by his name alone you shall swear. Do not follow other gods" (vv. 13-14).

One might propose then that "fear" really implies "reverence" or "awe," and these are useful understandings. Indeed, at one point at least, that is what *The Book of Common Prayer* has done: in Proper 7, the collect for the Sunday closest to June 22, the traditional form of the prayer begins, "O Lord, we beseech thee, make us to have a perpetual fear and love of thy holy Name"; the contemporary form of this prayer now begins, "O Lord, make us have perpetual love and reverence for your holy Name."[5]

On the other hand, there are Old Testament texts where, we must affirm, "fear" really does mean "fear." Jer. 5:21-23 is one of these: "Hear this, O foolish and senseless people, who have eyes, but do not see, who have ears, but do not hear. Do you not fear me? says the Lord; do you not tremble before me? [In Hebrew the pronouns in these phrases come first, in the emphatic position; they read literally: "Me do you not fear? says the Lord; before me do you not tremble?"] I placed the sand as a boundary for the sea, a perpetual barrier that it cannot pass; though the waves toss, they cannot prevail, though they roar, they cannot pass over it. But this people has a stubborn and rebellious heart; they have turned aside and gone away." Here the depiction is of the covenant people who do not have the sense they were born with, rebelling against God and overstepping all the boundaries God has set up; and here "fear" is paralleled by "tremble."

The Wrath of God

Before we raise the question of whether we really hear God today in the Old Testament injunction to fear God, we must discuss the related matter of the "wrath" or "anger" of God.[6] There are two principal Hebrew words at issue here. One is *ḥārôn*, a word that literally means "burning." It occurs 41 times in the Old Testament, and is used only of God's anger. The other word is *ʾap*, which literally means "nose" (Gen. 24:47). The two words are often combined, *ḥărôn ʾap*, literally "burning of the nose," to express "anger" or "wrath"; then *ʾap* by itself can mean "anger," sometimes of human anger (40 times) but mostly of divine anger (170 times).

God's anger is not only affirmed; there is a traditional creed that tries to measure it alongside of God's love: "The Lord, the Lord, a God merciful and gracious, slow to anger, and abounding in steadfast love and faithfulness, keeping steadfast love for the thousandth generation, forgiving iniquity and transgression and sin, yet by no means clearing the guilty, but visiting the iniquity of the parents upon the children and the children's children, to the third and the fourth generation" (Exod. 34:6-7). Here the inexplicable is laid out. God is merciful and gracious, but at the same time not exempt from the possibility of anger; loving to the thousandth generation (who could imagine so long-lasting a love?!) but at the same time not clearing the guilty, indeed pursuing them for three or four generations. (In Chapter 5 we shall explore the notion of "corporate personality," which gives some background to the pursuing of iniquity to the third and fourth generation; in Chapter 10, we shall see how that notion began to break down in the exilic and postexilic periods.)

The notion of the wrath of God is so insistent in the Old Testament that it is important for us to explore for a moment our attitudes toward it. Present-day Christians inevitably cling to the notion of the love of God and shrink from the notion of wrath. It is ironic, however, that the pre-exilic prophets, to whom many Christians are attracted in their concern for social justice, should stress so firmly the wrath of God. I have seen students who affirm both the love of God and the call to social justice helplessly torn when they work through the words of Amos or Isaiah. Listen to the opening oracle in the book of Amos: "Yahweh roars from Zion, and utters his voice from Jerusalem; the pastures of the shepherds wither, and the top of Carmel dries up" (Amos 1:2). Amos, a sheep-breeder, compares Yahweh's voice to the roar of a lion, who would be glad to take lambs for prey; when Yahweh speaks, the very grass on the moist mountainside of Mount Carmel turns brown. And this mood is sustained through virtually the whole book of Amos.

The same mood is set in the call of Isaiah, recorded in Isaiah 6. Christians are fond of the first eight verses of this passage: it has become a kind of model for worship. Isaiah sees God, high and lifted up; he affirms his sense of sin, from which he is then absolved, and he then accepts his call to go out and prophesy. But vv. 9-12 are less often read and pondered: "And he [God] said, 'Go and say to this people: "keep listening, but do not comprehend; keep looking, but do not understand." Make the mind of this people dull, and stop their ears, and shut their eyes, so that they may not look with their eyes, and listen with their ears, and comprehend with their minds, and turn and be healed.' Then I said, 'How long, O Lord?' and he said: 'Until cities lie waste without inhabitant, and houses without people, and the land is utterly desolate; until the Lord sends everyone far away, and vast is the emptiness in the midst of the land.'" (It should be said that v. 13 is so mangled in the Hebrew text that it cannot easily be interpreted; it is best to stay with the earlier verses.)

Christians are shocked; traditionally, Isaiah is celebrated as the prophet of hope, predicting the coming of the Messiah. What kind of call is this, to prophesy for the purpose of rendering the people steadily less capable of understanding? Isaiah himself is appalled: "How long, O Lord?" And the answer comes: until the people are wiped out. What kind of God is this, whose call to Isaiah really makes him out to be an anti-prophet? One can only conclude that, in Isaiah's understanding, God's people have become an anti-people, so that the only appropriate work for a prophet is as an anti-prophet. Our reaction to this is that it is monstrous. So we ask: Is there anything here for us?

It is best to approach these questions by asking what arouses God's wrath, in the understanding of the Old Testament. The answer, we should surmise after our discussion in Chapter 3, would be: breaking the law, the stipulations of the covenant. The analogy of the boys' choir is then no longer sufficient, because in the Old Testament the acts that arouse God's wrath above all are acts like disloyalty and betrayal, and whatever the peccadillos of which choirboys are guilty, they never amount to betrayal.

And it was precisely the prophets who portrayed this betrayal in the broadest strokes. The prophet Elijah, in the ninth century B.C., insisted that the Israelites should stop the worship of Baal, the Canaanite agricultural god that seemed to promise agricultural and economic security, and return to the covenant partner Yahweh. The prophet Hosea, in the eighth century, first used the analogy of husband and wife for the covenant between Yahweh and Israel, but for Hosea the whole point was that the wife was an erring wife, who had gone off after Baal (Hosea 2). The prophet Jeremiah, in the seventh century, continued to explore the analogy. "As a faithless wife leaves her husband, so you have been faithless to me, O house of Israel, says the Lord" (Jer. 3:20).

Wrath without Tantrums

I turn from the analogy of the boys' choir to another analogy, an incident shared with me by a friend. Some years ago, he and his wife and children took on a foster-daughter for several years. She was a teenager at the time, and in that family setting she manifested the kinds of behavior that suggested emotional deprivation from infancy onward: she had eating problems, for example, and she seemed to have helped herself to money belonging to other family members. After some years, she went to live elsewhere, but the family kept in touch with her. After she graduated from high school, she married, had a son, divorced, and had another son by a boyfriend. Eventually, her circumstances brought her to live nearby my friend.

One day she called him and asked whether he would co-sign a note at a local bank: she needed to buy a car for a job she had located, and she knew just the car; it cost $3,600. As a courtesy to her, he co-signed for the loan, which was to be paid back in thirty-six monthly installments of $130 or so.

Five months later, the bank called my friend: the young woman was behind in her fourth and fifth payments. He went to see her and confronted her with the matter. She burst into tears. Her situation, it turned out, was more chaotic than he had envisioned. After three months, she had sold the car (for only $1,800) to cover a hospital bill that was due, and without the car she had lost the job. Grasping at straws, she suggested turning over the child-support payments from her ex-husband to cover the bank payments. No: the child-support payments belonged to her son. Baffled by all this panicky and self-destructive behavior on the part of someone who had, after all, been a member of his family, my friend will never forget his words to her as she sat sobbing. "You betrayed me. I trusted you, and you betrayed me. I never expected to have to pay off your loan: I signed the note as a courtesy to you. Give me the payment book. I'm mad, but I'm not mean." And so he made 33 monthly payments of $130 to the bank, payments to buy nothing, not a car, not anything.

"I'm mad, but I'm not mean." Is this a clue to the wrath of God? So often, when we experience human anger, we experience the meanness of it. When we become angry, much of our anger is tied up with our own status, for example, or our unacknowledged conflicts that we project onto other people. We often overreact, and those on the receiving end of our anger sense the disparity between the immediate situation and our reaction to it. So much human anger is perceived as deplorable—mean, in fact. When we read about God's wrath, we envisage some kind of divine tantrum, and we wonder how a God who has created and loves human beings could turn about and fly into a rage (this was Lillian Smith's problem as a child). And since we take it for granted that a tantrum is unworthy of the author of the universe, we lay the whole notion aside as implausible.

God's Love and God's Wrath

The attitude of "mad but not mean" suggests that God's love and God's wrath might be intimately related. There are many Old Testament passages that suggest the matter; let me cite two. The first is Amos 3:1-2, a passage to which I briefly referred in Chapter 2. God addresses Israel: "You only have I known of all the families of the earth; therefore I will punish you for all your iniquities" (v. 2). To "know" implies covenant, choosing, intimacy—love, in fact; and that very intimacy leads God to punish when the people break covenant.

The second passage is Isa. 5:1-7, a song about a vineyard. Here the prophet Isaiah is evidently imitating the style of vintage songs; he may even have sung it at a harvest festival. But this is no ordinary vintage song, because the owner of the vineyard turns out to be God, and the vineyard is the covenant people (vv. 6-7). God will destroy the vineyard, it seems, because it has produced nothing but sour grapes. But if God will destroy the vineyard, God has also invested great effort in the vineyard: "He dug it and cleared it of stones, and planted it with choice vines; he built a watchtower in the midst of it, and hewed out a wine vat in it" (v. 2). One is invited to ponder the care and the love that Yahweh has bestowed on the covenant people before one hears the word of wrath.

Now let me pause to discuss another term that has caused grief to the Christians' view of God: the matter of the *vengeance* of God. If the phrase "wrath" of God conjures up for us the notion of a divine tantrum, the phrase "vengeance" of God conjures up for us the notion of God in a scheming vendetta, a heavenly version of the feuding of Hatfields and McCoys.

Let me state simply: we are wide of the mark in applying the term "vengeance" to God. Recently, a biblical scholar has offered a thoroughgoing study of the use of the Hebrew words in question (the verb and related nouns are from the root *nqm*), and his conclusion is that the verb describes not a new move in a mean-spirited vendetta but rather the action of a sovereign who is stirred to act to redress a wrong suffered by a subject who heretofore has not received justice.[7] The scholar writes, "In Isa. 61:1-4, the 'day of vengeance' has nothing to do with violent punitive actions against an enemy. The imperium rather is the ground for the events most needed by those who are in the greatest misery: the poor, the brokenhearted, the captives, and the grief-stricken."[8] The Hebrew term therefore needs an altogether new translation in English— "vindication," possibly. Indeed, translators have begun to deal with the issue. In the RSV, Jer. 46:10 begins, "That day is the day of the Lord God of hosts, a day of vengeance, to avenge himself on his foes"; the NRSV reads, "That day is the day of the Lord God of hosts, a day of retribution, to gain vindication from his foes." But much more work needs to be done on this matter if we are to purge our human notions of "vengeance" from our view of God.

Now let us return to the matter of the wrath of God. The Old Testament, I submit, suggests that God can exercise wrath without being mean, that wrath is the appropriate response in the face of betrayal by the covenant people. Jeremiah understands God to say, "They have turned their backs to me, and not their faces" (Jer. 2:27). How else is God to react, we must ask, when the covenant people turn their backs?

Signs of the Wrath of God?

The problem is, when we are faced with human anger, we perceive directly the words and the actions of the person who is angry; with God, direct perception is not so easy, and the question has always been: Is God angry, and how do we know? The natural conclusion is that disasters are evidence of God's anger: we have already looked at the sequence of disasters in Amos 4:6-11 as God's attempts to get the attention of Israel.

The disaster may be a personal one. Persons with handicaps were presumed to have been rendered so by God as a punishment (the narration of God's words to Moses in Exod. 4:11 implies it, as do Elisha's words in 2 Kings 6:18). But it was the great public disasters that caught people's attention.

Indeed, a great disaster was an occasion for a search for the cause of God's anger. "Now there was a famine in the days of David for three years, year after year; and David inquired of the Lord. The Lord said, 'There is bloodguilt on Saul and on his house, because he put the Gibeonites to death'" (2 Sam. 21:1).

A still more curious story is told in 2 Sam. 24:1-17. According to the narrative, "the anger of the Lord was kindled against Israel" (v. 1), the reason not being given. So Yahweh incites David to take a census, something evidently considered a sin (v. 10). Yahweh, speaking through a prophet, then offers David a choice of three punishments—three years of famine, three months of military defeat, or three days of plague. David chooses the plague. One may surmise what had happened: the onset of a plague cried out for an explanation, and prophetic groups brought forth an explanation: David's census, a measure that was doubtless for the purpose of royal reorganization, systematic taxation, and conscription—they would have viewed the census as an illegitimate innovation.[9] But those who were sympathetic to the king must have asserted that the census was not David's idea; rather, Yahweh incited him to the decision.[10] (This notion, which makes Yahweh out to have urged David to sin, was too much for the postexilic Chronicler; in his rewriting of the narrative, Satan incites David to take the census! [1 Chron. 21:1].) In such tangles, we see the effort of the Israelites to discern God's reactions.

Inevitably, there were permanent mysteries. The early tradition of Israel, preserved in what scholars call the Yahwistic and Elohistic Sources (see Chapter 1), understands Moses to have been Yahweh's unique servant. "When there are prophets among you, I the Lord make myself known to them in visions; I speak to them in dreams. Not so with my servant Moses; he is entrusted with all my house. With him I speak face to face—clearly, not in riddles; and he beholds the form of the Lord" (Num. 12:6-8; compare Deut. 34:10). Why, then, was Moses not allowed to enter the Promised Land? The Deuteronomic Source concluded not that Moses himself sinned but that he suffered vicariously for the sins of the Israelites at Kadesh (Deut. 1:37-38). On the other hand, the Priestly Source explained it by Moses' presumed lack of trust in Yahweh in the incident of the giving of the water at Meribah (Num. 20:10-13;

27:12-14; Deut. 32:48-52)[11] even though there is no narrative of Moses' actual disbelief.[12] We are left with the strong suspicion that these two explanations are *ad hoc,* late, and not overly convincing.

A similar mystery is the death of Josiah. Josiah was given an extraordinarily high estimation: "Before him there was no king like him, who turned to the Lord with all his heart, with all his soul, and with all his might, according to the law of Moses; nor did any like him arise after him" (2 Kings 23:25). Nevertheless, he was struck down at the battle of Megiddo (609 B.C.) at the age of 39 (2 Kings 22:1; 23:39). No explanation of why he might merit an early death was forthcoming, only a resounding silence.[13] It was not always easy to discern the reaction of God.

The view that there is a direct relation between a natural disaster such as an earthquake or a famine and the sins of the people who suffer continued for many centuries. One scholar has proposed that the earthquake in New England in 1727 precipitated the first "quickening" before the "Great Awakening," the great revival in American Protestantism.[14] The association between earthquake and the sins of the victims was in full force after an earthquake in Lima, Peru, in 1746 destroyed the cathedral and much of the city, with great loss of life; it was in full force after the great Lisbon earthquake of 1755 which, with the accompanying fires and tidal wave, killed 60,000 people. But then the French philosopher Voltaire wrote two works. The first, in 1756, was *Poème sur le désastre de Lisbonne,* in which he attacked the orthodox view of the origin of evil. Then, in 1759, came *Candide,* a novel that scathingly ridiculed the notion that every disaster was for a positive purpose: in chapter 5 of *Candide* the protagonist insists that the tidal wave in Lisbon harbor was specifically for the purpose of drowning Jacques, an Anabaptist. Such works, along with the works of English Deists and above all with the rise of modern science and the spread of scientific explanations, have removed to the edge of our consciousness any notion of a one-to-one correspondence between natural disasters and the sins of the victims.

So what are we today to say? Is a discernment of the wrath of God a will-o'-the-wisp?

Our current public stance is that God has no place in the causing of earthquakes. Earthquakes, we understand from the geologists, are the result of shifts in pressure in portions of the earth's plates. Nor, in our current public stance, does God have a place in weather patterns: the weather report on the nightly news accustoms us to meteorological analysis—rainfall is the result of low-pressure areas, not of God. Nevertheless, old habits die hard: prayers for rain are heard in our churches in times of drought, and insurance policies mention "acts of God"—damage from a falling meteorite, let us say.

The recently developed theory of chaos indicates that the weather will never be predictable in detail more than a couple of weeks in advance:[15] so, given the indeterminacy of it all, who knows what in ultimate truth the place of God in weather, or in earthquakes, will be? (I shall return in Chapter 7 to struggle further with the question of the tension between the Old Testament understanding of causation by God and our understanding of causation by natural forces.)

On the other hand, some large-scale disasters are the result not only of natural forces but of human foolishness and greed, and this is an aspect of the matter that the Old Testament does not glimpse. Floods, for example, may be the result not only of excess rainfall but of human acts of deforestation. There is much discussion these days of other ecological disasters—holes in the ozone layer from the discharge of chlorofluorocarbons into the atmosphere, or the possibility of global warming from an increase of carbon dioxide levels in the atmosphere. But the Old Testament is well aware that God may punish the covenant people through their own destructive deeds; Jer. 2:19, for example, sees God's punishment acting through the people's deeds: "Your wickedness will punish you, and your apostasies will convict you. Know and see that it is evil and bitter for you to forsake the Lord your God; the fear of me is not in you, says the Lord God of hosts."

The most creative kind of linking of God's punishment with disastrous human action in the Old Testament is that with political and military events and deeds of violence. The prophets understood God to be working through human agents, whether those agents are aware of it or not. For example, Isaiah understood that God would bring about civil war in Egypt (Isa. 19:2). But preeminently God was linked with the invasions by Assyria and Babylon of Israel and Judah, proclaimed by the prophets as God's judgment on the covenant people.

From the purely historical point of view, Israel had settled in the land of Palestine in the thirteenth century B.C., a time when neither Egypt to the southwest nor Assyria or Babylon in the northeast was active. But Assyria began to march west on punitive expeditions in the ninth century, and for conquest in the eighth century; Babylon did the same at the end of the seventh century. The march of these great powers was, in the proclamation of the prophets, God's judgment on the people.

We have seen that Amos listed military defeat and the overturn of cities along with agricultural disasters. But it was preeminently the prophet Isaiah, a few decades later, who set forth the onslaught of Assyria on Judah as the exercise of God's wrath. In Isa. 10:5-6, God is understood to say, "Ah, Assyria, the rod of my anger—the club in their hands is my fury! Against a godless nation

I send him, and against the people of my wrath I command him, to take spoil and seize plunder, and to tread them down like the mire of the streets." Though Isaiah proclaims Assyria to be the club in God's hands, the Assyrians did not know it—they simply pursued their campaigns of destruction (vv. 7-8; compare Hab. 1:10-11). But when God is finished punishing Judah, the Assyrians will in turn be punished for their haughty pride (Isa. 10:12). That is to say, Assyria exercises her human freedom to pursue her policies; but, at the same time, God is using the choices of Assyria to accomplish the punishment that is due the covenant people. It is important to note, however, that Isaiah evidently became convinced that though Assyria would conquer much of Judah, Jerusalem itself would not fall: God would use it as the nucleus for continuity with the future (Isa. 1:21-26; 37:33-35).

We have already touched on King Josiah's reform in Chapter 2: a century after Isaiah, in 622 B.C., Josiah sponsored a major reform of public worship (2 Kings 22–23), and soon thereafter (612) the power of Assyria collapsed. But after the death of Josiah (609) his reform lapsed, and in 605 the prophet Jeremiah proclaimed Babylon to be what Isaiah had proclaimed Assyria to be—the instrument of God's wrath on the people. Typical is Jeremiah's description of the "foe from the north," who sets out like a lion to destroy: all that the people can do is to lament and wail, "The fierce anger of the Lord has not turned away from us" (Jer. 4:5-8). But if Isaiah had been convinced that God would spare Jerusalem, Jeremiah was convinced that God would allow Babylon to take the city of Jerusalem. Thus, when the Babylonians were besieging Jerusalem, Jeremiah told King Zedekiah, "Thus says the Lord, the God of Israel: I am going to turn back the weapons of war that are in your hands and with which you are fighting against the king of Babylon . . . and I will bring them together into the center of this city. I myself will fight against you with outstretched hand and mighty arm, in anger, in fury, and in great wrath" (Jer. 21:3-5). Many citizens of Jerusalem must have maintained the conviction that Isaiah had proclaimed, that Jerusalem would never fall (compare Lam. 4:12, 17, 20); but, as we know, Jerusalem did fall to the Babylonians in 587, so Jeremiah's message proved true. I shall return to these prophetic texts in Chapter 6, where I discuss battles, and in Chapter 9, where I discuss the prophets.

Earlier we explored what, in the outlook of the Old Testament, arouses God's wrath; now let us return to the question, listening to what the prophets in particular have to say. In Isaiah, the accusations include the neglect of justice and righteousness (Isa. 1:17; 5:7), the selfishness of the rich (Isa. 5:8), violence toward the helpless (1:15-16; 3:14), negligent leadership (1:23), and the search for military security from Egypt instead of from Yahweh (30:1-2).

Jeremiah echoed many of these accusations (Jer. 5:26-28), but he stressed the way in which the people worshiped Baal instead of Yahweh (Jeremiah 2): indeed, the people's loyalty to "the queen of heaven," the consort of Baal, was in his mind the reason that Jerusalem fell (Jeremiah 44). The prophet Ezekiel proclaimed that Jerusalem fell because of "filthy lewdness," a shorthand phrase for worship of fertility deities (Ezek. 24:1-14).

Beyond these theological judgments, is there any objective historical validity to these accusations? It is clear that both Israel and Judah became more prosperous in the course of the eighth century, and, inevitably, the upper class benefited from the prosperity rather than the lower class. It is clear, too, that Baalism spread under Canaanite influence, particularly in the northern kingdom of Israel, but in Judah in the south as well.[16] These trends evidently continued in the seventh century.

What the prophets saw, then, was a breakdown of any solidarity within the covenant people—the disparity between rich and poor—and an increase in devotion to Baal at the very time when Assyria and then Babylon were hammering at the gates of Jerusalem. The prophets linked the two phenomena. Parenthetically, it should be said that those who worshiped Baal and the "queen of heaven" interpreted the same events in the opposite fashion: they maintained that all had gone well with the nation while they worshiped the "queen of heaven," but since King Josiah put a stop to their worship, they suffered nothing but disaster. (This is the argument cited in Jer. 44:15-18.) But the interpretation that Jeremiah offered of the fall of Jerusalem, echoed by the prophet Ezekiel, became the prevailing and definitive one (compare Lam. 4:12-13). (I shall discuss Baalism at greater length in Chapter 9.)

The fall of Jerusalem, then, was the example par excellence of God's wrath: as we look at Lam. 2:1-8, part of one of the laments over the fall of the city, we see the number of expressions for God's anger.

It is important to point out that, in all these battles that are understood to express God's wrath, many of those who suffer and die are innocent. This problem, touched on by Habakkuk, a contemporary of Jeremiah (Hab. 1:13-14), and reflected in an apocalyptic passage in the Gospels (Mark 13:17-19 and parallels), is never really solved at any point in the Bible.

Given this interpretation of the meaning of the fall of Jerusalem, the people took on the lesson: if God brought about not only the fall of the city but the destruction of the very temple where divine worship was centered, then the sins of the people must surely have been far greater than anyone had imagined. The lesson sank in. The years in exile seem really to have rid the Jewish people of any devotion to Baalism (as we shall see in Chapter 10, the references to Baalistic practices in postexilic passages like Isa. 57:3-8 are doubtless name-calling rather than historical fact). The years in exile brought about a deepening understanding of sin among the Jewish people: sin became a matter not of some single public matter like the census undertaken by King David, but of offenses that might be hidden even to oneself (Ps. 19:12). Indeed, the psalm sequences that emerged in the exilic or postexilic period, those like Ps. 19:7-14 and Psalms 51 and 103, often stress personal sin (51:1-9) and insist that God is more gracious than the people's sins merit (103:10-11).[17] The fact that the Day of Atonement is instituted only in late legal collections, in the Priestly Code (Leviticus 16) and in the Holiness Code (Lev. 23:26-32), suggests that it came into prominence in this period as a day of fasting and of purgation of the people's sins.[18]

Late in the postexilic period (probably in the first half of the fourth century B.C.), the book of Joel describes a catastrophic plague of locusts. This visitation was simply and immediately understood as the hand of God in punishment for sin, the beginning of the "day of the Lord"; it was therefore an occasion for public fasting and repentance (Joel 1:4, 15; 2:11-14).

New Testament Perspectives

The association between disaster on the one hand, whether public or personal, and punishment for sin on the other, has persisted for many centuries and is still part of the mental equipment of Jews and Christians, as witness the popularity of books like Harold Kushner's *When Bad Things Happen to Good People*.[19] But it is striking that Jesus seems to have refused to pronounce on the matter. One account, Luke 13:1-5, is worth citing in its entirety. "At that very time there were some present who told him about the Galileans whose blood Pilate had mingled with their sacrifices. He asked them, 'Do you think that because these Galileans suffered in this way they were worse sinners than all other Galileans? No, I tell you; but unless you repent, you will all perish as they did. Or those eighteen who were killed when the tower of Siloam fell on them—do you think that they were worse offenders than all the others living in Jerusalem? No, I tell you; but unless you repent, you will all perish just as they did." That is to say, whether it is a "natural" disaster like the collapse of a tower or an atrocity committed by tyrannical authority, we are not to speculate whether the victims were particularly sinful; instead we are to understand that all human beings are prone to sin, so that a violent death is an occasion to ponder the necessity to repent.

There is another narrative in which Jesus likewise avoids the issue, the narrative of his healing of the man born blind, in chapter 9 of the Gospel of John. The incident is presented in a typical Johannine fashion—the occasion offers Jesus an opportunity to manifest his identity, the one sent from God. But the first three verses of the chapter hit the same note as does that passage from Luke just cited. "As he [Jesus] walked along, he saw a man blind from birth. His disciples asked him, 'Rabbi, who sinned, this man or his parents, that he was born blind?' Jesus answered, 'Neither this man nor his parents sinned; he was born blind so that God's works might be revealed in him.'" Do not ask whose fault it is that the man was born blind: look instead toward healing.

On the other hand, Jesus seems to have anticipated that Jerusalem would be destroyed at a time soon after his day, and in this way he saw his ministry as analogous to the prophets of old, like Jeremiah, who pronounced the coming destruction of Jerusalem. We recall Jesus' word over Jerusalem in Luke 13:34, "Jerusalem, Jerusalem, the city that kills the prophets and stones those who are sent to it! How often have I desired to gather your children together as a hen gathers her brood under her wings, and you were not willing!" God sends the prophets to Jerusalem, but Jerusalem rejects them. This word is reinforced by the narrative of his weeping over Jerusalem after his entrance on Palm Sunday. We read, "As he came near and saw the city [of Jerusalem], he wept over it, saying, 'If you, even you, had only recognized on this day the things that make for peace! But now they are hidden from your eyes. Indeed, the days will come upon you, when your enemies will set up ramparts around you and surround you, and hem you in on every side. They will crush you to the ground, you and your children within you, and they will not leave within you one stone upon another; because you did not recognize the time of your visitation from God'" (Luke 19:41-44). Some of this diction, it is true, may have been shaped by Luke in the light of what happened in the Roman siege of Jerusalem in A.D. 70, but much of it must go back to Jesus: the "visitation" is the prophetic word through Jesus that Jerusalem ignores; Jerusalem then will be overthrown as it was in Jeremiah's day.

We must therefore ask: In the light of the New Testament, what becomes of the Old Testament notions of our fear of God and of God's wrath? Two convictions held in the New Testament (but not in the Old) are relevant to the discussion. The first, already mentioned, is a firm teaching about hell as eternal punishment for those whom God has condemned. The parable of the separation of the sheep and the goats (Matt. 25:31-46) may be a development by Matthew of material from Jesus' teaching rather than the direct teaching of Jesus himself, but sayings such as those in Mark 9:43-48 leave no doubt that Jesus taught the reality of hell.

The second conviction is that of original sin: we must understand that this conviction, developed by Paul (for example, in Rom. 5:12-21) from the narrative of the fall in Genesis 3, is deeper and darker than the Old Testament view of sin.[20] But though Paul developed the idea, it is not foreign to Jesus: one notes, for example, his teaching, "If you then, who are evil, know how to give good gifts to your children, how much more will your Father in heaven give good things to those who ask him!" (Matt. 7:11; compare Luke 11:13).

What we gain from the New Testament, both directly from the teachings and actions of Jesus and from the proclamation of the New Testament in general, is an overwhelming knowledge of the love of God, which far outmeasures the wrath of God. In this respect, the perspective of the New Testament matches the comparison of the love and the wrath of God set forth in the creed of Exod. 34:6-7, which I have already cited. God makes his sun rise on the evil and the good, and sends rain on the righteous and on the unrighteous (Matt. 5:45). God's love persistently seeks out those who would appear to be lost (compare the parables of the lost sheep, Luke 15:3-7, and of the lost coin, Luke 15:8-10); it is unforgettably set forth in the parable of the lost son (Luke 15:11-32). God's love is vividly expressed in Jesus' love, and that love is particularly directed toward those who are ill (Mark 1:31 and often), toward those who are possessed by demons, that is, who suffer from mental or moral-spiritual illness (Luke 8:2 and often). It is directed toward those who repent—men who have been tax collectors like Zacchaeus (Luke 19:1-10; compare Mark 2:16) and women who have been prostitutes (Luke 7:36-50): "Truly I tell you, the tax collectors and the prostitutes are going into the kingdom of God ahead of you" (Matt. 21:31).

Nevertheless, if Jesus showed an astonishing compassion for those like tax collectors and prostitutes who were scorned and rejected by the religious leaders of his day, the gospels record an array of woes that he pronounced against various classes of people. Thus, in Luke, there are woes against the rich, against those who have enough to eat, and against those of whom others speak well (Luke 6:25-26). Matthew preserves a whole series of woes (Matt. 23:1-36) directed to the "scribes and Pharisees, hypocrites," who lay heavy legal burdens on others, who seek praise in the marketplace, who are insensitive to God's purposes; for example: "Woe to you, scribes and Pharisees, hypocrites! For you are like whitewashed tombs, which on the outside look beautiful, but inside they are full of the bones of the dead and of all kinds of filth. So you also on the outside look righteous to others, but inside you are full of hypocrisy and lawlessness" (vv. 27-28). Here is wrath indeed!

And we do not forget Jesus' anger in driving out the money-changers from the Jerusalem temple (Mark 11:15-19 and parallels).

Jesus enjoins fear of God. "Do not fear those who kill the body, and after that can do nothing more. But I will warn you whom to fear: fear him who, after he has killed, has authority to cast into hell. Yes, I tell you, fear him!" (Luke 12:4-5). We are not to fear suffering and martyrdom, but we are to fear God.

Paul, for his part, speaks of the wrath of God, exercised on both the Gentiles (Rom. 1:28-32) and the Jews: "Do you not realize that God's kindness is meant to lead you to repentance? But by your hard and impenitent heart you are storing up wrath for yourself on the day of wrath, when God's righteous judgment will be revealed" (Rom. 2:4-5). And he gathers up a whole set of Old Testament texts that to him demonstrate that no one is righteous and that there is no fear of God before the eyes of anyone (Rom. 3:10-18).

Summary

We are not to assume that fearing God and loving God are opposites, or that a loving God does not exercise wrath. Do we hear God, then, in the texts of the Old Testament that speak of our fearing God and that speak of the wrath of God? We do, in the context of the overwhelming love of God for us and in the context of our experience of loving God. We hear God in the wrath he expresses through the prophets against those who, called to serve the true God, choose to serve false gods instead. We hear God in the wrath he expresses through the prophets against those in power who neglect the helpless and the marginalized in society, or even oppress them. Though we are not bound by the link that the prophets saw between the invasions of Israel and Judah by Assyria and Babylon on the one hand and the covenant people's neglect of the covenant on the other, we nevertheless ponder the possibility that God's punishing work continues today in the political and military affairs of nations, even though the nations today may be no more aware of the drama of God's love and wrath in their political and military affairs than were Assyria or Babylon of old. We may be enabled to hear God in these ways, and so we fear God, knowing from the New Testament that we can never be loving enough toward our fellow human beings, nor serve God with total fidelity, and so of necessity we are led simply to throw ourselves on God's mercy (Eph. 2:3-7), and in so doing we are reassured by the word in James 2:13, "Mercy triumphs over judgment."

But, it must be stressed, we do not hear God in the attempts offered in the Old Testament to identify God's wrath in disasters like earthquakes that overwhelm families or communities, nor do we assume that God does anything but weep over those innocent ones who suffer in war (see Chapter 6).

A Closing Thought: The "Dies Irae"

The wrath of God, and the fear that wrath engenders in us, must be seen in the context of the love of God. The wrath of God, and the fear that wrath engenders in us, expressed outside the context of the love of God, is epitomized in a poem from the Middle Ages, the "Dies Irae" ("day of wrath"). This Latin poem was evidently written in the thirteenth century in Italy, perhaps in Franciscan circles; that century was a period marked by dire uncertainty, terror, and death. The poem was based on Zeph. 1:14-15: "The great day of the Lord is near, near and hastening fast; the sound of the day of the Lord is bitter, the warrior cries aloud there. That day will be a day of wrath, a day of distress and anguish, a day of ruin and devastation, a day of darkness and gloom, a day of clouds and thick darkness." Zephaniah was a prophet of the seventh century B.C., and this passage presents his expectation of a culminating confrontation between God and God's enemies—a final battle, though not an apocalyptic overturning of history. The prophet Amos, a century before, had offered a shorter word along the same line (Amos 5:18-20).

The "Dies Irae" itself is a poem of 54 lines. It begins, *Dies irae, dies illa, Solvet saeclum in favilla Teste David cum Sibylla* ("Day of wrath, that day: the world will break up in ashes, David, with the Sibyl, being witness"). Though the poem has been popularly attributed to Thomas of Celano, an early Franciscan, no one really knows its origin. It began to be known outside of Italy in the fifteenth century and became part of the mass for the dead after the Council of Trent (sixteenth century).

It is an awesome poem; the fear it has generated through the centuries would be hard to imagine. In the revolutionary year 1848, the archbishop of Paris was at the barricades trying to put an end to the armed conflict, and he was shot and killed. At his Requiem in Notre Dame cathedral, the priests of the diocese sang the "Dies Irae" with overpowering effect. An English priest, William Josiah Irons, was present, and, moved by the service and by the tragic circumstances of the death of the archbishop, began a translation of the poem into English, which was published in 1849.[21] The first three stanzas are as follows: "Day of wrath! O day of mourning! See fulfilled the prophets' warning, Heaven and earth in ashes burning! O what fear man's bosom rendeth When from heav'n the Judge descendeth, On whose sentence all dependeth! Wondrous sound the trumpet flingeth; Through earth's sepulchers it ringeth; All before the throne it bringeth."[22]

There is a place, I would say, for such a hymn in Christian hymnody. It is appropriate to shudder at the martyr death of a churchman trying to bring peace amid violence, as we in our day have shuddered at the martyr death of Archbishop Oscar Romero of San Salvador; and it is appropriate to bring such deaths, for their witnesses, under the wrath of God.

It is certainly normal for human beings to fear death, and it is appropriate to be awestruck by the expectation of being judged by God at death. But it is monstrous to encourage a fear of death and of the judgment of God unless that fear is set in the larger context of the gracious love of God. For example, it is monstrous for churches to impose this kind of thing on children and on those who for whatever reason lack self-esteem. We must hear first how God loves us and hear of God's hopes for us and expectations from us; then we gain a sensitivity to how far we have fallen short. It is only at that point, where we can begin to make valid choices in our lives, that our fear of God and our understanding of the wrath of God become appropriate.

Notes

1. Lillian Smith, *Killers of the Dream* (New York: Norton, 1949), 79.
2. Useful here is Hans Ferdinand Fuhs, "*yārēʾ*," *TDOT* 6:300–15.
3. This is one of the prayers for the Fourteenth Sunday After Pentecost (Year C): see *Celebrate*, Vol. 23, No. 8, for September 13, 1992 (Minneapolis: Augsburg Fortress).
4. Herman Wouk, *The Caine Mutiny* (Garden City, NY: Doubleday, 1951).
5. *BCP* 178, 230.
6. Helpful here is Elsie Johnson, "*ʾānap*," *TDOT* 1:351–60.
7. George E. Mendenhall, *The Tenth Generation, The Origins of the Biblical Tradition* (Baltimore: The Johns Hopkins University, 1973), 69–104.
8. *Ibid.*, 100.
9. Bright, *History of Israel*, 206.
10. P. Kyle McCarter, Jr., *II Samuel* (AB 9; Garden City, NY: Doubleday, 1984), 514–18.
11. These verses in Deuteronomy are traced by scholars not to the Deuteronomic Source but to the Priestly Source: see Mayes, *Deuteronomy*, 394.
12. For these two explanations, see Samuel R. Driver, *Deuteronomy* (ICC; Edinburgh: T. & T. Clark, 1895), 26–27.
13. Stanley Brice Frost, "The Death of Josiah, A Conspiracy of Silence," *JBL* 87 (1968), 369–82.
14. Elizabeth C. Nordbeck, "Almost Awakened: The Great Revival in New Hampshire and Maine, 1727–1748," *Historical New Hampshire* 35/1 (Spring, 1980), 27–30.
15. See the work of Edward Lorenz and "The Butterfly Effect," Chapter 1 in James Gleick, *Chaos, Making a New Science* (New York: Penguin, 1988).
16. Bright, *History of Israel*, 255–62.
17. For the dating of Ps. 19:7-14, see Hans-Joachim Kraus, *Psalms 1–59* (Minneapolis: Augsburg, 1988), 267; for Psalm 51, see William L. Holladay, *Jeremiah 2*

(Hermeneia; Minneapolis: Fortress Press, 1989), 69, and Kraus, *Psalms 1–59,* 501; for Psalm 103 see Hans-Joachim Kraus, *Psalms 60–150* (Minneapolis: Augsburg, 1989), 290.

18. Compare Jacob Milgrom, "Atonement, Day of," *IDBSup* 82–83; Milgrom, however, sees its origin somewhat earlier.

19. Harold S. Kushner, *When Bad Things Happen to Good People* (New York: Schocken, 1981).

20. Simon J. De Vries, "Sin, sinners," *IDB* 4:370–75.

21. *The* [Episcopal] *Hymnal 1940 Companion* (New York: The Church Pension Fund, 1949), 290–91.

22. *The* [Episcopal] *Hymnal 1940* (New York: The Church Pension Fund, 1940), no. 468.

5

Narratives

~

Here we come to the heart of the matter. Whatever else the Old Testament is, its central essence is narrative. From creation to Abraham and Joseph, from Moses and Joshua to the kings of Israel, and on to the destruction of Jerusalem and the exile of the Jews and their subsequent return, the Old Testament is narrative. But the formation of narrative and the meaning of that narrative, it turns out, are complex questions. How may we hear God today in this narrative from far away and long ago?

"Anyone who tells a story speaks a world into being."[1] A few years ago, a story about computers was making the rounds: according to the tale, someone asked a computer expert whether computers could think. "Computers will show they can think," said the expert, "when, after you have asked the computer a question, the answer comes, 'That reminds me of a story.'"

Indeed, few words are so irresistible as "Let me tell you a story." While for many in our own culture the kind of oral storytelling implied by this invitation is confined, alas, to the days of childhood, nevertheless we all know how as adults we may enjoy a really good storyteller. Every human culture has told stories. Grimm's fairy tales are traditional stories that had been preserved by the German people, but we know that every culture across the world has had its own folklore. American children—and adults—are nourished on *The Wizard of Oz*, both the version in the book of L. Frank Baum (1900)[2] and the film version (1938). Such stories embody folk wisdom; they deal with the basic questions of good and evil, of jealousy and revenge, of anger and justice, of leaving home, of overcoming obstacles, of the movement into sexual awareness, of the meaning of death. Storytelling intertwines entertainment and the transmission of wisdom, and listeners wait eagerly for the word that the protagonists lived happily ever after.

Some narrative folklore is embodied in legends, stories that purport to deal with heroes of the past. Though these heroes may once have had a real historical existence, the legends about them belong more to folk wisdom than to historical reality.

Some narrative folklore across the world involves myths, in which deities are crucial to the action; these myths may offer explanations of the origin of the world and of human behavior.

Some of the narrative material in the Old Testament has functioned for Christians in the way such traditional tales do. One thinks of the stories of the animals entering Noah's ark two by two; Joseph and the coat his father gave him (whether it was of many colors or of long sleeves); Moses in the bulrushes; Daniel in the lion's den; Ruth, who followed her mother-in-law Naomi into a strange land.

But the stories of the Old Testament do not present themselves as imaginative fiction, as folklore so often does. Indeed, the narratives of the Old Testament raise for us in our day two interrelated issues, both of which need to be explored: (1) the claim to historicity and (2) the participation of God.

The Claim to Historicity

Most of the Old Testament consists of narrative with the claim to be historical. If the Pentateuch (Genesis through Deuteronomy) is roughly 47 percent laws (see Chapter 3), then the rest of it, roughly 53 percent, is narrative. The books of Joshua, Judges, Samuel, and Kings are almost entirely narrative. Ruth is a narrative. Most of Chronicles, Ezra, and Nehemiah are narrative. Among the prophetic books, Jeremiah offers large blocks of narrative. And it goes without saying that the New Testament shares with the Old Testament the claim to be historical.

For the moment, I set aside a category of material that arose in the postexilic period, what might be called historical fiction. This material—books like Jonah and Esther, and the first six chapters of Daniel—on the surface claims historical reality but offers clues that lead us to classify it as fiction. I shall examine this material in Chapter 7.

Returning to the claim of the Old Testament narrative to be history, our first question must be: Given this claim, is it really history? Our answer begins with an acknowledgment that the claim to historical validity of the narrative in the Old Testament can be affirmed for many events described in the later portions of that history. Thus, some of the events late in the monarchical period can be integrated by historians with evidence outside the Bible that has been unearthed by archeologists.

Let me give two specific examples to show what is involved. The prophet Jeremiah is said to have made use of a scribe named Baruch, the son of Neriah (Jer. 32:12; 36:4). There has recently turned up, in Jerusalem, a clay imprint of a stamp seal offering an inscription in Hebrew letters of the late seventh century B.C., "Berechiah the son of Neriah the scribe." There is no other Neriah mentioned in the Old Testament, and there is no other Baruch mentioned in the Old Testament. It is almost certain, then, that the name given in the Bible, "Baruch," is a shortened form of "Berechiah," and that what we can hold in our hand is the imprint of a stamp seal owned by Jeremiah's scribe.[3]

For a second example, a Babylonian document from Nebuchadnezzar's time lists among his court officials an officer named Nabuzeriddinam, who is given the archaic title "the chief cook" (the title, we presume, was honorary: he probably had no more to do with cooking than present-day stewards have to do with pigsties).[4] In Jer. 39:9-11, there is mention of a Babylonian officer named Nebuzaradan; though the NRSV translates his title as "captain of the guard," the Hebrew phrase in question means literally "chief of the butchers [or cooks]." There is little doubt, then, that the biblical Nebuzaradan and the Babylonian Nabuzeriddinam are the same man.

One can cite similar examples from the records of the Assyrian kings Sargon and Sennacherib and from the records of the Persian kings Cyrus and Darius: the clay tablets of the ancient Near East have confirmed and supplemented the Old Testament historical narratives at dozens of points.[5]

Our conclusion, then, is that for some portions of the Old Testament historical narrative, the historical claims of the narrative are secure. The Old Testament at these points is not fiction: it speaks of real people who are remembered as doing what is recorded.

On the other hand, for many of the most important characters in the Old Testament historical narratives we lack any outside validation: for example, outside the Bible there is no notice of Solomon, who looms large in the Old Testament. This is not to say that Solomon never lived but simply that the narratives about him lack any independent outside attestation.

It must also be said that the further we move back in time in the Old Testament historical narrative, the less we seem to be in touch with what we today can recognize as objective history. Here I must make a distinction between two related matters, historicity and credibility. By historicity I mean the historical reality of a given person or event; by credibility I mean the reliability of the narrated details. One could imagine the possibility of the historicity of someone named Methuselah but question whether he lived 969 years. (I am dealing at the moment with the question of historicity in the Old Testament narrative; I shall save until Chapter 7 a systematic exploration of the credibility of particular details in that narrative.)

The details of the question of historicity give rise to great differences of opinion among scholars. I can only sketch out brief suggestions here, but the general pattern would be agreed to by all but the most earnest biblical literalist. Let me offer my own judgment on several points.

A good example of the question is the matter of King David. The story of David takes up an enormous portion of the Old Testament, yet until 1993 there was no evidence outside the Old Testament of the historical reality of David. In the summer of that year, a fragment of an inscription in the Aramaic language, dating evidently from the ninth century B.C., was discovered in the archeological mound of Dan in northern Palestine; the inscription includes the words "king of Israel" and "house of David," "house" here meaning "dynasty," as in 1 Kings 12:19 and many other Old Testament passages. The inscription in question was shattered later in ancient times and reused in a wall. The archeologist, Avraham Biran, suggests that the inscription may well be connected with the incident described in 1 Kings 15:18-20. Asa, David's great-great-grandson, the king of the southern kingdom of Judah, sends a payment to Ben-Hadad I, king of the Arameans (whose capital was Damascus, and who used the Aramaic language), to bribe him into breaking his treaty with Baasha, king of the northern kingdom of Israel—a bribe that worked.[6] Whether that is the appropriate background for the fragment, it does indicate that roughly a hundred years after the presumed time of David, a foreign king referred to David's dynasty. This find reinforces the conviction of scholars that David was a completely historical figure who came to the throne of Israel about 1000 B.C.

A similar judgment can now be made about the Mesopotamian diviner Balaam, the son of Beor (Numbers 22–24). In 1967, fragments of an Aramaic inscription from the eighth century B.C. were excavated from a pagan sanctuary on the east side of the Jordan. They contained some oracles of Balaam, the son of Beor; that is to say, the memory of Balaam was preserved for several hundred years by a community of non-Israelites—strong evidence for the historical reality of Balaam, probably in the thirteenth century B.C.[7]

I assume Moses to be historical if only because the covenantal theology attributed to him is so distinctive (see Chapter 2); the pharaoh during whose reign Moses led the people out of Egypt is likely to have been Rameses II (1294–24 B.C.), though this is simply the prevailing suggestion of scholars.

But this is not to say that all the details of the narratives of Moses or Balaam are historical. With regard to Moses, it is striking that a narrative of the rescue of the hero, when still an infant, from a basket in the water, is recorded of Sargon of Akkad, an early ruler in Mesopotamia (modern Iraq) a thousand years before Moses' time.[8] A leader who is a hero in his adult life will have wonder-stories told about his childhood, and we are not surprised that the same narrative pattern turns up more than once.

Even though the narratives of Abraham, Isaac, Jacob, and Joseph in the book of Genesis are vivid and lifelike, there is no way to put a date to them, and the stories associated with them may bring together into a single family line events that originally took place within separate clans. The historian John

Bright guesses that Israel's ancestors (among whom these patriarchs are to be numbered, if they are historical) were in Palestine by the Middle Bronze Age (approximately 2000–1500 B.C.), but that is only a guess.[9]

Behind Abraham we lack all historical moorings. Attempts by archeologists to locate any remaining evidence of a universal flood that can be associated with Noah have failed. As one might imagine, there were, in those days, many floods that swept across the Tigris and Euphrates valleys in what is now Iraq, and any one of them, or more than one, might have given rise to a narrative about a universal flood, but we cannot attach any historical label to the flood in Genesis. Behind Noah lie those narratives of the earliest inhabitants of the earth; here the present-day historians of early humanity must part company with the narrative altogether.

But if we move back from the assuredly firm historicity of Nebuchadnezzar to the doubtlessly firm historicity of David and Balaam, to the probable historicity of Moses, to the possible historicity of Abraham, to the dubious historicity of Noah, to the nonhistoricity (in any meaningful sense) of Methuselah, we must at the same time take note of the fact that for the Old Testament itself its historical narrative is all of a piece. It is all held together by a chronology tight enough that Archbishop James Ussher of Ireland, in 1654, could state confidently that the creation of the world took place on October 26, 4004 B.C., at 9:00 A.M.[10] The Old Testament took the conviction that God entered history (see Chapter 2) and extended its story back to the beginning, to the origin of the world, with a chronological scheme it was convinced was valid, even if modern readers and hearers raise questions.

The Participation of God in the Narratives

As I have mentioned, there is a second and interwoven problem: the most distinctive characteristic of the Old Testament narratives is that God is affirmed to be a crucial participant in them. It is noteworthy that just as modern historians view the span of Old Testament narrative as appearing to manifest a variety of degrees of historicity (as we have just seen), so in the same way a careful reader may notice that the Old Testament narratives offer a variety in the degree to which God is affirmed to be a participant. In Genesis 1, God is obviously the only actor. In the rest of the Pentateuch, in Joshua and Judges, God is a major participant. By contrast, in the court history of King David, found in the books of Samuel and the first two chapters of 1 Kings, though God is a participant, that participation is largely behind the scenes. In the narratives of the early prophets like Elijah and Elisha, found in the books of 1 and 2 Kings, God is once more a major participant. But in the annalistic material of the kings of Israel and Judah, found in those same books, God rarely plays a major part. In the book of Ruth, God participates only implicitly. In the book of Esther, God plays no part at all—indeed there is no mention of God in the whole of that book; this is why, incidentally, the Septuagint Greek version of Esther expanded the book with prayers (see Chapter 1).

The variation in seeming historicity from later narratives to earlier ones, and the interwoven variation in the extent to which God is a participant, suggests to us that the narratives vary greatly in the *setting* in which they took shape and in the sensibility of the folk who first told them. Some narratives will be naive, others sophisticated; some will be traditional in form, others innovative; some will be the product of traditional village storytellers, others of urban chroniclers. Our sensibility about the variety of settings of these narratives will help to shape the way we hear them.

The Old Testament proclaims that God has entered history (and we affirmed this already in Chapter 1). For earlier generations of Christians, this proclamation was cause only for celebration: it was central to the faith. But that proclamation becomes problematic for many Christians in our day, because this is not the kind of history to which modern historians have accustomed us. In a way, we could deal with myth more easily: every traditional culture tells myths about the divine world and about the origin of the earth and of humankind. But the conventions of current historical writing are secular—they do not perceive or even look for the participation of God. History of the sort that is written today is a reconstruction of the affairs of men and women and their nations, and how they have interacted year by year. But to read or hear of the affairs of men and women and their nations and at the same time hear that God is involved—this can be disorienting to present-day readers and hearers, complicating the effort to hear God in the narrative.

Even when we find a way to understand the participation of God in the history narrated in the Old Testament, there is a further complication: How might we hear God speak to us at all through *narrative about* God? It is easier to understand how we might hear God in the oracles of the prophets such as we mentioned in Chapter 4 (we shall discuss them in detail in Chapter 9). After all, these oracles often begin with expressions like "thus says the Lord." Isaiah, for example, begins, "Hear, O heavens, and listen, O earth; for the Lord has spoken," and follows with words that are claimed to be those of God (Isa. 1:2). How might we hear God *today* through narratives that claim to set forth what God has done *in the past?*

Event and Interpretation

We shall begin to find our way through this maze of issues by making a clear distinction between event and interpretation. Let us keep it simple: let us assume that the event being narrated is an outward one, of the type that can be recorded today by video and audio tape. An infinite number of events impinge on us; to keep sane, we automatically pass by most of what happens to us, ignoring details that are not worth retaining. (We could, for example, try to record the license numbers of every vehicle that passes us as we drive along the highway, but it would do us no good and the data would soon swamp us.) Any segment of our history, then, whether it be our personal history or the history of our communities or nations, is made up of the finite number of events *that we choose to retain and remember* because they are significant to us—events, in short, that are memorable.

What the Old Testament does (and the New Testament, too, for that matter) is to select specific memorable events and offer for these events a specific interpretation—an interpretation that involves the covenanting God. We must recognize that every event is open to a variety of interpretations; the specific interpretation offered in the Old Testament for a given event is not *necessitated by* the event, though it is certainly *tied to* the event.

As an example, let us take it for granted that the deliverance of the Israelites from the Egyptian chariots at the Sea was an event that would have been recordable with a video camera. I shall return in Chapter 7 to the question of what the original event may have been, but for now we may assume that there was, indeed, some sort of recordable, objective historical event.

After the event, we might imagine Moses to have said, "Forget it: slaves make their escape all the time. There is nothing astonishing about this; let's put the past behind us and be on our way" (compare 1 Sam. 25:10b!). But this he did not do: he took it for granted that the event was *worth remembering.* But, given that it was worth remembering, he might have said, "How cunning we are! Pharaoh's charioteers were distracted and we made our escape." Or, alternatively, "How strong we are! We fought the forces of Pharaoh in a fair fight, and we won." Both these interpretations would have seen the event as the result of *Israelite prowess.* Or he could have said, "How lucky we are! All our auguries were favorable, and fate dealt us success." This interpretation would have seen the event as the result of *impersonal forces in the universe* that happened to benefit the Israelites. Instead, he is remembered to have said, "How blessed we are!—for Yahweh our God has brought us out of Egypt" (compare Exod. 16:6). Any one of these interpretations was possible, but the Old Testament chose to interpret the event as the prime gesture of the gracious and merciful God to the covenant people (Exod. 20:2).

It may be helpful at this point to look at the figure of Jesus in the New Testament with these same lenses, because one can actually find in the text itself a variety of interpretations about him. There is first of all the interpretation that said, "Jesus is in no way out of the ordinary; he is not worth remembering." This was the interpretation of his fellow-townspeople in Nazareth (Mark 6:1-6). Then there were those who took it for granted that he was extraordinary but were convinced that he was out of his mind—this was the interpretation of his family (Mark 3:19b-21). Then there were those who were convinced that he was extraordinary in that he had been sent by Satan; otherwise, how could he cast out demons? This was the interpretation of the scribes from Jerusalem (Mark 3:22). And there were those, finally, who accepted Jesus' own interpretation, that he was sent by God. The interpretation of the meaning of Jesus that is accepted by Christians was not the only possible interpretation of the historical Jesus, and not the only interpretation that he actually called forth: a specific interpretation of a given historical event is not *necessitated* by the event itself. So it is with the exodus from Egypt, and so it is with any other historical event narrated in the Old Testament.

To summarize: the Old Testament offers us a selection of events that it proclaims to be memorable, and then it offers an interpretation of these events in the light of convictions about Yahweh, the God who covenanted with Israel.

The Origins of Israelite Historical Narratives

Now we are ready to ask what we can discern of the process by which the Israelites brought to their present form the various portions of their historical narrative. Though I cannot be exhaustive, I can at least indicate some examples of how historical material seems to have arisen in Israel.[11]

For the reigns of the kings of Israel and Judah, and for the reign of Solomon before them, all found today in the books of 1 and 2 Kings, Israelite historians doubtless had access to royal archives. One suspects, however, that the narratives of prophets like Elijah and Elisha, likewise recorded in 1 and 2 Kings, were based on the oral tradition of prophetic circles. David's court history, now found in the books of 1 and 2 Samuel and in 1 Kings 1–2, was probably based on eyewitness accounts by those in one faction or another among his courtiers. For the period before the monarchy, when the judges ruled (roughly 1150–1020 B.C.), the tales that are recorded of individual leaders were doubtless handed down by professional storytellers.[12] These tales were collected and given a chronological framework much later, perhaps in the seventh century B.C.

For the narrative of Moses, and for the antecedent stories in Genesis, what we appear to have is what has been called the Israelite "epic": traditional oral material in which Israel preserved the story of its beginnings.[13] Just as, in the epic poetry of the Iliad, whose traditional author Homer may have lived in the

eighth century B.C.,[14] one hears of the heroes of the Trojan war (doubtless itself a historical event dating from the beginning of the twelfth century B.C.)[15]
and the interaction of gods and goddesses with them, so in the Israelite "epic"
one hears of the interaction of Yahweh with the founders of the faith. Pieces
of this epic must have taken shape in very early days, to be stabilized in written form probably during the reign of Solomon in the south in the tenth century B.C. (the "Yahwistic Source") and in the following century in the north
(the "Elohistic Source").

One must understand the purpose and spirit of this epic material. As we
have seen, the Israelite tradition (like the Greek one) is based on historical
events, but the material is not primarily concerned with a year-by-year
chronicle, as annals or archival material might be; rather, it is celebratory, reminding the hearers of the mighty acts of God on their behalf. In this way, it
is far more like the celebration held at a school after a football victory than
it is like the play-by-play account published the next day in the newspaper.

The central event celebrated in the Israelite epic was the deliverance from
Egypt. Not only do the events in the life of Moses extend over four biblical
books (we have already noted in Chapter 3 that the narrative of Moses' birth
is found in Exodus 2 and that of his death in Deuteronomy 34), but again and
again Yahweh is characterized in the Old Testament as the God of the exodus.
Thus, the Ten Commandments begin with "I am the Lord your God, who
brought you out of the land of Egypt, out of the house of slavery"
(Exod. 20:2). In Amos 3:1, we hear God say, "Hear this word that the Lord has
spoken against you, O people of Israel, against the whole family that I
brought up out of the land of Egypt." In Jer. 2:6, we hear God accuse the Israelite ancestors of forgetting their deliverance: "They did not say, 'Where is
the Lord who brought us up from the land of Egypt, who led us in the wilderness . . . ?'" Psalm 114 begins, "When Israel went out from Egypt, the house of
Jacob from a people of strange language, Judah became God's sanctuary, Israel his dominion."

This deliverance from Egypt is narrated in military terms: Yahweh is the
divine warrior, fighting on behalf of his covenant people. (I shall deal in more
detail with the motif of the divine warrior in Chapter 6.) This affirmation is
particularly clear in the so-called Song of the Sea, Exod. 15:1-18: "The Lord is
a warrior; the Lord is his name" (v. 3). The poem seems to presuppose the
conquest of the land of Canaan (vv. 13-17), so it cannot be attributed to
Moses himself, but scholars in recent years have acknowledged the antiquity
of the poem, dating it perhaps to the twelfth or eleventh century B.C.[16]

Around the central event of Yahweh's deliverance of Israel from Egypt
other events are associated in the Israelite epic: the giving of the law at Sinai

(as we saw in Chapter 3), and the giving of the land of Canaan— "I brought up into a plentiful land to eat its fruits and its good things" (Jer. 2:7). To the deliverance from Egypt are prefixed the narratives of Abraham and Jacob, to whom God promised offspring and land (Gen. 13:14-17; 28:13-15), narratives that thus point to their future (the segments cited here are assigned by scholars to the "Yahwistic Source," which probably dates, we recall, from the tenth century B.C.). Before the Yahwistic narratives of Abraham and Jacob are prefixed the Yahwistic narratives of Adam and Eve, of Cain's killing Abel, of the flood and the survival of Noah and his family, and the building of the Tower of Babel—all narratives that point toward the necessity for a solution for humankind such as God will bring beginning with Abraham. Indeed, these narratives of the earliest days of humankind are integrated closely with God's call to Abraham in Gen. 12:1-6: the counterpart of the expulsion of Adam and Eve from the Garden of Eden for the first sin (Gen. 3:23) is God's promise to Abraham of a land; the counterpart of Cain's killing his brother Abel (Gen. 4:2-12) is God's promise to make of Abraham a great nation; the counterpart of God's cursing the ground because of humankind (Gen. 8:21) is God's promise that Abraham will be a blessing to humankind; the counterpart of the effort by human beings to make a great name for themselves by building a tower (Gen. 11:4) is God's promise to make Abraham's name great (for the references to Abraham see Gen. 12:1-2).[17]

If we assume, as a working hypothesis, that around the early poem found in Exodus 15 the epic narrators in the time of David and Solomon, in the tenth century B.C., gathered together the traditions to which we have referred, traditions that formed the nucleus of the books of Genesis, Exodus, and Numbers, then there are two more major steps to which present-day scholars point as they seek to understand the development of the major narrative of the Old Testament. The first step is the extension of the narrative to the events after Moses: the collection of material concerning Joshua, the premonarchical judges, Samuel and Saul and David and Solomon, and the kings of Israel and Judah. This great work (which scholars have called the Deuteronomic history) appears to have been compiled in Jerusalem at the end of the seventh century. It was an attempt, given the great epic narrative of God's mighty act in delivering Israel from Egypt, to record the subsequent history of Israel in the land of Canaan;[18] I shall describe it in detail below. The other step is the enlargement of the early traditions of the Pentateuch (Genesis through Deuteronomy) by the "Priestly Source," an enlargement which, we recall, was evidently made in the course of the sixth century. This tradition not only added many of the laws (discussed in Chapter 3) but narrative as well; in particular, this tradition brought into the narrative the tight-knit genealogies with precise chronologies such as Genesis 5 represents. (I shall discuss the genealogies in Chapter 8.)

I cannot take time to discuss the matter here, but I must at least signal the obvious: in so many instances, the narratives of the Old Testament are the work of consummate artists. The telling detail, a small word-play, a bit of dialogue: all these move our emotions even as we seek understanding.[19]

Corporate Personality

It is important to call attention to one important contrast between ancient Israel's understanding of individual and family and the understanding normally held by us. In Israel, a person was understood to live on in the children and grandchildren of the next generation.[20] This is the background out of which God can be understood to visit the iniquity of the parents upon the children and the children's children, to the third and fourth generation (compare Chapter 4).

So far as we know, Israelites did not have a lively notion of individual life after death: one's identity survived in one's children. A simple expression of this conviction is found in Isa. 51:2: "Look to Abraham your father and to Sarah who bore you; for he was but one when I called him, but I blessed him and made him many." A more elaborate instance may be found in the story of Jacob. Jacob, at a climactic point in his life, received a new name, Israel (Gen. 32:28), and Jacob thus lives on in his children, the people Israel. This is nicely shown in the words God speaks to Jacob at Bethel (Gen. 28:14); in this pronouncement, "you" and "your" are singular in Hebrew, as the KJV indicates with "thou" and "thee" and "thy": "And thy seed shall be as the dust of the earth, and thou shalt spread abroad to the west, and to the east, and to the north, and to the south: and in thee and in thy seed shall all the families of the earth be blessed." Jacob, singular, will spread to the four points of the compass, because the people Israel are in fact understood to be identical with Jacob. We can note also the diction of the old creed recited at the time of bringing the fruit offering at the festival of weeks, which I shall mention in Chapter 7: "A wandering Aramean was my ancestor; he went down into Egypt and lived there as an alien, few in number, and there he became a great nation, mighty and populous. When the Egyptians treated us harshly and afflicted us, by imposing hard labor on us, we cried to the Lord, the God of our ancestors; the Lord heard our voice and saw our affliction, our toil, and our oppression. The Lord brought us out of Egypt with a mighty hand and an outstretched arm, with a terrifying display of power, and with signs and wonders; and he brought us into this place and gave us this land, a land flowing with milk and honey" (Deut. 26:5-9). We note the shift of pronouns: "he went down"; "he was an alien, few in number"; "treated us harshly."

This is why the prophet Jeremiah, in the sixth century B.C., can offer God's word of judgment on the people using a word-play on the name Jacob (Jer. 9:4): the phrase "for all your kin are supplanters" plays on the name "Jacob," as if to say that the behavior of the whole nation is nothing but the behavior of Jacob foreshadowed in his birth story—he "supplanted" his twin brother Esau (Gen. 25:26: see the footnote in the NRSV on that verse). The continuity of the people Israel is nicely illustrated by a verse in the book of Ecclesiasticus (Sirach), one of the extra books in Roman Catholic Bibles (see Chapter 1): "The days of a person's life are numbered, but the days of Israel are without number" (Ecclus. 37:25).

Another example may reinforce the matter. Paul in the New Testament pressed the notion of original sin by speaking of the sin of Adam (Rom. 5:12-21; 1 Cor. 15:22). To his way of thinking, it is not so much that original sin is passed on from generation to generation by some biological taint, as we might assume, but rather that all human beings *are* Adam in another form.[21]

Given this mentality, Israel's narrative history takes on a distinctive value for the Israelites: just as in the ancient creed of Deut. 26:5-9, the Israelites would understand the narrative not to be talking so much about individuals in the distant past as talking about "us" in our earlier embodiment. Given this understanding of history, how did historical narrative function for ancient Israel?

The Functions of Historical Narrative

I suggest that historical narrative carried one or more of three functions: celebration, instruction, and warning. I have already indicated one of the chief functions of history, namely *celebration*. An affirmation of the gracious acts of God in the past is an appropriate part of communal worship. Scholars have suggested that the Song of the Sea (Exod. 15:1-18) was originally sung at early celebrations of the feast of Passover, and that is an altogether plausible suggestion.[22]

There are other passages in which the mighty acts of God are celebrated: in poems such as the Song of Deborah (Judges 5), and in a variety of prose passages, some of which I have already mentioned—the tales in Genesis, the narratives of the deliverance from Egypt, events in the wilderness such as the victories over the kings Og and Sihon and Balaam's oracles (Numbers 21–25), and the fall of the walls at Jericho (Joshua 6).

Other narratives may offer a function related to that of celebration, namely *instruction*. Some instruction is pleasing—it is enlightenment that supplies the details of Israel's identity. The poem in Genesis 49, the so-called "Blessing of Jacob," is set forth as Jacob's deathbed testament, a set of characterizations of each of his sons that prefigure the nature of each of the tribes of Israel. The poem offers praise or blame for each tribe; one could imagine a set of epigrams arising in village life. But the poem hardly had a religious context to begin with—it offered the kind of judgment of each tribe that must have been at home in Judah, since we seem to have three Judah-sayings strung together (vv. 8, 9, 10-12).[23]

A special type of instruction in some of the earliest narratives in Genesis is what we call etiology: these are narratives that explain how some human trait or circumstance came to be. In this way, the narratives resemble Rudyard Kipling's *Just So Stories*. How did our human disobedience of God come into the world? Listen to the story in Genesis 2–3. How is it that some people are agricultural and others pastoral? The difference goes all the way back to Cain and Abel in Gen. 4:2. How is it that there are so many languages in the world? It is a consequence of the building of the Tower of Babel (Gen. 11:9).[24]

Still other narratives function as *warning*. One cannot prove that the story of the sin of Adam and Eve in the Garden in Genesis 2–3 was being circulated in the tenth century B.C. as commentary on the incident of King David with Bathsheba (2 Samuel 11–12), but there are phraseological parallels between the two narratives. And one cannot prove that the story of Cain's killing of Abel and its consequences gained a circulation at the time David's son Absalom killed his half-brother Amnon (2 Sam. 13:23-29; compare 14:6-7!), but again there are obvious thematic parallels. In any event, one may at least suspect connections: those old stories would have made altogether appropriate sermon illustrations.[25]

The Deuteronomic History

I turn now to a detailed discussion of the function and themes of the Deuteronomic history, the great historical work that makes up of most of Joshua, Judges, Samuel, and Kings, because this whole work appeared to have been compiled as warning. As we already noted in Chapter 3, a law-book was discovered in 622 B.C. in the temple in Jerusalem (2 Kings 22–23), a law-book that evidently embodied an early form of Deuteronomy (one presumes Deuteronomy 5–26 and perhaps 32); this discovery, essentially a kind of rediscovery of Moses, spurred King Josiah to a large-scale religious reform. Scholars have surmised then that scribal circles in Jerusalem, toward the end of the reign of King Josiah (about 610), convinced of the importance of the reform, sought to set down what one might term a "Josianic edition" of the history of the covenant people, that is, the first attempt at a narrative of their history in the promised land, gathering together material from various sources.

The story begins in anarchy: the book of Judges illustrates the theme that "in those days there was no king in Israel; all the people did what was right in their own eyes" (Judg. 17:6; 21:25; compare 18:1; 19:1). Its central event is the kingship of David, which takes up an enormous bulk in the work, from 1 Samuel 16 to 1 Kings 2. According to the narrative, David, as he dies, is said to have enjoined his son Solomon to "Be strong, be courageous, and keep the charge of the Lord your God, walking his ways and keeping his statutes, his commandments, his ordinances, and his testimonies, as it is written in the law of Moses, so that you may prosper in all that you do and wherever you turn" (1 Kings 2:2-3). The history continues with the glory of Solomon's kingship (1 Kings 2–8) and then reviews the progressive decline of the monarchy, now divided between north and south. But the history concludes, unexpectedly, with a surprising turnabout during the kingship of Josiah (640–609 B.C.): this kingship, anticipated in 1 Kings 13:1-3, comes to a climax in the judgment of 2 Kings 23:25: "Before him [Josiah] there was no king like him, who turned to the Lord with all his heart, with all his soul, and with all his might, according to all the law of Moses; nor did any like him arise after him." The purpose of this first edition of the history, then, was to set forth the story of the people when it seemed that the kingdom of Judah (the southern kingdom) might escape the fate of the kingdom of Israel (the northern kingdom).

Now let us see how this great history was presented for its hearers or readers. One theme can be spotted in the Deuteronomic framework in the book of Judges—for example, in Judg. 2:11-19. It affirms that whenever Israel abandoned Yahweh, Yahweh would give them over to their enemies, and that whenever they groaned in their misfortune, Yahweh would raise up for them a deliverer. This off-again-on-again scheme is set forth several times (Judg. 3:7-9; 10:6-16; 13:1). The assumption—that God rewards the covenant people whenever they are good and punishes them whenever they are evil— shapes the narration of the period of the monarchy as well. Since the Deuteronomic historians were committed to the Davidic dynasty, which ruled in the southern kingdom in Jerusalem, they were convinced that all northern kings by definition did evil in that they followed the example of Jeroboam, the northern king who originally broke away from the united monarchy (see, for example, 1 Kings 15:29-30, 34). Southern kings, by contrast, are portrayed as either evil or good. Examples of evil kings are Rehoboam, who succeeded Solomon (see 1 Kings 14:22-24), and Abijam, who succeeded Rehoboam (see

1 Kings 15:3); examples of good kings are Amaziah (2 Kings 14:3) and Azariah [Uzziah] (2 Kings 15:3). Though the narrative of the time of the judges and of the time of the divided monarchy offers many specific details of history, its overall framework affirms the reality of God's reward on the one hand or God's punishment on the other, within the life and affairs of each judge or king.

Within this Deuteronomic history, however, there is more extensive and varied narration of the reigns of David and of his son Solomon. The narration of David is embodied in what has been called his court history. In these chapters, though the righteousness of David is affirmed by the historian (see above), his story is not presented schematically at all but rather with all the variety that an eyewitness account could provide: what one has here is little short of astonishing. David's kingship is narrated not as a matter of power or prestige; instead, the king is portrayed as a monarch faced with both the necessity to innovate new procedures in Israel and the freedom to do so. He is a king who was master on the field of battle but at the same time far from master over the affairs of his complex, polygamous household, a king who was impelled to flee Jerusalem when his son Absalom revolted and who yet wept when he heard the news of Absalom's death. Here is narrative in which God is largely hidden, narrative that invites the hearer or reader to ponder right and wrong in the face of unprecedented circumstances.[26]

In contrast, what we have for David's son Solomon *is* a portrayal of the king's prestige and glory (1 Kings 2–11). The centerpiece of the narration of his reign is, as we might expect, the building and dedication of the Temple. Only in chapter 11 is there reference to the dark side of Solomon's reign.

In passing, it should be noted that when, much later, perhaps about 400 B.C., the anonymous writer whom we call the Chronicler re-presented the material about David in 1 Chronicles 11–29, he chose to omit altogether any mention of the episodes of Bathsheba and of Absalom, and he chose only to summarize David's military exploits (14:8-17; 18:1—20:8); instead, he concentrated on David's bringing the ark of the covenant to Jerusalem (chapters 15–16) and his organization of worship in Jerusalem. That is to say, the Chronicler offered what the Deuteronomic history had not offered: a portrayal of David's glory and prestige—David seen through the eyes of the post-exilic community.

If the first ("Josianic") edition of the Deuteronomic history was an expression of the optimism of the historians of the time that God would reward the people for the turn toward God led by King Josiah, then later expansions of that history, made in the light of subsequent events, show a darker view of the events of their history: Josiah fell in battle at the age of only thirty-nine; the policy of the kings that succeeded him wavered frantically between loyalty to Egypt and loyalty to Babylon; ultimately, Jerusalem fell, and it became clear that the south was to suffer just as the north had done. In fact, the fall of Jerusalem was even more tragic, because the south had evidently failed to learn anything from the fall of the north more than a century before.

These expansions were perhaps made in two stages. The first stage is exemplified by the account of Josiah's death in battle (2 Kings 23:28-30). In the decades after the fall of Jerusalem, there were further expansions. These expansions include not only an account of the fall of Jerusalem (2 Kings 23:31—25:30) but also an expansion of the prayer of Solomon (1 Kings 8:41-53) and Yahweh's reply (1 Kings 9:1-9), and a postscript on the summary about Josiah (2 Kings 23:26-27).[27]

Summary: The Nature of Old Testament History

Let me now summarize our discussion to this point. Any narrative is of necessity selective and tends to be stylized in one way or another. The narratives in the Old Testament evidently emerged from a variety of settings, but they were united by the efforts of generations of storytellers, historians, and scribes to record their understandings of the dealings of God with Israel. These storytellers, historians, and scribes were convinced they were recording history, but inevitably the connection with history as we understand it was less for the earlier periods of the narrative.

Hearing God in Celebration, Instruction, and Warning (1)

We are now in a position to undertake to answer the question how we ourselves might hear God through the narratives of the Old Testament. The first thing to say may seem so obvious as to be trivial, but it is not: the Old Testament is unique in that its core is a long narrative with a claim to be historical. The New Testament is similar in that it offers an extension on the historical narrative of the Old Testament: though the Gospels are not full biographies of Jesus, they do set down the memory of many of his acts and deeds and, at least for the last week of his earthly life, give a coherent account. The Acts of the Apostles offers a narrative of the first three decades or so of the emerging Christian church. But the events narrated in the New Testament occurred within a short enough span of time that Paul could summarize them in the statement, "But when the fullness of time had come, God sent his Son, born of a woman, born under the law, in order to redeem those who were under the law, so that we might receive adoption as children"

(Gal. 4:4-5). "Fullness of time" implies completion, but it also suggests the long process toward completion, alongside which the life of Jesus Christ may be seen as a single climactic event.

By comparison, the Muslim Qur'ān offers prophetic pronouncements on the meaning of events in the past as well as on human conduct and on the nature of God, but it offers no sustained narrative.

The Old Testament, by contrast, offers a narrative that (if one begins to reckon with Moses) covers almost a thousand years in the history of the people Israel, a period of time in which they underwent enormous shifts in their destiny. In all that period, the narrative undertakes to set forth the dealings of God with the people. This long narrative is, of course, a consequence of the notion of covenant (see Chapter 2): when a suzerain in the ancient Near East would covenant with his vassal, it became a crucial matter to take note how the vassal behaved and how the suzerain dealt with the vassal's behavior. So with God and Israel: if God has covenanted with Israel, then it becomes a crucial matter how Israel has behaved and how God has dealt with that behavior, and the record of the relationship becomes the raw material for Israel's self-understanding. Israel needed constantly to remember her history and to ponder it.

If Gentile Christians are the branches grafted onto the olive tree that is Israel (Rom. 11:17-24), then the history of Israel becomes our history as well. It is exactly like the immigrant to the United States who becomes a naturalized citizen and then exclaims, "Now George Washington is my first president!" The Old Testament narrative is not narrative only for Israel but for Christians as well.

Therefore, our first, approximate answer will be: Christians will hear God in the narrative just as the Israelites did—in celebration, in instruction, and in warning. I say "approximate answer" because we must still struggle with the question of whether God really acts the way the Old Testament proclaims. We shall return to this question below. For the moment, however, let us stay with celebration, instruction, and warning.

We can celebrate. Let us turn to the most celebratory occasion in the liturgy of the Roman Catholic church, the Easter vigil, the celebration on the eve of Easter Sunday of God's culminating mighty act in the resurrection of Jesus Christ. In the fullness of that liturgy there are seven readings from the Old Testament (though in practice some of them may be omitted). The last four of these are taken from the books of the prophets, but the first three are narratives: (1) Gen. 1:1—2:2, the first narrative of creation; (2) Gen. 22:1-18, the narrative of the testing of Abraham in his willingness to sacrifice Isaac; and (3) Exod. 14:15—15:1, the narrative of the deliverance of the Israelites from Pharaoh's chariots at the sea. (These same narratives, it should be said, are recommended for the Easter vigil in the Episcopal *Book of Common Prayer* as well.)

One can certainly understand how the first narrative, the account of creation, can be celebratory: as one hears the review of God's acts of creation, one by one, climaxed by the creation of humankind, one is moved to wonder and awe. It is the very first act of God in the long history, a history culminating for Christians in God's act of redemption of humankind by the resurrection of Jesus Christ.

And (to jump to the third narrative) one can understand how God's deliverance of Israel from Pharaoh's army at the sea can be celebratory: the account is, as we have seen, central to the proclamation of the Old Testament, God's liberation of Israel from oppression, a model for the hope in every generation that God will liberate oppressed people from their bondage. Again, it is appropriate at the Easter vigil, where Christians proclaim God's liberation of humankind from sin and death.

A Classic Problem Passage: The Narrative of God's Testing of Abraham (1)

With the second reading, however, the account of God's testing of Abraham, we face deep complications. On one level, it is one more narrative in the great story of salvation, and therefore cause for celebration. God had promised Abraham he would be the father of a multitude of nations (Gen. 17:5). Abraham's willingness to sacrifice his son Isaac is then not only a testimony of Abraham's faithfulness but resonates with the testimony of the New Testament that God was willing to give up Jesus Christ, the only-begotten Son, for the salvation of all nations. Above all, God's intervention to prevent the sacrifice of Isaac is an act of grace that allows God's purpose to go forward.

But as we take that narrative out of the context of the Easter vigil and listen to it in isolation, it offers other resonances. One can imagine it as an ancient polemic against child sacrifice. As we saw in Chapter 1, there were several instances recorded in which a king of Israel or Judah sacrificed one of his children, and the narrative in Genesis 22 could well have served to instruct (and warn) Israelites that God does not require such a dreadful act.

Yet the narrative continues to fascinate us and challenge us to grasp its meaning. Years ago, I was discussing this narrative with a class at the Near East School of Theology in Beirut, and one of the students, a young man from a Nilotic community in the southern part of Sudan, a convert to the Christian faith from his native animistic beliefs, offered this interpretation: "Abraham wanted to show that he was willing to give up as much to the true God as pagans were willing to give to false gods." And perhaps that is as good a summary as any.

But more must be said. The narrative threatens us with terrible thoughts. To put it most bluntly: if I saw a man walking down the sidewalk today holding a knife in one hand and his son in the other, proclaiming, "God has commanded me to kill my son as a sacrifice!" I would not wait for the fellow to hear a shift in God's command: I would call the police from the nearest telephone—and so would you.

Imagine the terror this passage might induce in a child's mind—we are back with Lillian Smith's observations about her notions of God in her childhood (see Chapter 4). The style of the narrative is not realistic: it is thoroughly stylized. No response from Isaac is recorded such as we might expect; nor from Sarah. We suspect that one of the great effects of the passage is the ambiguity of Abraham's reply to Isaac in 22:8. Is "my son" a vocative (word of address) or the identity of the burnt offering? (Indeed, the passage is full of verbal effects: another is the mention of the "knife" [Hebrew *maʾăkelet*] at the center of v. 10, and the "angel" [Hebrew *malʾāk*] as the agent who stays the knife.)

But this passage arouses in us a cluster of questions. Is God really like this? Does God demand something horrible, such as a teasing bully would, only to withdraw the demand at the last minute? Or did Abraham misunderstand God? I shall return to these questions at the end of the chapter.

Hearing God in Celebration, Instruction, and Warning (2)

Let me return now to the function of many narratives to lead the hearer to celebrate: whatever we will conclude about Gen. 22:1-18, there are surely many narratives that invite us to celebrate. One thinks of the story of Joseph, who did not die in the pit into which his brothers had lowered him but survived to save his family from famine (Genesis 37; 39–50). A whole series of heroic men and women are referred to in the long roll-call of Hebrews 11, heroic men and women whose faith allowed God to act through them. As we listen to these narratives, we are led to try to comprehend the kind of God who is involved in these events: this, the narratives say, is the God who is our author, our savior, and our destiny; listen, remember, and be in awe. God is like this! God has done this! Bow down and worship! Christian testimony offers all the more reason to celebrate, but it is important that that testimony begin not with the events of the New Testament but with testimony about the God who has always acted on our behalf, and we may therefore hear God today through such narratives as span history.

By the same token, just as much of Jesus' teaching is instruction and warning, so Christians may hear instruction and warning from God in Old Testament narratives. There is a narrative in 1 Kings 21 in which the prophet Elijah proclaims God's judgment on King Ahab of Israel in the affair of Naboth's vineyard. The king coveted the vineyard but was hesitant to expropriate it, whereupon his strong-minded wife, Queen Jezebel, found two men willing to bear false witness against its owner; Naboth was executed and the vineyard became the possession of the king. As we listen to the narrative, we are instructed by God through the words of Naboth to the king, "The Lord forbid that I should give you my ancestral inheritance"—that is to say, in Israel land stayed in the family, and the king had no right to expropriate it. God warns us through the evil acts of Ahab and of Jezebel, who, it seems, was a devotee of the god Baal. We are led to ponder how one's heart can be shaped by the character of the deity one worships. God, we hear in this narrative, is not on the side of the powerful but on the side of those who are humble and righteous.

I turn now to a very short portion of narrative, actually a song embedded in the narrative describing the immediate descendants of Adam in Genesis 4, the Song of Lamech (vv. 23-24). "Lamech said to his wives: 'Adah and Zillah, hear my voice; you wives of Lamech, listen to what I say: I have killed a man for wounding me, a young man for striking me. If Cain is avenged sevenfold, truly Lamech seventy-sevenfold.'" Here is nothing but savagery. What can we hear of God in this brutal song? Lamech, according to the narrative, was a sixth-generation descendant of Adam; he praises himself as the prototype of limitless violence. The poem, coming on the heels of Cain's murder of Abel, suggests the increasing evil of humankind. But what may not be apparent to present-day hearers and readers is that the poem breaks the expected pattern of parallelism with numbers: the expected pattern is x followed by x + 1 (one notices "three" followed by "four" in Prov. 30:21 and Amos 1:3, and "six" followed by "seven" in Prov. 6:16). But "seven" followed by "seventy-seven"? Even in the pattern of his poem, Lamech breaks all measure! I propose that the way one hears God in this poem is through Jesus' response when Peter asks about forgiveness (Matt. 18:22): not "seven" but "seventy-seven." Jesus obviously had Lamech's song in mind. As Lamech broke all bounds in violence, we are to break all bounds in forgiveness. Indeed, some ancient manuscripts read "seventy times seven" (the preferred reading in the RSV), in which case Jesus would exaggerate even more in the positive direction than Lamech did in the negative.

Extended Instruction and Warning: The Court History of David

Let us turn now to the tenth century B.C., to the court history of David. This narrative affords us a large-scale opportunity for instruction and warning. Many years ago, one of my students preached a sermon in the seminary chapel on the theme of David. David was the great leader of his people; David was the great warrior against the Philistines; David was the great singer of psalms: we should all look to David as our model. When I discussed his sermon with him afterward, I asked, "But what about the affair with Bathsheba? Should David be our model in that regard?" The student was, of course, dismayed: No, he assured me, we are not to take David for our model in the incident with Bathsheba. So I had to point out: the Old Testament is not a scrapbook of example-stories, a series of "good guys" (and "gals") we are to emulate, and "bad guys" (and "gals") we are to shun emulating; instead, it offers men and women in whose lives one may ponder the work of God.

But, as we have already seen, the court history of David is not a sequence of narrative in which God figures as a central actor. How, then, are we to ponder the work of God in David's story?

Let us look at a few episodes in the story of David. An early one is his fleeing to the protection of Achish of Gath (1 Sam. 21:10-15). We are in the midst of Israel's wars with the Philistines, a Greek people whose power center was in what we today call the "Gaza Strip" and who were evidently doing their best to conquer Palestine. Saul is the reigning king but, according to the (pro-David) narrative, has been "rejected" by God (13:7-15; 15:1-35). David has therefore been (privately) anointed king (16:1-13), marked for his destiny. He steps forward to kill the Philistine giant (17:1-58), has great success in battle, and arouses Saul's jealousy (18:6-11) even as he marries Michal, one of Saul's daughters (18:20-29). Saul begins to spend more energy seeking to kill David than battling Philistines, and eventually David, in order to buy time and find a safe haven, flees to the coast, to the Philistine city of Gath, and puts himself under the protection of its king, Achish. Achish, of course, assumes that David has switched sides and expects him to fight on behalf of the Philistines against Israel. To avoid such a circumstance, David pretends to be insane whenever Achish and his servants are present: he scratches meaningless marks on the doors of the gate and drools into his beard. Eventually, he drifts back into the territory of Judah and becomes a kind of Robin Hood character, taking from the rich and giving to the poor, steadily gaining support among his own clan and people. There comes a time when Saul acknowledges that David is to be king (24:20), and eventually Saul dies in a battle against the Philistines at Mount Gilboa (31:1-13).

What might we make of David's sojourn with the Philistine king? More specifically, what instruction or warning might God want us to take from this episode? There is no mention of God in the narrative itself. David is blessed by God: that is the implication of "he was ruddy, and had beautiful eyes, and was handsome" (16:12); and, since he has been anointed king, he must preserve himself for his calling. But by any means—in this instance by misrepresenting himself to the enemy of the Israelites? We wonder.

David has a great appetite for women. Most people remember the episode with Bathsheba (2 Samuel 11–12), because she became the mother of Solomon (12:24). But there is a curious episode earlier, with Abigail (1 Samuel 25). Abigail is the wife of Nabal, a landowner rich in property and sheep and goats, who does not respond to the requests of David and his servants for "gifts"—bread and meat and wine. But Abigail, his wife, does bring provisions to David and his men, makes peace with them, and makes the point that Nabal lives up to his name (v. 25: Nabal means "fool" in Hebrew). When Nabal recovers from a drunken feast and Abigail tells him what she has done for David and his men, "his heart died within him; he became like a stone," and he dies about ten days later (vv. 37-38); whereupon Abigail becomes David's second wife.

So again we wonder what God intends us to hear. Nabal had dismissed David as a lawless nobody (vv. 10-11), whereas Abigail is portrayed as giving voice to David's destiny to be king (v. 28). We wonder, are we to understand Abigail as taking her destiny into her own hands, rejecting her loutish husband to share the destiny of the handsome David? As always, we are fascinated by David, who seems to lead a charmed life: he and his men get provisions for feasting, and he himself gains a wife. And so we wonder again, with David is it a matter of "anything goes"?

Plainly not, in the episode with Bathsheba. David is now king. Can the king do no wrong? The answer is clear: the king can indeed do wrong, and does so in this instance. He has taken Bathsheba to bed and she conceives. He then tries to get her husband Uriah, home from battle, to go home to her so that the unborn child will appear to be his; failing that, he contrives to have

Uriah fall in battle, whereupon he takes Bathsheba as wife. But now God's word is manifested through the prophet Nathan. Nathan tells the king a parable of an act of injustice; David responds to the parable and so finds himself accused. And now an amazing thing happens: David does not condemn Nathan to die (compare Deut. 18:20)—rather, he admits his guilt: he says to Nathan, "I have sinned against the Lord" (12:13). God punishes David: the baby falls ill and eventually dies. And David's conduct is curious: while the baby is still alive, David fasts and weeps, but when the baby dies, the king washes and anoints himself and changes his clothes—he recognizes that the books are balanced, he has paid for his sin and is now free.

David has had no solid role model for kingship—certainly not Saul, for Saul's kingship had been idiosyncratic and *ad hoc*. David then has been innovating a completely new pattern. Might kingship then involve what kingship involves in the rest of the Near East, namely the notion that "the king can do no wrong"? No, not in Israel: God has spoken. God sets limits to the conduct even of the king who has carried the divine blessing through all the years.

David (and we) learn further lessons: he may crave an array of wives (six are listed in 2 Sam. 3:2-5), but the wives are rivals and their children as well, so that the palace is heavy with jealousy and intrigue. David cannot master this jealousy and intrigue, even though he mastered the affairs of men in the field of battle. Emblematic of the state of affairs is the narrative, in 2 Samuel 13, of how Tamar, a daughter of David's wife Maacah, was raped by her half-brother Amnon, a son of David's wife Ahinoam; the rape is avenged by Tamar's full brother Absalom: he has Amnon killed. Absalom then flees from David's presence, and these events bring on a political crisis: at one point, Absalom proclaims himself king and David is forced precipitously to flee Jerusalem (2 Samuel 15). Eventually, Absalom himself is killed, but this death only brings on David's uncontrolled weeping (2 Sam. 18:33).

So again, what are we to learn? That David's sexual appetite was not the best model for his son and ultimately led to strife within his household? True. That political affairs (then and now) are messy, heavy with plots and intrigue and struggles for power? Also true. But beyond these obvious matters of morality and conduct, one grasps for an understanding of God's purpose in this man David.

I have noted several times that David was moving into fresh domains where there were no role models. How does God lead us into fresh territory? We are often called into fresh territory where there are no role models. Dietrich Bonhöffer, the German church leader, became convinced that it was his

Christian duty to join the plot to kill Hitler. What guidance could his church tradition give him for such a venture?

Kingship in Israel, a Good Thing or a Bad Thing?

There is an even more basic problem. The narrative of David's kingship, undergirded by Nathan's oracle to David that he will be the founder of a great dynasty (2 Samuel 7), gives the impression that the institution of the Davidic monarchy is God's will for Israel. And that is the assumption for the circles in Jerusalem that produced the Old Testament as we now know it. But at the edges of the Old Testament are evidences of other opinions. The prophet Samuel, back in the eleventh century, before Saul is declared king, seems to have been at least ambivalent about kingship: one source, reflected in 1 Sam. 9:1—10:16, portrays him as being agreeable to choosing Saul so long as the latter is called "ruler" (a neutral term) rather than "king" (a term with overtones of oppression). Another source (1 Samuel 8) portrays him as granting kingship only as a concession to people's sin, and warning them about the dread consequences of their request. Beyond the uneasiness of Samuel in the early days is the opinion recorded in the book of the prophet Hosea in the eighth century, reflecting the anarchy of kingship in the north in the decades before the north fell to Assyria. Hosea understands God to associate kingship with idolatry, "They made kings, but not through me; they set up princes, but without my knowledge. With their silver and gold they made idols for their own destruction" (Hos. 8:4).

So: did God will kingship for Israel, or not? The Old Testament clearly is not univocal on the matter. George Lindbeck, a Lutheran church historian at Yale University, compares the monarchy in Israel with the institution of the papacy in the Middle Ages: in both instances, though the institutions were not intended by God, they were (perhaps reluctantly) used by God.[28] If this is a useful formulation, then one might conclude that once Israel had embarked on kingship, God expected a kingship that would be in accordance with the norms of the covenant with Israel: the king no less than the commoner is subject to God's norms of righteousness and justice (compare the prophetic word in Isa. 11:1-5).

Our pondering of God's will in the institution of kingship leads us to an important generalization: it is not only in matters of personal conduct that God instructs us and warns us in Old Testament narratives; we also gain instruction (and warning) in regard to institutional affairs. This, it should be stressed, is one of the crucial contributions of the Old Testament to the

Christian faith. In the New Testament one hears Jesus preaching and teaching to crowds of villagers in a Palestine that is under the occupation of the Roman army; one reads Paul's letters written to small conventicles of Christians in various cities in the eastern Mediterranean. In few cases in the New Testament do we have any words directed to those who lead great political, economic or ecclesiastical institutions. In the Old Testament, by contrast, we ponder various solutions to the issues of leadership in Israel. We have already glimpsed the debate over whether kingship is a good thing or a bad thing. But if kingship is a good thing, then shall it remain within a single dynasty, that of David, as was the assumption in the south, or shall it shift from family to family on the basis of prophetic designation—or of power struggles, for that matter, as was the assumption in the north? What is to be the relationship between king and prophet, between prophet and priest? How shall the people of God function when kingship is at an end? Indeed, what is the relation to be between the people of God and pagan nations? Though the institutions of Israel were on a small scale in comparison with present-day institutions, nevertheless these narratives offer clues to the will of God in the life and institutions of Israel and the nations.

What Is Our Own Identity within These Narratives?

The question of the relation between Israel and pagan nations brings me to the last question I want to touch on in this chapter: What is our own identity as we seek to hear God in these narratives of Israel's history? The point is this: mostly, when today we hear the accusations that the prophet Nathan levels at King David, or the accusations that the prophet Jeremiah levels at King Jehoiakim (Jer. 22:13-17), we wonder what accusations might be leveled at our current head of state, the President of the United States (or whoever). That is to say, we assume an analogy between Israel or Judah on the one hand and our own political state.

But this, I propose, is not appropriate, for several reasons. One is simply a matter of size. Israel (north and south together) had an area roughly the size of the state of Vermont, or of New Hampshire, and its population in David's day must have been very limited (the population level of the city of Jerusalem in David's day was about 2,000). Judah (the southern kingdom) had a area not too much larger than the present state of Rhode Island; the population level of Jerusalem in Jeremiah's day was about 30,000.[29] Alongside these territories and populations the empires of Egypt, Assyria, and Babylon loomed enormous. As we think about Israel and Judah alongside the great world empires in ancient times, it is more appropriate to think of a Central American republic like Guatemala or Nicaragua alongside the enormous size and power of the United States.

Quite aside from size, this analogy is theologically wrong. The narrative is not primarily concerned with Israel and Judah as political units but rather as the people of God, and the New Testament analogue of Israel (and therefore our analogue) is the Church (Gal. 6:16). Calvin is clear about this: again and again in the course of his commentary on the Psalms, he refers to David and the Church (meaning Israel), a reference that to us sounds anachronistic. To cite one example out of dozens: in his commentary on Psalm 14, Calvin writes, "We have much need to be fortified from the example which David here sets before us: so that, in the midst of the greatest desolations which we behold in the Church, we may comfort ourselves with this assurance, that God will finally deliver her from them."[30] It is then as members of the Church, not as citizens of the political entity to which we belong, that we should hear God in these narratives. What kind of leadership does God intend for our churches? How faithful are we at living out our mandate to be the covenant people in the institutions of our churches? How does God deal with us when we fail in our calling to be the covenant people? Indeed, I have sometimes thought, as we read the Old Testament, that it would be useful to view our present *political entities* as the analogue of ancient Assyria or Babylon, against which Israel and Judah (the analogue for which is the Church) needed to maintain their integrity. (I shall return to this matter in Chapter 9.)

Let me summarize this portion of the chapter. If the narratives of the Old Testament offered Israel the occasions for celebration, instruction, and warning, they offer us the same occasions. The narratives of celebration afford the opportunity to be moved to awe and worship by the testimony of what God has done. Narratives of instruction and warning invite us to watch God at work with the covenant people as they respond, or do not respond, to the divine expectation. In some narratives, like that of the Song of Lamech or Naboth's vineyard, it is easy to understand what God approves of, and does not approve of; but other narratives, like the long court history of David, invite us to try to discern, behind the episodes of the history, the will of God for the covenant people and for us.

The Narrative of God's Testing of Abraham (2)

But there are narratives in which God's alleged actions leave us bewildered, narratives like that of Abraham's attempted sacrifice of Isaac. I have already suggested, in regard to that narrative, that if we came on such a scene today we would call the police. The difficulty with the narrative is put in bold relief in a recent novel by Anne Tyler. A teenage girl is expressing her objections to her uncle's insisting that she go to church, and she first finds fault with the narrative of Jesus' cursing the fig tree. She then continues, "Or Abraham and Isaac. That one *really* ticks me off. God asks Abraham to kill his own son. And Abraham says, 'Okay.' Can you believe it? And then at the very last minute God says, 'Only testing. Ha-ha.' Boy, I'd like to know what Isaac thought. All the rest of his life, any time his father so much as looked in his direction Isaac would think—" at which point her uncle moves to mollify her.[31]

I have raised the question whether Abraham did not misunderstand God. But the narrative itself neither suggests child abuse (in the way the Song of Lamech suggests overweening violence) nor suggests that Abraham misunderstood; instead, we have a scene inspiring awe. In Heb. 11:17-19, in the midst of the roll-call of men and women of faith, we find the incident mentioned: "By faith Abraham, when put to the test, offered up Isaac." There is no suggestion here that Abraham misunderstood God. So again we raise the question: Does God really act this way?

I suggest that we not try too hard to make rational sense out of the narrative, nor to make God reasonable after our own standards. If we follow the lead of the Old Testament, we are talking about the author of all creation, who is in no way an equal partner in debate with us. Does God test those called to faithfulness? Is a change of mind on God's part possible? We do not hear, clearly, and we wonder. All we know is that we ourselves are called to faithfulness, that much of God remains a mystery to us, and that we seek to follow Jesus Christ, who is himself remembered as calling out in his agony on the cross the first phrase of Psalm 22, "My God, my God, why have you forsaken me?" (Mark 15:34). The story of God's dealings with the covenant people is not reasonable.

But there remain two large issues raised by the narratives of the Old Testament that bother us today, issues that I have only skirted in this chapter. The first is God's sponsorship of battles; the matter was raised by the Easter Vigil reading of Exodus 14, but it is by no means limited to that passage. There are lots of battles in the Old Testament. This question is crucial enough to demand special treatment, and I shall fill that need in the next chapter. The second is: What do we do when we find ourselves unable to believe some narratives? This is the matter of credibility. What are we to do when we seem to be required to suspend our disbelief? We touched on this matter in Chapter 1, and we shall discuss it in Chapter 7.

Notes

1. Michael E. Williams, "Voices from Unseen Rooms: Storytelling and Community," *Weavings, A Journal of the Christian Spiritual Life,* 5/4 (July/August 1990), 22.

2. L. Frank Baum, *The Wonderful Wizard of Oz* (Chicago, New York: G. M. Hills, 1900).

3. See conveniently William L. Holladay, *Jeremiah 2* (Hermeneia; Minneapolis: Fortress Press, 1989), 215–16.

4. *ANET,* 307b.

5. See in detail Bright, *History of Israel, passim.*

6. Avraham Biran and Joseph Naveh, "An Aramaic Stele Fragment from Tel Dan," *Israel Exploration Quarterly* 43 (1993), 81–98.

7. See conveniently André Lemaire, "Fragments from the Book of Balaam Found at Deir Alla," *Biblical Archaeology Review* 11/5 (Sept./Oct. 1985), 26–39, and in detail Jo Ann Hackett, *The Balaam Text from Deir ʿAllā* (HSM 31; Chico, CA: Scholars, 1984).

8. *ANET,* 119.

9. Bright, *History of Israel,* 96.

10. *The New Encyclopedia Britannica* (15th ed., 1974), 16:748.

11. Besides commentaries and introductions on specific books of the Old Testament, the reader should consult introductions like Otto Eissfeldt, *The Old Testament, An Introduction* (Oxford: Blackwell, 1965).

12. Robert G. Boling, *Judges* (AB 6A; Garden City, NY: Doubleday, 1975), 32.

13. For the notion of Israelite epic, see particularly Frank M. Cross, *Canaanite Myth and Hebrew Epic, Essays in the History of the Religion of Israel* (Cambridge, Mass.: Harvard University, 1973).

14. Anthony M. Snodgrass, "Central Greece and Thessaly," in *The Cambridge Ancient History* (2nd ed.), III/1, 679.

15. Frank H. Stubbings, "The Recession of Mycenaean Civilization," *The Cambridge Ancient History* (3rd ed.), II/2, 342–50.

16. Childs, *Exodus,* 246; compare Richard J. Clifford, "Exodus," *New Jerome,* 50a.

17. Compare Gerhard von Rad, *Genesis, A Commentary* (OTL; Philadelphia: Westminster, 1961), 23, 155; B. Davie Napier, *Song of the Vineyard, A Theological Introduction to the Old Testament* (New York: Harper, 1962), 56–60, and *Come, Sweet Death, A Quintet from Genesis* (Boston, Philadelphia: United Church Press, 1967).

18. Otto Eissfeldt, *The Old Testament, An Introduction* (Oxford: Blackwell, 1965), 241–48; David Noel Freedman, "Deuteronomic History," *IDBSup* 226–28.

19. For an accessible presentation of the matter, see Robert Alter, *The Art of Biblical Narrative* (New York: Basic Books, 1981).

20. The classic statement of the matter is H. Wheeler Robinson, *Corporate Personality in Ancient Israel,* first published in 1936; see conveniently the republication (Philadelphia: Fortress Press, 1964).

21. Compare the discussions of Joachim Jeremias, "Adam," *TDNT* 1:141–43; Brevard S. Childs, "Adam," *IDB* 1:44a.

22. James Muilenburg, "A Liturgy on the Triumphs of Yahweh," *Studia Biblica et Semitica Theodoro Christiano Vriezen . . . Dedicata* (Wageningen, Netherlands: Veenman, 1966), 236.

23. Claus Westermann, *Genesis 37—50* (Minneapolis: Augsburg, 1986), 222; George W. Coats, *Genesis, With an Introduction to Narrative Literature* (FOTL 1; Grand Rapids, Mich.: Eerdmans, 1983), 307–11.

24. See conveniently John F. Priest, "Etiology," *IDBSup* 293–95.

25. For the details of these parallels, see John Craghan, *Love and Thunder, A Spirituality of the Old Testament* (Collegeville, Minn.: The Liturgical Press, 1983), 81.

26. *Ibid.*, 75–86.

27. Compare John Gray, *I & II Kings* (OTL; Philadelphia: Westminster, 1970), 6–9; Freedman, "Deuteronomic History."

28. George Lindbeck, "The Church," in Geoffrey Wainwright (ed.), *Keeping the Faith, Essays to Mark the Centenary of Lux Mundi* (Philadelphia: Fortress Press, 1988), 188.

29. Magen Broshi, "Estimating the Population of Ancient Jerusalem," *Biblical Archaeology Review* 4/2 (June, 1978), 10–15.

30. James Anderson (tr.), *Calvin's Commentaries: Psalms* (Edinburgh: Calvin Translation Society, 1843–55; repr. Grand Rapids, Mich.: Eerdmans, 1948–49), I, 189.

31. Anne Tyler, *Saint Maybe* (New York: Knopf, 1991), 198.

6

Those Battles

~

Few features of the Old Testament bother Christians today as much as the narrative of battles commanded by God. Though a life of nonviolence is hard for us to live out, we have at least heard of Jesus' teaching and the commandment to love. We live in a violent world, but it is difficult to make any sense of the notion that the God of all humankind might sponsor one side of a war against the other or actively fight for one side against the other.

When I was pastor of a congregation many years ago, one of the church school teachers telephoned me one Sunday afternoon; she taught a class of fourth-grade boys, and she said the class had posed a problem she could not answer. They had been studying the events of the book of Joshua, particularly how Joshua led the Israelites to take possession of the land of Canaan. "But," the boys objected, "didn't the land belong to the Canaanites?" "Yes," she admitted. "But that isn't fair!" they all agreed. So here was her question: "What," she asked, "am I to tell the class?" It is indeed a problem, when the ethical sensitivity of a group of nine-year-old boys exceeds that of Joshua. And, it should be added, the ethical issues involved in the Canaanites' loss of their land in ancient times are given resonance in our own day by the seeming parallel of "ethnic cleansings" that we witness. So: How, if at all, can we hear God today in the narratives of those battles of old?

Implications of the Metaphor of Covenant

We begin where we begin so often, with the notion of covenant between God and Israel. If the covenant between God and Israel was modeled on the suzerainty treaties of the ancient Near East, then God was the government, carrying all the functions of a human king (as we found in Chapter 2). If Israel kept the stipulations of the covenant, God was understood to guarantee prosperity and peace for the people, just as a king undertook to keep the peace of those who owed loyalty to him. But a king also had the responsibility of keeping enemies at bay, and so, by the theology of the covenant, God was understood to have that responsibility as well.

This notion is well illustrated in the blessings and curses of Deuteronomy 28 (as again we found in Chapter 2). "All these blessings shall come upon you and overtake you, if you obey the Lord your God: Blessed shall you be in the city, and blessed shall you be in the field. Blessed shall be the fruit of your womb, the fruit of your ground, the fruit of your livestock, both the increase of your cattle and the issue of your flock. Blessed shall be your basket and your kneading bowl" (vv. 2-5): that is to say, God will guarantee peace and prosperity at home. Then, "Blessed shall you be when you come in, and blessed shall you be when you go out. The Lord will cause your enemies who rise against you to be defeated before you; they shall come out against you one way, and flee before you seven ways" (vv. 6-7): God will guarantee the defeat of their enemies. On the other hand, of course, "if you will not obey the Lord your God" (v. 15), then your life at home will be cursed (vv. 16-18), and "the Lord will cause you to be defeated before your enemies; you shall go out against them one way and flee before them seven ways" (v. 25).

The Deliverance from Egypt (1)

As we have already seen in Chapter 5, the defining act of God for Israel and the centerpiece of the old Israelite epic is the deliverance of Israel from Egypt, and the event that made the deliverance possible was the battle at the Sea between the Israelites and Pharaoh's chariots (Exodus 14). Let us lay aside our concern in Chapter 5, the question of the historical event that lay behind the biblical narrative, and concentrate rather on the details of the narrative itself in Exodus. In the first place, the Israelites have been enslaved: "The Egyptians became ruthless in imposing tasks on the Israelites, and made their lives bitter with hard service in mortar and brick and in every kind of field labor" (1:13-14); "the Israelites groaned under their slavery, and cried out" (2:23). Moses emerges; he kills one of the cruel Egyptian overseers and must flee (2:11-15). God hears the cries of the Israelites (2:23; 3:7) and is determined to deliver them (3:8); God's agent will be Moses (3:10).

Second, the Egyptians are depicted not only as ruthless but at the same time as those whom the Israelites can outwit. Moses asks that the Israelites be given leave to go three days' journey into the wilderness to sacrifice to Yahweh—clearly a ruse; and Pharaoh, who has never heard of Yahweh, refuses (5:1-5). Moses and his brother Aaron summon up plagues against the Egyptians; the first plagues could be duplicated by Pharaoh's magicians, but they could not duplicate the plague of gnats (8:18-19). A plague of flies causes

Pharaoh to agree to allow the Israelites to offer a sacrifice to God, but only within the land of Egypt (8:25). Moses replies that such a sacrifice would be offensive to the Egyptians, and that they must go a distance of three days (8:26-27). Pharaoh then agrees, provided they "do not go very far away," and then he adds, astonishingly, "Pray for me" (8:28). How is this to be taken? Sardonically? Or as a word for the Israelite faith on the lips of a pagan, an Old Testament analogue to the word of the Roman centurion at the crucifixion (Mark 15:39)? Moses takes the request as one made sincerely and prays that the flies be taken away (8:30).

As the narrative progresses, Pharaoh's heart grows steadily harder (8:32), or, alternatively, Yahweh hardens Pharaoh's heart (9:12)—I shall discuss this matter below. And so more plagues ensue. Pharaoh proposes to allow the Israelite men to go to sacrifice, if they leave the women, children, and livestock behind (10:8-11), obviously as hostages. There is another plague, and Pharaoh agrees to allow their families to accompany them, only requiring that they leave their livestock behind (10:24). Moses insists that they must take their livestock with them, since they will need to choose animals for sacrifice on the spot (10:26). Pharaoh refuses. There is a last plague, the death of the firstborn: "Then he [Pharaoh] summoned Moses and Aaron in the night, and said, 'Rise up, go away from my people, both you and the Israelites! Go, worship Yahweh, as you said. Take your flocks and your herds, as you said, and be gone. And bring a blessing on me too!'" (12:31-32)—another prayer for Pharaoh! They leave, pausing only to ask and take silver and gold from their fellow Egyptians, plundering them (12:35-36). There follows the great victory at the Sea: the Israelites, on foot, get away, while the Egyptian chariotry is swallowed up by the water.

This is narrative *as told by the underclass*. With God's help, the Israelites steadily outwit their oppressors. But many of the Christians who read this work will have had no experience as part of an underclass. Members of racial minorities or other persecuted groups will understand to some degree. But unless one has been a prisoner of war, or an inmate in prison, one is not likely in our day to empathize easily with that sense of helplessness, the sense that one's back is to the wall; or with the need to tell jokes and to play pranks, sometimes cruel, on one's overlords—anything in order to maintain one's integrity or indeed one's identity. African Americans understand; as slaves they told Br'er Rabbit stories. They sang, "Go down, Moses, 'way down in Egypt land; tell ol' Pharaoh, to let my people go." This is the context of the contest between Moses and Pharaoh. According to the triumphant narrative, God heard the cry of the oppressed and rescued them. There was no one else who could rescue; in the words of Ps. 73:25a, "Whom have I in heaven but you?"

The Hardening of Pharaoh's Heart

Let us pause to consider the matter of the hardening of Pharaoh's heart. Nine times it is said that Pharaoh hardened his heart or that Pharaoh's heart was hardened (from 7:13 to 9:35). This mode of expression we can understand; many times in our lives we have known people who become more and more fixed in their resolve and less and less able to hear the wishes of others. But six times it is said that Yahweh hardened Pharaoh's heart (9:12 to 14:8), and this is the expression that causes us difficulty. A deacon in one of my congregations, years ago, told me he was more troubled by this phrasing than by anything else in the Bible. Did God really harden Pharaoh's heart? Why would God want to do a thing like that? If we say, "Yes, God did," then we make God out to be a monster, but if we say, "No, God did not," then we contradict one of the main motifs of the story.

The reason God is said to have hardened Pharaoh's heart is given in Exod. 10:1-2: "Then the Lord said to Moses, 'Go to Pharaoh; for I have hardened his heart and the heart of his officials, in order that I may show these signs of mine among them, and that you may tell your children and grandchildren how I have made fools of the Egyptians and what signs I have done among them—so that you may know that I am the Lord.'" As I have said, this is history told by the underclass.

My search for an answer for us will be roundabout. I begin with Luke 22:3, "Then Satan entered into Judas called Iscariot, who was one of the twelve; he went away and conferred with the chief priests and officers of the temple police about how he might betray him [Jesus] to them" (compare John 13:2). This we can understand; whether we believe in the reality of Satan or not, we can accept the expression at least metaphorically: we know how an evil impulse might come over someone to become an enemy of God. I then turn to two parallel passages in the Old Testament, a pair already mentioned in Chapter 4. In 1 Chron. 21:1 we read, "Satan stood up against Israel, and incited David to count the people of Israel." In 2 Sam. 24:1, an account of the same incident, we read, "Again the anger of the Lord was kindled against Israel, and he incited David against them, saying, 'Go, count the people of Israel and Judah.'" As we have seen, taking a census was understood to be against God's will, but the question at issue here is: Which supernatural figure incited David to take the census, God or Satan? The early account, in 2 Samuel, presumably from the tenth century B.C., has no problem with the idea that God incited David to do something wrong. (This is not the only such passage; in 1 Sam. 18:10 we read, "The next day an evil spirit from God rushed upon Saul, and he raved within his house.") The late account, in 1 Chronicles, from the end of the fifth century B.C., is not willing to attribute such an action to God, attributing it instead to Satan, a figure not commonly mentioned in the Old Testament but common in the New.

The existence of these three passages, in Luke 22:3, in 1 Chron. 21:1, and in 2 Sam. 24:1, then leads us to wonder: if the pattern of the narrative of Moses and Pharaoh had not been so fixed in the tradition, someone in the fifth century B.C. might not have affirmed that it was Satan who turned the heart of Pharaoh against the Israelites.

After all, the epic story of God's bringing the Israelites out of Egypt was just that—epic: it was shouted and sung and celebrated. And thus it was told in broad strokes—Moses and Aaron the heroes, Pharaoh and his servants the villains, and God in charge of it all. Given the broad strokes of the narrative, we cannot expect the intricacies of motive such as we found in David's court history. Just as Judas' betrayal of Jesus was told as part of a cosmic drama, so in the epic of the exodus the motif of Pharaoh's hardness of heart was central to the cosmic drama. God was in charge of it all, and so it was said: God hardened Pharaoh's heart.

Can we leave it there? Can we say: We should prefer not to affirm that God willed Pharaoh's steadily increasing insensitivity, but we honor the testimony of those ex-slaves, our ancestors in the faith, who were convinced that God was in charge, that God contrived every step of the great drama that was to lead to their liberation—can we say that? Let us recall what was said in Chapter 1, that all God-language is metaphorical, and that we are trying to reduce to a minimum the wrongness of our affirmations. One more point: the notion that God hardens people's hearts is hinted at in the New Testament as well: in 1 Pet. 2:8, those who reject Jesus Christ are said to "stumble because they disobey the word, as they were destined to do." Here is comfort for Christians: their enemies are not out of control, but are under the control of God.

The Deliverance from Egypt (2)

I return now to the question of God's sponsorship of battles, and specifically to the battle at the Sea. Again and again we are told that God participated in the battle. "As the Egyptians fled before it, the Lord tossed the Egyptians into the sea" (Exod. 14:27); "Thus the Lord saved Israel that day from the Egyptians" (14:30). Indeed, in Exod. 15:3, part of the so-called Song of Moses, we hear (literally), "Yahweh is a warrior, Yah is his name" ("Yah" being a short form of Yahweh). Here, then, is God the divine warrior. Can we hear God today in this testimony?

Generations of Christians have heard it: we saw in Chapter 5 that the narrative has been the third Old Testament reading for the Easter vigil liturgy for Roman Catholics. It is crucial that those who are oppressed be able to know that God, who marks the sparrow's fall (Matt. 10:29), hears the cry of the oppressed and comes to their rescue, even if they cannot count on any human intervention. This is the quintessential word of hope for all those individuals and groups who cry out for rescue. From the point of view of historical fact, the Egyptian troops who died in the encounter were doubtless innocent, falling in a battle that was not of their making, as so many men (and women and children) have fallen in the midst of battles before and since that were not of their making. And doubtless a sensitive Christian will be aware of all the innocent folk who fall on both sides of any battle. Nevertheless, the Israelite battle epic still should stir us with a knowledge that God intervenes in history on the side of the oppressed.

The Wilderness Wanderings

While in the wilderness, the Israelites are recorded as having sent out spies to spy out the land; they report back that the land is filled with giants, and the Israelites despair. "Then all the congregation raised a loud cry, and the people wept that night. And all the Israelites complained against Moses and Aaron; the whole congregation said to them, 'Would that we had died in the land of Egypt! Or would that we had died in the wilderness'" (Num. 14:1-2). There is no room here for Israelite self-exaltation; they remember only their grumbling and despair in the wilderness period. They do not remember themselves as having any faith in God's leadership at all. Moses is recalled as saying, "But you were unwilling to go up. You rebelled against the command of the Lord your God; you grumbled in your tents and said, 'It is because the Lord hates us that he has brought us out of the land of Egypt, to hand us over to the Amorites to destroy us. Where are we headed?'" (Deut. 1:26-28a).

Nevertheless, they record further victories in their wanderings in the Transjordan area, notably against Sihon, king of the Amorites, and Og, king of Bashan (Num. 21:21-35), two names long remembered (see, for example, Ps. 135:11). The narratives about both these kings resemble the narratives about Pharaoh: Sihon is portrayed as inhospitable (Num. 21:23), and there was a tradition that Og was gigantic, since his iron bedstead was nine cubits long and four cubits wide (Deut. 3:11)—a cubit is the distance from the elbow of an adult to the end of the middle finger, about a foot and a half, so we are talking about a bed thirteen feet long and six feet wide. Then there is the tradition about Balak, the king of Moab, who hired a Mesopotamian prophet named Balaam to curse the Israelites, only to hear the curses turn to blessings. So again the foreign kings can be held in derision, as Pharaoh was.

The Conquest of Canaan

Let us turn now to Joshua and the battles for the land of Canaan, the battles that so troubled the fourth-grade boys' class. Here we come to the heart of the matter, but the matter is not so simple. We need to review what the narrative in the book of Joshua says, we need to establish what happened historically, so far as we can, and we need to understand the setting in which the book of Joshua took shape.

In the first chapter of the book it is said that God spoke to Joshua, "Be strong and courageous; for you shall put this people in possession of the land that I swore to their ancestors to give them" (1:6). Joshua's conquests are narrated in chapters 6—12. One of the most detailed narratives, and one of the most brutal, is of the fall of Jericho (chapter 6). Spies had earlier been sent to spy out Jericho (chapter 2), and they were sheltered by Rahab, a prostitute. (Prostitutes, then as now, had no social status, and the fact that there was solidarity between a prostitute and the Israelite spies indicates the sensibility of the underclass on both sides; I shall return to this matter in Chapter 12.) At the time of the siege of the city, Joshua gave orders, "The city and all that is in it shall be devoted to the Lord for destruction. Only Rahab the prostitute and all who are with her in her house shall live because she hid the messengers we sent" (6:17). Further, he ordered that all the silver and gold and the vessels of bronze and iron would be sacred to God. And so, according to the narrative, it was done: "Then they devoted to destruction by the edge of the sword all in the city, both men and women, young and old, oxen, sheep and donkeys" (6:21).

Later, at Ai, in the central hill country (chapters 7—8), the Israelites were at first defeated, but the reason given is that a man named Achan had taken for himself some of the booty from Jericho—silver, gold, and the like. The Israelites killed Achan and his family and his livestock by stoning, and thereupon they gained victory at Ai.

In chapter 9, we hear of men from Gibeon, who come to the Israelites resorting to a ruse to keep from being slaughtered; they are enslaved instead. Chapters 10 and 11 offer summaries of campaigns in the south and in the north respectively, and chapter 12 is a list of Israel's victories.

Perhaps the first thing to say about the narrative is something that would not necessarily occur to modern readers: its format is very much like the format used for narrating military conquests in Assyrian, Hittite, and Egyptian accounts. In those accounts too, one finds not only the intervention of the deity but exaggerated details as well: this is simply the mode of presenting conquest narratives in this period.[1]

What actually took place, historically, when Israel entered Canaan? This is a surprisingly difficult matter to establish, in spite of the forthright narrative in the book of Joshua. There is evidence even within the Old Testament that the taking over of the land was not a simple sudden conquest: Judg. 1:27-36 lists many territories that the Israelites were not able to conquer, and 2:21-23 reinforces this conclusion. The evidence from archeology is again mixed. The site of Hazor, a great city mentioned in Josh. 11:10-11 as having been burned by the Israelites, does give archeological evidence of having been destroyed at about the time one would expect from the biblical account. But other sites, such as Jericho and Ai, were not occupied at all during the period associated with the Israelite takeover.[2]

How was the takeover accomplished? Scholars do not agree. Some simply see a relatively peaceful immigration of Israelites into areas thinly populated by Canaanites.[3] Others see coming into the land a small group of Israelites fired with the new faith in Yahweh and sparking a kind of "peasants' revolt" of the local inhabitants, who thereupon became part of the Israelite identity.[4] One scholar in particular notes that the kings of many of the Canaanite cities at that time had foreign names; some of them may have been military adventurers who had come south from the Anatolian plateau (present-day Turkey) and oppressed the local population. There would then have been good reason for local peasants to make common cause with the newly arrived Israelites to overthrow these kings.[5] The narrative of the covenant ceremony in the northern city of Shechem (Joshua 24) may point in that direction: Shechem is one of the cities in Canaan that offer no archeological evidence for a destruction layer in this period, and the narrative may reflect a covenant between the Israelites and the local inhabitants.[6]

There were undoubtedly battles for some of the cities, not only at Hazor but elsewhere. Bethel offers archeological evidence of destruction at this period, but we must remind ourselves that the evidence does not allow us to prove that it was the Israelites who were responsible for the destruction.

Let us return to two matters raised by the narrative in the book of Joshua. The first is the "devotion" of a city "to destruction," such as is narrated of the Israelites at Jericho. What is involved here? Josh. 6:17 reads literally in Hebrew, "The city and all that is in it shall become *ḥērem* to Yahweh." The word *ḥērem* refers to what is utterly prohibited for common or private use (the word is related to the Arabic word from which we get "harem," that is, the separate and exclusive place for the women of the palace). What is *ḥērem* is devoted to Yahweh; men, women, and children cannot be allowed to survive as slaves, nor animals to survive for profit, so both categories therefore are to be put to death (Lev. 27:28-29), and silver, gold, and the like are to be deposited in the cultic area.[7] When God was credited with giving the city to those who took it over, then the human beings, animals, and goods of the city are "off limits" and belonged to God, not to those who took the city over. We must understand that the human beings and animals that were destroyed were not considered a *sacrifice*—they were not a gift to the deity, because they did not belong to the conqueror in the first place. This policy of extermination was a real fact in the ancient Near East: in an inscription of the Moabite King Mesha (ninth century B.C.), he affirms having practiced it.[8] Thus, if the Israelites remembered having made a practice of devoting a city to destruction, then doubtless it was a fact; Deuteronomy preserves a legal tradition about the custom (Deut. 7:2).

The second matter is the more general one of the notion of holy war. Actually, "holy war" is not a biblical phrase, but the idea is embodied in the procedure set forth in Deuteronomy 20, instructions purportedly given by Moses to the Israelites before they occupy the land of Canaan. They are not to fear when they go into the land; Yahweh will fight on their behalf (v. 1). When they draw near to a town, they are to offer it terms of peace; if the town surrenders, the people shall be put to forced labor. If they do not surrender, the males are to be killed and the women, children, livestock, and other goods are to be taken as spoil (vv. 10-14). These instructions differ in detail from those for "devotion to destruction" but are no less brutal. Again, though the book of Deuteronomy took shape centuries after the takeover of Canaan (see Chapter 5), these instructions doubtless reflect the real practice of the Israelites at some times and places.

Let me now summarize to this point our understanding of the conquest of the land. The actual historical events may have been heterogeneous. Israelites came across the Jordan from east to west, fired with the new faith in Yahweh as the leader of the new covenant people and perhaps arousing local people to join their movement. The Israelites were convinced that God continued to act on their behalf as had happened at the Sea a generation earlier. Where they met opposition, they were often able to take over a city, with dire consequences to its former inhabitants.

Two questions then remain with regard to the conquest: (1) How did the book of Joshua come to narrate the events as it does? and (2) What are we on our part to say about God's will in the matter? First, the book of Joshua. In Chapter 5, I explained the origin of the so-called Deuteronomic history, of which the book of Joshua forms the first section. The history was prepared in

the first instance about 610 B.C. as instruction about the history of the Israelite people in the period after Moses and as warning of the regression of
the nation until the rediscovery of the law of Moses and the consequent reform that King Josiah undertook.

The most important issue facing the kingdom of Judah at that time, according to Jeremiah, a prophet of the time, was the temptation to abandon
Yahweh and to be devoted instead to the god Baal and the goddess Astarte,
the so-called "queen of heaven," fertility deities who were therefore understood to promote economic security; see the accusation in Jer. 2:5-13, among
many. Indeed, the threat of this alternative religious devotion had been present for centuries, for Baal and Astarte were the gods of the Canaanites who
inhabited the land before the Israelites entered it (see Judg. 2:6-15). It was a
central issue for the prophet Elijah in the ninth century (see 1 Kings 18), and
for the prophet Hosea in the eighth century. One can gain an idea of the beliefs of the devotees of Baal and Astarte at the time of Jeremiah from the
speech recorded in Jer. 44:15-19, speech of Jews who had fled to Egypt after
the fall of Jerusalem in 587 B.C. (I have mentioned the worship of Baal in
Chapter 4, and I shall discuss the worship of Baal and Astarte more extensively in Chapter 9.)

The book of Joshua, then, is somewhat like a sermon, prepared in Josiah's
day as a cautionary tale to those who heard it. In effect, it says: have nothing
to do with Baal worship, be as firm in your convictions as our ancestors were
who first entered the land, who would have nothing to do with the Canaanites
or their gods. Read Josh. 24:1-28, hearing it as earnest rhetoric composed in
Josiah's day. No wonder the "sermon" that is the book of Joshua stressed an
all-or-nothing-at-all attitude toward the inhabitants of the land, holy war and
all. The extent of real historical memory in Joshua will be debated by scholars, but what cannot be debated is the sense one has that the listener must
make a choice and take a stand.

Where does this discussion leave us in regard to hearing God in the book
of Joshua?

Did the Israelites Need Land?

Before we tackle the question, let us pause to deal with the whole question of
the assumption that the Israelites needed land. The promise of land to Israel
is embedded in the narratives of the patriarchs. The memory of Israel is that
their ancestors were nomads, aliens moving from one pasture to another, depending on the tolerance of the local population. (Compare the old testimony
at the offering of first fruits, which begins, "A wandering Aramean was my

ancestor" [Deut. 26:5].) In order to bury his wife Sarah, Abraham needed to purchase a burial place (Gen. 23:1-20). We hear God's promises for offspring and for a land of their own: God calls Abraham "to the land that I will show you" (Gen. 12:3), and God's covenant with him includes a promise both of offspring (17:5-7) and "the land where you are now an alien, all the land of Canaan, for a perpetual holding" (17:8), and these promises are repeated to Jacob (28:13-14). Moses, before his death, was allowed to see the promised land from across the Jordan (Deut. 34:1-4). The dream of land is the dream of the underclass: to belong, like everybody else; and the land of Canaan is always understood as a gift (or loan) from God, an act of God's grace, not as a prize of conquest. But nothing is ever said about the rights of the earlier inhabitants of the land, or their lack of rights, for that matter; no thought is given to the point of view of the Canaanites.

Let us ponder the periods when Israel did not have a land. The generations before Moses, when they were landless slaves in Egypt, were remembered as being anticipatory, and the forty years in the wilderness were remembered as a transitional period, when they tiptoed past other nations. Much later—after the takeover of the land, after the period of the judges and of the kings—in the sixth century, the leaders of Judah would endure a half-century of exile in Babylon, and through these leaders the community was able to survive. By that time, they evidently possessed some of the written material that was later incorporated into the Old Testament, written material that helped to maintain the people in the absence of territory and national shrine and kingship. After the exile, they were allowed to return to Jerusalem, and though they were not politically independent, they were allowed to rebuild their temple, and the temple symbolized their sense of home. The temple served as a symbolic center even for those many Jews who lived outside Palestine, both in Egypt and in Babylon. A second destruction of Jerusalem in the first and second centuries A.D. meant that, until modern times, only a small population of Jews remained in Palestine; the majority of Jews were scattered throughout the world, sustained by their law and by the hope within their tradition for a better future.

It is hard to imagine how the Israelites might have maintained themselves in the thirteenth, and twelfth, and eleventh centuries without a sense that they were identified with the land. Few if any of them were literate; beginning in the twelfth century, they were subject to the depredations of the Philistines, an enemy who was able to steal the very central symbol of the presence of Yahweh, the ark of the covenant (1 Samuel 4–6). The Israelites were united by their oral tradition of God's great act of deliverance, but they could hardly have survived without a location in which to belong.

Do Christians Need Land?

What is the Christian understanding of the relation of the covenant people—the Church—to the land? Jesus, for his part, had nowhere to lay his head (Matt. 8:20; Luke 9:58), and the tradition remembers his telling the Samaritan woman that God will be worshiped neither in Jerusalem nor on Gerizim, the mountain sacred to the Samaritans (John 4:21). Paul was instrumental in planting the faith in cities all across the eastern Mediterranean area, beginning a process of the spread of the faith that continues to this day. For the first three centuries, the communities of Christians were sustained not by territory at all but simply by their faith in Jesus Christ embodied in common Scripture and sacraments. Indeed, the Letter to the Hebrews, picking up a saying attributed to Jesus, hints that Jesus himself is the functional equivalent of the land. One of the purposes of the giving of the land in the Old Testament is "rest," that is, freedom from the threat of the enemy; Joshua is remembered as saying, "Remember the word that Moses the servant of the Lord commanded you, saying, 'The Lord your God is providing you a place of rest, and will give you this land'" (Josh. 1:13). The saying of Jesus is "Come to me, all you that are weary and are carrying heavy burdens, and I will give you rest." Hebrews says, "Therefore, while the promise of entering his rest is still open, let us take care that none of you should seem to have failed to reach it" (Heb. 4:1).

No sooner had the Christian faith become legal in the fourth century, however, than assumptions were made about the necessity to identify the faith with territory. Such assumptions persist to this day (the Roman Catholic Church in Ireland, the Orthodox Church in Greece): one has only to ponder the endless religious wars in the Middle Ages and in the century after the beginning of the Reformation. Only with great difficulty have some Christians learned how a church might be self-sustaining without being identified with a particular land, and those in our day who maintain, for example, that the United States is a "Christian nation" have still not grasped the possibility. Every nation with a majority of Christians is tempted to assume that God is on that nation's side in any war (recall the slogan, "Gott mit uns" [God with us] on the belt-buckles of German soldiers in the First World War, for example).

Who Were Jesus' Enemies?

Let us turn now to the identity of Jesus' enemies, and how he dealt with them. Several human enemies are named in the course of the gospel narrative—Judas, Annas and Caiaphas, and Pontius Pilate, but the enemies against whom he is constantly portrayed as fighting are Satan and the demons in Satan's kingdom (this is a matter to which I shall return in Chapter 13). I am not asking the readers of this book to accept the objective reality of Satan and the demons, but it is difficult to read the gospel accounts without taking them into at least symbolic account.

The gospel narrates Jesus' encounter with Satan in the temptations in the wilderness (Mark 1:13, and, in more detail, Matt. 4:1-11 and Luke 4:1-13). People in Jesus' day who were mentally ill were understood to be possessed by demons, and Jesus' healings often involved the exorcism of demons (for one example, Mark 1:21-28). Jesus is remembered as greeting the return of the seventy with the testimony, "I watched Satan fall from heaven like a flash of lightning" (Luke 10:18), and he is remembered as saying that "it is by the finger of God that I cast out demons" (Luke 11:20). Jesus then is portrayed as in battle with Satan and his demons, and the Letter to the Ephesians takes up the description of the battle with different terms for the cosmic forces of darkness: "Our struggle is not against enemies of blood and flesh, but against the rulers, against the authorities, against cosmic powers of this present darkness, against the spiritual forces of evil in the heavenly places" (Eph. 6:12).

Christians, then, have understood themselves to be in a struggle against God's cosmic enemies. The first four questions put to candidates for baptism in *The Book of Common Prayer* are as follows: "Do you renounce Satan and all the spiritual forces of wickedness that rebel against God? Do you renounce the evil powers of this world which corrupt and destroy the creatures of God? Do you renounce all sinful desires that draw you from the love of God? Do you turn to Jesus Christ and accept him as your Savior?" This rhetoric bears a close resemblance to the urgings of Joshua to the people at Shechem to renounce foreign gods and serve Yahweh (Joshua 24). It also bears a resemblance to the rhetoric in Deuteronomy, where Moses is portrayed as saying, "When the Lord your God brings you into the land that you are about to enter and occupy, and he clears away many nations before you . . . , and when the Lord your God gives them over to you and you defeat them, then you must utterly destroy them. Make no covenant with them and show them no mercy. Do not intermarry with them . . . , for that you turn away your children from following me, to serve other gods. Then the anger of the Lord would be kindled against you, and he would destroy you quickly" (Deut. 7:1-4).

Summary: The Conquest of Canaan

I summarize here, in five propositions, the belief system that gave rise both to the actions of the Israelites in their battling for the land and to the narrative in the book of Joshua regarding those actions.

1. There are enemies of God. In the New Testament, these enemies are given the designations of Satan, the demons, and the like. Whether they are "real" in the way believers believe God to be real, at least it may be said that many communities of Christians have affirmed the reality of an organization of evil beyond the evil impulses of individuals that may be commonly acknowledged.

2. In the realm of worship, the main rivals to Yahweh, from the first years of the Israelites in Canaan until the fall of Jerusalem in 587 B.C., and in particular in the seventh century, when the book of Joshua was compiled, were the fertility gods Baal and Astarte. Since the first of the Ten Commandments forbids Israelites from having any other gods before Yahweh (see Chapter 3), Baal and Astarte and any other such gods are understood to be enemies of Yahweh, or Old Testament equivalents of the demons in the New Testament. Indeed, Paul equates demons and pagan gods (1 Cor. 10:19-21).

3. Baal and Astarte were gods to whom the Canaanites had been devoted. Since there was understood to be a strong association between consorting with pagans and adopting their gods (compare the notation on Solomon's foreign wives, 1 Kings 11:1-13), the Israelites demonized the Canaanites themselves, understanding them to be enemies of God. It was believed then that it was God's will to free the land of them and thus to kill them.

4. The Israelites remembered themselves to have been very much the weaker power militarily in comparison with the Canaanites; their victories were therefore credited to God, the divine warrior, who acted on their behalf.

5. In the same way, they understood God to have given them the land, which they were convinced they had been promised, as an act of grace. They never claimed that God was rewarding their superior righteousness by their victories or the gift of the land.[9]

Hearing God in the Narratives of the Conquest

Given this particular belief system, what can we as Christians say? One solution, developed in the course of the late nineteenth and early twentieth centuries, was the notion of progressive revelation. By this view, the Israelites were at a primitive stage of development at the time of Joshua, scarcely to be distinguished in moral development from the other peoples of the region. Yahweh was a tribal God, much as Chemosh was the deity of the Moabites (I shall discuss the Moabites and Chemosh more extensively in Chapter 11). Thus, the barbarous notion of conquest by holy war, unworthy of Christians, was part of the moral landscape of the time. Only in later centuries, under the moral influence of the classical prophets, did Israel begin to develop the kind of sensitivity to others that would finally flower in Jesus.[10] By this approach, one assumes that, as time passed, either the Israelites learned more and more about God or God shared with them more and more self-revelation.

There are two difficulties with this approach. The first is that there is no hint of such an understanding in the New Testament. In Acts 13:16-19, we read the beginning of Paul's address to those in the synagogue at Antioch in Pisidia, and it is the same testimony we read in Joshua: "You Israelites, and others who fear God, listen. The God of this people Israel chose our ancestors and made the people great during their stay in the land of Egypt, and with up-lifted arm he led them out of it. For about forty years he put up with them in the wilderness. After he had destroyed seven nations in the land of Canaan, he gave them their land as an inheritance. . . ."

The second difficulty with such a reinterpretation is simply that it takes no account of the theological motifs of the narrative of the conquest—Israel's sense of obligation to God, the necessity of obedience to God, and of God's grace to Israel. Perhaps no text collocates the barbarism of the command to annihilate the Canaanites with the sense of God's grace as much as does Deuteronomy 7, the first few verses of which we have already cited. In vv. 1-6 we hear the command to annihilate ("you must utterly destroy them," v. 2); in vv. 7-8 we hear, "It was not because you were more numerous than any other people that the Lord set his heart on you and chose you—for you were the fewest of all peoples. It was because the Lord loved you and kept the oath that he swore to your ancestors, that the Lord has brought you out with a mighty hand, and redeemed you from the house of slavery, from the hand of Pharaoh king of Egypt." One does violence to this testimony if one separates its two halves. Instead, I propose the following three propositions for our hearing God in the narratives about the conquest.

1. The narratives are most emphatically not a literal model for Christian action, and so in this respect at least we do not hear God in them. Christians do not need to conquer land for their needs. Christians are never to demonize communities that become their adversaries, even though, as a matter of fact, they have done so again and again in the course of Christian history. Jesus extended the notion of "neighbor" to its farthest limits (compare the parable of the Good Samaritan), so that the Christians' watchword becomes "You shall love your neighbor as yourself" (Lev. 19:18).

2. The Israelite passion for loyalty to God, reflected in the narratives of the conquest, and their affirmation that their strength is from God, becomes a model for Christians, so in this respect we may hear God in the narratives.

3. Though all statements about God are to some degree metaphorical (see Chapter 1), it may be said that God always wills that the covenant people do the least wrong thing possible, and the Israelites' conquest of the land of Canaan in holy war, however gradually or abruptly it was actually accomplished, appears to have been the least wrong action possible. This is an extension of another statement I made in Chapter 1, that theology is learning how to say the least wrong thing about God. Wrong it most emphatically was, to kill Canaanites for God. But God willed what God could, given the limited options of the Israelites.

This has been a long discussion of the narrative in Joshua: could one find a simple way of saying it to the fourth-grade boys' class, who claimed that what Joshua did wasn't fair? Perhaps this: "No, you're right, it wasn't fair at all. But in those days people hadn't learned so well what was fair, and God wanted to give the Israelite people a chance to stay together long enough to learn better how to behave, and God couldn't figure out any other way to do that than to give them the right to the land. At the same time, God must have been deeply sorry at all the hurt and death that was caused by their taking the land over." More might be said, but that is a start.

Later Battles

The battles narrated in the books of Judges and 1 Samuel can be analyzed in much the same way I have done for the battles in the book of Joshua. We are horrified by Samuel's hewing Agag, the king of the Amalekites, in pieces, after Saul is accused of disobedience in the matter (1 Samuel 15); beyond the cruelty of the age, we may understand this chapter as one attempt to understand why God presumably rejected Saul's status as king. But there is an earlier attempt to understand why God rejected Saul: by this account, it was because Saul himself offered a sacrifice before embarking on holy war instead of waiting for Samuel to arrive and offer it (1 Sam. 13:7b-15a). The historian wanted to pin *something* on Saul.

We are struck by the savagery of the interminable wars with the Philistines. To take but one detail: the Philistines, we are constantly reminded, were uncircumcised (*e.g.,* 1 Sam. 17:26, 36), and Saul, seeing that his daughter Michal loved David, was determined to control him; for a marriage present, therefore, he asked for one hundred foreskins of Philistines, assuming that David would surely fall in battle before the score of one hundred was reached (1 Sam. 18:20-29). But David kills one hundred Philistines to gain the marriage present (the Hebrew text actually says "two hundred," v. 27). It was a crude age.

There was cruelty on every hand. Nahash, the king of the Ammonites, is said to have gouged out the right eye of every Israelite living east of the Jordan River (1 Sam. 10:27: the last paragraph of 1 Samuel 10 in the NRSV, not found in previous English translations, has been restored to the text from the evidence of one of the Dead Sea Scrolls, reinforced by the ancient Jewish historian Josephus). We must remind ourselves that many battles had no blessing from God. In wars between Judah and Israel (1 Kings 15:6-7, 16), we confront the tragedy of two wings of the covenant people at war with each other.

It is striking that the last mention of the custom of "devoting to destruction" is in the narrative of the wars of King Ahab of Israel with King Ben-Hadad of Syria (ninth century). Ahab was magnanimous to the Syrian king (1 Kings 20:31-34), but, in a weird narrative, a member of a prophetic guild entrapped the king in guilt in his sparing of Ben-Hadad (vv. 35-43), insisting that God commanded he be devoted to destruction. Prophets were not always compassionate! One wonders, then: Did the notion of devoting to destruction, and of embarking on holy war, fade in the hearts and minds of the Israelites with the passing of the years?

An astonishing development took place in the eighth and seventh centuries. The prophets, notably Isaiah and Jeremiah, reconceived the idea of holy war and Yahweh the divine warrior; now they proclaimed that Yahweh was behind the armies of Assyria and Babylon in their march *against* the covenant people! I have already discussed the matter in Chapter 4, where I pointed out that God's wrath toward Israel is often exercised through military events. Readers who are repelled by the narratives in the book of Joshua and elsewhere, in which the divine warrior fights on behalf of the chosen people against the rest of the nations, need to notice this development by the prophets, and so I choose to reinforce the matter here—even though much of the evidence is not in narrative but in prophetic oracles (see Chapter 9).

One of the characteristics of the ideology of holy war in the Old Testament is that, when the enemy sees that Yahweh the divine warrior is about to fight in reinforcement of Israel, the enemy succumbs to panic. With regard to the battle at Gibeon (Josh. 10:10) we read, "And the Lord threw them into a panic before Israel, who inflicted a great slaughter on them at Gibeon, chased them by the way of the ascent of Beth-horon, and struck them down as far as Azekah and Makkedah." But, in Jer. 30:5-6, Yahweh mocks the cries of Judah, "We have heard a cry of panic, of terror, and no peace. Ask now, and see, can a man bear a child? Why then do I see every man with his hands on his loins like a woman in labor? Why has every face turned pale?" That is to say, Yahweh, through the march of Babylon upon Judah, creates the same kind of panic that Israel's enemies had experienced in the days of Israel's conquest of Canaan. In Lam. 3:46-47, the inhabitants of Jerusalem bewail, "All our enemies have opened their mouths against us; panic and pitfall have come upon us, devastation and destruction."

Most telling is Jer. 21:4-5, a passage I cited in Chapter 4: God speaks through the prophet Jeremiah to King Zedekiah, the last king of Judah, "I am going to turn back the weapons of war that are in your hands and with which you are fighting against the king of Babylon and against the Chaldeans who are besieging you outside the walls; and I will bring them together into the center of this city. I myself will fight against you with outstretched hand and mighty arm, in anger, in fury, and in great wrath." There are two features of this passage that need exploration at this point. The first is the verb translated "turn back": it literally means "turn (180 degrees) around"—that is to say, God will take the very weapons in the hands of the defenders of Jerusalem and turn them around to point at the defenders themselves. The other feature is the phrase "outstretched hand and mighty arm." The usual phrasing is "mighty hand and outstretched arm." That is the expression used for the action of the divine warrior in the exodus and conquest, for example in Deut. 7:18-19, "Just remember what the Lord your God did to Pharaoh and to all Egypt, the great trials that your eyes saw, the signs and wonders, the mighty hand and the outstretched arm by which the Lord your God brought you out. The Lord your God will do the same to all the peoples of whom you are afraid." Jer. 21:5 is the only passage in the Old Testament where the adjectives are reversed with the respective nouns, as if the reversal of God's rhetoric itself indicated that God had changed sides.

Let us now summarize. The battles of the exodus and conquest are understood to be God's battles on behalf of a formerly enslaved people with whom God has covenanted. We cannot assume that the Israelites simply projected onto God their own nationalistic ideology, not if they were also able to honor and preserve prophetic pronouncements that understood God on occasion to function as a divine warrior in holy war *against* the covenant people to punish them.

Our discussion of the battles of the Old Testament suggests two related topics. The first is the reappearance of Yahweh the divine warrior in apocalyptic visions of the end-time; I save that topic until Chapter 10. The other is equally a problem for sensitive Christians: the self-righteousness that appears to be so common in the Old Testament, particularly in the Psalms. I save this topic to discuss in connection with worship, in Chapter 13.

Notes

1. K. Lawson Younger, Jr., *Ancient Conquest Accounts: A Study in Ancient Near Eastern and Biblical History Writing* (Journal for the Study of the Old Testament, 98; Sheffield: 1990).

2. Robert North and Philip J. King, "Biblical Archaeology," *New Jerome*, 1208; Roland E. Murphy, "A History of Israel," *New Jerome*, 1228a; Michael David Coogan, "Joshua," *New Jerome*, 116a.

3. Martin Noth, *The History of Israel* (London: Adam & Charles Black, 1960), 68–84; Manfred Weippert, *The Settlement of the Israelite Tribes in Palestine, A Critical Survey of Recent Scholarly Debate* (SBT, 2nd Series, 21; Naperville, Ill: Allenson, 1971).

4. Norman K. Gottwald, *The Tribes of Yahweh, A Sociology of the Religion of Liberated Israel, 1250–105 B.C.E.* (Maryknoll, NY: Orbis, 1979), especially 210–19.

5. George E. Mendenhall, *The Tenth Generation, The Origins of the Biblical Tradition* (Baltimore: The Johns Hopkins University, 1973), 1–31.

6. Coogan, "Joshua," *New Jerome*, 130b.

7. Marvin H. Pope, "Devoted," *IDB* 1:838–39.

8. *ANET*, 320.

9. For a good discussion of these matters, see Robert G. Boling and G. Ernest Wright, *Joshua* (AB 6; Garden City, NY: Doubleday, 1982), 5–37; for suggestions on the kind of sermon that might be preached from the book of Joshua, see John Bright, *The Authority of the Old Testament* (Nashville and New York: Abingdon, 1967), 241–51.

10. For a classic presentation of this approach, see Harry Emerson Fosdick, *A Guide to Understanding the Bible* (New York and London: Harper, 1938), esp. 6–8.

7

Signs and Wonders

~

What do we do with a narrative that to us is simply unbelievable? We read along, doing our best to hear God in an Old Testament narrative, and then we come across some detail that stops us cold: the fall of the walls of Jericho at the blast of the trumpets (Josh. 6:20), or the sun's standing still at the behest of Joshua (Josh. 10:12-13), or whatever. Our reaction is: "That couldn't have happened the way it is told!" What are we to do then? Many of us are troubled by narratives in the Old Testament that lack any plausibility.

There are two groups of people *not* bothered by the problem. In the first group are those who accept the Bible without any questions: it is so written, and therefore it must have been. Who are we to question the testimony of Scripture? The second group consists of those who have a rationalist outlook and for whom the whole biblical testimony is dubious: the Bible is full of odd affirmations from far away and long ago, and particularly implausible details in a narrative come as no surprise. Why trouble ourselves over this or that dubious claim?

There are others, however, who want to take the Bible seriously but keep stumbling; they are the present-day descendants of the father of the epileptic child who said to Jesus, "I believe; help my unbelief!" (Mark 9:24). It is for those folk that this chapter is written.

Two things need to be said at the outset. The first is that, in this regard, the Old Testament is of a piece with the New Testament; indeed, in certain respects, the narratives of the four Gospels and of the book of Acts bring more frequent challenges to our belief system than the Old Testament does. In one, we are told that Moses turned the water of the Nile into blood (Exod. 7:14-24); in the other, we are told that Jesus in the course of the wedding at Cana turned water into wine (John 2:1-12). Let me then say at the outset that I am not going to deal in a substantial way with such matters in the New Testament, although clearly much of what I say will apply to both Testaments.[1]

The second thing that needs to be said is that there are interlocking questions here, from two sources, and I am not going to try with any thoroughness to answer them. The historian asks: "Did this event happen the way it is told? Could it have happened?" This questioning revolves around assumptions of the orderliness of nature and the way we understand the natural world to work. The theologian asks: "Did God do it this way? Could God have done it this way?" This questioning assumes the existence of God and then assumes either an interruption in the natural order or else the exploitation by God of some feature of the natural order unrecognized by us.

As I have said, I am not going to try to answer these questions. The extent to which there are laws of nature to which God always adheres or which God may interrupt—indeed, what God can or cannot do—these have been issues for centuries, and all kinds of approaches, philosophical and theological, have been proposed to deal with them. Because I am not trained at all in these matters, I shall not make bold to adopt any given approach, let alone try to propose a new one. Instead, I shall make some modest suggestions that may help readers to clarify what is at stake in whatever stance they take with problematic narratives. These suggestions revolve around some of the contrasts between our own cultural assumptions and the assumptions of the ancient Israelites with regard to how reality is perceived.

Historical Fiction

Before we deal with the problem of incredible details in narrative with a claim to historical reality, we must look at some examples in the Old Testament of what may be called historical fiction. For the Old Testament, this description is something of a contradiction: the ancient hearers of this material would not perceive it as being anything but part of the overall historical narrative. Nevertheless, it is a useful distinction to make.

Job is an example; as I shall indicate in Chapter 11, the framework of the story of Job is set with the implication of far away and long ago.

There are narratives, evidently drafted in the postexilic period, that locate the stories they tell in historical contexts of the past—specifically, the books of Jonah and Esther and the first six chapters of the book of Daniel. As for Jonah, 2 Kings 14:25 mentions a Jonah, the son of Amittai, in the eighth century, but that verse suggests no awareness of the story preserved in the present book of Jonah; scholars who have examined the phraseology of the book have concluded that it was drafted much later, at the end of the sixth century or perhaps in the fifth. It offers several items of fantasy. The city of Nineveh is said to be "three days' walk across" (Jon. 3:3), suggesting a city some sixty miles wide, whereas excavations of historical Nineveh, the final capital of the Assyrian empire, have revealed a city with walls somewhat less than eight miles in total circumference.² Further, the story tells of a bush that grew up overnight (Jon. 4:10). Thus, the fish that swallowed Jonah whole and vomited him up three days later is not the only detail that would bring wonder and amusement to the hearer. The story was circulated to challenge the narrowness of some factions within the postexilic Jewish community. Jonah hates Nineveh: as one writer has recently said, it is a story about the joy of hatred.³

An analogy to such historical fiction from American experience would be the story of George Washington and the cherry tree. That story was offered by Mason L. Weems in 1800 as part of the effort to render Washington a suitable hero for emulation by the young. George Washington is a historical figure, but the story of the cherry tree is not.⁴

The book of Esther is evidently another instance of historical fiction. "Ahasuerus" is the biblical form of the name of the Persian king Xerxes I, who ruled in the fifth century B.C. But Xerxes' queen was Amestris, not Vashti,⁵ and scholars have found no historical evidence for the events portrayed in the book. And what are we to do with the gallows prepared for Mordecai's hanging but used for Haman's instead—a gallows described as being fifty cubits high (Esth. 5:14). A cubit is about a foot and a half (see Chapter 6), so we are dealing here with a gallows seventy-five feet high! We have, then, a comedy based on life in the Persian court to tell the story of a heroine who rescues her people (compare Chapter 12) and, incidentally, to validate the feast of Purim, a holiday that became part of the Jewish calendar.

The first six chapters of the book of Daniel are likewise historical fiction (the last half of the book is apocalyptic—I shall deal with it in Chapter 10). These chapters offer hero tales of Daniel and his friends at the court of Nebuchadnezzar, the king of Babylon. In chapter 1, Daniel rejects the rich food of Nebuchadnezzar's court in order to obey kosher food laws. In chapter 2, he interprets Nebuchadnezzar's dream of a composite statue. Chapter 3 tells the story of the three youths in the fiery furnace. In chapters 4 through 6 respectively, Daniel interprets Nebuchadnezzar's dream of the great world tree, interprets the handwriting on the wall at Belshazzar's feast, and survives the lion's den. As with the book of Esther in relation to the Persian court, these tales do not reflect the history of the real Babylonian court in the sixth century B.C.; rather, they were circulated when Jewish patriots were struggling against the Hellenistic Seleucid king Antiochus IV (Epiphanes) about 165 B.C.—the so-called Maccabean revolt, which was triggered when the king profaned the Jerusalem temple in 167 B.C. (The later Jewish rededication of the temple is the occasion celebrated in the Jewish feast of Hanukkah.) When Jews of the time heard "Nebuchadnezzar," therefore, they thought "Antiochus."

I suggest, then, that we need not fret over the dimensions of the gullet of the fish that swallowed Jonah or the temperature of the furnace prepared for Shadrach, Meshach, and Abednego. These stories entertain, but they also serve the same functions as does historical narrative (see Chapter 5): celebration, instruction, and warning.

Fiction that purports to be history, however, is not our main concern; rather, we are concerned with the implausible events within narratives that have been recalled as historical, such as Moses' parting of the Red Sea in Exodus 14, or the sun's standing still.

We have already touched on some of the issues that swirl around this problem. In Chapter 4, in our discussion of God's anger, we took note of the way we ourselves have recourse to science to explain the occurrence of catastrophes, and, in Chapter 5, we took note of the way in which current notions of history deal entirely with natural and human events without any notion of the participation of God. Now we need to explore a range of related questions in detail.

Our Assumption: We Are Mostly in Control

I choose to begin not with the outlook of the Old Testament but with a brief exploration of the general outlook of our own culture. I shall concentrate on how we act, our assumptions about the way our lives run, rather than on what we say we believe about how the world runs (the extent to which we say we believe in scientific explanations, for example).

I first note the curious phenomenon of simultaneity. When we look forward to watching a particular television program, we find out that it begins at 8:30 P.M., we check our watches, and we turn on the TV at 8:30 with the assumption that the program will indeed begin at that time. This assumption is based in turn on the assumption that the watch consulted and the clock at the TV station point to the same minute, an assumption based in turn on the possibility of standard time, itself an invention in the latter part of the nineteenth century, necessitated by the scheduling of railroad trains. (Before then, all time was local time.) Ships in the nineteenth century carried carefully constructed chronometers that maintained the local time of Greenwich, England, but such chronometers, necessary for the calculation of longitude, became available only in the eighteenth century. Standard time assumes the accuracy of astronomical measurements, based in turn on the assumption of regularity in the movements of heavenly bodies; and the ability to stay with standard time is likewise based on the universality of electrical power and a consequent communications network. We can assume that children can get to school on time, that adults can get to work on time, and that buses, trains, and aircraft will move according to schedule. All of this precision can be typified by the ability of astronomers to predict eclipses to the minute in future centuries, or to calculate, to the minute, eclipses that have taken place in past centuries.

If we assume that some matters are precisely predictable, we assume others are dependable. We take it for granted that one book from a press run is identical to another book from the same press run, an assumption traceable to the process of printing from movable type, developed in the fifteenth century; and we take it for granted that a manufacturer's car parts purchased in Chicago are identical with those sold by the same manufacturer in New York, an assumption based on the system of mass production of interchangeable parts, a development that began in the gunsmithing industry in the nineteenth century. We assume the reliability of the banking system we use, and the acceptability of the credit cards we hold. We assume that quality control measures protect the canned foodstuffs we buy and the purity of our water supply. We assume the general reliability of the weather predictions and of the news of the past day or two in our newspapers. We assume the general dependability of our postal service. We take for granted that there will be a supply of fuel for our cars at service stations along the way of our travels. We assume the general reliability of medical services available to us, and the accessibility of police and firefighting protection. All of these assumptions, I point out, are shared by almost everyone in our culture, whatever our beliefs about God may be; only a few groups like the Amish deliberately exclude themselves from aspects of this network of availabilities.

Beyond these dependabilities in our lives, most of us live as if we will live long lives. Deep down we know that death is certain; nevertheless, we live with a working assumption of certainty about our future. If I assume that my monthly income is dependable, then I assume that my food supply is assured. We may make appointments in our appointment books several months or even a year or two in advance, confident that we will be there when we say we will. Some of us take out thirty-year mortgages from our banks; though we may not live to make the final payment, the bank takes it for granted that some executor or heir will. We are aware of risks in our lives, but insurance policies of various sorts are available to minimize financial loss.

Such a confident outlook is often marred. For decades, we have been aware of the threat of nuclear war; true, since the recent collapse of the Soviet Union, we perceive that threat to have abated, but we know that most of those weapons are still in existence. There is always the possibility of some natural disaster: a hurricane, earthquake, or flood may destroy the confidence of a whole community, and economic disasters, such as a massive loss of jobs during a depression, or a runaway inflation in prices, may have the same effect. The recent rise of violence and sudden death in our city streets, particularly among young men, has caused a widespread sense of nihilism and despair about the future among many young people. Nevertheless, I would maintain that most of the behaviors I have described are adhered to by most of the population of North America and Europe. These behaviors are those of middle-class (and upper-class) life, and the readers of this book will doubtless recognize themselves in these descriptions.

It goes without saying that these behaviors are based on the practical applications of science in our lives, notably in technology and medicine; these applications have been developed in the past few centuries but are ultimately derived from the philosophical inquiries of the Greeks. Indeed, we are all children of the Greeks, whether we recognize it or not. It is appropriate here to recall an event in the life of Alexander the Great. As the Greek conqueror was marching eastward, doing battle with the Persians, just after he crossed the Tigris River, a nearly total eclipse of the moon took place (it was September 20, 331 B.C.). As one authority describes the event, "Alexander, with a characteristic blend of science and religion, sacrificed to the Moon, and also to the Sun and Earth, because they are said to cause this phenomenon."[6] Alexander was a perfect ancient exemplar of the attitude toward life that I have been setting forth.

A Different Assumption: "God Willing"

From 1963 until 1970, I lived with my family in Beirut, Lebanon. In notable respects, the life I lived there was analogous to life in the United States at that time: Beirut has been, of course, a cosmopolitan city. Beyond the universal predictability of eclipses, in Lebanon as in the United States, there was the same dependability of identical copies of books published either in Beirut or elsewhere; car parts, imported from abroad, were identical to those in Europe and North America. By and large, the airline system was dependable, and I could do my banking at the absolutely dependable local branch of the British Bank of the Middle East. The health care available to us was excellent, thanks to the American University Hospital.

But, in other equally important respects, the details of living were not nearly so dependable in the ways to which we had become accustomed. We kept a five-gallon canister of water in the closet, and kerosene lanterns handy, inasmuch as either the water system or the electricity, or both, could fail for an hour or a day. The postal system appeared undependable enough that, when I would send successive portions of a book manuscript to the publisher in Europe, I would place them in the care of some acquaintance I had met who was flying there rather than risk mailing them locally. During those years, we witnessed the Middle East war of 1967, and both before and after that war there were various kinds of skirmishing among Lebanese political forces, or between the government and militias operating out of local Palestinian refugee camps. Curfews and other interruptions of the normal flow of life were fairly frequent.

In these circumstances, we Americans quickly learned the Arabic expression *in ša² Allāh* (contracted to *inšallāh* and pronounced *inshallah*), literally, "If God wills." (It is the exact equivalent of the Latin phrase *Deo volente*, "God willing," often abbreviated "D.V.," which appears occasionally in the correspondence of pious Roman Catholics.) The Arabic phrase is used by both Muslim and Christian Arabs, but it is not a simple expression of fatalism, as one might think. In my experience, it was used in the course of conversation about the near future as a cautionary expression, and the striking thing was that it was freely used by Americans in Beirut talking to each other, even by those who had no lively belief in God. Doubtless it was sometimes used with a mocking air, but we used it simply because there was no English expression that quite fit the local situation. "I'll meet you for lunch tomorrow, *inshallah*," we would say, meaning, "if the government does not impose a curfew, or whatnot." Even those of us who did believe in God would not hold God specifically responsible for any given interruption of our plans; the expression simply fit our perception of the uncertainties of our days. Our plans were often thwarted, even to the matter of tomorrow's luncheon appointment.

This kind of world, in which one's future is not primarily in one's own hands is, we recognize, the world today of so many in the Third World, so many even of the poor and of members of ethnic minorities within our own land, whatever may be the specific beliefs of the folk involved—whether one's future is thought to be a matter of fate, or of the position of the planets, or the favor or disfavor of one or more gods, or of the God of the Bible, for that matter. These folk know that they are not the masters of their fate or the captains of their souls.

The Assumption of the Israelites:
God Is Completely in Control

Now, take away the electric power grid, airline schedules, and timepieces; take away the banking system, insurance, and minted coinage; take away interchangeable manufactured goods, books bound at the spine, and, to a large extent, literacy; take away health care, a water distribution system, and the ability to deal with infestations of rodents, and one has the world of the Old

Testament. (For the rodents, see 1 Sam. 6:4-18: the "mice" mentioned there may have been rats that spread the plague.)

It was a world with a tragically high infant mortality rate (compare Isa. 65:20); a world whose horizons were by our standards extremely limited (the territory of biblical Israel was roughly the size of the state of Vermont or of New Hampshire); a world that, in comparison with our experience, was strikingly underpopulated (we recall from Chapter 5 that the city of Jerusalem in King David's day had a population of only about two thousand people; the extent of the city at that time was roughly twelve acres).[7]

It was a world understood to be constructed in three stories: the heavens above, consisting of a "firmament" (dome) with the waters of the heavens poised to come down through its windows; the flat disk of the earth beneath, set on its foundations, and then waters below and at the edge of the earth (compare Gen. 1:6-10; 7:11; 8:2; Exod. 20:4; Pss. 104:7-9; 148:4; Prov. 8:29; Isa. 40:22; Mal. 3:10).[8] It was a world in which the ratio of the circumference of a circle to its diameter could be taken as precisely three (1 Kings 7:23); eclipses could be a source of public panic (Jer. 10:2); a major event, the reading of the law every seven years, would be scheduled not for a given hour or even a given day, but simply for a given week (Deut. 31:10-13, compare 16:13-15).

Yet one would have a completely distorted picture of the world of the Old Testament if one were to dwell only on what, from our point of view, was lacking. On its own terms it was a culture as rich and intense as any other. Men and women and children struggled to survive, they laughed and loved, despaired and hated, intrigued and reconciled as people always do. If many were unlettered, we may be sure that many were wise (on the matter of wisdom, see Chapter 11). If people lacked instant communication across great distances, still there would be rumors and reports that traveled along the caravan tracks of merchants or the roads of royal messengers, and people would hear and assess what they heard (2 Kings 19:7; Jer. 51:46). Oral tradition must have been varied and compelling, given what we can discern of it behind the written deposit we have in the Old Testament (I shall return to this matter below).

The important matter for our purposes, however, is that it was most emphatically a world of *inshallah*, "God willing." We will plant next month, if God sends the rain. The harvest will allow us to survive, if God does not send blight, or mildew, or locusts. We shall make a pilgrimage to Jerusalem next year, if God does not overthrow the city by the Assyrian army. Our children will live to see our old age, if God does not send a pestilence. (For all these concerns, see Amos 4:6-11, a passage discussed in Chapter 4.)

God was understood to be immediately and intimately in charge of everything—of inanimate nature, of the animal world, and of the world of human beings. The best presentation of God's governance of the inanimate world is found in Job 38, where we hear God tell of laying the foundations of the world, of the storehouses of the snow and hail "which I have reserved for the time of trouble, for the day of battle and war." The best presentation of God's governance of the world of animals is to be found in the subsequent chapter, Job 39: God is affirmed to know the gestation period of the mountain goat and to be the source of the horse's strength. We find reflections of this governance elsewhere as well. Jeremiah, for example, notes that God has set a barrier for the sea and sends the rain in its season (Jer. 5:22-25), and that the birds know their time of migration (8:7). The point of both these passages is that the covenant people are compared unfavorably with the sea and with the birds: the people disobey God, whereas the sea and birds are obedient, so Jeremiah implies that it is God who has taught the birds their time of migration. It follows then that the people of the Old Testament did not develop any notion of the regularity of nature unrelated to God's immediate will—rather, it was understood to be God who brings everything to pass.

In regard to human affairs, it was taken for granted in the Old Testament to be God's will whether a wife could conceive or not (Gen. 29:31; 30:2, 22; 1 Sam. 1:5, 19-20), and whether a child lived or died (2 Sam. 12:15-19; 2 Kings 4)—indeed, whether anyone lived or died (Ps. 30:3). Even a random bowshot was ultimately directed by the will of God (1 Kings 22:17-18, 34).

To sum up: People lived their lives with the conviction that every contingency is in God's hands.

Ordinary and Extraordinary

It is important to stress that in this governance of the world God is not capricious: this is implied by what we have already said. God did not create the earth to be a chaos, but to be inhabited (Isa. 45:18); to that end, one must be able to count on the general dependability of the world. The dawn knows its place (Job 38:12). There is a fixed order of the sun, the moon, the stars, and the sea (Jer. 31:35-36), and God has promised that seedtime and harvest, cold and heat, summer and winter, day and night shall not cease as long as the earth endures (Gen. 8:22). One can set forth the habits of the ant, the locust, the lizard, the badger (Prov. 30:24-28), or any other animals, for God has taught them their ways (again, Job 39). Yet into this fixed order God may intervene, for example, by bringing on sudden events like earthquakes (Isa. 29:6). Nothing is too hard for God (Jer. 32:17, compare Gen. 18:14).

The Old Testament understands, then, that life is filled in general with ordinariness and dependability, punctuated by extraordinary events through which God is manifested in presence and power. These extraordinary events are again and again called "signs and wonders" (see, for example, the traditional confession in the first-fruits ritual, Deut. 26:8, which I shall paraphrase below).

It is possible that, as the centuries passed, there was a shift in perception on these matters—in the pre-exilic period, there may have been a greater sense of God's intervention, and in the postexilic period, a greater sense of a fixed order. Thus, it is instructive to set the pre-exilic description (eighth century) in Mic. 1:3-4, "For lo, the Lord is coming out of his place, and will come down and tread upon the high places of the earth. Then the mountains will melt under him and the valleys will burst open, like wax near the fire, like waters poured down a steep place," alongside Isa. 64:1-3, a postexilic (sixth century) passage, "O that you would tear open the heavens and come down, so that the mountains would quake at your presence—as when fire kindles brushwood and the fire causes water to boil—to make your name known to your adversaries, so that nations might tremble at your presence! When you did awesome deeds that we did not expect, you came down, the mountains quaked at your presence." One might conclude that, for the author of Isaiah 64, the "awesome deeds that we did not expect" were not to be seen in his generation. Nevertheless, I shall not attempt to arrange these sensibilities on a time scale: the general pattern of the ordinary and the extraordinary holds for all periods.

The Lack of Distinction between Objective (Photographable) and Subjective (Nonphotographable) Events

The Old Testament makes no explicit distinction between what is seen with the physical eyes and would therefore be photographable by us and what is "seen" with the inner eye, nor between what is heard with the physical ears and would therefore be recordable by us and what is "heard" with the inner ear. Visions and auditions are referred to with the same vocabulary as are the sights and sounds of the ordinary workaday world. In either case, the verbs are "see" (Hebrew *r'h*) and "hear" (Hebrew *šm'*).

In 1 Kings 20:13, we read that "a certain prophet came up to King Ahab of Israel and said, 'Thus says the Lord, Have you seen all this great multitude?'" The "great multitude" is the army of the Syrian king Ben-hadad; we are dealing with objective seeing of what is photographable. By contrast, in Zech. 5:2, an angel asks the prophet, "What do you see?" And the prophet's answer is, "A flying scroll; its length is twenty cubits [thirty feet] and its width ten cubits [fifteen feet]." Here we are dealing with an unphotographable visionary experience (I shall return to this flying scroll in Chapter 10).

146 Long Ago God Spoke

And the situation is similar with hearing. In 1 Kings 3:11-14, we hear the contents of what God said to Solomon; in v. 15, we learn that God spoke in a dream. We recall, too, the story of the boy Samuel in the sanctuary at Shiloh: Samuel himself evidently confused an audition from God with a recordable voice. Apparently, Samuel's experience with God involved a vision as well as auditions (1 Sam. 3:10).

Factors That Raise the Possibility of Visionary Experiences

There have been people in every age and in a variety of cultures who have testified to visionary experiences. Many people today testify to such experiences and credit them as marking a turning point in their lives. Sometimes they are vivid dreams or hallucinations, but sometimes there are no adequate external explanations for these experiences.

It may be useful at this point to ponder various circumstances that may well have raised the possibility of visionary experiences among the Israelites. There are, first of all, specific external circumstances. There were no corrective lenses for people with poor eyesight, and for such folk what they believed they saw might well have depended on distortions of physical vision. The lack of adequate illumination at night might well have contributed to such conclusions about what they experienced.

One's inner emotional state, perhaps of fear or exaltation, likewise helps to shape what one perceives. The presence of a fever during illness surely heightens the possibility of visions, and so does fasting from food.

Cultural expectations play a profound role in bringing people to extraordinary experiences of the divine. (I shall return to this matter in Chapter 9 when I discuss the experience of the prophets.) I want to press particularly in the direction of group experience of visions, a phenomenon that is perhaps less familiar to us. For this purpose, I describe a seventeenth-century movement within Judaism among the followers of a man named Sabbatai Ṣevi, whom they declared to be the Messiah. In the years 1665 and 1666, Sabbatai lived in Smyrna (present-day Izmir, on the west coast of Turkey). I quote from a recent biography. "Smyrna was in a festive mood, and the believers moved in a dizzy whirl of legends, miracles, and revelations. Abraham Yakhini, who was in Smyrna at the time, well summed up the mood of the period when, a few years later, he spoke of 'those blessed days'. . . . Collective enthusiasm quickly surrounded events with a halo. Tales of the appearance of a pillar of fire and similar miraculous signs became indubitable facts. The people of Smyrna saw miracles and heard prophecies, providing the best possible illustration of Rénan's remark about the infectious character of visions. It is enough for one member of a group sharing the same beliefs to claim to have seen or heard a supernatural manifestation, and the others too will see and hear it. Hardly had the report arrived from Aleppo that Elijah had appeared in the Old Synagogue there, and Elijah walked the streets of Smyrna. Dozens, even hundreds, had seen him . . . Solomon Cremona, one of the wealthiest Jews in Smyrna, had invited friends to a great feast. One of the guests, his gaze falling on the shining brass plates hanging on the wall, started from his seat and, bowing deeply, exclaimed: 'Arise brethren and behold the prophet Elijah'—and all rose, bowed, and beheld Elijah."[9] We are very close to the spirit of the Old Testament when we read an account like this.

The Lack of Explicit Distinction between Natural and Supernatural

It would appear that our distinction between the natural order and the supernatural world is not crucial to the Old Testament, or at least that the distinction is not made clear in the language. One notable example is the Hebrew word *maḻāk,* which may be translated either "messenger" or "angel." Jacob sent messengers—human, photographable servants (Gen. 32:3, 6). In Isa. 44:26, God is said to have sent messengers, and in this verse the implication is that these are the prophets, human and photographable. But the word is also used of heavenly messengers: in Genesis 18–19, it is said that there are "three men" (18:2), who appear to be God (18:13) along with two servants (compare 18:33 with 19:1), and the two in 19:1 have always been understood to be "angels" (so say the English translations). Whether these personages are photographable or not, they are understood to be supernatural. The angel of God that spoke to Hagar in Gen. 21:17 spoke "from heaven" and therefore was hardly understood to be photographable. In sum, the distinction that is so crucial to us between a "messenger" and an "angel" was not crucial to the Israelites.[10] (In passing, it may be noted that the Greek word *angelos* in the New Testament lacks the distinction as well: in Luke 7:24 the word refers to the messengers John sends to Jesus, but most of the occurrences of the word in the New Testament refer to "angels," as in Luke 2:9-15.)

Signs and Wonders[11]

I return to the lack of an explicit distinction between natural and supernatural; this lack is likewise clear with respect to the nouns that are central to the concerns of this chapter—above all, the phrase "signs and wonders." Though this phrase translates two Hebrew words that appear to be a fixed pair (the words are the plural of 'ōt and môpēt respectively), these are not the only terms that appear in these contexts: there are at least two other such words. One is the plural of niplē't, translated "wonders" or "wondrous things" in the NRSV (for the first rendering, see Exod. 3:20; for the second, see Ps. 72:18). The other is the plural of nôrā'â, translated "awesome things" (Deut. 10:21). These four words then claim our attention.

The word 'ōt has a good equivalent in the English word "sign." "Signs" in the Old Testament may be completely natural. In Num. 16:38, bronze censers have been declared to be "holy," that is, set aside for God's purposes, and they are then made into a covering for the altar, as a "sign" to the Israelites—that is, as a reminder, a warning, or the like (compare v. 40)—of God's power and presence. Indeed, the sun and the moon were created as "signs" (Gen. 1:14), as bodies to keep chronological order. But the phrase "the signs of the heavens" may refer not only to heavenly bodies that mark the seasons but also to sudden signs that are omens of things to come; superstitious people could be dismayed at them (I have already cited Jer. 10:2 in this regard). The reference then is to unexpected phenomena like eclipses, comets, or particular astrological portents.

"Signs" from God may be, from our point of view, altogether "natural" or altogether marvelous. Thus, in Exod. 3:12, God explains that after the deliverance from Egypt, the return of the Israelites to Sinai to worship will be a "sign" that it was God who effected the deliverance. But then in Exod. 4:8-9 the word "signs" refers to the marvels that God enables Moses to perform, such as the staff that turned into a snake and then became a staff once more, and to his hand that became leprous and was then healed. The important thing about a "sign" from God is not whether it is "natural" or contrariwise is "against the laws of nature," but rather what it signifies of the presence and the power of God, or what it indicates of future events.

A môpēt (usually translated "wonder") is scarcely to be distinguished from an 'ōt "sign." This pair of words occurs in Isa. 20:3 (NRSV "a sign and a portent") to refer to a completely natural phenomenon—Isaiah's walking naked and barefoot for three years. But môpēt ("wonder"), even more than 'ōt ("sign"), is used for marvelous displays of God's power (Exod. 4:21), particularly for the so-called "plagues" in Egypt (Exod. 11:9-10).

The third word I have cited, niplē't, is a participle of a verb meaning "to be too difficult (to do)," "to be extraordinary or marvelous." The finite verb is the one that occurs in Gen. 18:14 and Jer. 32:17, already cited: "Nothing is too hard for God." The participle of the verb means "something too difficult, something extraordinary, marvelous." This word, then, approaches more specifically to the notion with which we are grappling in this chapter—

namely, matters "too hard to believe." This word, too, is associated with the deliverance from Egypt (Exod. 3:20; 15:11), but it is not necessarily confined to those events (see Ps. 139:14). As one might imagine, the word is almost entirely confined to the deeds of God.

The fourth word is a participle of the verb "fear, be in awe of": it refers to "fearful" or "awesome" phenomena. This word may in flattery refer to the deeds of the king (Ps. 45:4), but it almost always refers to God's deeds, notably to the deliverance out of Egypt (Ps. 65:5) but then to other deeds of God as well (see Isa. 64:3).

If these words point toward the issues we are facing in this chapter, what may we conclude? I offer four interrelated conclusions.

1. The Old Testament appears to make no distinction at all between phenomena on the one hand that are *in accord* with what we understand to be the laws of nature, and presumed phenomena on the other hand that are understood to *break* the laws of nature. All four of these words—"signs," "wonders," "wondrous things," and "awesome things"—refer without distinction both to natural events and to presumed unnatural events.

2. What concerned the people of the Old Testament was another matter altogether: the way in which they understood striking events to be communication from *God*. Overwhelmingly, these words betoken God's activity; we have already pondered the way in which natural events like earthquakes were understood to signal God's anger (see Chapter 4). But God's favor was remembered above all, especially in the rescue from Egypt (see Chapter 6), and that rescue was remembered as marked by signs and wonders.

3. The mention of "signs and wonders" suggests a tone of celebration. The Israelites testified to, indeed celebrated, the presence and power of God in specific historical circumstances, and, as we recognized in Chapter 5, testimony at celebrations does not always meet the specifications of the historian.

4. If the model for "signs and wonders" was the rescue from Egypt, the phrase refers not only to the crossing at the Sea but also to the previous "plagues" of Egypt that were associated with the rescue. In another direction, the phrase refers not only to the battle at the Sea but to subsequent battles in the conquest of the land. An important part of the testimony about the God of battles is that God does not need large armies. We are told that God twice reduced the number of men Gideon had at hand to fight the Midianites (Judges 7). There is similar testimony regarding a later incident, during the reign of Saul. When his forces were fighting the Philistines, only six hundred Israelite fighters were left. Without telling the king, Jonathan determined to march into Philistine territory: "It may be," he said to his armor-bearer, "that

the Lord will act for us; for nothing can hinder the Lord by many or by few"
(1 Sam. 14:6). That is to say, for God's people victory or defeat is always in the
hand of God.

A Dialogue of the Deaf?

As we imagine ourselves making inquiry of the ancient authors with regard to
their testimony concerning events we find hard to believe, we seem to find
ourselves reduced to a kind of dialogue of the deaf. We say, "What happened
at the rescue of Israel at the Sea?" They say, "Rejoice! God heard our voice and
saw our affliction, our toil, and our oppression, and brought us out of Egypt
with a mighty hand and an outstretched arm, with a terrifying display of
power, and with signs and wonders, and brought us into this place and gave
us this land, a land flowing with milk and honey" (compare Deut. 26:7-9).
"Yes, that's all very well," we say briskly, "but what really happened at the Sea?
Did you catch the whole thing on your video camera? What actually took
place?" "Celebrate, celebrate," they say; "God has given us victory!" By and
large, as we search in their testimony for answers to our questions, we search
in vain. We have our notions about what is possible in this world, but what we
hear is simply the Israelites' testimony about the event, a testimony that does
not seem to answer the questions we crave to put.

At this point, I pause to suggest that what is needed is for us to honor the
integrity both of the Israelites' testimony on the one hand and of our questions on the other, and not to seek too soon to insist either that their testimony is somehow misguided, or contrariwise to be told that our questions are
illegitimate.

Clues in the Testimony: Two Examples

Even if it appears that we are in a dialogue of the deaf, occasionally a literary
analysis of the testimony itself suggests fresh modes for our understanding. I
offer two examples—the rescue at the Sea (Exod. 13:17—14:31) and the narrative of the sun's standing still (Josh. 10:12-14). I shall deal first with the
narrative in Joshua, inasmuch as the literary problems are simpler.

We are told that the sun stood still when Joshua and the Israelites fought
the Amorites (Josh. 10:12-14). But if we look carefully, we will see that what
we have in these three verses is a poem (vv. 12b-13a) consisting of some kind
of command to the sun and moon, followed by a poetic affirmation that the
sun and moon obeyed the command, followed by a comment in prose on
the event (vv. 13b-14). We might conclude that the first portion of the poem,

the command, was an original kernel, and the second part of the poem a later extension; and we might conclude, too, that the two portions of the prose comment (vv. 13b and 14) may be from different writers. But let us keep it simple and deal with two portions only, the poetry as a whole and the prose as a whole. The later prose writer (or writers) clearly assumed some kind of extraordinary astronomical event, but it is far from clear that this is the assumption in the poem itself.

At issue here are the meanings of the two verbs that appear in the poem, the verb "stand still," twice used of the sun (Hebrew *dmm*), and the verb "stop," used of the moon (Hebrew *ᶜmd*). These verbs are clearly in poetic parallelism, and the same parallelism is found in 1 Sam. 14:9, where the NRSV translates *dmm* as "wait" and *ᶜmd* as "stand still." The commoner verb (*ᶜmd*) is the one used of the moon; it is used to mean "stop moving," but it is also used of a servant or inferior standing alert over the master (for example, in 1 Kings 1:28), or of someone waiting (for example, 1 Kings 20:38). The verb used of the sun is not so common; it is used of having rest (Job 30:27) or keeping silent (Lev. 10:3). A recent commentary translates the first two lines of v. 13 as "Sun was stilled, and Moon stood fixed,"[11] and perhaps this is as good as we can do.

Translating the verbs rightly, however, does not fill out for us the thought-world represented by the poem. But we can be reasonably sure of several things. First, it would be understood that God is in charge of the heavenly bodies, and that the heavenly bodies may play their part in victory: it is said in v. 11 that Yahweh sent down hailstones to bring the victory, so one is already dealing with intervention from the heavens. And we may compare the ancient Song of Deborah in Judges 5, where we hear that the stars fought against the Canaanite general Sisera. Second, a look at a map of biblical sites shows that Aijalon is about ten miles west of Gibeon. One might therefore understand Joshua to appeal to the rising sun on the east and to the setting just-past-full moon on the west to stand guard over the battle.[13] It is conceivable that the verbs may also have had some astrological content that escapes us.[14] But I suggest that what we have here is a poem that appeals to the sun and moon to take their part in the battle, a poem that later generations understood as an astronomical marvel.

My second example is the narrative of the rescue at the Sea (Exod. 13:17—14:31). We are told that the Israelites "went into the sea on dry ground, the waters forming a wall for them on their right and on their left" (14:22). This detail can well strike the modern reader as bizarre, the stuff of cartoons. Indeed, I have in my file a cartoon from *The New Yorker* showing precisely that scene: the Israelites are trudging along between two walls of water, and a man at the front is saying to his wife, "Of course it's damp underfoot! That strikes me as a very petty complaint to make at a time like this." Again, how might we deal with the narrative?[15]

For over a century, scholars have noticed unevennesses in the narrative of the rescue at the Sea. It is said on the one hand that the crossing of the sea was made possible by God's driving the sea back by means of a strong east wind (the middle portion of Exod. 14:21); on the other hand, it is said that Moses split the waters which, as we have already noted, formed a wall to the left and the right of the fleeing Israelites (the beginning and end of 14:21, and all of 14:22). Two different reasons are given for the detour in the route taken by the Israelites: in 13:17-18a, God led the Israelites by a roundabout way so that they might avoid a direct confrontation with the Egyptians; on the other hand, in 14:1-4 God led them back to the main road so that they would be seen by the Egyptians, so that the latter would attack and be defeated, so that God would "gain glory." Scholars are generally agreed that 13:17-18a and the middle portion of 14:21 are part of the earlier "Yahwistic Source," to which we have given a date of the tenth century B.C., and that 14:1-4 and the beginning and end of 14:21 and 14:22 are part of the later "Priestly Source," to which we have given a date of the sixth century B.C. (for both Sources, see Chapter 5). An early and relatively naturalistic account was evidently expanded in a later century with more details that appear to us to go against nature. Though it is impossible to be precise about the geographical details, one could imagine a skirmish between the Israelites and the Egyptian forces in the swampy area of Lake Balaḥ on the eastern edge of Nile Delta (30° 50' N., 32° 22' E.);[16] there the east wind could well have dried the shallow water temporarily.

To our inability to reconstruct the geography with any certainty, a further difficulty is added: the meaning of the Hebrew expression *yām-sûp*. This is the expression translated "Red Sea" (for example, in Exod. 13:18). There has been widespread support in the past few decades for an understanding of this expression as "Sea of Reeds" (the alternative translation in the NRSV); if "Reed Sea" was the original meaning of the expression, then there is encouragement to look for the escape across the water in the marshy area I have indicated. But the expression occurs in Jer. 48:21 with reference to the Edomites, and there it surely means "Red Sea." The Septuagint Greek translation (about 250 B.C.) understood its occurrences in Exodus to mean "Red Sea." It is likely that the Priestly Source so understood the expression; and if the Priestly Source understood the rescue to have taken place at the Red Sea, then, given the depth of that sea, that understanding would have encouraged the notion of walls of water in 14:22. If the Israelites' geographical knowledge was as limited as it seems to have been, then it is altogether plausible that, whatever the original meaning of *yām-sûp* was for the generation that experienced the deliverance firsthand, later generations of Israelites, after they had settled in Canaan, would have assumed that the great deliverance took place in the great body of water to the south—the Red Sea.[17]

What we seem to see in both these narratives—the sun's standing still and the rescue at the Sea—is a process of the heightening of the marvelous details by those who repeated the stories later on. For the other "signs and wonders"—for the plagues in Egypt, the pillar of cloud by day and pillar of fire by night that guided the Israelites, and all the rest—many naturalistic explanations have been advanced. But we lack any convincing reconstruction of what we ourselves might have recorded with a video camera, and we must be content simply to listen to the ancient narrative with an ear sympathetic to the celebratory tone intended by the original narrators, understanding the human urge to underline the wonder of whatever God was understood to have done.

The Nature of Oral Tradition

Behind the written sources that preserve these early narratives of the rescue from the Sea, Joshua's appeal to the sun and moon, and the rest, we must assume an extended period of oral tradition. Because these celebratory narratives must have been passed on orally from one generation to the next, we need to give some thought to how oral tradition works.

Any oral narrative tends to take on a particular *shape* as it is passed on. Watch how we narrate a collision of vehicles, or a house-fire. What are the conventions of the collision-of-vehicle narrative? "I was just driving along, minding my own business, when this truck appeared out of nowhere. . . ." Of the house-fire narrative? "So I said to my husband, 'Do you smell smoke?' . . . ." And we find that by the time we have told our narrative three times we have selected the details and the phrases of its telling, and thereafter we do not change the telling. Oral tradition *shapes,* and then *conserves.* It shapes and conserves even when the total reality of the event may be somewhat different.[18]

The professor under whom I studied in Holland once gave us a striking example of this process. During the time of the German occupation of Holland, in the Second World War, he was a leader in the Dutch resistance, and at one point he was captured by the Germans and escaped. The news of the Dutch resistance was spread essentially through oral tradition. Some irregular newsletters were reproduced on mimeograph machines in hidden corners of churches, but the radio was controlled by the Germans, and the news of the resistance therefore traveled from mouth to mouth. My professor, after he escaped, moved by night from barn to barn, and after a couple of weeks was able to return home for a quick visit. He discovered that news about him had preceded him: everyone knew he had been captured and escaped. But, he told us, every detail people told of the matter was wrong: the only details they got right were that he had been captured and escaped. He could correct the facts because, of course, he knew them. But the way people told the story made the incident far more plausible than the way it had actually happened. Oral tradition shapes and conserves; we must bear in mind this dynamic of stories as we deal with the narratives of the Old Testament.

The Importance of Not Drawing the Wrong Conclusion

At this point, it would be easy for readers to conclude that I am suggesting that these implausible events were just the product of the Israelites' imaginations. But to reduce our understanding of these events to "just imagination," "just hallucinations," or "just" anything, is one more example of the "it's-just-a" reaction I discussed in Chapter 1. I am suggesting that the present form of these narratives reflects: (1) at least in part the lack of a clear distinction between the natural order and what is presumed to be an interruption of that order, (2) patterns of oral tradition, and (3) other features in the culture of the Israelites. None of us was there at the time, and we must at least begin by listening to the ancient tradition if we would participate in its testimony.

A current historian has hit the right note. Caroline Walker Bynum, in her book *Holy Feast and Holy Fast, The Religious Significance of Food to Medieval Women*, makes this comment: "It should hardly be necessary to comment that I am not concerned with whether medieval accounts of phenomena such as stigmata, levitation, miraculous bodily changes, extended inedia, visions, and food-multiplication miracles are 'true.' As a phenomenologist would say, I 'bracket' the question of cause, either natural or supernatural, for such events. I am interested in what medieval people experienced; and while I have a historian's skepticism about all evidence, I also, as a historian, prefer to start my study of the past with what people in the past said themselves. . . . Thus when I say, for example, that a certain holy woman lived for years without eating, I do not mean to imply that this statement is true (or false) by twentieth-century standards of reporting or of scientific verification. I mean that such a story interested medieval people enough for them to record it and that it expressed a way of finding value and giving meaning that holy women, their chroniclers, and their admirers all shared."[19]

By the same token, those of us who hope to hear God in these narratives— or in our understanding of these narratives—may still do so. One of my colleagues once said that he lost his faith for the first time when he read the works of Sigmund Freud. When he had regained his faith, he had another look at Freud, and his reaction was, "Oh, so *that's* how God does it!" God may use our unconscious minds, our dreams, our shared visions. (Christians might add that Satan may use them as well, but that is another story.)

How then might we hear God in the implausible narratives? By listening to them with an open mind; by not closing off too soon our notions as to how God might have worked with our ancestors in the faith; by watching for signs and wonders in our own lives, and listening for the testimony of signs and wonders in the lives of our fellow Christians; and by disciplined cultivation of the response of gratitude and celebration for God's power and grace. Then we can participate in the process the psalmist depicts in his address to God: "One generation shall laud your works to another, and shall declare your mighty acts" (Ps. 145:4).

Notes

1. For a thorough exploration of the so-called "miracles" of Jesus, see now John P. Meier, *A Marginal Jew, Rethinking the Historical Jesus* II (New York: Doubleday, 1994), 509–1038.

2. Ephraim A. Speiser, "Nineveh," *IDB* 3:551.

3. Stewart Brand (ed.), *The Next Whole Earth Catalog* (Sausalito, Calif.: Point, 1980), 449–61.

4. Weems's book went through many editions in a few years, with variations in title. The edition in 1800 was titled, *A History of the Life and Death, Virtues and Exploits of George Washington* (Philadelphia: 1800); I have consulted Mason L. Weems, *The Life of Washington* (ed. Marcus Cunliffe; Cambridge, Mass.: Harvard University, 1962), 12. That edition is based on the ninth, titled *The Life of George Washington, With Curious Anecdotes, Equally Honourable to Himself and Exemplary to his Young Countrymen* (Philadelphia: 1809).

5. Herodotus, *Hist.,* 7.61.

6. Andrew R. Burn, *Alexander the Great and the Hellenistic World* (New York: Collier Books, 1962), 108; see Arrian, *Anabasis* 3.7.

7. See the maps in any standard biblical atlas, such as G. Ernest Wright and Floyd V. Filson (eds.), *The Westminster Historical Atlas to the Bible* (Philadelphia: Westminster, 1946), Plate XVII, or Herbert G. May (ed.), *Oxford Bible Atlas* (London and New York: Oxford University, 1974), 81.

8. For an illustration, see Theodor H. Gaster, "Cosmogony," *IDB* 1:703.

9. Gershom Scholem, *Sabbatai Ṣevi, The Mystical Messiah, 1626–1676* (Bollingen Series 93; Princeton: Princeton University, 1973), 417.

10. For a useful survey, see Gerhard von Rad, "*maPāk* in the OT," *TDNT* 1:76–80.

11. A useful survey is Bernhard W. Anderson, "Signs and Wonders," *IDB* 4:348–51.

12. Boling and Wright, *Joshua,* 274.

13. *Ibid.*, 288.

14. This is the view of John S. Holladay, Jr., "The Day(s) the *Moon* Stood Still," *JBL* 87 (1968), 166–78.

15. In what follows, I am heavily dependent on Childs, *Exodus,* 218–30; see also G. Ernest Wright, "Exodus, Book of," *IDB* 2:193; Richard J. Clifford, "Exodus," *New Jerome,* 49–50; P. Kyle McCarter, Jr., "Exodus," James L. Mays (ed.), *Harper's Bible Commentary* (San Francisco: Harper & Row, 1988), 144–46.

16. Clifford, "Exodus," 49.

17. See Bernard F. Batto, "The Reed Sea: *Requiescat in Pace,*" *JBL* 102 (1983), 27–35.

18. For a thorough investigation of the process, see Jan Vansina, *Oral Tradition, A Study in Historical Methodology* (Chicago: Aldine, 1965).

19. Caroline Walker Bynum, *Holy Feast and Holy Fast, The Religious Significance of Food to Medieval Women* (Berkeley: University of California, 1987), 8.

8

Lists

One kind of material in particular seems to get in the way of any smooth reading of the Old Testament: I refer to *lists*. Lists, it is true, do not bulk large in the Old Testament, but they certainly seem devoid of any value for our understanding of God.

There are first of all those long lists of names of people or names of places. In Genesis there are, for example, several genealogies. Genesis 5 gives ten names of the descent from Adam to Noah. It is here that one comes upon Methuselah, who is said to have lived 969 years (v. 27). Genesis 10 appears to be another genealogy, descendants of Noah's sons—but many of the names are nations in disguise (v. 6, "The descendants of Ham: Cush, Egypt, Put, and Canaan"). Gen. 11:10-32 offers another genealogy, in the style of Genesis 5, this time from Shem, the oldest son of Noah, down to Abram (= Abraham), again ten names. In Gen. 25:1-18, we have two genealogies: vv. 1-4 tell of descendants of Abraham by a wife Keturah, of whom we otherwise hear nothing (she is called a "concubine" in 1 Chron. 1:32), and vv. 12-18 list the descendants of Ishmael, Abraham's son through his concubine Hagar. Most baffling of all, the long chapter 36, containing 43 verses, consists of a genealogy of the descendants of Esau, verse after verse of tongue-twisting names.

One may also note in passing Gen. 46:8-27, a list of Jacob's descendants, set forth as a list of those who went down to Egypt, and Exod. 6:14-27, a list (curiously) of the sons of Reuben, Simeon, and Levi only. The list in Exodus 6 agrees with that in Genesis 46 for these three sons of Jacob, but the Exodus 6 list is more extended for Levi in order to give the genealogy of Aaron and Moses.

Genealogies appear elsewhere in the Old Testament too: the first nine chapters of 1 Chronicles are in part a summary of family lists one has already had. In the first chapter, the first four verses bring us from Adam down to the sons of Noah, and v. 27 brings us down to Abraham. Subsequent chapters list genealogies of the various sons of Jacob.

But the lists of the Old Testament are not confined to genealogies. In Numbers 1, we have a census tally of the Israelites at Sinai; in Numbers 2, there is a list of the arrangements of the tribes while encamped or on the march; and in Numbers 3, a reckoning of the Levites, clan by clan. Numbers 26 gives a second census list, one of the next generation. Numbers 32 indicates an allotment of the land in Transjordan to those tribes that will settle on the east side of the Jordan, and Numbers 33 contains an itinerary, a listing of the camping spots of the Israelites on their way from Egypt to Canaan.

Joshua 12 names the kings (and their territories) east of the Jordan whom Moses conquered (vv. 1-6), and then lists 31 cities west of the Jordan whose kings Joshua defeated (vv. 7-24). In chapters 13–21 of that book, there are territorial lists of the allocation of land west of the Jordan, so that again we have the lists of the villages belonging to the various tribes.

In the book of Judges, the bulk of chapter 1 is a list of cities in Palestine that the Israelites did *not,* as a matter of fact, conquer; this list is in contrast to the narrative in the book of Joshua.

Some "judges" are mentioned without any record of incidents in their lives: Tola and Jair in Judg. 10:1-5, and Ibzan, Elon, and Abdon in 12:8-15. The only detail remembered about Jair is the picturesque note that "he had thirty sons who rode on thirty donkeys, and they had thirty towns, which are in the land of Gilead" (10:4).

There is a roster of King David's warriors in 2 Sam. 23:8-39, and in 1 Chronicles 23–27 are lists of other functionaries traditionally appointed by David: Levites (chapter 23), priests (chapter 24), musicians (chapter 25), gatekeepers, treasurers, and other functionaries (chapter 26), and military and civil leaders (chapter 27), though as a matter of fact all these are given a descent from Levi.

In 1 Kings 4:7-19 is a list of the administrative districts established by King Solomon: these do not conform to the old tribal boundaries.

In Ezra 2 is a census of those who returned from Babylon to Jerusalem in the first return in the sixth century B.C.; the same list is duplicated in Neh. 7:6-73. The list even includes the number of animals that were brought back (Ezra 2:66-67; Neh. 7:68-69)! In Ezra 8:1-29 is a census of those who returned from Babylon to Jerusalem with Ezra in the fifth century B.C. In Ezra 10:18-44 is found a list of descendants of priests who had married foreign women. Nehemiah 3 lists 41 work details, the crews assigned by Nehemiah to rebuild the walls of Jerusalem, and the sections of the wall to which they were assigned. In Neh. 10:1-27 is a long list of the signatories to a covenant to support the second temple, a covenant evidently initiated by Nehemiah; Nehemiah 11 is a census list, and Neh. 12:1-26 is a census list from earlier times, evidently supplementing Ezra 2:36-40.

Beyond lists of names of persons or places, there are other lists in the Old Testament. One curious one is in Isa. 3:18-23, a list of types of garments, jewelry, and other accessories.

Beyond lists in the narrower sense, another type of material can be almost as tedious to the modern reader: the description of various details of the tabernacle in the wilderness, the temple of Solomon, the second temple, and the equipment of these structures and their priests. For example, there are in Exodus 25–28 directions for making the ark of the covenant, the table for the holy bread, the lampstand, the tabernacle, the altar, and the priestly vestments. The directions for the ark begin, "They shall make an ark of acacia wood; it shall be two and a half cubits long, a cubit and a half wide, and a cubit and a half high. You shall overlay it with pure gold, inside and outside you shall overlay it, and you shall make a molding of gold upon it all around" (Exod. 25:10-11). (As I explained in Chapter 6, the cubit is about a foot and a half in length.) The narrative of the construction of these objects largely repeats the instructions (Exodus 35–39). In Exod. 38:21-31, we even have a list of the amounts of metals used in the construction. Numbers 7 lists offerings from tribal leaders: the chapter contains 89 verses.

In 1 Kings 6–7, we have details of the building of Solomon's temple, and of his palace and other administrative buildings. In Ezekiel 40–48, we have a whole series of plans. The first four of these chapters (Ezekiel 40–43) set forth plans for a temple to replace Solomon's temple. "These are the dimensions of the altar by cubits (the cubit being one cubit and a handbreadth): its base shall be one cubit high, and one cubit wide, with a rim of one span around its edge . . ." (Ezek. 43:13). In Ezekiel 45–48, we have other plans: for the distribution of land to the Levites and priests (45:1-9), for the secular tribes (48:1-7), and so on. None of these plans in Ezekiel 40–48 was ever carried out.

Any of these lists that contain the names of men or women, or of places, are particularly hard to read aloud. Passages that contain the details of construction are tedious: who needs all those cubits? And so we ask ourselves, What can modern readers find in passages like these? In particular, can modern readers hear God in passages like these?

I begin by noting that not all the genealogies are in the Old Testament: the Gospels of both Matthew and Luke begin with genealogies of Jesus through Joseph, the husband of Mary. In Matt. 1:1-17, we have fourteen generations from Abraham to David, fourteen generations from David to the Babylonian exile, and fourteen generations from the Babylonian exile to Jesus. In Luke 3:23-38, the genealogy goes in the other direction, from Jesus, through Joseph, and back to Abraham, and behind Abraham back to Adam (and it is obvious that the two genealogies do not agree). Furthermore, the book of Revelation lists the number of those saved out of each tribe of Israel (Rev. 7:4-8).

It must be noted further that the lists, both in the Old and the New Testaments, are open to discrepancies; as I have said, it is clear to everyone that the genealogies of Jesus in Matthew and in Luke are not in agreement, though each purports to set forth his patrilineal descent. By the same token, the list of the twelve tribes of Israel in Revelation 7 is curious in that it omits the tribe of Dan altogether and then makes up the twelve by including both Manasseh and Joseph: we recall that, in Genesis, Manasseh was a son of Joseph.

Neither do the lists within the Old Testament agree. To take a simple example, the Hebrew text of Gen. 10:4 reads, "The sons of Javan: Elishah and Tarshish, Kittim and Dodanim" (and that is the rendering of the KJV), but 1 Chron. 1:7 reads "Rodanim" instead of "Dodanim," and since the Samaritan Pentateuch and the ancient Greek Version also read "Rodanim" in the Genesis passage, the RSV and NRSV have corrected the reading in Genesis to "Rodanim" (*r* and *d* are easily confused in the Hebrew alphabet). Nor, in a given passage, do the various traditions always agree about a given name: one wonders, for example, whether, in 1 Chron. 2:42, the first name that begins with "M" is Mesha (the traditional Hebrew reading) or Mareshah (the traditional Greek reading)—see the footnote in the NRSV. One can imagine how this kind of confusion might arise for an ancient copyist when faced with a long sequence of proper names. But such variation makes more urgent the question of what possible value such lists have for us.

Before we arrive at an answer to that question, however, we must ask what value the lists had for the first writers or reciters and the first audiences, and to answer the latter question, we must ask the origins of these various lists. Determining the origins of the lists, then, is our first task. But it must be admitted that scholars cannot supply complete information about the origin of every list and I shall offer, instead, a few examples that give an indication of how some of these lists came to be.

Origins of the Lists

Let us turn first to the genealogies in Genesis. It is easiest to begin with the genealogies in Genesis 5 (Adam to Noah) and 11:10-32 (Shem, the son of Noah, to Abraham): both these genealogies have the same style and format (for example, 5:12-14: "When Kenan had lived seventy years, he became the father of Mahalalel. Kenan lived after the birth of Mahalalel eight hundred and forty years, and had other sons and daughters. Thus all the days of Kenan were nine hundred and ten years; and he died"). Scholars have attributed these genealogies to the so-called "Priestly Source," one of the strands of tradition that fed into the present text of the first five books of the Old Testament (see Chapters 1 and 5), and, as we recall, they date the incorporation of the Priestly Source into Genesis to be during the Babylonian exile in the sixth century B.C. There is no way to establish the historical validity of Abraham (see again Chapter 5), let alone a secure date for him (though some have guessed at perhaps 1800 B.C.), so we are not justified in giving any *historical* value to the names in a genealogy before Abraham: its value is schematic (ten names plus ten names from Adam to Abraham), and the data of years given for these ancestors also indicate the genealogy's artificial nature.

It is also easy to see that the Priestly Source used these genealogies as summary transitions between the narratives of the creation of humankind and the narrative of Noah, and again between the narrative of Noah and the narrative of Abraham.

It is another matter with the so-called "Table of Nations" in Genesis 10. Rather than a vertical genealogy (father-to-son-to-grandson), this is a horizontal genealogy (multiple descendants in each generation), an attempt to understand the reality of the various lands, peoples, and languages known in Old Testament times by resort to a threefold division of humankind classified by a presumed descent through the three sons of Noah (Shem, Ham, and Japheth). What has evidently happened is a combining of a list from the Priestly Source (we remind ourselves, probably brought into Genesis in the sixth century B.C.) with fragments of an older list from the Yahwistic Source (shaped probably in the tenth century B.C.). The Priestly material consists of vv. 1a, 2-7, 20, 22-23, and 31-32; the fragments of the Yahwistic material consist of vv. 1b, 8-19 (the descendants of Ham), 21, and 24-30 (the descendants of Shem).

Scholars have long noted that genealogies both in the ancient Near East and in non-Western societies today have a function not so much to chart literal biological family trees as to set forth the social relationships that are perceived between clans and tribes at a given period.[1] This seems to be the case with the genealogy in Genesis 10. What purport to be "descendants" (literally "sons") of each of the sons of Noah, when identifiable, are cities, peoples, or nations. They are not divided up by language group, as we might expect. Thus, the descendants of Shem (vv. 21-31) include not only the peoples that we know spoke "Semitic" languages (for example, in v. 22, Asshur = Assyria, in present-day Iraq; Aram = the Arameans, in present-day Syria), but also those who did not: Elam (v. 22) was a people centered in the southwest of the Iranian plateau, and they spoke a language unrelated to any other known. On the other hand, Canaan (v. 6) is reckoned among the sons of Ham, though the language of the Canaanites we reckon today as one of the Semitic languages. Some of the "descendants" of Ham (vv. 6-20) are nations in the center of attention for Israel, like Egypt (v. 6), but many of the other names are vague terms for peoples to the south and east of Israel: Cush (v. 6), for example, is a general term for dark-skinned peoples to the south of Egypt. Surprisingly, the name Lud (v. 22) is pluralized to Ludim (v. 13) and given contrasting ancestry: the name evidently refers to the Lydians, a people in Asia Minor (present-day Turkey). The "descendants" of Japheth (vv. 2-5) are a very mixed lot indeed. Javan (v. 2) must be identified with the Ionians, that is, Greek-speaking people, but Madai (v. 2) are the Medes, a people living in the northwest of the Iranian plateau, and Ashkenaz (v. 3) are evidently the Scythians, a people centered in what is now southern Russia and the Caucasus. In short, these lists reflect a lively, if primitive, notion of the relation of nations as known by Israel, and the two sources evidently reflect the knowledge of the Israelites at two different periods in history: the commercial relations Israel had with other nations in Solomon's time, in the tenth century B.C. (the Yahwistic Source) and the knowledge of other nations gained during the Babylonian exile in the sixth century B.C. (the Priestly Source). Many of the names in the Priestly material here are identical with names found in Ezekiel, who was a prophet during the Babylonian exile.

The origin of the listing in Gen. 25:1-4 is a mystery; the names suggest an Arabian locale. It may be noted in passing that Sheba and Dedan (v. 3) occur also in 10:7 with another ancestry.

Both Gen. 25:12-18 (the descendants of Ishmael) and Genesis 36 (the descendants of Esau) are from the Priestly tradition. The first of these points to various tribal groups in Arabia. The second is an elaborate reckoning of Edomite lineages, which may in some way have come into the possession of authorities in Jerusalem.[2]

The list of names in Gen. 46:8-27 evidently had a complicated history. There is a close relationship between it and the census list in Numbers 26, and at least one scholar suggests that the list in Genesis 46 is derived from that in Numbers 26.[3] In Genesis 46, it appears to be an addition to the Priestly tradition; on the other hand, many of the names seem to be old, the types of names current in the time of the judges (eleventh century B.C.).[4]

Some of the genealogies in 1 Chronicles 1—9 reproduce names from earlier material in the Old Testament (the Pentateuch, Joshua, Judges, Samuel, and Kings), but other names are found nowhere else, and, interestingly, from time to time particular sources are cited. For example, in the section on the tribe of Simeon (4:24-43), we have first a family list (vv. 24-27) that is based on Gen. 46:10 = Exod. 6:15 and on Num. 26:12-13. Then there follows a list of towns and cities belonging to Simeon (vv. 28-33), which is based on Josh. 15:26-32, 42 and 19:2-7. Thereafter, there is a statement that the tribe of Simeon kept a genealogical record (v. 33): that record is doubtless reflected in the fresh material that follows, namely a list of leaders and clans of the tribe (vv. 34-43) who were half nomads.[5]

Let us turn now to lists other than genealogies. With regard to the census list in Numbers 1, scholars are not sure how old the list is: some of the names are of a type that is very old, like Amminadab (Num. 1:7),[6] but other names, like Nethanel (Num. 1:8), are of a type that seems to have been current only in the postexilic period (for Nethanel, compare Ezra 10:22; Neh. 12:21);[7] we surmise therefore that what we have here is a late construction in which some very old names are supplemented by names current when the construction was made.

Both the land allotments in Numbers 32 and the itinerary from Egypt to Canaan in Numbers 33 appear to combine early material from the Yahwistic Source (tenth century) and late material from the Priestly Source (sixth century), but it is impossible now to establish the antiquity or the reliability of the lists.

The list in Josh. 12:9-31 (the 31 cities whose kings were defeated by the Israelites) must be a very ancient list: it disagrees with the "standard" story set forth in chapters 1—11.[8] As for the list of land allotments west of the Jordan, in Joshua 13–21, it is evidently a combination of a number of documents. For example, the old detailed boundary lists preserved for Judah (15:1-12), Ephraim (16:1-8), Manasseh (17:7-11), and Benjamin (18:12-20) seem to derive from a boundary document from a time before the monarchy (eleventh century B.C.). On the other hand, the province list of the cities of Judah (15:20-63), which defines a larger area than that set forth in vv. 1-12 (see above), appears to derive from a reorganization of administrative districts made during Solomon's time (tenth century B.C.).[9]

The listing of David's warriors in 2 Samuel 23 must be very old: the first ten warriors in the list after Asael (v. 24) come from Judah—indeed, most are from towns within a narrow radius of Bethlehem, David's birthplace, and there is no indication in the total list of an attempt to gather names representing "all Israel."[10] On the other hand, the long lists of David's Levitical personnel in 1 Chronicles 23–27 clearly reflect the organization of temple officiants at the time the books of Chronicles were prepared (probably the end of the fifth century B.C.), all shaped by earlier genealogies such as that of the Levites in chapter 6, and anachronistically put back into the time of David (tenth century B.C.).

The census lists and similar lists in Ezra and Nehemiah are doubtless derived from historical documents of the time, but there is also evidence that the lists come from a variety of sources and are not always internally consistent.

The specifications of the tabernacle and its furnishings (Exodus 25–28) and the notice of the construction of these objects (Exodus 35–39) are derived, as one might expect, from the Priestly Source. Scholars suggest that an ancient "tent of meeting" tradition was historically derived from the days of Israel's wilderness wandering; that the tent of meeting tradition was overlaid by a "tabernacle" tradition, which may reflect a shelter for the ark of the covenant at Shiloh or a shrine erected by David for the ark; and that the tabernacle tradition in turn was evidently overlaid by details in Solomon's temple, as retained by the Priestly Source in the sixth century B.C.[11] In short, this material has a complicated history of transmission covering several centuries. The details of the building of Solomon's temple in 1 Kings 6–7 are attributed by some scholars to temple archives, but the way in which the details do not cohere and the remarkable fact that the statement about the foundation and actual building of the temple comes at the end of chapter 6, not at its beginning, have led others to suggest that what we have here is a digest of the oral tradition of various craftsmen.[12] The material in Ezekiel 40–48 on the plans for a new temple and other details for a rebuilt Jerusalem is based on a vision of the prophet Ezekiel about the future Jerusalem: since Ezekiel had been a priest (Ezek. 1:3), one can understand how this material would have been produced.

To summarize: The greater proportion of the lists that occur in the Pentateuch (Genesis through Deuteronomy) are to be attributed to the Priestly Source (sixth century B.C.), but the fact that these lists were collected and became part of the Pentateuchal tradition at a particular time does not imply that they were created out of whole cloth at that time; to the contrary, many of them give evidence of great antiquity. Only rarely can we trace intact lists from earlier traditions, as we can in the genealogy of Genesis 10. Some of the lists in Joshua and Judges reach back to pre-monarchical times, and some of the lists in Samuel and Kings maintain the historical value of the times to which they pertain—and the same may be said of the later material from Ezra and Nehemiah. On the other hand, the lists in Chronicles, which purport to reach back to high antiquity, have been thoroughly reshaped by the interests of the time of their preparation (fifth century B.C.). In short, sometimes these lists reflect historical reality, and sometimes they reflect the perceptions of a late period about what that late period understood to be the reality centuries earlier.

Motivations for the Lists

Now we are in a better position to try to set forth some reasons why those who compiled, collected, and preserved the lists did so. I can think of five motivations, which are not mutually exclusive, for these lists: (1) exuberance, (2) orientation, (3) legitimation, (4) completeness, and (5) antiquarianism.

1. *Exuberance* is perhaps the least important of the motivations, and it may only rarely be relevant, but I cannot rule it out altogether. Exuberance is the impulse that moves a reciter or author to expand a category as far as possible. Garrison Keillor, the host of the radio show "Prairie Home Companion," has perfected the recitation of all 87 counties of Minnesota in alphabetical order in less than a minute. Such a feat, of course, has no utilitarian value at all, but it brings astonishment nonetheless. People in oral cultures pride themselves on their capacity for memorization, and that trait can easily lead to expansionist lists. The long list of various garments and adornments in Isa. 3:18-23 is an interpolation in the midst of the poem in 3:16-17 + 24, and I can think of no other motivation for it than the exuberance of a redactor or copyist.

2. *Orientation* is a far more common motivation. There were no wall maps in those days, but with a listing of the territories distributed to the tribes west of the Jordan, one could be oriented to one's location within the tribal holdings. One could know where one fit geographically. By the same token, the details of construction of Solomon's temple in 1 Kings 6 could remind hearers of the plan of a shrine that they had visited only from time to time, or could give an impression of the temple to those who had never seen it.

Similarly, the genealogies gave Israelites an awareness of how their clans were related to each other, instructing hearers how they were connected to their fellows. In a long recitation of a genealogy or of a census list, one could listen for the mention of one's own lineage. The lists thus gave to everyone the chance to be located within one's people and within one's land.

3. *Legitimation* allowed the genealogies of those in power to be used as credentials for their power. A famous example is the genealogy of Zadok, the priest in David's time. Zadok's father is given as Ahitub in 2 Sam. 8:17, and his descent is given twice, in 1 Chron. 6:3-8 and 50-53 (compare 24:1-3); there is a strong suspicion among scholars that the genealogy in Chronicles is

a traditional attempt to legitimate Zadok as a descendant of Aaron,[13] over against the priest Abiathar, who was banished by Solomon (1 Kings 2:26). In the postexilic period, such a priestly genealogy became crucial when priests of the Zadokite lineage were reestablished in Jerusalem at the time of the building of the second temple (compare Ezek. 40:46; Ezra 7:2).

There was doubtless much tension between those who returned from exile, who are listed in the census lists of that time, and those more humble folk who remained in the Jerusalem area; the term "people of the land" was used in the time of Ezra (fifth century B.C.) to refer to the heterogeneity of the half-heathen population with whom the returned Jews had intermarried (Ezra 10:2). The genealogies and census lists would then have been useful in that period for the returnees and their families to legitimate their descent.

The motive of legitimation is turned in an ironic direction in the book of Ruth, which tells how the Moabite Ruth became a great-grandmother of King David (Ruth 4:17). This notion of a non-Israelite ancestor for David needed at a later time to be supplemented by the patrilineal genealogy of David from Judah (4:18-22).[14]

4. *Completeness* describes a mentality of meticulousness that is represented particularly by the Priestly Source in the Old Testament. This mentality takes it for granted that careful recording, accuracy in detail, and a standard operating procedure all redound to the glory of God. This mentality encourages the compilation and preservation of lists.

One notable way that this urge for completeness functions in Genesis is in giving an account of descent for collateral figures in genealogies that are not in the direct line of the promise. Thus, even though it is through Abraham that the promise will be fulfilled, and Abraham's descent is reckoned from Noah's son Shem (Gen. 11:10-32), the descendants of Noah's sons Ham and Japheth are also given (Gen. 10:2-20), as are the descendants from Abraham's brother Nahor (Gen. 22:20-24). Again, although the promise continues with Isaac, the son born to Abraham and Sarah, we have a genealogy of the descendants of Abraham from his wife Keturah (Gen. 25:1-6) and from his son Ishmael, born of his concubine Hagar (Gen. 25:12-18). Finally, even though the promise continues through Isaac's son Jacob, descendants are supplied of his twin brother Esau as well (Genesis 36).

In this mentality, as we have seen, there is a belief that, along with the names and numbers of the various groups that came back in the first return from Babylon to Jerusalem, it is important to record the numbers of animals as well (Ezra 2:66-67).

5. *Antiquarianism,* simply collecting all one can from the past, is surely the motive for the genealogy from Adam to Noah (Genesis 5): by the logic of the

narrative itself, all those except Noah were destroyed. There must have been an insistent urge to gather up archival material preserved in Jerusalem, when the city was about to fall in 587 B.C. And surely an antiquarian interest led to the preservation of the genealogies and the land allotments of the northern tribes, since the fall of Samaria in 721 B.C., the fall of Jerusalem in 587 B.C., and the effort to reconstruct life in Jerusalem to the exclusion of the north after 538 B.C. would render the northern material steadily less urgent for any current usefulness.

Hearing God in the Lists

We are now in a position to ask the crucial question of this chapter: Can we hear God in any of these lists, and if so, how? The first thing to be said is that Jesus, according to the tradition about him, rejected any status based on family relationships. ". . . A woman in the crowd raised her voice and said to him, 'Blessed is the womb that bore you and the breasts that nursed you!' But he said, 'Blessed rather are those who hear the word of God and obey it!'" (Luke 11:27-28). Again, "A crowd was sitting around him; and they said to him, 'Your mother and your brothers and sisters are outside, asking for you.' And he replied, 'Who are my mother and my brothers?' And looking at those who sat around him, he said, 'Here are my mother and my brothers! Whoever does the will of God is my brother and sister and mother'" (Mark 3:32-34). For Jesus, what is crucial is not his family identity but his response to God, and the relationships in the Kingdom of God replace family ties.

On the other hand, we must take note that Matthew and Luke are just as concerned to offer genealogies for Jesus as the Old Testament is to offer genealogies for Abraham, Moses, David, or any other central figure. We must hold in tension Jesus' rejection of biological family relationships and the evangelists' concern for Jesus' descent to satisfy the Old Testament expectation that the Messiah will be a son of David.

Jesus' own lack of interest in his genealogy is congruent with the remark recorded of John the Baptist about the complacency of his hearers in their ancestry. "Do not begin to say to yourselves, 'We have Abraham as our ancestor'; for I tell you, God is able from these stones to raise up children to Abraham" (Luke 3:8).

Jesus was not interested in the details of the construction of the temple in his day. "As he came out of the temple, one of his disciples said to him, 'Look, Teacher, what large stones and what large buildings!' Then Jesus asked him, 'Do you see these great buildings? Not one stone will be left here upon another; all will be thrown down'" (Mark 13:1-2). Jesus is remembered as judging the temple to be doomed; the details of the building plans of the temple that are recorded in the Old Testament will then have hardly been of great moment to him.

One may assume then that the lists in the Old Testament would not have been of prime importance to Jesus. Even given this assumption, however, we may still discern some positive theological value in some of them.

Let us begin with the genealogies; I offer four observations about them.

First, with few exceptions, they pay no attention to descent through females. The participation of women in the array of generations is almost ignored altogether. Even in the notice given of Jesus' siblings in the Gospel of Mark, we have the names of each of his four brothers but only the collective notice of his "sisters" (Mark 6:3). From this perspective, a perusal of the genealogies is an occasion to confess the sin of male domination, a sin that is still very much with us.[15] We shall return to this matter in Chapter 12.

Second, the genealogies remind us of our own mortality and of how quickly our names are forgotten. A century ago, our great-grandparents were roughly as old as we are today. Yet very few of us can name all eight of our great-grandparents, including the maiden names of our great-grandmothers. This suggests that a hundred years from now our very names will have been forgotten by all but a few. Yet, here in the Old Testament are arrays of hard-to-pronounce names of people who lived 75 or 100 generations ago. These people may not be our ancestors, but they are remembered as *somebody's* ancestors, and the preservation of these names reminds us of the immensely complex network of human relationships, all those folk who have contributed to our gene pool. That reminder can give even the list of Edomite names in Genesis 36 some redeeming purpose for us.

Third, the genealogies in Genesis 10 relate all of humankind to each other. Paul's word at Athens, that "from one ancestor he [God] made all nations to inhabit the whole earth" (Acts 17:26), is set forth schematically in Genesis 10. Every human being is a cousin of every other human being.

Fourth, the genealogies in the Old Testament concentrate on the specific lines of those whom God has chosen. According to the testimony of the Old Testament, in Noah's line God chose Abraham. In Abraham's line God chose Jacob. In Levi's line God chose Moses and Aaron, and in Judah's line God chose David. God is not neutral in regard to the array of humankind but chooses specific people for the divine purpose. That mystery of divine choice has already been touched on in Chapters 2 and 5. It is grace, however, and not privilege: we recall Amos's pronouncement (Amos 3:1-2), and John the Baptist's remark about "children of Abraham."

In these ways, then, the genealogies can remind us of God's purpose.

By the same token, the allocation of tribal territories in Numbers 32 and Joshua 13–21 remind us of the way in which the covenant people functioned in history. It is hard to imagine how the covenant people could have survived, at least for several centuries, without a specific territory in which to live through their history (we discussed this matter in Chapter 6). Their history was lived at a specific time and in a specific place, and as God has chosen a people, so he has chosen a land for that people. Christians are no longer tied to a specific land; we recall Jesus' word to the Samaritan woman, recorded in John 4:21, "Woman, believe me, the hour is coming when you will worship the Father neither on this mountain [Gerizim] nor in Jerusalem" (see Chapter 6), but issues such as a clean environment, right use of economic resources, and an adequate food supply continue to be central for us, and to that degree the specificity of land allocations is at least symbolically useful as a reminder: we must not spiritualize our faith.[16]

The presumed details of the tent and tabernacle in the wilderness, the plans of Solomon's temple, and Ezekiel's vision of a restored temple in a restored Jerusalem are clearly no more directly relevant to Christians than the laws of animal sacrifice are (see Chapter 3). Indeed, we recall that the temple of Herod was destroyed in A.D. 70 at the conclusion of the first Roman–Jewish War. But it must not be overlooked that Rev. 11:1-2 preserves the memory of a time when the notion of measuring the temple was still important, even to Christians. The "temple" in this passage is evidently intended symbolically to refer to the holy and righteous Christians; later in the chapter (11:19) we hear of the heavenly temple being opened—the heavenly archetype for any earthly one. These passages in the book of Revelation then suggest that the old passages of measuring the temple continued to shape the imagination of Christians even after the Jewish temple had been destroyed.

There is no simple answer to the question of whether we can hear God in the lists of the Old Testament. We cannot ignore them in favor of a "religion in general"; but we cannot insist either that they are all heavy with revelatory power. They are reminders of the specificities of the Old Testament faith, wherein God is understood to have chosen specific people and specific places for the living of covenantal obedience, reminding us in turn of our calling to be responsive to God in our own times and places.

Notes

1. See Robert R. Wilson, "Genealogy, Genealogies," *ABD* 2:929–32, and, in more detail, Marshall D. Johnson, *The Purpose of the Biblical Genealogies, With Special Reference to the Setting of the Genealogies of Jesus* (Cambridge: Cambridge University,

1969, 1989); Robert R. Wilson, *Genealogy and History in the Biblical World* (Yale Near Eastern Researches 7; New Haven: Yale University, 1977).

2. Claus Westermann, *Genesis 12–36* (Minneapolis: Augsburg, 1985), 561.

3. Ephraim A. Speiser, *Genesis* (AB 1; Garden City, NY: Doubleday, 1964), 347.

4. Claus Westermann, *Genesis 37–50* (Minneapolis: Augsburg, 1986), 159.

5. Jacob M. Myers, *I Chronicles* (AB 12; Garden City, NY: Doubleday, 1965), XLVI–XLVII, XLIX–LIII.

6. Martin Noth, *Numbers* (OTL; Philadelphia: Westminster, 1968), 18; for the first part of the name, see Herbert B. Huffmon, *Amorite Personal Names in the Mari Texts, A Structural and Lexical Study* (Baltimore: The Johns Hopkins University, 1965), 196–98.

7. John Sturdy, *Numbers* (The Cambridge Bible Commentary on the New English Bible; Cambridge: Cambridge University, 1976), 14.

8. J. Alberto Soggin, *Joshua* (OTL; Philadelphia: Westminster, 1972), 143; compare Boling and Wright, *Joshua*, 322.

9. Boling and Wright, *Joshua*, 70.

10. P. Kyle McCarter, Jr., *II Samuel* (AB 9; Garden City, NY: Doubleday, 1984), 500–501.

11. See G. Henton Davies, "Tabernacle," *IDB* 4:498–506; Childs, *Exodus*, 530–37.

12. John Gray, *I & II Kings* (OTL; Philadelphia: Westminster, 1970), 157–58.

13. See the discussion in Myers, *I Chronicles*, 45–46; Richard W. Corney, "Zadok the priest," *IDB* 4:928–29. But a different explanation is offered in Cross, *Canaanite Myth and Hebrew Epic*, 207–15, followed by McCarter, *II Samuel*, 255–57.

14. Edward E. Campbell, Jr., *Ruth* (AB 7; Garden City, NY: Doubleday, 1975), 168–69, 172–73.

15. For this matter, see Alice L. Laffey, *An Introduction to the Old Testament, A Feminist Perspective* (Philadelphia: Fortress Press, 1988).

16. For an exploration of these issues see Walter Brueggemann, *The Land* (Philadelphia: Fortress Press, 1977).

9

The Prophets

~

From modes of narrative we turn to the words of the prophets. At first glance, one would assume that it is easier to hear God in the discourses of the prophets than in narrative: after all, the prophets often begin their words with "Thus says the Lord," or at least they imply it. How easy, we may assume, to hear God in God's own words! But as we shall see, there are a variety of theological tangles here too.

For Christians, the prophets have always loomed large in the Old Testament: beside the Psalms and perhaps the narratives in Genesis, it is the books of the prophets that Christians read and use more than all other Old Testament material. Shelves of books have been published for Christians on how to read the prophets, particularly in the past few decades. Even so, there are many aspects of the material in the prophets that Christians may misunderstand, and it is useful to try to clarify not only the significance of prophetic material for ancient Israel but how Christians may hear God in it today.

I begin with a matter that always leaves me astonished: the prophets' self-understanding, given the understanding of "word" in the Old Testament. I touched on this matter of "word" in Chapter 1; I cited Isa. 55:10-11 as an illustration of the sense Israel had of the power of words to do good or ill, and above all, of course, the power of God's word to do good or ill. God's word gets things done. But what, one must wonder, was the prophets' understanding of what they were doing? They must have been awe-struck at their own calling. At the moment of Isaiah's call, he experienced a divine seraph taking a glowing coal with tongs from the sacrificial altar of the temple and touching his lips to make them fit to voice the word of God (Isa. 6:6-7). When Jeremiah experienced a call from God to be a prophet, his only thought was that he did not know how to speak for God because he was too young (Jer. 1:6). Ezekiel, in exile in Babylon, experienced an awesome vision of God's throne chariot (Ezekiel 1; I shall discuss that vision in Chapter 10), and when the spirit of God sent him to his fellow exiles, he sat stunned for seven days (Ezek. 3:15). What thoughts went through the minds of the prophets, convinced as they were that they were charged to speak the very words of God Almighty? And what thoughts went through the minds of their listeners, if they took the prophetic claim seriously? We need to hold these questions in our own minds as we ponder the words of the prophets.

I shall not attempt a full history of the prophets; there are plenty of treatments of the topic.[1] As far back as we can trace in the Syria–Palestine area, there were prophetlike figures, men and women who were believed to bring messages from a given deity (the documents from Mari, in northeast Syria, in the eighteenth century B.C., give evidence of these), or who fell into trances, thus leaving bystanders convinced they were in touch with a deity (the Egyptian story of Wen-Amun, from the eleventh century B.C., gives an amusing example of such a prophet in Phoenicia, present-day Lebanon).[2]

In the tradition of Israel, one source calls Abraham a prophet (Gen. 20:7), and Aaron and Miriam are called prophets (Exod. 7:1; 15:20), as indeed is Moses himself (Deut. 18:18). Samuel was known as a prophet (1 Sam. 3:20) as well as serving as a judge (1 Sam. 7:15-17, compare 8:1). Saul, before he became king, is said to have fallen in with a group of prophets, who appear to have been ecstatics (1 Sam. 10:5-13). There are extensive narratives of the prophet Nathan in David's court (2 Samuel 7; 12; 1 Kings 1, tenth century), of the prophets Elijah and Elisha (1 Kings 17-19; 21; 2 Kings 1–9, ninth century), and of many other named and nameless prophets in these centuries—for example, Ahijah, who designated Jeroboam to revolt against Rehoboam and become king over the northern kingdom after Solomon's death (1 Kings 11:26-40).

Then, during the next four centuries, a whole series of figures arose whose words were deemed memorable enough to be gathered in separate, named collections. In the eighth century, there were: Amos, a southerner who went north to preach; Hosea, a northerner; Micah, a rural southerner; and, above all, Isaiah, who had an enormous and continuing impact. The seventh century saw others; most notable was Jeremiah, but there were also collections made of the sayings of Zephaniah, who prophesied a few years earlier than Jeremiah, and of Nahum and Habakkuk, who were contemporaries of Jeremiah. From early in the sixth century, we have Obadiah and another figure whose impact was decisive, Ezekiel. Ezekiel had been a priest in Jerusalem and was deported in 597 B.C. to Babylon, where he prophesied. Then, still among the exiles at the end of that period (about 540 B.C.) we hear a nameless prophet whose words were preserved in Isaiah 40–55: scholars call him "Second Isaiah" or "Deutero-Isaiah." At the end of that century, three other figures emerge who prophesied to those who returned from exile: Haggai, Zechariah, and a nameless prophet whom scholars call "Third Isaiah" or "Trito-Isaiah," whose utterances are preserved in Isaiah 56–66 (see Chapter 10). The words preserved in the book of Joel and of Malachi probably date from the following (fifth) century. (As we saw in Chapter 5, the books of Daniel and Jonah, though reckoned among the prophetic books, are of a different sort.)

The collections of these oracles (prophetic utterances), unlike books of more recent times, underwent much editing in the ensuing centuries, in the course of which time, evidently, the books were often expanded by adding oracles from other, anonymous prophets who may have been disciples or followers of the tradition of the named prophets. Scholars have expended great effort to try to discern the dates and contexts of these various oracles, but their results often remain more a matter of probability than of certainty. I shall tread lightly on these matters in this chapter, referring the reader to commentaries on the specific prophetic books.

I discuss in this chapter some key matters that bear on our hearing God today through the prophets: the prophets as predictors; the prophets as social reformers; the question of the mode by which the prophets gained their revelation; and the time-boundedness of the prophets. I then suggest how Christians today might hear God in the oracles proclaimed by the prophets. I save until the next chapter a consideration of a related matter, the development of the apocalyptic outlook.

The Prophets as Predictors

Our current usage of the word "prophet" suggests predicting: we speak of economic prophets, or weather prophets. Christians for centuries understood the biblical prophets to be predicting events of later centuries, notably the coming of Jesus Christ. Many handbooks concentrate on these so-called "messianic" prophecies—passages that are understood to point to Jesus Christ. Indeed, the New Testament itself affirms this approach: in 1 Pet. 1:10-11 we read, "Concerning this salvation, the prophets who prophesied of the grace that was to be yours made careful search and inquiry, inquiring about the person or time that the Spirit of Christ within them indicated when it testified in advance to the sufferings destined for Christ and the subsequent glory."

The book of Isaiah in particular has been used by Christians in this way— for example, the "Immanuel" passage in Isa. 7:14 (compare Matt. 1:23), the passages announcing that "The people that walked in darkness have seen a great light" (9:2-7) and "a shoot shall come out from the stump of Jesse" (11:1-9), and, above all, the description of the suffering servant in 52:13—53:12. Indeed, the book of Isaiah has seemed to be so full of such predictions that this prophet was mentioned above all in the traditional schemes; for example, the second stanza of the Christian carol "Lo, How a Rose E'er Blooming" begins, "Isaiah 'twas foretold it." But Isaiah is not the only book that has been used this way; in Mic. 5:2 is the prediction of the birth of the Messiah in Bethlehem, interpreted in Matt. 2:6 as referring to Jesus.

Since the advent of the historical-critical method, however (see Chapter 1), it has been understood that the prophets' eyes were on their own day and their own immediate future. They spoke out on the issues of their own time—the oppression of the poor by the rich, false worship, and, in general, the immediate destiny of the covenant people. By this understanding, the literature of the prophets is seen to be not a sequence of scarcely read writings punctuated by the few passages that resonate with Christian events, but, rather, a rich array of pronouncements relevant to the life of the historical periods in which the given prophets lived.

What then becomes of prophetic passages that have been taken to refer to events in the New Testament? This question becomes a major riddle for students in my classes who struggle to maintain the integrity of their faith-understanding of these passages. Some will ask: Could the Holy Spirit not bring material to the lips of the prophet, the meaning of which only became apparent with the coming of Jesus Christ? I try to press these questioners. Can one imagine a given prophet puzzled by the meaning of his own utterance, and, in effect, simply urging an equally puzzled audience to remember and record a given oracle in the assurance that centuries after it was uttered its meaning will finally become clear?

Such a scenario is unacceptable. It is more fruitful to try to understand these passages—the ones that have been understood to predict Jesus Christ— as we do the rest of the utterances of the prophets, as utterances meaningful in their own time, and then see how such passages have been interpreted in later centuries, especially by the New Testament and the early Christian church. Such an exercise broadens our awareness of how such texts may work.

Let us try the exercise with Isa. 9:2-7. Verse 2 (along with v. 1, not ordinarily linked to the passage in reading) is cited in Matt. 4:15-16: there, Jesus' action in moving from Nazareth to Capernaum is understood to fulfill Isaiah's words. The passage has been a traditional text for Christmas eve; it appears in Handel's *Messiah* (though without the more militaristic vv. 3-5) as part of the Christmas section of that work. But how might it have been intended and heard in Isaiah's own day?

In the year 733 B.C., the Assyrian king Tiglath-Pileser III conquered the northern Israelite territories of Zebulun and Naphtali; it was a time of low morale even in the south, in Jerusalem, where Isaiah was active. The prophet alludes to the old tradition of holy war (see Chapter 6) by which Yahweh had brought Israel victory, by the leadership of the judge Gideon, over the Midianites, a people from the east (Judges 6–8). Such a victory, according to the passage in Isaiah, will happen again under a new king who is coming on the scene. Whether the passage assumes that the king has just been crowned and will bring military victory by God's guidance, or whether it assumes that a royal son has just been born who will grow up to be the king who brings victory, is uncertain from the text. In Israel, as in other nations in the ancient Near East, a king, on his coronation day, was understood to have been adopted as a son of God (this is the meaning of Ps. 2:7, part of a coronation psalm), so the passage in Isaiah may be a coronation ode. On the other hand, it may be a birth ode. In any event, the throne names of the new king will reflect both his prowess in war and peace ("Wonder of a Counselor," "Prince of Peace") and the marvels of God ("God is Almighty, Father Forever"). Whether the new king to whom Isaiah is referring is Hezekiah, who came to the throne about 715 B.C., or some other ruler is impossible to say.

This poem was too marvelous to forget. No matter how disappointing a given king's reign has been, one can always hope and pray for better when a new king comes on the throne, and to that end Isaiah's ode continued to be useful. When kingship came to an end, as it did in 587 B.C., then the survivors of the fall of Judah remembered Isaiah's ode as a promise of better days ahead when God would restore kingship once more. And this was how people understood the ode through all the centuries ahead.

Christians have solved the kingship problem, since Jesus Christ is remembered as having come into Jerusalem peaceably riding on an ass, following the words of Zech. 9:9 (I shall discuss this passage in Chapter 10); for Christians, Jesus Christ is king of kings and lord of lords (Rev. 19:16) and more a prince of peace than any king in Isaiah's day could ever have been. In this way, Isaiah's ode, full of meaning when it was first used, has take on a new life for Christians and is therefore an utterly appropriate reading for Christmas eve.

Similar remarks may be made regarding Isa. 11:1-9. This passage, too, speaks of an ideal king who will rule with justice, and the peace of paradise will return in his reign (vv. 6-9): "the wolf will live with the lamb, the leopard shall lie down with the kid" (v. 6). I would understand these phrases to be metaphors for international peace, wherein the great empires no longer prey on small nations (compare the description in 5:29 of Assyria as a lion seizing her prey). This kind of thinking is appropriate to Isaiah in the eighth century B.C.

The passage in Isa. 7:14 ("the young woman is with child and shall bear a son, and shall name him Immanuel") is more complicated for Christians to sort out. The whole passage, vv. 1-17, describes an encounter between Isaiah and the young king Ahaz of Judah, who is unnerved by the threat of the king of Syria (Rezin) and the king of (the northern kingdom of) Israel (Pekah); these latter kings threatened to invade Judah and depose Ahaz unless he agreed to join their coalition against the growing threat of Assyria, farther to the east. Isaiah tries to reassure Ahaz by giving him a "sign," something on which he can set his mind that will remind him of God's concern. The sign, it turns out, is the birth of a baby who will be called "Immanuel." It is not a miraculous birth; the designation of the mother is not "a virgin," as the KJV has it, but "the young woman." Strikingly, "Immanuel" in Hebrew means not only "God is with us" but "God is against us"; that is to say, *God is involved with us one way or the other*, but how God is involved with us depends to a great degree on how Ahaz himself will respond.

Matthew took v. 14 and quoted it in the version he knew, the Septuagint (Greek) translation, which, as we recall, had been made about 200 B.C. in Alexandria, Egypt (see Chapter 1). In that version, curiously, the "young woman" had been rendered as "virgin"; Matthew was therefore able to use the passage to reinforce his testimony about the virgin birth of Jesus. Furthermore, as we know, Matthew took the more hopeful meaning of "Immanuel," that is, "God is with us." Where does this leave Christians? What, we may ask, does Isa. 7:14 *really* mean?

We can say this. Matthew is on fire with the good news of the coming of Jesus, and, of all the gospel writers, he favored most particularly the use of Old Testament texts to reinforce his news. Some of the texts he quotes fit better than others. Isa. 7:14 is one of those texts which, because of the shift in the Greek version, has in Matthew's reappropriation of it drifted appreciably from the intention of Isaiah. But this is not the only time Matthew offers something other than the Old Testament situation: Matt. 27:9-10 cites as words of Jeremiah a passage about thirty pieces of silver and applies it to Judas' betrayal of Jesus. But the nearest one can find to such a thing in Jeremiah is his purchase of a field from a cousin for seventeen shekels of silver (Jer. 32:9-15). Zech. 11:12-13 mentions thirty shekels of silver, but that passage, too, is not very close. So, in regard to Isa. 7:14, I think we will simply have to say that in our understanding of the text we will want to be faithful both to Matthew's intention and to Isaiah's. A passage had one meaning in the eighth century B.C. Matthew took it in his own understanding and gave it a new use in proclaiming the gospel. The new use does not cancel the old.

There are different issues to discuss with respect to the "suffering servant" passage in Isa. 52:13—53:12, and I shall postpone the matter until later in this chapter.

Beyond the use of passages of the prophets to predict Jesus Christ, there are passages that have been given a specific interpretation in international politics in our own day. Thus, there are Christians who until recently proclaimed that "Meshech," in Ezek. 38:2, 3, is to be identified with (the similar-sounding) Moscow, and that Gog, of the land of Magog (Ezekiel 38–39), describes the threat of the Soviet Union. This is simply misuse of Scripture (I shall discuss these passages in Chapter 10).

We must conclude, then, that the prophets were not conscious of any commission to predict events centuries ahead. It must be said plainly, they *did* predict: part of their task was not only to diagnose what was wrong with the society of the covenant people in their day but to offer a prognosis of what was to happen in the short run if the covenant people did not change their ways. The prophets laid before the eyes of their people a whole array of scenarios of what God might well do; we shall return to this matter later. In particular, the notion of a coming "messiah" is far more complicated than a simple matter of a scenario matched by Jesus Christ; I shall develop this matter both in this chapter and in Chapter 10.

To conclude: the notion that the prophets understood themselves to be predicting events centuries ahead is not part of their own self-understanding. It is, rather, an expression of the conviction of the faith communities of later centuries that treasured the prophetic books, notably (from our perspective) the convictions of the New Testament community, which looked back on the prophetic words of the past and understood them to be relevant to the events of their own day.

The Prophets as Social Reformers

During the past century, many Christians, spurred by the so-called "social gospel," have discovered the prophets in a new way, in the conviction that they were social reformers; this understanding is relevant particularly to the prophets of the pre-exilic period. In the eighth and seventh centuries, Israel and Judah witnessed a growing disparity between rich and poor; the pre-exilic prophets, by this understanding, came as reformers to call the people to social justice, a call that is relevant in our own day, perhaps more than ever. And there is certainly a truth to this: one recalls the text of Amos used by Martin Luther King, Jr.: "Let justice roll down like waters, and righteousness like an everflowing stream" (Amos 5:24). The book of Amos is filled with this kind of call to justice. The prophet begins an indictment of Israel with these words: "They sell the righteous for silver, and the needy for a pair of sandals—they who trample the head of the poor into the dust of the earth, and push the afflicted out of the way" (2:6b-7a). The indictment continues with specificities, mentioning girls who are taken advantage of sexually, and garments left by poor people as pledge for unpaid debts that are then misused in riotous living. Amos mentions corruption in the law courts (that is the meaning of 5:10, 12 and 15), bribery (5:12), and false weights and measures (8:5). Passages in the first three chapters of Micah and in Isaiah 1–39 are just as specific and vivid, and they seem as relevant today as they were twenty-six hundred years ago.

The notion of the prophets as social reformers is only a small part of the truth, however, and there are three considerations that render it somewhat out of focus. First, what they proclaimed was not really new in their day: they were insisting on the same ethical standards that had been a part of the covenant with God since Moses' time. Indeed, Hosea accused Israel of breaking many of the Ten Commandments (Hos. 4:2), and Jeremiah repeated the same accusation in the following century (Jer. 7:9). Given the new prosperity of the upper class, the prophets' accusations of the breaking of covenant norms may have come to the ears of the people with fresh urgency. In other words, it may have been "harder to be good" than it had been in earlier centuries, but the norms were the same. In this respect at least, the prophets were not really announcing anything new.

A second consideration is that, though the prophets did speak of social injustice, their message covered many other issues. Amos, Isaiah, and Jeremiah accused the nation of spending more energy on the details of sacrificial worship than on justice (Amos 4:5; 5:21-23; Isa. 1:10-17; Jer. 6:20; 7:21-24); we discussed these passages in Chapter 3. Hosea and Jeremiah, in passage after passage, accused Israel of abandoning Yahweh in favor of the false god Baal. Their concerns therefore were wider than social injustice alone.

A third consideration is that the prophets' emphasis was always on God, and not on their own personalities or insights. They urged repentance on the people and proclaimed that, in the absence of repentance, God would come to judge the people for their wrongdoing. In short, the prophets were proclaimers of God's urgent words to the people rather than teachers of fresh notions about how to organize society.

The Mode by Which the Prophets Gained Their Revelation

This is not, strictly speaking, a question that involves any distortion in our understanding of the prophets' functioning, but it is certainly a question that illuminates how we might hear God in the prophets. Interestingly, it is the one question that always comes up when I discuss the prophets in church or classroom: How did the prophets receive their messages? The same question could be asked about Moses or any other biblical figure whose words we ponder, but it comes to mind particularly in connection with the prophets, who stand forth and speak so directly and distinctively.

I am not sure why the question comes up so steadily. In part, I attribute it to simple curiosity. In our age, when the reality of God has faded for so many, the process by which these speakers for God could be so convinced that their word was really from God becomes a matter of interest to us. Perhaps behind the question is an assumption that if the mode of reception of the message was striking or dramatic enough, the very mode of reception would in itself be a convincing reassurance of the reality of God. But in this matter, as in so many others, we find ourselves at great remove from the world of the Old Testament, because it is a question in which the Old Testament evinces no interest whatever, nor indeed is it a question about which we have much direct information.

We may get at the matter indirectly by first exploring a problem about which the Old Testament was indeed concerned: How can one tell true from false prophets?[3] One way or another, various prophets became convinced, or convinced themselves, that they had received divine revelation, whereupon they stood forth and proclaimed these messages. Most of these prophets were undoubtedly sincere, though sincerity by itself does not guarantee the absence of self-deceit. But the Israelites who heard the messages were convinced that some prophets were "true"—they really did speak God's word—while other prophets were "false"—they claimed their messages were from God but, as a matter of fact, they were not.

We must continue to remind ourselves that evidently all kinds of people made prophetic claims: we think again of the band of ecstatics with whom Saul prophesied (1 Sam. 10:9-13). We must assume, therefore, that through the decades there were prophets who functioned in groups and prophets who were solitary, prophets who spoke in ecstasy and prophets who spoke in sobriety, prophets in villages and prophets in the city, prophets who were associated with places of worship and prophets who were associated with the court.

The problem of who really speaks for God, out of all those who claim to speak for God, surfaced early. The matter is dramatized by the narrative, in 1 Kings 22, of the prophet Micaiah son of Imlah (ninth century). Ahab, king of Israel, thinks it is time to retake the city of Ramoth-gilead from Aram (= the Syrians), and he has as an ally the king of Judah, Jehoshaphat. The latter suggests that before they undertake the battle they consult the word of the Lord, and so Ahab gathers his band of prophets together; according to the narrative, there are four hundred of them! They reply unanimously that the Lord will give the city into the hands of the king. Jehoshaphat, perhaps thinking that the answer has come too easily, asks if there are any other prophets who might be consulted. There is one more, admits the king, Micaiah son of Imlah, "but I hate him, for he never prophesies anything favorable about me, but only disaster" (v. 8). Nevertheless, a messenger is sent to summon Micaiah, and the messenger tells him he would do well to answer as the others have done. So when Micaiah comes before the king, he does answer at first as the previous prophets have done, but he evidently does it tongue in cheek, because the king says to him, "How many times must I make you swear to tell me nothing but the truth in the name of the Lord?" (v. 16). Micaiah thereupon offers a sincere description of what he has seen. "Therefore hear the word of the Lord: I saw the Lord sitting on his throne, with all the host of heaven standing beside him to the right and to the left of him. And the Lord said, 'Who will entice Ahab, so that he may go up and fall at Ramoth-gilead?' Then one said one thing, and another said another, until a spirit came forward and stood before the Lord, saying, 'I will entice him.' 'How?' the Lord asked him. He replied, 'I will go out and be a lying spirit in the mouth of all his prophets.' Then the Lord said, 'You are to entice him, and you shall succeed; go out and do it.' So you see, the Lord has put a lying spirit in the mouth of all these your prophets; the Lord has decreed disaster for you" (vv. 19-23). The chief of the four hundred prophets then comes forward and slaps him on the cheek and says, "Which way did the spirit of the Lord pass from me to speak to you?" (v. 24). Micaiah answers that the chief will find out on the day disaster strikes and he will be hiding in his bedroom. The king orders Micaiah to be locked up and put on bread and water till the king returns "in peace"—that is, safely. Micaiah answers, simply enough, "If you return in peace, the Lord has not spoken by me" (v. 28). The king is uneasy enough to disguise himself in battle, but a random bowshot strikes him mortally, and he dies that evening, as his army scatters.

This picturesque tale offers several matters for the reader to ponder. To the same question, four hundred prophets say yes, and one prophet says no: how is that possible? The majority, clearly, is not always right. But Micaiah does not say the four hundred are *false* prophets: according to him, the four hundred do speak for God, but they say yes because God intends to *entice* Ahab into falling at Ramoth-gilead. It is a "lying spirit" that God puts into the mouths of the four hundred.

Israelites in later centuries were not comfortable with this explanation of prophets who do not speak the straight word of God: how could one deal with a God who would deliberately set out to deceive the covenant people? The problem remained: Which prophet could one trust in a given instance? The prophet Micah, in the eighth century, contrasted himself with "prophets who lead my people astray, who cry 'Peace' when they have something to eat, but declare war against those who put nothing into their mouths" (Mic. 3:5). The sun shall go down on these prophets, he declares, and they shall all cover their lips, for there is no answer from God (vv. 6-7). "But as for me, I am filled with power . . . and with justice and might, to declare to Jacob his transgression and to Israel his sin" (v. 8). Micah declares that false prophets are willing to offer good news when they are paid by those who want to hear the good news, but the result of such a situation is that no word from God will come out of their mouths; by contrast, Micah declares that he speaks convincingly ("with power and justice and might") to declare a word of judgment. But alas, this test is not airtight: good news is not always false, and we cannot doubt that sometimes even false prophets are convinced that they speak with power (and are thus convincing to others).

The book of Deuteronomy struggles with the same question, how to tell true prophets from false. "Any prophet who speaks in the name of other gods, or who presumes to speak in my name a word that I have not commanded the prophet to speak—that prophet shall die. You may say to yourself, 'How can we recognize a word that the Lord has not spoken?' If a prophet speaks in the name of the Lord but the thing does not take place or prove true, it is a word that the Lord has not spoken. The prophet has spoken it presumptuously; do not be frightened by it" (Deut. 18:20-22). This is no more help than the test of convincingness: we cannot afford to wait to find out how the matter will turn out in the end—we need to know now whether the word is true or false.

The prophet Jeremiah struggled with the issue of true and false prophecy in the context of his understanding of his own calling. At one time, he assumed, as Micaiah had, that optimistic prophets were sent by God to deceive Jerusalem with good news (Jer. 4:9-10). On the other hand, there were times in his career when, certain as he was that he himself was speaking God's word, he was convinced God had revealed to him that those prophets who said the opposite were not sent by God at all but rather deluded themselves and indeed deluded those who listened to them (Jer. 14:13-16; 23:16-17).

At still another point in his life, Jeremiah shifted in his outlook, wondering whether God was not deceiving him, after all, by the constant bad news he was convinced he had received (Jer. 20:7)—because, although the news did actually turn out to be bad, it was not altogether bad. The city of Jerusalem fell to Nebuchadnezzar in 598 B.C., but thereafter life continued more or less on an even keel: the Babylonian monarch did exile King Jehoiachin and strip much of the treasure from the temple, but he maintained the continuity of Davidic kingship by putting Jehoiachin's uncle on the throne. Then, four years later, in the summer of 594 B.C., convinced as Jeremiah was that the nation must ultimately submit to the Babylonian king Nebuchadnezzar, he confronted an optimistic prophet named Hananiah (Jeremiah 28). The latter, by contrast, was convinced that within two years events would take a sharp turn for the better—that the exiles and loot that Nebuchadnezzar had taken from Jerusalem in 598 would be returned to Jerusalem, and everyone would live happily ever after. Jeremiah, who had been wearing yoke-pegs on his neck as a symbol of the coming submission to the yoke of Nebuchadnezzar, replied, "Would that it were so!" but suggested that inasmuch as true prophets in earlier times spoke bad news, any good news spoken by a prophet should be listened to with caution. Hananiah then went up and broke Jeremiah's yoke-pegs, and for the moment all Jeremiah could do was go his way: at that point, the optimistic prophet had the last word (v. 11). Later, however, Jeremiah perceived God to tell him that his wooden yoke-pegs were to be replaced by iron ones, and, so emboldened, Jeremiah shared the word with Hananiah that he, Hananiah, had not been *sent* by God at all, but that within a year God would *send* him off the face of the earth. Here then was another confrontation between a prophet who said yes and a prophet who said no. Jeremiah, it turned out, was validated in the short term when, two months later, Hananiah dropped dead (v. 17), and he was validated in the long term when, seven years later, Jerusalem fell for the second time to Nebuchadnezzar, for this time the kingdom of Judah was at an end.

We may conclude that, at a given moment, it was not an easy matter to tell true prophet from false. Hananiah, we are sure, was sincere, and we might go further and say that his word was not so different from that of Isaiah, a hundred years before, who in his day had declared that Jerusalem would not fall to Assyria (Isa. 37:33-35). Jeremiah, for his part, was saying by implication that God had now shifted intention, and Jerusalem would fall after all. (We recall the discussion in Chapter 6 of Jeremiah's proclamation that God had taken the step of embarking on holy war against the covenant people.)

These passages that speak of true and false prophets give us some clues by which to try to understand how the prophets gained their messages. The behavior of those prophets who were accused of being false, or finally recognized as being false, was no different from the behavior of those understood to be true—otherwise, there would have been no problem in distinguishing the one from the other. Bearing in mind our earlier caution that there must have been wide variation in the behavior of prophets, let us nevertheless see what we can affirm about how at least some prophets received their messages.

Some of these clues are to be found in a long passage in Jeremiah 23. Jeremiah raises the question, "Who has stood in the council of the Lord so as to see and to hear his word?" (v. 18). What might it mean, to "stand in the council of the Lord"? It is, like all such expressions, metaphorical, but it is possible that a prophet could testify to a vision of standing in the heavenly court; Jeremiah at another point understands God to tell him that if he turns to God,

God will accept him and he will *stand before God* (15:19). Later, in chapter 23, the prophet understands God to say, "I did not send the prophets, yet they ran; I did not speak to them, yet they prophesied" (Jer. 23:21). The verb "ran" is curious; what would it suggest? Did the prophets in Jeremiah's day continue to cultivate ecstatic behavior? These verses at least suggest the possibility of visionary experiences of some sort. Chapter 23 continues, "I have heard what the prophets have said who prophesy lies in my name, saying, 'I have dreamed, I have dreamed!' How long? Will the hearts of the prophets ever turn back—those who prophesy lies, and who prophesy the deceit of their own heart? They plan to make my people forget my name by their dreams that they tell one another, just as their ancestors forgot my name for Baal. Let the prophet who has a dream tell the dream, but let the one who has my word speak my word faithfully. What has straw in common with wheat? says the Lord. Is not my word like fire, says the Lord, and like a hammer that breaks a rock in pieces? See, therefore, I am against the prophets, says the Lord, who steal my words from one another. See, I am against the prophets, says the Lord, who use their own tongues and say, 'Says the Lord.' See I am against those who prophesy lying dreams, and who tell them" (23:25-32). Beyond the possibility of visionary experiences, then, we may conclude that some of the prophets, at least, believed that through dreams they could gain a revelation that was thought to come from God; on the other hand, if prophets could be accused of stealing dreams from each other, it is possible that some shammed the experience in order to claim their access to divine revelation. Two prophets whom we honor as true prophets, Micah and Jeremiah, insisted that there is no comparison between true and false revelation, because true revelation comes with power ("wheat" in comparison with "straw"; "fire"; "a hammer"). On the other hand, the sensitive prophet Jeremiah was not always sure that the word he had from God really represented God's sincere intention (Jer. 20:7); at least for him, the experience of receiving revelation did not always carry with it incontrovertible convincingness.

I offer one more clue. At some point after the final fall of Jerusalem, Jeremiah found himself among a group of refugees, led by a Judahite military officer, who were attempting to stay clear of the struggle in Judah between the occupying Babylonian power and those who were trying to continue resistance. The military officer in charge of the refugees asked Jeremiah to seek the will of God as to whether they should pursue plans to migrate to Egypt (Jer. 42:2-3). Jeremiah agreed to pray for guidance (v. 4), but the answer from God was not forthcoming until ten days had passed (v. 7). Jeremiah did not understand himself to be so closely in touch with the word of God that he could expect an instant answer to his prayer.

So how did the prophets receive their revelations? Let me offer some general considerations. In every culture that assumes there is intercourse between the supernatural world and human beings, there are particular modes by which communication from the supernatural world is both sought for and understood to be received: the mediators (priests, prophets) may eat or drink preparations that have hallucinogenic properties; they may be stirred by dancing or drumming or the like; they may fast or sit in isolation or darkness; they may sleep in a sacred area with the expectation that the deity will speak through a dream. Every culture that seeks divine revelation develops such modes, and within that culture those modes are understood to be valid. But within a given culture, some persons will be more sensitive, will be more adept, at using such practices to gain revelation; of these, some might be considered by us to be psychologically "normal," while others might be considered mentally abnormal in some way ("schizophrenic," for example). The particular culture, in subtle ways, encourages those mediators who are recognized to be adept and trustworthy in bringing revelation, so that the culture can maximize its sense of access to the supernatural world.

In these matters, ancient Israel was no different from any other culture: the difference was not so much in the *modes* of reception of the revelation as in the perceived *validity* of the revelation in the long history of Israel and the relevance of that revelation to our own faith community.

An analogy from a different realm of life may help our understanding here. Through what means did Franz Schubert get his inspiration? Where did his music come from? In his short 31-year life, he poured out hundreds of songs and dozens of chamber music works, as well as nine symphonies. (How, indeed, one might ask, did he have time even to write out the manuscripts of all these compositions?) All we can say is that he grew up in a culture saturated with music, that he had an astonishing gift of melody, and that this music simply came to him full-blown, as it were.

By contrast, we know a little more about the process by which Schubert's contemporary and fellow-countryman, Ludwig van Beethoven, worked out his musical ideas, because we have some of Beethoven's notebooks. We can trace the evolution, over a month, of the main theme in the second movement of his Fifth Symphony, from a fairly uninteresting melody to the one he finally used. This does not make Beethoven's inspiration any the less marvelous; it simply gives us direct access to some of the process by which he hammered out his ideas.

It was little different, I submit, for the Old Testament prophets whose words have survived for us. They evidently received their revelation through a combination of (1) a thorough awareness of their religious and cultural tradition,

(2) a steady and persistent attention to the religious, economic, political, and military issues of their day, (3) common sense and insight (whatever they are), and (4) the specific techniques that their culture offered them and that their personal preferences urged on them—whether dreams and the cultivation of visions, or the sudden conviction that comes in the course of times of solitary prayer. And, it must be added: in Jeremiah's case at least, the prophet was not immune from self-doubt.

The Time-Boundedness of the Prophets

Here, we come to the heart of the question of how we might hear God in the prophets. If the prophets are of their own time and spoke out on the issues of their own day, then in what way, if at all, are their words authoritative today for us?

One might maintain that their words are in no way authoritative over us. Their circumstances, one might say, are so different that there is no safe link between their words and our situation. More than once I have cited the beginning of the Letter to the Hebrews, "Long ago God spoke to our ancestors in many and various ways by the prophets, but in these last days he has spoken to us by a Son" (Heb. 1:1-2a). From this passage one might conclude that Jesus Christ, the full word of God, has replaced all the previous partial words from God spoken through the prophets.

And, it must be said, on this whole question, the guidance of later generations within the Old Testament and of the New Testament is of little direct help to us. Later generations of the Old Testament took it for granted that the prophetic words of earlier generations continued to communicate to them, or else they would not have been preserved; they certainly were not retained simply as historical relics. Even though, at the time the prophets' words were uttered, they were understood to be Yahweh's fresh words for fresh circumstances—in contrast to the laws, which were understood to be valid for all time (see Chapter 3)—later generations preserved the words of the prophets in the same way as they preserved the laws. Admittedly, in doing so, they were ignoring any differences in historical context between the time the prophets spoke and their own day: they simply heard them as words for their own day. As I have indicated, the time came when the early New Testament church simply took it for granted that the words of the prophets were long-term *predictions* that were to be understood as relevant to their own later day, an approach that paid no attention to the original intention of the prophets.

The Jewish community and the Christian community have preserved the words of the prophets, yet, given our understanding of the specific historical circumstances of the prophets, we are impeded from understanding the words as direct communication to us. Does God communicate to us through these old words, and if so, how are we to hear that communication? Can we untie the boat marked "Isaiah" from its moorings in the eighth century B.C. and take it down the lake to a mooring in the twentieth century A.D. and still recognize it as "Isaiah"? How might this be done?

Our first task is to reinforce what has been said before in this work (see Chapter 5); words addressed to Israel must be heard by us in the first instance as words to us in our identity as *the Christian church.* Because so many of the words of the pre-exilic prophets deal with particular matters of public policy for which the kings of Israel had responsibility, because in our own day matters of public policy are dealt with by secular governments, and because the churches are so often marginal by comparison, we tend to think first how the words of the prophets (particularly their appeals for social justice) might be addressed directly to the secular governments of our day. But, we remind ourselves, the prophets understood themselves to be those who spoke God's words to the people of God, and therefore we must start by hearing these words as addressed to the church, the "Israel of God" (Gal. 6:16).

The question of secular governments, however, leads us at least to pause for a moment to consider the present-day relations between church and state. For most of Christian history, church and state have been so intimately related that the words of the prophets could be heard by the church and related to the state in ways not too different from the ways that prevailed in ancient Israel. Beginning with the Protestant Reformation, and at a growing pace in the past two hundred years, however, churches have become separated from the state; this is particularly the case in the United States, where this separation has been reinforced by the great variety of Christian churches. On the other hand, three simultaneous developments in the past century or two have brought about an unprecedented situation: (1) the rise of modern secularism, which allows our cultures and societies to be organized without regard to any divine claims; (2) the evolution of the modern political state, with its geometrically increasing military capacity; and (3) the evolution of economic corporations, especially those with international reach. All these developments have tended to marginate the Christian churches in the attention of public life, particularly as that life is reflected in books, magazines, and the various communications media.

At the same time, it must be stressed that not only do the books, magazines, and various other media reflect public life; they also, from time to time, criticize that public life, and to that degree they serve some of the function that the prophets served in ancient Israel. Here is a simple example. The first paragraph of a newspaper article: "University of Massachusetts trustees have agreed to pay the school's new president $175,000 a year—about 35 percent more than the previous president received—to lead a teaching staff demoralized by four years of no pay raises."[4] The editorial writers, the "Op. Ed." columnists, and the political cartoonists of our newspapers may all function to varying degrees in the way the Old Testament prophets did.

It is worth noticing that when present-day governmental authorities seek perspective on public issues, they frequently draw on scholars in our universities and "think-tanks"; on the other hand, the professors in our universities often challenge those in government on public issues whether the political leaders want to listen to them or not. The activity of such scholars, like that of the media, is thus parallel to the activity of the prophets in ancient Israel, except for the most crucial matter of all: present-day professors rarely think to speak in the name of God, any more than the media do. At the most, such public figures appeal to the fate of the planet: I think of such works as Rachel Carson's *Silent Spring*,[5] or Jonathan Schell's *The Fate of the Earth*,[6] These matters are crucial to all human beings but are not ultimate in the light of the Christian faith. Christians do not deny that God can speak through secularists, who do not acknowledge God, and through them to people who do not acknowledge God either; but that does not exclude the obligation of the churches to hear God and to speak the word of God to the world. I shall return to the question of God's word to secular governments below.

Hearing God in Prophetic Accusations and Appeals

Let us now turn to the prophetic oracles themselves. What kinds of utterances have been preserved from the prophets, and how might God speak to us through them? Most of their judgment oracles, as we might imagine, were directed to their own people, in Israel and Judah, and so I begin with these.

In Chapter 4, in pondering the matter of God's wrath, we examined the prophetic accusations that threaten God's wrath, and so we have only to review them here. There are, first of all, their appeals to social justice and their accusations that the covenant people are remiss in exercising that justice: here, as we have affirmed, the prophets appear to communicate directly from their day to ours. We hear, in Amos 5:24, "Let justice roll down like waters, and righteousness like an everflowing stream." In spite of the distance of centuries, these words come stinging at us. Listen to Isa. 10:1-4: "Ah, you who make iniquitous decrees, who write oppressive statutes, to turn aside the needy from justice and to rob the poor of my people of their right, that widows may be your spoil, and that you may make the orphans your prey! What will you do on the day of punishment, in the calamity that will come from far away? To whom will you flee for help, and where will you leave your wealth, so as not to crouch among the prisoners or fall among the slain? For all this his anger has not turned away; his hand is stretched out still." These words need no interpretation. God's demand for justice must be heard within the churches. God demands fairness and trustworthiness from church members both in their dealings with each other and in their dealings in the wider world. God expects the church to manifest a concern for the marginated within its membership and in the wider world, whether that concern be expressed in a literacy program, a soup kitchen, work with battered women, or any other of innumerable modes of ministry. And God expects the church to continue to hammer at these issues so that secular institutions too may manifest a greater measure of social justice. Though almost everyone agrees on these matters in outline, carrying them out in practice causes difficulties.

I turn now to another kind of oracle of the prophets: appeals to stay loyal to Yahweh, and accusations that the covenant people have not been loyal to Yahweh. The collections of the oracles of Hosea and Jeremiah are particularly full of these admonitions: according to these prophets, the people have abandoned Yahweh for the fertility god Baal. Listen to Jeremiah, where God is recorded as saying, "The prophets prophesied by Baal, and went after things that do not profit"; "You said, 'It is hopeless, for I have loved strangers, and after them I will go'"; "They have turned their backs to me, and not their faces" (2:8, 25, 27). These words are the prophetic equivalent of the first commandment, which we discussed in Chapter 3: "You shall have no other gods before me."

I referred briefly to the religion of Baalism in Chapter 4 when discussing what it was that was understood to arouse Yahweh's wrath, and in Chapter 6 when discussing how the prophets understood God to be punishing Israel and Judah by the battles waged by Assyria and Babylon; now we must examine the matter more closely.[7] The Canaanites worshiped various gods, but chief among them was Baal, a god of storm and fertility, and his consort Astarte (1 Kings 11:5), sometimes called the "queen of heaven" (Jer. 7:18). Actually, "Baal" is simply a generic term for "master" or "lord," and the name of the storm and fertility god was Hadad (compare the reference to the god Hadadrimmon in Zech. 12:11), but the generic term became the common one at the time the Israelites came into the land.

The farmers in Egypt could count on a supply of water by irrigation from the Nile, and those in Mesopotamia from the Tigris and Euphrates, but there were no steady rivers in Palestine, and rainfall could not always be depended on; we recall recurrent notices of droughts in the Old Testament—for example, in the narrative of Elijah (1 Kings 17:1). The Canaanites therefore had elaborated myths and rituals that were believed to reinforce the activity of these deities to bring rainfall and fertility to the land, rituals that evidently included the drinking of wine and sacred prostitution (compare the implications of Hosea 2; 4:10-14). We must bear in mind that these myths and rituals arose in a world without bank accounts or insurance policies or retirement plans. The survival of any family depended on the adequacy of their harvests and the plenitude of their flocks and herds, and ultimately on the birth and survival of children who could support their parents in old age. All of this required rainfall and the fertility of fields and of animals and of the marriage bed.

The Israelites, when they came into the land, were relatively untutored in agriculture, and there was a strong tendency for them in their new situation to adopt Canaanite fertility worship in their efforts to gain fertility from the land (compare the story of the altar to Baal erected by Joash, the father of Gideon, Judg. 6:11, 25-32). King Saul named one of his sons Ishbaal, a name compounded with "Baal" (1 Chron. 8:33). (We must note in passing that the NRSV uses that form of the name not only in 1 Chronicles but also in 2 Samuel—for example, in 2 Sam. 2:8 and elsewhere—even though the Hebrew text in 2 Samuel has "censored" the name to "Ishbosheth" [so the RSV], substituting the Hebrew word *bōšet* "shame" for the name of the Canaanite god.) Saul worshiped Yahweh (1 Sam. 10:1; 13:12), so why, one might ask, did he name one of his sons a name compounded with Baal? There is no reason to think that he also worshiped Baal as a separate deity. Rather, in Saul's day, the worship of Yahweh may have taken on the characteristics of Baal worship in a kind of syncretism, and since the word Baal means "lord," Saul could well have assumed that "Baal" was a title for Yahweh. Indeed, the whole point of the challenge by the prophet Elijah of the prophets of Baal in the days of King Ahab (see 1 Kings 18) was that the people must *choose* between Yahweh and Baal (v. 21) rather than assume they were somehow equivalent.

The prophets maintained that the religious systems of Baal and Yahweh were as different as night and day. It was not so much the excesses of wine and sexual indulgence in the fertility rituals that bothered the prophets—though, as we have seen, these matters were part of their accusation. Rather, it was the fact that the religion of Baal made no ethical demands on its adherents: there was no notion of a covenant with a deity that implied the ethical requirements of law. Baal, in fact, was a kind of projection onto the cosmic sphere of the craving for economic and political security that the people naturally exhibited. The people craved fertility and prosperity, and they prayed to Baal to bring it. Baal, we might say, was understood to be a kind of cosmic bellhop, at the beck and call of people. Yahweh, however, was no projection of the people's cravings; to the contrary, as we already saw in Chapters 2 and 3, Israel proclaimed that Yahweh had brought the people into existence, made a covenant with them, and made high demands on them.

This is why the prophets insisted that people had to choose which deity they worshiped. Jeremiah mocks the expectations of Baal worshipers. Of course the people need water, he says, but the people have deserted Yahweh, who is the constantly dependable running spring of water, and then, lacking water, they have gone off to dig out cisterns. Cisterns do not produce water— they can only retain the water that is poured into them, except that these cisterns leak (Jer. 2:13). It would be hard to imagine a more contemptuous dismissal of the claims of Baal worship than this depiction of Baal as a leaky cistern. If the people have abandoned the true source of security, the dependable running spring of water that is Yahweh, and if the cisterns that are Baal leak, then their only recourse is to go off to Egypt to drink Nile water, or go off to Assyria to drink Euphrates water (Jer. 2:18)—that is to say, to seek the military and political security that vassalage to Egypt or to the power in Mesopotamia might bring.

These appeals and accusations, so vivid at the time, seem actually no longer to have been necessary after the Babylonian exile—the impression we gain from the biblical record is that the worship of Baal faded after the exile (I shall deal with the accusations preserved in Isa. 57:3-10, which are postexilic, in Chapter 10). One assumes that the fall of Jerusalem was such a shock to Jews that those who held to the traditional religion at all had no heart to be tempted by Baalism.

Now what of us? Are we in the churches in danger of forgetting our obligation to the true God? The easy answer is to say no; the churches to which most of the readers of this work belong are attempting to be faithful to God, listening to Scripture, preserving the tradition that has been entrusted to this generation of Christians. On the other hand, there is always the danger, as Jesus insisted, of saying "Lord, Lord" and not doing the will of the heavenly Father (Matt. 7:21). What might the modern equivalent of Baalism be—our own urges for economic and military security? To what degree do these urges shape the policies of our churches? To what degree do the impulses of narrow nationalism, or of social prestige, or of complacency, infect our church life? Given the fact that Christian churches are found in every nation of the world, does the American flag, given perhaps by a local American Legion post, belong in the sanctuary of American churches? These can be troubling questions. A missionary wrote from China, in the midst of the Christian conflict there just after World War II, that Christians are people who are completely fearless, absurdly happy, and in constant trouble.[8] Measured by that standard, many congregations might fall short; if that description is the measure of faithfulness to the God of the Bible, then that faithfulness is never easy.

Hearing God in Prophetic Judgments

In another category of prophetic utterances are those that announce God's angry judgment against the covenant people, with descriptions of a variety of fearsome punishments.

There is really nothing quite like these passages. One can listen, for example to Isa. 2:5-21, which ends, "On that day people will throw away to the moles and to the bats their idols of silver and their idols of gold, which they made for themselves to worship, to enter the caverns of the rocks and the clefts in the crags, from the terror of the Lord, and from the glory of his majesty, when he rises to terrify the earth" (vv. 20-21). Purely as rhetoric, this is awesome: but is God speaking to us today through such passages of judgment as these?

I offered a discussion of the wrath of God in Chapter 4, including several prophetic passages of this sort, and I touched on the matter again in Chapter 6 when discussing the battles mounted by Assyria and Babylonia, but I skirted in those chapters the basic question: How are these awesome pronouncements of judgment relevant to Christians today? Do we hear God in them? Most Christians, I suppose, take it for granted that the coming of Jesus Christ has removed God's wrath, and passages like Paul's word in Rom. 8:1 ("There is now no condemnation for those who are in Christ Jesus") lend support to that view. On the other hand, Paul warns against overconfidence: "God was not pleased" with most of the Israelites in the wilderness, and "these things occurred as examples for us, so that we might not desire evil as they did" (1 Cor. 10:5-6). I suggest, therefore, that prophetic passages declaring God's anger are to be heard by us as reminders of the seriousness of God's expectations for us. We cannot take it for granted that we are immune to God's wrath.

Words of Hope beyond the Judgment

Beyond the awesome pronouncements of the prophets regarding justice, fidelity to God, and scenarios of God's coming judgment against the people, we find among the pronouncements of the prophets bright promises for the future that offer hope for their hearers. Often, such passages were added to earlier collections expressing judgment, and these additions were made during the exilic and postexilic period. For example, the book of Amos consists almost entirely of a sequence of expressions of God's anger spoken through that eighth-century prophet, but the last five verses of the book offer two little passages of hope: a word about the restoration of the Davidic monarchy and revenge against the rival Edomites (9:11-12), and a word telling of the restoration of the exiles on their land and the fertility of that land (9:13-15). Many scholars have concluded that these last five verses are not from the prophet Amos himself, but from a writer perhaps in the sixth century B.C.[9] Even though I agree, I would also suggest that without these five verses the words of Amos might not have been preserved for us: the five verses are like the hot pad by which we are able to take a casserole out of the oven. The people of the exilic and postexilic period must have pondered the high expectations of God and the anger God expressed when they fell short, but just as Christians in worship, having confessed their sins, need to hear the words of the gospel that they have been forgiven, so the Israelites, having heard words of judgment from God, needed to hear hope as well. Without the last five verses, the words of Amos would have been too hot to handle.

Sometimes, the chapters of the prophets offer a dizzying alternation of words of judgment and of restoration. For example, in Isaiah 31–32, one hears, judgment against those in Judah who depend on Egyptian military aid (31:1-3), followed by reassurance to Jerusalem that it will not fall to the Assyrians (31:4-9), followed by an assurance that an age of justice is coming (32:1-8), following by a judgment against the complacency of Judah's women (32:9-14), followed by a reassurance that the spirit of God will come and transform all creation into a time of happiness (32:15-20). This kind of format leads us to ask: How shall we hear such an oscillation? Some of it, I suspect, is the result of the accidents of the kind of "scrapbook" way the collections of the prophets evolved—passages were added on the basis of association of "catchwords" or simply on the basis of the availability of a half-column of empty papyrus at the end of a scroll. But we must still ask: What word does God intend us to hear, a word of judgment or of reassurance? Do we sometimes need to hear the judgment, and sometimes the reassurance, or do we need to hear both at the same time? How can we be sure?

The American newspaper columnist Finley Peter Dunne, at the end of the nineteenth century, invented an Irish immigrant character named Misther Dooley, who remarked that it was the mission of a modern newspaper to "comfort the afflicted and afflict the comfortable."[10] This might well be the task of the Old Testament prophets for us. Are we comfortable? Then let us hear the affliction of God. Are we afflicted? Then let us hear the comfort of God.

Even Jeremiah, who spun out judgment after judgment against his people, found himself, in the circumstance of the fall of Jerusalem, voicing hope for his people. These expressions of hope are found particularly in chapters 30–31 of the book of Jeremiah, and of these passages none has taken on so much importance as the passage that announces a new covenant (31:31-34),[11] a passage already discussed in Chapter 2. Let us review what was affirmed there, and press some matters further. The passage affirms, first of all, that the covenant between God and Israel concluded by Moses is irretrievably broken—drastic news indeed, considering all the assumptions about that covenant we have already explored. But then it goes on to affirm that, in time to come, God would replace it with a new covenant with the people, by means of a law not written on tablets of stone, as the old one was, but rather written in the hearts of the people. Indeed, the Hebrew text says "heart," singular, as if the people were to have one heart, one mind, one will. When that time comes, the people will obey God not because they are supposed to, bound by external law, but because they want to, impelled by God's will planted within them, and thus there will be no more struggle between God and the covenant people.

This radical notion lay unexploited for many centuries. Eventually, it was picked up by the Dead Sea Scrolls community, which affirmed itself to be the people of the new covenant, but it was particularly the New Testament that took it over. Jesus is remembered as having referred to the new covenant in his blessing over the wine at the Last Supper (1 Cor. 11:25), and the whole Jeremiah passage is cited in the Letter to the Hebrews (Heb. 8:8-12). Indeed, it is not too much to say that the Jeremiah passage was one of the really formative passages for the New Testament, as we have already seen. This passage expresses comfort, and it is good for Christians to understand themselves as a community freshly created by God after the pattern set forth in Jeremiah, but it is sobering to ponder the assumptions of that passage: that in the community of the new covenant there will be no necessity of explicit instruction in the faith, but rather that children will grow up in the community obeying God by their very inner nature. In order to embody that vision, Christian communities still have a distance to go.

There are marvelous words of hope to be found in the book of Jeremiah's younger contemporary, Ezekiel. Ezekiel was exiled to Babylon in the first deportation, in 598 B.C., prophesied words of judgment to his fellow exiles, and then, after the final fall of Jerusalem in 587 B.C., began to prophesy hope for the future. Ezekiel therefore nicely fulfills the mandate to "comfort the afflicted and to afflict the comfortable." But I shall save a consideration of his

words of hope until Chapter 10 because his use of words points us in the direction of the apocalyptic worldview.

The Pre-eminent Prophet of Hope: "Second Isaiah"

The most sustained sequence of comfort to be found in the prophets is the six-
teen chapters that have come to be called "Second Isaiah," the work of an
anonymous prophet who prophesied at the end of the period of the Babylonian
exile (about 540 B.C.), now found in Isaiah 40–55. The sequence begins, "Comfort, O comfort my people, says your God. Speak tenderly to Jerusalem, and cry
to her that she has served her term, that her penalty is paid, that she has received from the Lord's hand double for all her sins" (40:1-2). A deaconess in a
church I served years ago used to say, "I just love the book of Isaiah." She was a
widow in her 60s, crippled with arthritis, and she was nursing her widowed
mother. I knew she did not mean the passage about the moles and the bats from
chapter 2, but rather the sequence that begins, "Comfort, O comfort my people." These chapters seem to need little commentary: almost every human life
endures pain and loss, and comfort is always welcome.

Nevertheless, these words become even more vivid when they are understood in the context of the exile of Jews in Babylon. The exiles had endured
almost a half-century away from their home; a new generation had grown up,
and few among them remained who could remember Jerusalem firsthand.
Rarely have the metaphors of faith been so cogently employed. A highway will
be built across the desert (40:3-4)! The creator God is still present (40:12-17)!
God will bring the princes of the world to nothing (40:21-24)! God will not
forget the covenant people (40:27-31; 41:8-10)! The pagan nations of the
earth will not survive a showdown with God (41:1, 21-24)! God is going to
bring you home (43:1-7)! The God of Israel is the only true God, while the
idols of the nations are nothing (44:1-22)! (We touched on this affirmation in
Chapter 2.) God has raised up Cyrus of Persia to be the agent of your deliverance from Babylon (44:24-28; 45:1-7)!

It is appropriate to pause here to notice two remarkable things about these
passages that mention Cyrus. First, Cyrus is called God's "anointed" (45:1),
using the Hebrew word normally rendered "messiah"; the prophet is suggesting that the community will be restored not by a king in the line of David but
rather by an alien king, the king of Persia: it is he who is God's anointed. Here
we see how flexible was the notion of "messiah" in the Old Testament; I shall
discuss that flexibility further in Chapter 10.

Second, in Chapter 4, in discussing Isa. 10:5-8, I pointed out that Assyria,
in pursuing her imperial plans, could be the tool of God's judgment without

being aware of it. Now, almost two centuries later, Second Isaiah could make the same kind of observation about Cyrus of Persia, this time not for the judgment but for the restoration of the covenant people. "Thus says the Lord to his anointed, to Cyrus, whose right hand I have grasped to subdue nations before him and to strip kings of their robes, . . . so that you may know that it is I, the Lord, the God of Israel, who call you by your name. For the sake of my servant Jacob, and Israel my chosen, I call you by your name, I surname you, though you do not know me" (45:1, 3b-4). For Second Isaiah in the sixth century, God does a work of compassion through the unaware foreign power Persia precisely as the original Isaiah had proclaimed in the eighth century God's work of judgment through the unaware foreign power Assyria. In these ways, then, the passages in Isaiah 40–55 may nourish our sensibilities.

The Suffering Servant

One particular matter in these chapters needs special discussion: the suffering servant passage in 52:13—53:12. I mentioned it early in this chapter, but I have postponed discussing it until this point. The passage was understood in the New Testament to refer to Jesus (Acts 8:26-35; 1 Pet. 2:22), and for centuries it has been used as a text on Good Friday. Christians assume that, at least here, the prophet would surely seem to be predicting Jesus Christ! Actually, there are four servant sequences in these chapters: the first three are 42:1-4; 49:1-6, and 50:4-11, and this passage is the fourth. Though the prophet in general identifies Israel as God's servant (41:8; 44:1; 45:4), in these four passages the servant is not identified[12] and indeed seems to be different from Israel (49:6). Immense efforts have been made to try to discern the intention of the prophet in these songs. My own view is that his audience was left just as unsure as we are: the prophet's hold on his rhetoric is so sure that, if he does not identify the servant in these songs, then it is his intention that his audience should ponder who the servant might be. But though he leaves the servant unidentified, he makes quite clear the task of the servant: deliberately to accept suffering as a means of bringing salvation.

In Chapter 4, we explored the question of how suffering was understood to be punishment for sin: Israel took it for granted that any suffering or disaster the people experienced was God's judgment on them for some offense they had committed. True, some suffering was assumed to be warning (compare Amos 4:6-11, and, on the human level, Prov. 10:13). But Second Isaiah suspected that there was no one-to-one correspondence between suffering and what was deserved: we note again, in 40:2, "that she [Jerusalem] has received from the Lord's hand double for all her sins"—she has suffered twice as much as she deserves to suffer.

Isa. 52:13—53:12, then, sets forth a view completely at odds with Israel's traditional understanding of suffering: a servant of God, by deliberately accepting a vocation to suffering, could bring health to the nations. Who then, in the mind of the prophet, was the servant? Was it to be the nation Israel, or a faithful remnant of that nation? If so, Israel ignored that portion of the prophet's message. They gladly heard his message that God was still in control and they would be going home, but there is no trace in later portions of the Old Testament that Israel had any taste for a vocation to suffer innocently.

I suggest, then, that it is not so much that the prophet peered into the future to predict Jesus Christ, as that Jesus deliberately accepted the job description for his own calling. In his temptations in the wilderness (Matt. 4:1-11), he pondered how he would exercise his vocation, and there were passages of Scripture that came to his mind that he rejected as from Satan. Just as he would take Isa. 61:1-2 as a model (see Luke 4:16-21), so, I suggest, he took Isa. 52:13—53:12 as his own: if he rejected the role of simply feeding the hungry, the role of being a wonder-worker, and the role of exercising political power, then he accepted the role of bringing salvation by becoming God's servant in the acceptance of suffering.

Hearing God in the Prophetic Judgments against Foreign Nations

The prophets did not confine their activity to Israel and Judah. The book of Obadiah is a judgment against Edom, and Nah. 1:15—3:19 is a description of God's punishment against the capital of Assyria. Beyond these specific passages, the books of Amos, Isaiah, Jeremiah, and Ezekiel each contain collections of oracles against a variety of foreign nations, mostly oracles of judgment. Thus, at the beginning of the book of Amos, there is a sequence of short sayings against Damascus, Gaza, Tyre, Edom, the Ammonites, and Moab (Amos 1:3—2:3). There are similar sequences in Isaiah (chapters 13–21 and 23), in Jeremiah (chapters 46–51) and in Ezekiel (chapters 25–32), and in the collections in these books the prophetic words against the great powers of the day, Egypt to the southwest and Assyria and Babylon to the northeast, loom especially large.

Let us look first at the sequence in Amos 1:3—2:3, a series of oracles against the immediate neighbors of Israel, all of which were of roughly equal size. One has the impression that these oracles against foreign nations—Damascus to the northeast, Gaza to the southwest, Tyre to the northwest, Edom, the Ammonites, and Moab to the southeast—were offered in order to attract the attention of Israel: following the sequence of these utterances is a long judgment oracle addressed to Israel that begins with the same format (2:6-16). The point would seem to be that everyone enjoys hearing of the wickedness of other nations, but Amos wants to be sure that the Israelites know that their own nation is not exempt from the judgment of God. One can imagine that the audience must have delighted in eavesdropping, so to say, on what God was saying to foreign nations. Yet these oracles were not understood to be for the ears of Israel alone: we recall again what was said in Chapter 1 when we studied Isa. 55:10-11, a passage in which God sets forth the power of the divine word to be effective. The Israelites believed that words were effective at a distance, so that though Amos's words were of course not outwardly audible in Damascus or in Gaza, the Israelites who did hear them would assume that they would effectively reach their ultimate target.

According to the judgments Amos utters against foreign nations, of what are they guilty? Essentially, various war atrocities. The Syrians, in Damascus, have been cruel toward the Gileadites to their south (1:3); the Ammonites have ripped open pregnant women, again in Gilead (1:13). Amos proclaims Yahweh to be about to judge foreign nations for these gross cruelties. Here, one suspects, is one of the roots of the notion of natural law: there are some deeds that any human culture knows to be wrong, no matter what its particular moral code might be. Alongside Yahweh's judgment for these atrocities is Yahweh's judgment on Israel, a much more fine-tuned judgment, inasmuch as Israel is obligated to obey covenant law: Israel is accused of injustice toward the poor and helpless (2:6-8), as we have seen.

Can we find any analogy today to these nations named by Amos that adjoin Israel? I suggest, that in North America at least, there are a whole range of institutions that in some respects parallel the churches: labor unions, public hospital boards, public schools and colleges, newspapers, public affairs groups like the League of Women Voters. Such groups as these, which are not charged with proclaiming the gospel, may nevertheless be expected to adhere to basic standards of behavior—honesty, fairness, and concern for equal rights for minorities. These oracles against foreign nations in the book of Amos may well remind us that God will judge these institutions too, if their behavior falls below a minimum level. (In Chapter 13, I shall suggest a different modern analogy for Edom.)

Hearing God in the Prophetic Words against Babylon: The Exile as a Model for Churches

I now turn to the oracles of judgment against the great powers of the day and take as a sample Jeremiah 50–51, a series of oracles against Babylon. These two chapters are enormous, a total of 104 verses (excluding 51:59-64, which is a separate narrative). It is almost as if the extent of this material matched the looming bulk of the Babylonian empire itself.

The Babylonian empire succeeded the Assyrian empire in the year 612 B.C. and continued until it was conquered by Cyrus of Persia in 538 B.C. As we have already noted, Jerusalem fell to the Babylonian army twice, in 598 B.C. and in 587 B.C., and on both occasions the Babylonians took Judahite leaders into exile. The destiny of the Babylonian empire was therefore of intense interest to the Jews during the whole three-quarters of a century of its existence. Some scholars have questioned whether any substantial part of Jeremiah 50–51 is from the prophet Jeremiah; my own conclusion is that most of the material is indeed genuine to the prophet,[13] but for purposes of the present discussion it is not necessary to make a decision on the question.

The oracles in the two chapters are heavy with descriptions of the cruelty and pride of Babylon (see, for example, 50:11, 31), battle orders to her attackers (50:14-16, 35-38; 51:11-12), and gloating descriptions of her coming downfall (50:2, 12, 23-24; 51:41-44). One also hears a reassurance to the Jews that they will ultimately go home to Jerusalem once more (50:4-5; 51:50-51).

How might we hear this material today? One clue is found in the New Testament, where "Babylon" is a symbol for Rome, the great power within which the first-century church emerged (1 Pet. 5:13; Rev. 17:1—18:24). I propose then that we ponder the possibility of seeing our own nation-state as an analogy of Babylon. This notion will strike many of us as implausible or even wrong-headed: we are accustomed to viewing our nation as a Christian nation, and we have been raised to see its founders as exemplars of virtue and its present leaders as churchgoers. Nevertheless, at least in the United States of America, we have slowly been persuaded that the policy of our government has been based at least in part on deceit, corruption, and the exercise of power for its own sake, and it may therefore be a useful exercise to ponder the place of the church within our nation-state after the analogy of the Jews in Babylonian exile. (As with Edom, I shall suggest a different identity for Babylon in Chapter 13.)

This notion stands in contrast to a use of the Old Testament by Christians that has been current for several decades: I refer to the analogy of the exodus. This analogy has been a favorite among those who have developed liberation theology. By this understanding, those peoples and groups in our world who are oppressed and marginated—the poor, the homeless and the dispossessed—may look to the God of liberation: as God brought the Israelites out of the house of slavery in Egypt, so God will bring today's oppressed out of their present situation of neglect. God has a "preferential option for the poor."[14] This theme is central for the Old Testament (see Chapter 6).

But it is not the only theme, and it is striking that the other great historical moment in the Old Testament, the exile, has not been drawn on to the same extent. If we explore the analogy, we will be uneasy with governmental pretentions of virtue, and we will be distressed but not surprised when some new governmental scandal or horror, long covered up, comes to light. We will not necessarily sit back in the expectation that the government will pioneer in social justice. We will not despair when we in our churches perceive ourselves to be marginal, knowing as we do that once upon a time the Jews saw themselves as forgotten people in Babylon, far from home (Isa. 40:27). Instead, we will continue to work, in our churches, to become the kind of community that God has in mind for us. Above all, we will long for the day when the vision of the book of Revelation comes to pass, "The kingdom of the world has become the kingdom of our Lord and of his Messiah, and he will reign forever and ever" (Rev. 11:15), and we will pray for it and work for it.

There is one more matter to consider in this chapter; in a way, it is the most important matter of all. In Jesus' own self-perception, the role of prophet loomed large. We think of several sayings that suggest this. As he preached in the synagogue at Nazareth, he remarked, "Prophets are not without honor, except in their hometown, and among their own kin, and in their own house" (Mark 6:4). In his lament over Jerusalem he is remembered as saying, "Jerusalem, Jerusalem, the city that kills the prophets and stones those who are sent to it! How often have I desired to gather your children together as a hen gathers her brood under her wings, and you are not willing!" (Luke 13:34). His remark about Nineveh and Jonah (Luke 11:32) points in the same direction, as does the response of the people in John 6:14. This suggests that we may be able to get a better grasp on Jesus' self-understanding as we gain understanding of the Old Testament prophets.

In this regard, I think particularly of the prophet Jeremiah. Matthew preserves a tradition that Jesus reminded some people of Jeremiah (Matt. 16:14), perhaps because Jeremiah was remembered as having predicted the fall of Jerusalem, as Jesus did centuries later. But one may also take note of Jeremiah's struggle with God over his calling as a prophet, a struggle preserved in a whole series of laments, some of which have recorded answers from God (Jer. 11:18-23; 12:1-6; 15:10-21; 17:14-18; 18:18-23; 20:7-18). If Jesus' public career is spanned by the temptations in the wilderness at the beginning (Mark 1:12-13 and, in more detail, Matt. 4:1-11 and Luke 4:1-13) to the cry of dereliction from the cross at the end, "My God, my God, why have you forsaken me?" (Mark 15:34), then we may be allowed to ponder how Jesus might have struggled to discern God's will as we ponder Jeremiah's struggle.

Can we hear God today in the words of the ancient prophets? We can and must.

There is one more important kind of oracle that the prophets offered to Israel: the visionary word of God's ultimate acts, which we call apocalyptic. Because the issues presented by these oracles deserve special treatment, I discuss them in the following chapter.

Notes

1. Useful are B. Davie Napier, "Prophet, prophetism," *IDB* 3:896–919; Martin J. Buss, "Prophecy in ancient Israel," *IDBSup* 694–97; Bruce Vawter, "Introduction to Prophetic Literature," *New Jerome*, 186–200; John J. Schmitt, "Prophecy, Preexilic Hebrew," *ABD* 5:482–89; John Barton, "Prophecy, Postexilic Hebrew," *ABD* 5:489–95; and the bibliographies offered with these articles. Many excellent recent commentaries on the individual books of the prophets are available.

2. Herbert B. Huffmon, "Prophecy in the ANE," *IDBSup* 697–700; "Prophecy (ANE)," *ABD* 5:477–82. For the text of Wen-Amun, see *ANET*, 26b.

3. See conveniently James L. Crenshaw, "Prophecy, false," *IDBSup* 701–2.

4. Frank Phillips, *The Boston Globe*, 19 August 1992, 27.

5. Rachel L. Carson, *Silent Spring* (Boston: Houghton Mifflin, 1962).

6. Jonathan Schell, *The Fate of the Earth* (New York: Knopf, 1982).

7. See conveniently John Gray, "Baal (deity)," *IDB* 1:328-29; "Ashtoreth," *IDB* 1:255–56.

8. Paul R. Clifford, *The Mission of the Local Church* (London: SCM, 1953), 81.

9. For this judgment, see Hans Walter Wolff, *Joel and Amos* (Hermeneia; Philadelphia: Fortress Press, 1977), 352–53. For the contrary view, see Shalom M. Paul, *Amos* (Hermeneia; Minneapolis: Fortress Press, 1991), 288–95.

10. John K. Winkler, *W. R. Hearst, An American Phenomenon* (New York: Simon & Schuster, 1928), 12.

11. See conveniently William L. Holladay, "New covenant, the," *IDBSup* 623–25.

12. In 49:3, many scholars believe that the word "Israel" is a secondary addition.

13. William L. Holladay, *Jeremiah 2* (Hermeneia; Minneapolis: Fortress Press, 1989), 401–8.

14. The idea was expressed at the conference in 1968 of Roman Catholic bishops in Medellín, Colombia: there the phrase was "preference to the poorest and most needy sectors." The phrase "preferential option for the poor" was coined at the meeting of the bishops in 1979 in Puebla, Mexico: see *Puebla Final Document*, Part 4, Chapter 1. On all this, see conveniently Gustavo Gutiérrez, *A Theology of Liberation; History, Politics and Salvation* (revised ed.; Maryknoll, NY: Orbis, 1988), and see further, Richard J. Neuhaus (ed.), *The Preferential Option for the Poor* (Encounter Series; Grand Rapids, Mich.: Eerdmans, 1988).

10

Apocalyptic

∽

There gradually emerged in the course of the postexilic period a type of literature, new to Israel, which we call apocalyptic. This literature is not easy to define in short compass. It often embodies visions vouchsafed to the seer, either directly from God or mediated by an angel. Such visions frequently employ vivid and even bizarre images. When apocalyptic material refers to events or persons in the writer's past or present, it often refers to them in code; for example, Daniel 7 describes four beasts, which represent four successive world kingdoms. But it more typically concerns God's climactic plans for the future, a scenario of final events; this scenario is likely to describe a last judgment, the destruction of the enemies of God, and the establishment of new, ideal living conditions for the covenant people, conditions that presuppose a transformed heaven and earth.[1]

A half-century ago, scholars customarily understood apocalyptic literature to have arisen under the stimulus of Persian religion (Zoroastrianism). That religion is strongly dualistic—it understands the universe to be the scene of a cosmic struggle between the good deity (called Ahura Mazda) and the evil deity (called Ahriman), and indeed declares that every human soul is subjected to that same struggle. While not denying that Persian dualism reinforced the tendencies toward apocalyptic to be found in postexilic Judaism, scholars today view apocalyptic literature much more as a natural development of the outlook of the Old Testament prophets in that period. It is therefore appropriate for us, having surveyed the prophetic literature in the last chapter, to turn to apocalyptic at this point.

Can we hear God in the apocalyptic literature of the Old Testament? When we ask that question, we are confronted by a difficult set of problems. Let me offer a cluster of them here. One can use the approach of the historical-critical method to trace the social and historical situation in the postexilic period that gave rise to apocalyptic literature. We shall do so, but, as we have seen in dealing with other kinds of material in the Old Testament, that method by itself cannot tell us whether we may hear God in the material, and if so, how. As we saw in Chapter 9, the prophets kept their eyes on the events of history, but apocalyptic literature envisages a new heaven and a new earth beyond the possibilities of history as ordinarily experienced. How might one trust such visions? The passages of apocalyptic material in the various collections cannot be made to fit into any single scenario; indeed, some of them appear to us more like dream material than anything else with which we may be familiar. Furthermore, such material in the Old Testament stands in some tension with similar material in the New Testament (the latter material, of course, has taken precedence for Christian understanding). And because apocalyptic literature, by definition, offers visions of what is not yet, it is difficult to know how, if at all, to hear the authoritative voice of God in these sections of the Old Testament.

In the New Testament, apocalyptic literature is represented by the book of Revelation (sometimes called the Apocalypse), and in shorter span by Mark 13 (and its parallels in Matthew 24 and Luke 21:5-36); but beyond these literary units, apocalyptic ideas are to be found everywhere in the New Testament. For example, the term "day of the Lord" appears several times in the epistles (1 Cor. 5:5; 1 Thess. 5:2; 2 Thess. 2:2; 2 Pet. 3:10; compare 1 Cor. 1:8; 2 Cor. 1:14). In the Old Testament, apocalyptic literature is represented by the book of Daniel (especially chapters 7–12) and the book of Zechariah (especially chapters 9–14), and in shorter span by Isaiah 24–27.

Old Testament Apocalyptic in Contrast to Both the New Testament and Current Notions

It is important at the outset to indicate how distinctive are the motifs of Old Testament apocalyptic literature: it is useful to contrast them with the beliefs in earlier, pre-exilic Israel, with the beliefs of the New Testament, and with the beliefs current among Christians today, with regard to eschatology ("last things"), because all four of these belief systems are in contrast with each other. Let me begin with the conventional beliefs of Christians today (or at least with the conventional beliefs of the kind of Christians who are likely to read this work!). These beliefs are doubtless both various and fuzzy; part of the difficulty in defining them is that many Christians now focus so thoroughly on this world that their beliefs about matters beyond this life are not in the center of their attention except at the time of a funeral service, or when their own time of death approaches. But if one is guided by the assumptions of current funeral services, present-day beliefs usually include an assumption that the individual who has died has gone to be with God, and with Jesus, and has thus joined those who have died previously, in the realm called heaven, where he or she will dwell for eternity. Any belief in hell has faded: hell is largely the stuff of cartoons and jokes and of phrases of slang and insult. This notion of the destiny of the individual at death is, however, at some dissonance with the metaphor that the individual is "asleep" in the grave, and with corresponding affirmations made by Christians who recite the creed in the course of worship, the affirmation that Jesus "will come again to judge the living and the dead," and the affirmation in the "resurrection of the dead" (or "of the body").

The New Testament offers various affirmations about eschatology, affirmations that are not always coherent with each other, but they stand in some contrast to the conventional beliefs of Christians today. Some traditions about Jesus suggest that he took it for granted that a person goes immediately to heaven or hell upon death—the parable of the rich man and Lazarus (Luke 16:19-31) implies this. Thus, heaven is described as "the bosom of Abraham" (v. 22: see the footnote in the NRSV), hell is described as a torment of flames (vv. 23, 24), and we notice that the rich man has five brothers who are still living. (Compare Matt. 8:11, in which heaven is described as feasting with Abraham.) On the other hand, the parable of the great judgment (Matt. 25:31-46) assumes that those destined for heaven and those destined for hell are separated not at the death of the individual but at the end of time. But Jesus is remembered as assuming that the end was coming quickly: "Truly I tell you, there are some standing here who will not taste death until they see that the kingdom of God has come with power" (Mark 9:1).

A belief in the resurrection of the dead was current among many Jews in Jesus' day—we recall the tradition that some people believed Jesus was John the Baptist alive once more (Mark 8:28), and we recall also that Paul, testifying before the Sanhedrin, was able to set Sadducees against Pharisees by raising the question of the resurrection of the dead (Acts 23:6-10). But *Christians'* belief about the resurrection was of course grounded on their testimony of Jesus' own resurrection (Rom. 8:29; Col. 1:18). It is also important to stress that the New Testament writers expected an imminent, dramatic, visible return of Christ to usher in the new age (see 1 Thess. 1:9-10 and often). The earliest New Testament writings expected the end of the age to come quickly, but there is clear evidence of tension in later strata of the New Testament when the end of the age appeared to be deferred (2 Pet. 3:1-18). And there are traces in the Gospel of John that suggest an alternative belief, namely that eternal life begins for the Christian at the point when he or she accepts the gospel; for example, John 5:24: "Very truly, I tell you, anyone who hears my word and believes him who sent me has eternal life, and does not come under judgment, but has passed from death to life."[2]

The set of beliefs about death in the pre-exilic period in the Old Testament is very different. In that period, so far as we know, there was no notion of life after death. The dead were gathered in Sheol, which was understood to be a kind of super-grave. Most references to Sheol, such as in Gen. 37:35, offer no description of it, but there are a few passages that elaborate on the matter; one thinks of Isa. 5:14, and particularly Isa. 14:9-20. There are references to Sheol in the Psalms, too, that are suggestive, especially the descriptions of it (and synonyms for it) in Psalm 88. Since early Israel took for granted the notion of corporate personality (see Chapter 5), it was understood that it was through one's descendants that one lived on—an assumption that reinforced the obligation in the Old Testament to produce children.

The Loss in the Exilic and Postexilic Periods of the Sense of History

I begin by stressing what I have said so often in this work: the central affirmation of the Old Testament is that God has entered history. We saw it as a consequence of the notion of covenant (Chapter 2), we saw it in our discussion of Old Testament narratives (Chapter 5), notably in the battles (Chapter 6), and it was a central presupposition of the prophets whom we have discussed, who announced God's judgment on the covenant people and God's restoration of the covenant people at the end of the exile (Chapter 9).

This preoccupation with history was given a framework in the institution of the monarchy and in the succession of the kings of Israel and Judah. The chronological framework of these kings gave a firm basis for testimony about God's acts in history—we have seen the difficulties faced by present-day scholars when they try to establish the specifics of the history for the period *before* the monarchy, the period of Moses and Joshua and the "judges" (see Chapter 5). But with the succession of the kings of Israel and Judah the covenant people maintained a chronological framework for their historical narrative, and though scholars may quibble about small details in the chronology, few doubt that the succession of kings occurred as the narrative affirms. This Israelite concern for history was not focused on local events alone; it involved the kings of Egypt and Assyria and Babylonia and the kings of other states in the eastern Mediterranean. Given the Israelites' theological assumption of God's involvement with history, then, there was a preservable sequence of events into which to affirm the entrance of God.

This preoccupation with history faded in the exilic and postexilic periods, after the end of the monarchy: dated events become much rarer in the record. Once the biblical narrative has recorded a third deportation of Jews to Babylon in 582 B.C. (Jer. 52:30), we have no further record of historical events in the exilic period. It is true that we have dates of various revelations to the prophet Ezekiel, down to 571 B.C. (Ezek. 29:17), but these dates do not mark events of public experience such as are afforded by the advent of kings or the fighting of battles. We do have records of a few scattered events dated by the regnal years of Persian kings. Thus we have the notices of the end of the Babylonian captivity in the first year of Cyrus (538 B.C.: Ezra 1:1) and the consequent re-turn of a group of exiles to Jerusalem under the leadership of a "prince" named Sheshbazzar, who cleared the foundation of the old temple (Ezra 1:8; 5:14-16); of the renewal of efforts to rebuild the temple in the second year of Darius (520 B.C.) under the leadership of Zerubbabel, who was a nephew of Sheshbazzar, and of a priest named Jeshua (Ezra 3:8), and under the prodding of the prophets Haggai and Zechariah (see the notations in the prophetic books of those names); and of the completion of the temple in 515 B.C. (Ezra 6:13-18). We have in the next century the notice of the coming from Babylon to Jerusalem of Ezra the priest with a copy of the book of the law in the sev-enth year of Artaxerxes I (458 B.C.: Ezra 7:7) and of the coming of Nehemiah the governor in the twentieth year of Artaxerxes I (445 or 444 B.C.: Neh. 1:1). But alongside these scattered dates, two facts stand out. The first is that the chapters of the books of Ezra and Nehemiah are in disorder; the second is that, even though the high priests in Jerusalem were the de facto leaders of the community, the succession of whom might offer the chronological equivalent of the sequence of kings in the monarchical period, as a matter of fact we cannot construct a complete sequence of high priests.[3] To put it an-other way: we know far more about the events in Jerusalem during the eighth and seventh centuries than we do about events there during the fifth and fourth centuries. The Jewish concern to record history had receded; in-deed, it might almost be said that that history itself seemed to afford few events worthy of record.

I took note in Chapter 9 that we could characterize the task of the Old Tes-tament prophets to be "to comfort the afflicted and to afflict the comfort-able." The task of the prophets was to proclaim the unexpected news: in times of confidence, that God's judgment was coming, and in times of demoraliza-tion, that God's rescue was ahead. We saw in Chapters 4 and 9 the various shapes that God's judgment might take—invasion by foreign armies, or nat-ural disasters such as earthquake, drought, locusts, or plague. All of these dis-asters were recurrent: such events were bound to happen in the course of time. They were part and parcel of the world as it was (and is) constituted; people who are prosperous and confident and secure have only to wait, and something terrible is bound to happen eventually, inevitably. It was only the

interpretation of these events as the judgment of God that made them something extraordinary.

But the reverse is plainly not true: people who are poor and oppressed and
demoralized cannot expect that good fortune will automatically come if only
they wait. People who are poor and oppressed and demoralized will probably
stay that way; indeed, they may see even greater misery as they wait. This obvious contrast indicates why the pre-exilic prophets who tended to predict
doom could see God intervening in history, while the exilic and postexilic
prophets who tended to predict salvation more and more saw God bringing in
a new heaven and earth. The matter was not so simple that we can make an
easy contrast between two sorts of prophets, but the tendency was as I describe it.

Origins of Apocalyptic Motifs

As we attempt to trace the rise of the motifs of apocalyptic literature, we find
their roots in the very beginning of Israel's memory. Two of these motifs are to
be found in the earliest testimony of Israel and indeed have antecedents in the
world of pre-Israelite myths. Both of them, as a matter of fact, are illustrated in
an early song attributed to Moses that depicts God's deliverance of Israel at the
sea, Exod. 15:1-18. The first of these is the motif of the divine warrior, which
we discussed in Chapters 5 and 6. In the epic literature of the Canaanites, the
god Baal battled against the gods Mot ("Death") and Yamm ("Sea").[4] This
motif became historicized in Yahweh's fighting on behalf of the Israelites at the
Sea and God's fighting on their behalf as they moved toward Canaan.

The second mythic motif is the depiction of the creator deity freely shifting the elements of heaven and earth: in Exod. 15:8 we hear that "the floods
stood up in a heap." Other early songs offer similar images: in another poem
attributed to Moses, the fire kindled by God's anger "sets on fire the foundations of the mountains" (Deut. 32:22); and in the Song of Deborah in Judges
5, probably the earliest extensive poem in the Old Testament (twelfth century
B.C.?), "the stars fought from heaven, from their courses they fought against
Sisera [the enemy general]" (v. 20). Such phrases as these may be understood
as poetic metaphors (and might have been so understood originally), but they
do suggest a mentality that sets no limits on what Israel could testify to be
possible for God in this world. If God is creator of heaven and earth, then the
elements of heaven and earth are always subject to God's beck and call: we explored this in Chapter 7.

In Chapter 7, we also explored the relation between ordinary and extraordinary events in the Old Testament. The people of the Old Testament were

slow to develop any notion of a *fixed order* in the world. It is true, one does find in Jeremiah an awareness of the regular migration of birds: "Even the stork in the heavens knows its times, and the turtledove, swallow and crane observe the time of their coming; but my people do not know the ordinance of the Lord" (Jer. 8:8), but an expression of the fixed order of the present world like that found in Jer. 31:35-36 probably belongs to the fifth century B.C., long after Jeremiah: "Thus says the Lord, who gives the sun for light by day and the fixed order of the moon and the stars for light by night, who stirs up the sea so that its waves roar—the Lord of hosts is his name: if this fixed order were ever to cease from my presence, says the Lord, then also the offspring of Israel would cease to be a nation before me forever."[5] One wonders: Is the idea expressed in this verse a reflection of the awareness of the regularities of the heavenly bodies known in Babylonian astronomy?

The idea of a culminating intervention of God is likewise found deep in Israel's past. I have mentioned the phrase "the day of the Lord" in the New Testament, but that phrase is already found in the prophet Amos, in the eighth century B.C. Amos mocked those who assume that the day of the Lord would be good news: "Alas for you who desire the day of the Lord! Why do you want the day of the Lord? It is darkness, not light; as if someone fled from a lion, and was met by a bear; or went into the house and rested a hand against the wall, and was bitten by a snake. Is not the day of the Lord darkness, not light, and gloom with no brightness in it?" (Amos 5:18-20). We do not conclude that in Amos's day the "day of the Lord" was thought to be an apocalyptic last judgment, but we may assume at the very least that it was thought of as a historical landmark, a reckoning in which God would reward his people. The people's assumption that they deserved to be rewarded was of course what Amos was challenging.

The characteristic details of the apocalyptic visions of the Old Testament are various enough and curious enough so that we must survey at least the main bodies of material one by one if we are to have any hope of answering the question how we might hear God in the material. It is to this survey then that we turn.

Visionary Motifs in the Pre-exilic Prophets

There must have been many visionaries in the early days of Israel, but among the pre-exilic prophets Isaiah (eighth century) was certainly one of them—or at least his call is couched as a vision report in a passage that is often cited: "In the year that King Uzziah died, I saw the Lord sitting on a throne, high and lofty; and the hem of his robe filled the temple . . ." (Isa. 6:1). And Isaiah, like

Amos, spoke of God's "day" of judgment, and in terrifying terms: see, for example, 2:5-21, a passage we looked at in Chapter 8, where the reference to the "day" of God's judgment occurs four times (vv. 11, 12, 17, 20). Similarly, Jeremiah in the seventh century referred to a "day" or "year" or "time" of calamity or punishment (Jer. 10:15; 11:23; 18:17; 23:12). These phrases were not meant to refer to an apocalyptic last judgment, any more than Amos's expression was, but they were certainly available when such notions of a last judgment became current.

The Jews in the early years of the Babylonian exile understood these prophetic pronouncements about God's day of judgment to refer to the fall of Jerusalem, an event that marked a watershed in their history. We see this in the books of the prophets Jeremiah and Ezekiel, and we see it in the book of Lamentations, a collection of laments over the fall of the city.

As for Jeremiah, it is clear, again as we saw in Chapter 8, that beyond the judgment that he announced, he announced hope for the future: the exiles would remain away from Jerusalem for "a long time" (Jer. 29:28) but eventually they would return (compare the joyful poem in Jer. 31:7-9, which can hardly be denied to the prophet). And the book of Lamentations offers several references to the day of Yahweh's anger (1:12; 2:1, 21, 22).

Ezekiel

Jeremiah's younger contemporary Ezekiel was crucial in stimulating the rise of apocalyptic literature, so we need to take some time to examine his words. Ezekiel, as we have seen, was among the exiles in the first deportation from Jerusalem (598 B.C.). He had been a priest (Ezek. 1:3), doubtless having served at the temple in Jerusalem, and five years after the deportation he began to prophesy. Like Isaiah, he was a visionary; indeed, the vision report of his prophetic call takes up the entire first three chapters of the book called by his name. Whether it was his previous experience as a priest that caused him to be so systematically specific in his visual descriptions, or whether he was stimulated to that end by the appearance of the monumental Babylonian bas-reliefs around him, or whether his descriptions are simply the expression of his personal makeup, is of course impossible to say, but the fact remains that his descriptions are astonishing in their elaboration. We glanced in Chapter 1 at the first chapter of Ezekiel, especially at v. 28 of that chapter, when we discussed the metaphorical nature of language for God; but when one reads the whole description he offers of his vision of the throne chariot of God (Ezek. 1:4-28), one realizes that something new and unique has entered the testimony of the covenant people: God's chariot is described in detail, including the working of its wheels, its spokes whirring and flashing in the sun, and then we have Ezekiel's description of God: "Upward from what appeared like the loins I saw something like gleaming amber, something that looked like fire enclosed all around; and downward from what looked like the loins I saw something that looked like fire, and there was a splendor all around. Like the bow in a cloud on a rainy day, such was the appearance of the splendor all around" (1:27-28). Even if, as some scholars believe, the material in the book of Ezekiel underwent later editorial expansion after the original words of the prophet were recorded, one catches some sense of the awe with which Ezekiel described what he had seen when God appeared to him, and, too, what he had heard (1:24) and even tasted (3:3).

One might wonder: How would Ezekiel's fellow-exiles have received these words? We have a brief glimpse of people coming to him for an explanation of his behavior (24:18-19), so one assumes that a significant number of his fellow-exiles took his words and actions seriously; certainly his words were remembered and recorded and preserved with the conviction that his testimonies, including his vision reports, were revelations from God.

A small detail from my own history may offer some indirect light on the matter. I had grown up in a comfortable middle-class home, so that the rudeness and lack of privacy I experienced when I was drafted into the army in 1946 was something of a shock. I found myself in those early weeks of army service looking forward to the night and to sleep, not so much out of fatigue as out of a craving for my dreams, because at least my dreams were my own, something beyond the control of the first sergeant. So I have wondered whether the disorientation experienced by the exiles in Babylon, far from their accustomed ways, did not predispose them not only to listen to Ezekiel's vivid visions but to treasure and preserve them. Again we may think of African American slaves, making Ezekiel's vision their own: "Ezekiel saw the wheel, 'way up in the middle of the air." They, in their own experience of disorientation and oppression, could identify themselves with the visionary prophet of long ago.

Much of the material in the first twenty-four chapters of Ezekiel is devoted to oracles of judgment on the people, the details of which need not detain us here. We do, however, need to take account of an issue related to judgment, and that is the extent to which the *individual* in those days was to be held accountable for sins committed. I alluded in Chapter 4 to the old creed in Exod. 34:6-7, in which God is described as visiting the iniquity of the parents upon the children and the children's children, to the third and fourth generation, and as keeping steadfast love for the thousandth generation; and I described in Chapter 5 the notion of corporate personality, by which a whole family or clan or tribe manifests a single identity. By this notion, the Israelites of pre-exilic times could assume that God's justice would work itself out within this world: a wicked man himself might live to an old age and die prosperous, but his children would surely pay for his wicked deeds, and contrariwise a righteous man might die early and poor, but his children would doubtless be rewarded. In this way, conventional beliefs could be sustained: "Whoever is steadfast in righteousness will live, but whoever pursues evil will die" (Prov. 11:19). A remark of a psalmist says it even more strongly: "I have been young, and now am old, yet I have not seen the righteous forsaken or their children begging bread" (Ps. 37:25).

In a stable community, this set of beliefs might have continued indefinitely, but the fall of Jerusalem and the consequent exile tore the community apart. One result of this dislocation was evidently that people began to question the validity of the assumption of corporate personality: people began to wonder whether the locus of responsibility was not the individual rather than the family or clan.

In Ezekiel 18, the prophet gave voice to this new perception: "The word of the Lord came to me: What do you mean by repeating this proverb concerning the land of Israel, 'The parents have eaten sour grapes, and the children's teeth are set on edge'? As I live, says the Lord God, this proverb shall no more be used by you in Israel. Know that all lives are mine; the life of the parent as well as the life of the child is mine: it is only the person who sins that shall die" (vv. 1-4). In the remainder of the chapter, Ezekiel goes on to work out various scenarios, that of a good father, who has a bad son, who in turn has a good son; of a wicked man who finally repents, and contrariwise of a righteous man who goes bad, all to demonstrate how God judges one's own actions at a given time, rather than the actions of one's parents or even one's own actions at an earlier stage in life. Now the fact that we have this chapter does not mean that Ezekiel has persuaded his Jewish community to turn its back altogether on the notion of corporate personality but rather that the door is now open to the notion of individual responsibility in one's standing before God.

The notion of individual responsibility brings with it the very real problem of God's reward of the righteous and punishment of the wicked: it becomes hard to continue to affirm a verse like Ps. 37:25, cited just above. The problem of the suffering of righteous persons, and of the lack of punishment of wicked persons, becomes acute, and if one assumes that God is all-powerful, then only two solutions become possible: either one accuses God of being unjust, which is the accusation leveled by Job, an accusation to which we will give attention in Chapter 11, or else one looks forward to God's rewards and punishments beyond this life. The latter solution eventually emerged in the Old Testament, but only gradually, as we shall see.

Like Jeremiah, Ezekiel was moved, after the final fall of Jerusalem in 587 B.C. (Ezek. 33:21-22), to voice hope to his people, and these words of hope are to be found particularly in chapters 33–39; several of these passages become food for our thought. In chapter 34, he announces God's judgment against the "shepherds" of Israel ("shepherds" is a metaphor for rulers): these shepherds have exploited and neglected their "sheep" (the people). The solution is that God will take over the shepherding of the covenant people directly and will appoint a new David who will be a faithful shepherd (vv. 23-24). In the years after the exile, such a passage would reinforce the people's hope for the restoration of the Davidic monarchy.

In 37:1-14, we hear Ezekiel's well-known vision of the valley of dry bones. "The hand of the Lord came upon me, and he brought me out by the spirit of the Lord and set me down in the middle of a valley; it was full of bones" (v. 1). I never read this verse without thinking of the Armenian martyrs' shrine next to the Armenian cathedral in Antelias, just north of Beirut, Lebanon. This shrine contains skulls and tibia bones collected in the Syrian desert, bones of Armenians sent out in 1915 by the Turks to die. "Can these bones live?" (v. 3). It may be that the genesis of Ezekiel's vision was the common remark he cites, "Our bones are dried up, and our hope is lost; we are cut off completely" (v. 11). In any event, one should read the whole awesome passage aloud. Look particularly at the last two verses: "'And you shall know that I am the Lord, when I open your graves, and bring you up from your graves, O my people. I will put my spirit within you, and you shall live, and I will place you on your own soil; then you shall know that I, the Lord, have spoken and will act,' says the Lord."

A minister of the United Church of Christ, whom I know, has been able in his ministry to use Scripture passages in innovative ways. One Sunday morning, the Scripture lesson was Ezekiel's vision of the dry bones. He read it aloud and then said, "We will all sit quietly, pondering these words. And when any of you can affirm that your bones have begun to live, will you please stand up." And he waited until perhaps two-thirds of the congregation, one by one, had stood up, after which they all sang the Doxology. On such an occasion the power of this passage is manifest.

How might Ezekiel and his hearers have understood these words? In spite of the message of chapter 18, one suspects not that he had in mind some kind of notion of individual resurrection but rather that he was affirming a belief that God will bring the nation to life once more. It is noteworthy that the preceding chapter (chapter 36) is a vision of the restoration of Israel on its land,

and that the following vision (37:15-28) portrays the reunification of north and south—these kingdoms, separated for 350 years, would be joined together once more (see below).

To return to the valley of dry bones: how are the bones of the nation to come to life once more? Is it to be by a photographable miracle of skeletons taking on sinews and flesh and breath once more, or is this description a metaphor for a new beginning for the nation in the natural course of events? There is no way to know; on the one hand, Ezekiel and his listeners would never set any limit on what God is able to do; on the other hand, because Ezekiel himself understood the inadequacy of language in talking about God (we recall once more our discussion of Ezek. 1:28 in Chapter 1), we cannot discount the possibility that his vision was not to be understood so much literally as symbolically—Ezekiel's effort to speak about the unspeakable.

I should make mention here of the symbolic act reported in 37:15-28. Ezekiel is told to take two sticks—one marked "Joseph," representing the northern kingdom, and one marked "Judah," the southern kingdom—and to join them together to signal the coming reunification of the people under a Davidic king. This passage is noteworthy as a vehicle for Ezekiel's optimism, but we will find, when we analyze Zechariah 11 (see below), that the symbolism is the background for a far darker vision.

Other hopeful visions in the book of Ezekiel similarly hover between history and nonhistory. I mentioned in Chapter 9 the misuse made recently by Christians who took "Meshech" in 38:2, 3 to refer to Moscow, and therefore "Magog" as well. Meshech appears to be a real people, the Mushki, a tribe identified with the Phrygians in the area of present-day Ankara, Turkey. But even though Magog, like Meshech, also appears in Gen. 10:2, there is no land or people with which modern scholars can identify Magog, and one is therefore led to believe that Ezekiel's vision of the punishment of the wicked "Gog, of the land of Magog," has more to do with a mythical people off the edge of the map than it has to do with a group with any historical identity.

I must now say a further word about chapters 40–48, which I have already mentioned in Chapter 8. They offer a description of the future temple and future Jerusalem, and though some scholars have assumed them to be an anonymous addition to the book, it is safer to attribute them to Ezekiel himself.[6] The plans for the temple are ideal ones (and were not carried out when the temple was finally rebuilt). The future Jerusalem too was to have an altered geography (45:1-8), and there would be a broad river emerging out of the temple and flowing to the east, to freshen the Dead Sea (47:1-12). So these chapters too offer an ideal, transformed reality. What is important for our purposes is that Ezekiel's visionary language, exhibited throughout his book, encouraged Jews to shape a way of talking about ultimate matters in terms that pointed away from ordinary history.

Once More: "Second Isaiah"

I turn once more to discuss the words of comfort in Isaiah 40–55, words of Second Isaiah, whom we discussed in Chapter 9. This prophet, we recall, prophesied in Babylon at the end of the exilic period. He spoke of God's creating something new (43:18-19; 48:6-7), but in Second Isaiah that new thing was his one anchor to current history, namely God's calling of Cyrus, king of Persia (41:25-26; 44:28; 45:1), to bring liberation to the covenant people. Beyond the one anchor to the advent of Cyrus, Second Isaiah's words made the minds of his contemporaries and of those who came after him hospitable to the categories of apocalyptic in this way: his descriptions of the transformed land, simply as descriptions, soared high above any reality experienced by those who returned from exile. Listen; God speaks: "I will lay waste mountains and hills, and dry up all their herbage; I will open rivers on the bare heights, and fountains in the midst of the valleys; I will make the wilderness a pool of water, and the dry land springs of water. I will put in the wilderness the cedar, the acacia, the myrtle, and the olive; I will set in the desert the cypress, the plane and the pine together" (41:18-19); "For you shall go out in joy, and be led back in peace; the mountains and the hills before you shall burst into song, and all the trees of the field shall clap their hands" (55:12). These words, spoken only a year or two before the first group of exiles made their way back to Jerusalem, not only must have raised their spirits but must have raised them to expectations far above what their real world was able to offer, and to this degree the words would have encouraged their hearers to ponder and entertain possibilities beyond the history they were experiencing.

"Third Isaiah"

I now turn to passages contained in the last eleven chapters of Isaiah, Isaiah 56–66, material that scholars are accustomed to attributing to a "Third Isaiah." These chapters were written later than those of Second Isaiah (chapters 40–55); they were written in Jerusalem by a prophet who had returned there from Babylon along with other Jews, evidently within the years 530–510 B.C. Although some scholars (myself included) suspect that Third Isaiah is actually Second Isaiah speaking once more some decades later, it is safer to refer these chapters to a separate prophet who was a disciple of Second Isaiah. With Third Isaiah, as the scholar Paul Hanson has recently suggested, we are at the dawn of apocalyptic:[7] in 65:17 we read, "For I am about to create new heavens and a new earth; the former things shall not be remembered or come to mind." This shift in mentality is important enough so that we need to explore the context of these eleven chapters.

It is clear that this prophet understood himself to speak for fellow Jews whom he judged to be oppressed; the verses in which he testifies to his call are the verses that Jesus would later cite when he read from the scroll of Isaiah in the synagogue at Nazareth: "The spirit of the Lord God is upon me, because the Lord has anointed me, he has sent me to bring good news to the oppressed, to bind up the brokenhearted, to proclaim liberty to the captives, and release to the prisoners, to proclaim the year of the Lord's favor" (61:1-2). (We notice in passing that Third Isaiah claims an *anointing* from God, that is to say, he claims to be a metaphorical "messiah." We shall return to this matter presently.) But there are many other passages within these chapters that stress God's love for the poor; for example, "For thus says the high and lofty one who inhabits eternity, whose name is Holy: I dwell in the high and holy place, and also with those who are contrite and humble in spirit, to revive the spirit of the humble, and to revive the heart of the contrite" (57:15).

There are also a whole array of passages in which the prophet understands God to inveigh against haughty leaders who claim ritual holiness. For example, in 65:1-5, God is represented as waiting in vain for people to pray to him, people "who say, 'Keep to yourself, do not come near me, for I am too holy for you'" (v. 5). The target for these attacks is clearly the priests of the temple, either just rebuilt or about to be rebuilt. But, astonishingly, the prophet accuses these priests of gross pagan practices, even the eating of pork (v. 4). Accusations of pagan practices are found elsewhere in these chapters: in 57:3-8, where the leaders are accused of child sacrifice and fertility worship, we find language as abusive as any in Scripture. The question immediately arises: Were temple priests really guilty of child sacrifice, fertility worship, and the eating of pork? It is doubtful: the fall of Jerusalem sixty years before, and the explanation offered by the prophets Jeremiah and Ezekiel for the fall of the city—that it was the result of the people's worship of Baal—would make it unlikely in the extreme that these accusations are to be taken literally. Instead, Third Isaiah seems to have drawn on the accusatory vocabulary of pre-exilic times to express his angry judgment on the quality of worship in his day—and on the quality of leadership as well, for he calls the leaders "children of a sorceress, offspring of an adulterer and a whore" (57:3). He is using the language of invective.

He is particularly concerned to challenge the exclusivity and centrality of the newly rebuilt temple. He understands it to be God's will that the temple be open to foreigners (56:6-8); he hears God say, "Heaven is my throne and the earth is my footstool; what is the house that you would build for me, and what is my resting place?" (66:1). Indeed, he seems to understand God to level a scathing criticism at the whole sacrificial system (66:3).

By contrast, he speaks several times of the righteous as God's "servants" (63:17; 65:8, 13-14). He appears then to have identified himself and his followers with the suffering servant depicted in 52:13—53:12. As that servant is pictured as suffering, so the righteous have suffered. Indeed, 65:13-16 illustrates a remarkable feature of this material: to those to whom the passage is addressed, judgment is proclaimed, while to God's servants, salvation is proclaimed. This oracle (and others like it) announces judgment and hope simultaneously to contrasting segments of the community.

We need to pinpoint more precisely the background of the social conflict reflected here. The scholar Paul Hanson has suggested that what we see here is a result of the demotion of the Levites. At the end of the pre-exilic period, when the book of Deuteronomy was published, the Levites had had priestly status (Deut. 18:1-8). In the exilic and early postexilic periods, they were being demoted to subpriestly status: by the time of which we are speaking, only those of the lineage of Zadok held full priestly rank (Ezek. 45:15). (We recall our discussion about the descent of Zadok in Chapter 8.[8]) The priests against whom Third Isaiah directed his oracles were therefore Zadokites. But because Third Isaiah offers two of the few references to *Moses* in the prophetical books (63:11 and 12), and because Moses was a Levite (Exod. 2:1), Hanson proposes that Third Isaiah was himself a Levite whose oracles were a reaction to the new, lower status to which the Levites were demoted in the process of rebuilding the temple.[9]

In any event, we may conclude that the oracles of Isaiah 56–66, written in the period 530–510 B.C., reflect a community that was deeply divided in its religious outlook, a community whose power resided in a circle of temple priests who had grown fat (56:11-12) and haughty (65:5) and were concerned for their own privilege (58:13), who seemed only to go through the motions of ritual (58:5), and who neglected the most basic matters of social justice (58:6-9; 59:14-15); it was a community in which the angry prophet spoke on behalf of the poor and neglected and raised the question, on at least one occasion, whether the temple was necessary at all (66:1).

In the conviction of Third Isaiah, what, in this situation, was God to do? In the day of Second Isaiah, God's new act of creation had been the coming of Cyrus, king of Persia (45:1, 4), who indeed went on to free the covenant people from their exile in Babylon, so that those who wished to could return to Jerusalem. But the Jerusalem to which they had returned was now ruled by these haughty and thoughtless priests. What was God to do? The prophet could sing of God's glory to arise on Jerusalem: "Arise, shine, for your light has come, and the glory of the Lord has risen upon you. For darkness shall cover the earth, and thick darkness the peoples; but the Lord will arise upon you, and his glory will appear over you" (60:1), a Jerusalem acknowledged as the center of the world by all nations: "Nations shall come to your light, and kings to the brightness of your dawn" (60:2), but when, indeed, would this wonder take place? The prophet insisted that he would continue to speak out until it happened: "For Zion's sake I will not keep silent, and for Jerusalem's sake I will not rest, until her vindication shines out like the dawn, and her salvation like a burning torch" (62:1). Indeed, he would continue to remind God to do what was promised: "Upon your walls, O Jerusalem, I have posted sentinels; all day and all night they shall never be silent. You who remind the Lord, take no rest, and give him no rest until he establishes Jerusalem and makes it renowned throughout all the earth" (62:6-7). It will be "the year of the Lord's favor, and the day of vengeance of our God" (61:2). But when will it be? "Soon": "Maintain justice, and do what is right; for soon my salvation will come, and my deliverance be revealed" (56:1). But how? One must ask, how? By a still newer creative act of God. What is that newer creative act to be? "For I am about to create new heavens and a new earth; the former things shall not be remembered or come to mind. But be glad and rejoice forever in what I am creating; for I am about to create Jerusalem as a joy, and its people as a delight" (65:17-18).

Strikingly, from our own vantage point in history, the array of characteristics of the new heaven and new earth which the prophet offers begins rather modestly. There will be no more weeping (65:19), nor infant mortality, nor indeed shall anyone die before his or her time (65:20). "They shall build houses and inhabit them; they shall plant vineyards and eat their fruit. They shall not build and another inhabit; they shall not plant and another eat" (65:21-22). Imagine being able to build a house and plant a vineyard and know that one will live to enjoy them and not see them taken over by a foreign conqueror! "They shall not labor in vain, or bear children for calamity" (65:23). These poignant lines speak volumes about the griefs, the pains, and the dashed hopes of the Jews of those days. Further, God will always be available to answer the covenant people: "Before they call I will answer, while they are yet speaking I will hear" (65:24): there will no longer be any barrier between God and the people. Finally, and remarkably, the prophet summarizes Isa. 11:6-9, "The wolf and the lamb shall feed together, the lion shall eat straw like the ox; but the serpent—its food shall be dust! They shall not hurt or

destroy on all my holy mountain, says the Lord" (65:25). If, as I have surmised, those phrases in 11:6-9 were, for the original Isaiah, metaphors for international peace (see Chapter 9), they now move beyond metaphor to offer a
description of shifted relations in the animal world: if the array of characteristics of the new heaven and the new earth began modestly, it ends stunningly.
Such, for Third Isaiah, is the new creative act of God.

Haggai and Zechariah 1–8

I turn next to two contemporaries of Third Isaiah, the prophets Haggai and
Zechariah. At the outset of our discussion of these two prophets, two things
must be explained. First, of the fourteen chapters of the book of Zechariah,
only chapters 1–8 may be attributed to the prophet himself; the last six chapters in the book are anonymous additions from later times, which we shall
take up later. Second, not only do we have books containing the oracles of
these two prophets, but the two men are also mentioned in association with
each other in the book of Ezra (Ezra 5:1; 6:14).

Haggai and Zechariah proclaimed very different sets of messages from the
ones proclaimed by Third Isaiah. If Third Isaiah had questioned the very need
for the rebuilding of the temple, Haggai and Zechariah encouraged and led
the people in completing the rebuilding (Ezra 6:14); indeed, the first eleven
verses of the book of Haggai record an oracle of that prophet that urged that
task on the people.

These two prophets were likewise associated in another project, the proclamation of the messiahship of Zerubbabel. We must pause here to fill in a few
historical details. Zerubbabel was a grandson of Jehoiachin, the next-to-last
king of Judah, whom Nebuchadnezzar had taken into exile in Babylon in 598
B.C. (1 Chron. 3:17-19), and he was evidently appointed governor in
Jerusalem under the Persian king Darius (Hag. 1:1), for he appears in the second year of Darius (520) to undertake the completion of the temple (Ezra
5:2). Because he was of royal lineage, some of the community were moved to
crown him king and thus restore the Davidic monarchy. This would be a signal act of God within history!

Both prophets drew on phraseology preserved in the book of Jeremiah.
Listen to Haggai, in an oracle of 520 B.C.: "The word of the Lord came a second time to Haggai on the twenty-fourth day of the month: Speak to Zerubbabel, governor of Judah, saying, I am about to shake the heavens and the
earth, and to overthrow the throne of kingdoms; I am about to destroy the
strength of the kingdoms of the nations, and overthrow the chariots and their

riders; and the horses and their riders shall fall, everyone by the sword of a comrade. On that day, says the Lord of hosts, I will take you, O Zerubbabel my servant, son of Shealtiel, says the Lord, and make you like a signet ring; for I have chosen you, says the Lord of hosts" (Hag. 2:20-23). The mention of "signet ring" is significant: Jeremiah had compared Zerubbabel's grandfather Jehoiachin to a signet ring on God's right hand, soon to be torn off (Jer. 22:24). Now, it seems, the signet ring is to be restored. One could take Haggai's notion of the overthrow of chariots to be a statement that God will redeem the covenant people as happened with the overthrow of Pharaoh's chariots at the exodus from Egypt—that is to say, an event within history. But the phrase "I am about to shake the heavens and the earth" makes one pause: clearly Haggai saw in the restoration of the Davidic throne not merely an act of God within history but (at least symbolically) a cosmic shift. It is possible that just as Second Isaiah had seen the Babylonian empire fall with the advent of Cyrus of Persia, so these prophets thought they were witnessing the tottering of the Persian empire: Cyrus's successor Cambyses had died in 522, a usurper named Gaumata had ruled for six months, and the throne had then been seized by Darius; all these might well have been taken as signs of a shift in the whole order of the world.[10]

The prophet Zechariah joined Haggai in these predictions: in Zech. 3:8, the prophet refers to a figure called the "Branch," using an expression for the messianic king already mentioned in Jer. 23:5. But the move to make Zerubbabel king ultimately failed: the Davidic monarchy was not reestablished. The wording of Zech. 6:11-13 may offer a clue on the matter. In that passage, too, Zechariah refers to the Branch, but the wording of the passage appears to be muddled: "[The word of the Lord came to me:] Take the silver and gold and make a crown, and set it on the head of the high priest Joshua son of Jehozadak; say to him: Thus says the Lord of hosts: Here is a man whose name is Branch: for he shall branch out of his place, and he shall build the temple of the Lord. It is he that shall build the temple of the Lord; he shall bear royal honor, and shall sit and rule on his throne. There shall be a priest by his throne, with peaceful understanding between the two of them." Now it should be explained that the priest Joshua (or Jeshua) and the governor Zerubbabel were associated with each other in the rebuilding of the temple—earlier in this chapter we mentioned the reference to the two of them in Ezra 3:8. But in Zech. 6:12 it looks very much as if the original intended recipient of the crown was not Joshua but Zerubbabel—that is, Zerubbabel was the "Branch"—and as if an original reference to Zerubbabel in the text was later changed to Joshua when the attempt to restore the monarchy failed.[11]

In the meantime, the prophet Zechariah was mediating several visions to his people. Eight of these are recorded in Zech. 1:7–6:8: (1) divine horsemen patrolling the earth (1:8-17); (2) four horns and four smiths (1:18-21); (3) a man going to measure Jerusalem (2:1-5); (4) Joshua and Satan (3:1-10); (5) a golden lampstand and two olive trees (4:1-14); (6) a flying scroll (5:1-4); (7) a woman in an ephah (a unit of measure, roughly two-thirds of a bushel, 5:5-11), and (8) four chariots (6:1-8). In general, the visions depict Zechariah's concern for a purified community of Jews. For example, Jerusalem is to be resurveyed; it will remain without physical walls because its true protection will be God, who will be a wall of fire around it (2:1-5).

These visions offer new modes of expression derived from night dreams (see 1:8). But if Ezekiel's visions, such as that of the dry bones, resembled dreams, at least their symbols were publicly accessible; the material in Zechariah's visions is private and hidden, needing the interpretation of a mediating angel (1:9 and often). Even with angelic explanations, however, these visions are perhaps as opaque to a modern reader as anything in the Old Testament. Let us see what we can do with a couple of them.

First, the vision of a flying scroll (5:1-4). The scroll is odd in three different ways: (1) it soars, (2) it is enormous and out of proportion (roughly thirty feet long and fifteen feet wide), and (3) it is unrolled without being held by anyone.[12] This scroll is the vehicle for God's punishment on those who have stolen. Who might these people be? Ezek. 11:15 suggests that, in Ezekiel's day, the land near Jerusalem owned by those who had been sent into exile was being appropriated by those who were able to stay behind, and that process may have continued in the ensuing decades. Claims for the ownership of property in Zechariah's day, then, may have been as tangled as they are today in the eastern portion of Germany. The scroll is also a vehicle for punishment of those who were guilty of false oaths. In short, by mentioning stealing and false oaths, the vision suggests that God was punishing those who had broken one or another of the Ten Commandments: here Zechariah was stressing the validity of that core of the law even under conditions in which there would be folk who assumed the community was making an altogether new start.[13]

Second, the vision of a woman in an ephah (5:5-11). An "ephah," as we have noted, was a bulk measure, roughly two-thirds of a bushel. Because a specific measure is used—a measure that was often falsified (see Amos 8:5)—one could imagine that Zechariah has in mind the problem of false measures. This ephah, we are told, is "iniquity in the land." The cover of the ephah is lifted; strangely, the cover is not of pottery or the like but of lead. Inside there appears a woman—but a woman of normal stature would not fit in so small a space, so again, as with the flying scroll, we have a vision with a distortion of dimension. The woman is called "Wickedness"—alas, one more example of the constant tendency in the Old Testament to associate evil with the female gender. Was the story of Eve in Genesis 3 already being interpreted as meaning that primal sin was her fault? (We shall discuss the matter in Chapter 12.) The lead cover, now called a "weight," is quickly replaced. Is the reference to a "weight" intended to be associated with the ephah measure, both open to being falsified? The prophet then sees two women with wings carrying the container off to "Shinar"; the wings are those of pelicans, an unclean bird. Shinar is an old name for Babylon; it is doubtless used here to remind the listeners of the story of the Tower of Babel, which was built on a plain in the land of Shinar (Gen. 11:1). There a "house," that is to say, a temple, will be built for the ephah, as if it is to be worshiped like an image. One has here then an impression that the prophet perceived Jerusalem still to be polluted, that Babylon is the land of pollution par excellence, and that the prophet has in mind a kind of exchange of population: as the Jews have come back from Babylon to Jerusalem, so personified evil is to be taken from Jerusalem to Babylon. This evil that is to be transferred cannot be touched by God directly, but the transfer to Babylon is nevertheless supernatural, flying through the air between heaven and earth.[14]

So the outlook of the prophets Haggai and Zechariah is in stark contrast to that of Third Isaiah: whereas Third Isaiah questioned the need for a temple altogether, Haggai and Zechariah urged the completion of the temple and supported the Zadokite priesthood, specifically the high priest Joshua (or Jeshua). One wonders whether Third Isaiah's affirmation that Yahweh had *anointed* him was an announcement that was intended to be heard as a counterpoise to Zechariah's sponsorship of Zerubbabel, to be *anointed* the new Davidic king?

As we know, the priestly party won the struggle, and the community in Jerusalem found its focus in the second temple. But Third Isaiah's words were nevertheless preserved: his faction continued to prize them. And in spite of their differences, it is striking that both Third Isaiah and Zechariah resorted to language that moved beyond the ordinary stuff of history. Third Isaiah did so in part because of his conviction that God must surely bring vindication to the suffering, righteous poor: the day of the Lord was soon to come. Zechariah for his part does not speak of a coming of the day of the Lord. The apocalyptic imagery that he used was evidently in the service of the priestly party, though we cannot discount the possibility that he used it in part because of the disappointment he and his followers must have sustained when their move to reestablish the Davidic monarchy failed. The fact that such contrastive bodies of material both became part of the canonical prophets in the Old Testament is indirect evidence of the struggle the community underwent at the end of the sixth century to clarify the will of God.[15]

Zechariah 9–14

I now turn to the material in the last six chapters of Zechariah; in spite of the difficulty of these chapters, there is value in examining them in some detail because they illustrate so well the nature of apocalyptic.[16] In contrast to Zechariah 1–8, they give several descriptions of a coming manifestation of God. Indeed, as I have already noted, these chapters offer a very different style and content from the style and content of chapters 1–8.

Chapter 9 is a hymn to God the divine warrior. That motif is an old one in Israel—indeed, it is already found in the Song of Moses in Exodus 15 (see Chapter 5). But whereas Exodus 15 celebrated the primal act of Yahweh in history, that is, the rescue of Israel from Egypt, in Zechariah 9 the motif of the divine warrior re-emerges to celebrate an act of God in the future without any mooring in history. One might think that we are in touch with history: vv. 1-7 name several enemy peoples—Damascus, Tyre, and Sidon, and various Philistine cities. But these areas had ceased to be independent enemies of the covenant people in the eighth and seventh centuries B.C.; for our prophet, these names are simply interchangeable designations for lands that God will liberate for the covenant people. God will bring a king who, in the well-known description (v. 9), enters Jerusalem humbly riding on an ass. The fact that Jesus is remembered as drawing on that verse does not moor the chapter to history: in the mind of the prophet, God will permanently give to the covenant people the territory "from the River [Euphrates] to the ends of the earth" (v. 10). It will be a kingdom whose territory surpasses that of David! The final manifestation of God is told in language that could have been used of the Canaanite Baal, a manifestation in lightning, thunder, and whirlwind.[17]

Chapter 10 is another hymn to the divine warrior, though now it is mixed with accusations against wicked leaders (vv. 2-3a). These accusations remind hearers of Ezekiel 34, including the reference to "he-goats" (the NRSV translates "leaders," v. 3; see the footnote there), a reminiscence of Ezek. 34:17. But whereas Ezekiel 34 railed against negligent kings of the prophet's immediate past, "shepherds" in this period must refer to negligent priests. Do we have here the same polemic as we found in Third Isaiah? Again the divine warrior will fight against enemies (vv. 5-6) and bring the scattered Israelites home again. We notice that the divine warrior is victor over the sea (v. 11) just as Baal was in the Canaanite myth.[18]

Zech. 11:1-3 is a judgment against metaphorical tall trees, a symbol of pride, and a command of the shepherds to wail; once more, we seem to hear polemic against negligent priests.[19]

Verses 4-17 continue the negative tone with a discourse that can only be taken as savage irony. The anonymous prophet is himself commissioned to be a shepherd because the current shepherds are exploitive and negligent (v. 5); but the commissioning is a mockery: the flock is doomed to die (v. 4). We are reminded of Isaiah's call to be a prophet who would increase people's lack of understanding, so that Yahweh might punish them (see Chapter 4). In vv. 7-14, the shepherd renders up his report: he takes two staffs, named Favor and Unity, and tends the sheep (v. 7). The whole passage again reminds one of Ezekiel's discourse on the wicked shepherds (Ezekiel 34) and of his mention of the two sticks "Joseph" and "Judah" (Ezek. 37:15-28). But in the present passage the shepherd breaks his two staffs (vv. 10, 14): so much for Ezekiel's vision! The culminating surprise is that when the shepherd is paid for his work, he throws the money into the temple treasury—he has been in the pay of the temple leadership all the time. No wonder his commissioning was a mockery, no wonder the passage ends with a scathing woe-oracle against the existing shepherd. This bitter passage underlines the continuation of the struggle between visionaries like Third Isaiah and the priestly party who held power in the community.[20]

The wording of Zechariah 12 is not altogether clear, but we must again picture a culminating battle. The nations of the world rush against Jerusalem and Judah; then God the divine warrior enters the scene, striking the horses and riders (of the foreign nations) with confusion (vv. 2-4) and giving attention particularly to the clans of Judah (v. 5). These clans of Judah are the means of God's judgment, becoming the victor in competition with the inhabitants of Jerusalem (v. 7). One may detect here again the anonymous prophet's perception of God's rage against the powers-that-be in Jerusalem: the "clans of Judah" may well be his archaic code word for his own party, the faithful in the land. The reference to "the one whom they have pierced" (v. 10) reminds hearers of the suffering servant in Isaiah 52:13—53:12. If Third Isaiah and his followers took that image as a description of themselves, then this anonymous prophet continues the identification. Finally, then, Jerusalem and the whole land will mourn the martyred prophetic party whom they have hurt and will thus be delivered. Zech. 13:1-6 depicts the purification of Jerusalem—these verses may be a later addition to the sequence in chapter 12. The short sequence in 13:7-9 reverts to the figure of the shepherd in 11:4-17. Two-thirds of the population is to be destroyed, one-third is to be saved; once more we gain a sense of conflict within the community.[21]

The last chapter, Zechariah 14, depicts again the final battle of the divine warrior. The rest of the nations are lined up against Jerusalem (v. 2), and God fights against the nations (v. 3). God will then rearrange the geography of Jerusalem and make an entrance along with the "holy ones" (vv. 4-5), who may be either angelic beings or the faithful saints. Heaven and earth will be rearranged so that there will no longer be cold, or night, and rivers shall flow out of Jerusalem both to the Dead Sea and the Mediterranean (vv. 6-8: compare Ezek. 47:1-12). God alone will reign (v. 9), Zion will be raised on high (v. 10), and the city will dwell in security (v. 11). God's enemies will be destroyed (vv. 12-15), all nations will recognize God's reign (vv. 16-19), and there will be a final sacrifice and banquet (vv. 20-21).

Isaiah 24–27

I shall not deal in such detail with Isaiah 24–27, another late, apocalyptic sequence. In chapter 24, a description of rejoicing (vv. 14-16) is sandwiched between two passages describing cosmic destruction (vv. 1-13, 17-23); there will be a destruction of the "city of chaos," a kind of generalized city of the enemies of God, and there will be a destruction even of the "host of heaven" (v. 21) (the sun, moon, and stars), perhaps because people had been tempted to worship them; thereafter, God is enthroned (v. 23). Chapter 25 begins with hymnic material (vv. 1-5) and a description of a final banquet (25:6-10a) and ends, astonishingly, with an oracle against Moab, to be trodden down like straw in a dung-pit (vv. 10b-12). What in the world, one wonders, is the relevance of this here? Chapter 26, like the previous chapter, begins with hymnic material, something like a processional psalm (vv. 1-6). Verses 7-19 embody a prayer that expresses the emotions of the righteous as they shift from the old verities ("You make smooth the path of the righteous," v. 7) to the reality of their oppression by the wicked ("If favor is shown to the wicked, they do not learn righteousness; O Lord, your hand is lifted up, but they do not see it," vv. 10a, 11a), a prayer that finally, given the strain between the old verities and reality, affirms a belief in resurrection ("Your dead shall live, their corpses shall rise," v. 19a). Whether that resurrection is understood as fresh life for the nation, as Ezek. 37:1-14 seems to indicate, or whether it is understood as the revivification of individuals, is not clear from the text, but the latter is certainly possible, and the text certainly encouraged a belief in resurrection among many Jews in the centuries thereafter. Verses 20-21 affirm God's punishment of the wicked; the present wrath will last only "for a little while." Does "enter your chambers" mean "accept death (temporarily)"? The first verse of chapter 27 affirms that God will slay the sea monster, an affirmation analogous to the Canaanite myth of Baal's victory over Yamm (the sea). The rest of the chapter offers some appendices. Verses 2-6 offer a counterpoise to Isaiah's song of the vineyard (5:1-7), which we discussed in Chapter 4: here, God does not tear up the vineyard which is Israel but rather will keep it until the whole world is filled with its fruit. Verses 7-9 speak of the punishment of enemies and the purification of Israel. Verses 10-11 speak of the destruction of a fortified city: is this Jerusalem, or is it not rather the "city of chaos" of 24:10? Finally, in vv. 12-13 there is a description of the ingathering of all the scattered exiles.

Daniel 7–12

I touch now with equal brevity on the last six chapters of the book of Daniel. I mentioned Daniel 1–6 in Chapter 5: there we discussed these chapters as historical fiction, tales set in the court of Nebuchadnezzar to strengthen the resolve of Maccabean patriots struggling for their integrity against the Hellenistic Seleucid King Antiochus IV (Epiphanes) in the early part of the second century B.C. Chapters 7–12, by contrast, offer a series of apocalyptic visions. In chapter 7, we hear how Daniel himself dreamed of four beasts, who, it seems, represent four successive empires: (1) the Babylonians, (2) the Medes, (3) the Persians, and (4) the Greeks; the ten horns of the last beast represent the ten successive kings of the Greek kingdom, beginning with Alexander the Great and ending with Antiochus IV (the "little horn," v. 8). This vision is notable for its description of God sitting on a throne ("an Ancient One," v. 9). In chapter 8, we hear of a vision of a ram (representing the Medes and Persians, v. 20) and a he-goat (represting Alexander the Great, v. 21).

In chapter 9, we have a prophecy of Daniel explicating the reference in Jer. 25:11, 12 and 29:10 to the "seventy years" that would elapse before the restoration of Israel. Since, as a matter of fact, the restoration did not take place, Daniel explains that the seventy years are really "seventy weeks" (of years: v. 24), that is to say, 490 years. The chronology does not work out exactly, but the writer evidently had in mind 49 years from the presumed date of Jeremiah's words to the advent of Zerubbabel (v. 25), 434 years from then until the coming of Antiochus (v. 26), and seven years during which the oppressions of Antiochus would cease (v. 27). Finally, in chapters 10–12, we have a vision of the last days. The introduction of the vision takes up all of chapter 10. Chapter 11 consists of a symbolic recitation of the events of world history beginning with the Persian empire. Most of the figures in this chapter can be decoded by historians. Chapter 12 announces the present tribulation (that is, the oppression under Antiochus IV); in the vision, this tribulation is followed quickly by the resurrection of the dead (v. 2).

Further Apocalyptic Literature

As we conclude our survey of apocalyptic material in the Old Testament, it is perhaps useful to add that many other apocalyptic books were written in this period. Fragments of some of them have turned up among the Dead Sea Scrolls, but most were not ultimately accepted into the canon of Scripture. One notable exception is the book of Enoch, a long work (108 chapters) that, as I mentioned in Chapter 1, was preserved as scriptural by the Ethiopic church (Jude 14 in the New Testament quotes Enoch 1:9 as if scriptural). And, in surveying apocalyptic material, we must not forget such material in the New Testament—the book of Revelation and shorter sequences in the Gospels, as I have already mentioned.

The Difficulties of Hearing God in the Apocalyptic Literature

Now that we have sampled this literature, we face the steady question of this book: Can we hear God in this material, and if so, how? There are several considerations that render an answer difficult. Let me describe three of them.

1. By definition, this material is not verifiable by historical methods in the way historical narrative is. Assuming we can establish the historical reality of Jeremiah's scribe Baruch or the name of one of Nebuchadnezzar's officers (see Chapter 5), we cannot verify the angel Michael (Dan. 12:1) in the same way. This does not render apocalyptic material "untrue" (whatever may be our definition of truth), but it makes it hard to establish a generally agreed-upon base for answering our question.

2. The material is clearly time-bound, even though it is not always easy for us to pinpoint the date for a given unit. We have paid particular attention to material from the period 520–515 B.C., when there was controversy within the community surrounding the rebuilding of the Jerusalem temple, and material from around 165 B.C., when the Maccabean revolt was under way; and we can at least surmise historical circumstances between these dates when some of our apocalyptic material might have arisen. The fact that every passage is time-bound does not automatically exclude its relevance to us in our day, but its time-boundedness does raise the issue of whether there is permanent value here.

3. Given the fact that there are features of apocalyptic discourse that recur, that become clichés, nevertheless one could make the case that much of

the material finds its ultimate origin in dreams. This is particularly the case for Zechariah 1–8, but it appears to be true for material outside those eight chapters as well. God can well make revelation known through dreams, and indeed dreams are a well-known medium for revelation in the Bible; but Jeremiah's oracle against false prophets who claim revelation through dreams (Jer. 23:23-32) should make us cautious. Dreams may reveal God's will, but dreams may also be the vehicle for impulses of hatred and revenge—impulses that, at a given time, may galvanize the nascent impulses of a whole community.

The Possibilities of Hearing God in the Apocalyptic Literature

How can we find our way in all this? I begin by stating what is implicit in this whole chapter: apocalyptic literature is an expression of the people's hunger for justice in the context of disorientation and powerlessness. If God is just and if justice has at least for the moment been denied, then the covenant people have been impelled to look for God's intervention on their behalf beyond the norms of history as it has been experienced. In the disorientation of the exile in Babylon, Ezekiel drew on the symbols of his inner world, and Second Isaiah offered his rhetoric of a desert transformed into fertile fields. In the powerlessness of the early postexilic period, Third Isaiah dreamed of a new heaven and a new earth, and in his train came the anonymous visionaries whose words are preserved in Zechariah 9–14, Isaiah 24–27, and Daniel 7–12. Even the prophet Zechariah himself, who backed the priestly party in power, felt the vulnerability of a Jerusalem without walls and gave voice to a vision of God as the wall of fire around the city (Zech. 2:5). We may surmise that he and his supporters endured frustration at the failure of the crowning of Zerubbabel.

Christians affirm that God is just, and they also, even while achieving (and hoping to achieve) moderate islands of moderate justice within history, affirm their ultimate powerlessness. Reinhold Niebuhr wrote in 1952, "Nothing that is worth doing can be achieved in a lifetime; therefore we must be saved by hope. Nothing which is true or beautiful or good makes complete sense in any immediate context of history; therefore we must be saved by faith. Nothing we do, however virtuous, can be accomplished alone. Therefore we are saved by love."[22]

This powerlessness is of many sorts. Many Christians, through history, have had only marginal control over their destinies, and many other Christians will be in that position in the future. Some of these folk have had little or no share in what we take to be a just measure of health or wealth. And even those who have had or will have a measure of health or wealth face and then undergo, like everyone else, the powerlessness of death; and, in this world, oblivion, and, finally, so far as our scientific knowledge can tell, the destruction of this world in an ultimate explosion of the sun.

To this powerlessness, under a just God, the faith of Christians answers with the assurance of the resurrection of the dead, a resurrection confirmed by the resurrection of Jesus Christ. Minimally, this means that God loves us and does not abandon us or forget us, and that in God's economy there is both restitution for wrongs and scope for joy in community with each other and with God. Given this assurance of God's restitution for wrongs and the scope for joy with God, what place is there for the apocalyptic material of the Old Testament? Does it hinder this Christian assurance or enrich it? How can we tell?

One answer would be that apocalyptic material of the Old Testament that is in conformity with the New Testament would enrich rather than hinder. We must not forget the various apocalyptic remarks that the New Testament remembers as having been delivered by Jesus. Doubtless many of these remarks were elaborated by the second generation of Christians, but there is little doubt that the apocalyptic outlook was congenial to Jesus.

But we face a practical difficulty: the body of New Testament material that is most like the apocalyptic material of the Old Testament is to be found in the book of Revelation, a book that is not central for many Christians.

This study is not the place to explain or even defend the book of Revelation. But if it is true that all God-language is metaphorical, as was affirmed at the beginning of this study, then, most emphatically, any description of the details of God's final acts, the restitution of wrongs, and the scope God gives for joy, will be in metaphors, whether the metaphors of the book of Revelation are to our taste or not. Ultimately, words fail. With these provisos, let us see how we might hear God through some of the motifs of Old Testament apocalyptic material that we have examined.

Let us begin with the motif of the day of the Lord. This notion began, as we have seen, as a reference to a time when, as we might say, God would balance the accounts, but not necessarily to a *last* judgment accompanied by the destruction of heaven and earth (Amos 5:18-20; Isa. 2:5-21). In postexilic material, however, it became the latter (Zechariah 12; 14). The gospels enlarge on the motif ("But about that day or hour no one knows, neither the angels in heaven, nor the Son, but only the Father. Beware, keep alert; for you do not know when the time will come," Mark 13:32-33), and therefore it is appropriate to use such passages in the Old Testament as reminders of God's final summing up, as descriptions that underline the seriousness of our ultimate destiny.

Christians may likewise find New Testament legitimation for the motif of a purified Jerusalem. In the New Testament, "Jerusalem" became a standard metaphor for the church: we may recall the vision of the new Jerusalem in Rev. 21:1—22:5. It was the perception of the apocalypticists that there was impurity in Jerusalem and that the city therefore needed to be purified (Isaiah 65; Zech. 11:4-17); it was Jesus' perception that the wheat and the weeds exist side by side in the field until God separates them at the close of history (Matt. 13:24-30); and it is the perception of present-day Christians that good and evil continue to coexist in the church. The vision of a double river flowing out of Jerusalem (Zech. 14:8) is a refreshing reinforcement of this complex of ideas. But my own judgment is that the association of pollution with the female gender, such as is found in Zechariah's vision of the woman in the ephah (Zech. 5:5-11), is destructive for Christian mentality today—and the same may be said of Isa. 4:2-6, a similar late passage.

What do we do with the motif of the divine warrior? What was said about the God of battles in Chapter 6 is valid here: if God the divine warrior has acted within history (Exodus 15), God the divine warrior may likewise act beyond history (Zechariah 14). Some readers may be surprised to notice that the book of Revelation casts Jesus Christ in the role of divine warrior: Rev. 19:11-21 depicts Christ riding on a white horse, putting down "the beast and the kings of the earth" (v. 19). Here is the background for the lines in the hymn "Onward, Christian Soldiers," "Christ the royal Master, Leads against the foe." But the theme appears outside Revelation: one may ponder the meaning of the saying of Jesus recorded in Matthew, "Do not think that I have come to bring peace to the earth; I have not come to bring peace, but a sword" (Matt. 10:34). The saying at the very least suggests that the proclamation of the Kingdom of God brings division, and that to it some will say yes, and some will say no. The parable of the Great Judgment (Matt. 25:31-46) casts Jesus in the role, if not of divine warrior, then certainly of divine judge who condemns the wicked to eternal punishment and accepts the blessed into eternal joy. Given these strands of tradition in the New Testament, it is appropriate to listen to scenarios in the Old Testament of the divine warrior putting down the enemies of God. Such scenarios may provide a final hope for many folk in this world.

By the same token, though it is important to proclaim God's ultimate defeat of the enemies of the covenant people, many of such proclamations in the Old Testament are too ugly to be immediately helpful in this regard. I am thinking of the description of the defeat of the Moabites, trodden down as straw is trodden down in a dung-pit (Isa. 25:10b-12), or of the description of the plague visited on the enemies (Zech. 14:12): "Their flesh shall rot while they are still on their feet; their eyes shall rot in their sockets, and their tongues shall rot in their mouths." There are more useful passages in the Old Testament for such a purpose: for example, the description of the steadfast love God will show to Israel and the corresponding shame that will be experienced by Israel's enemies (Mic. 7:8-20). It is good to be reminded, too, that these enemies are not primarily terrestrial (Isa. 24:21-23). We shall return to the identity of God's enemies in Chapter 13.

One may draw on the descriptions of resurrection of the dead in the Old Testament; it is important to ponder and even to experience for ourselves the despair that lay behind the vision of the dry bones in Ezekiel 37 and the sense of helpless rage that lay behind the affirmation in Isaiah 26, as well as the serene confidence expressed in Dan. 12:2-3. As we hear Jesus' anticipation of the eschatological feast in the New Testament (Luke 13:29; 22:30), it is good to be reminded of the description of that feast in the Old Testament (Isa. 25:6-10a), "a feast of rich food, a feast of well-aged wines, of rich food filled with marrow, of well-aged wines strained clear" (v. 6). What a wonderful description of the full life for a people who were so often hungry! It is worth noting, in passing, that this marvelous passage immediately precedes the passage about the Moabites and the dung-pit: the Old Testament is a real checkerboard; we may hear God clearly in one passage, while in the next passage our chances of hearing God are small.

The affirmation to which we must hold in Old Testament apocalyptic is that of the ultimate kingship of God: "And the Lord will become king over all the earth" (Zech. 14:9). Jesus points to it in his teaching of the kingdom of God, and we can rejoice that the Old Testament offers passages that affirm that sovereignty as firmly as do passages in the New Testament. One well-known verse in Revelation was incorporated by George Frederick Handel into the "Hallelujah" chorus of his *Messiah:* "The kingdom of the world has become the kingdom of our Lord and of his Messiah, and he will reign forever and ever" (Rev. 11:15).

Notes

1. For guidance on the question of the definition of apocalyptic literature, see Paul D. Hanson, "Apocalypse, genre," and "Apocalypticism," *IDBSup* 27–34, and "Apocalypses and Apocalypticism, the Genre and Introductory Overview," *ABD* 1:279–82.

2. For an accessible treatment of New Testament beliefs in this regard, see John Wick Bowman, "Eschatology of the NT," *IDB* 2:135–40, and Adela Yarbro Collins, "Apocalypses and Apocalypticism, Early Christian," *ABD* 1:288–92.

3. For an attempt to bring some order out of the scattered accounts of events in this period, see Shemaryahu Talmon, "Ezra and Nehemiah," *IDBSup,* 317–28.

4. See Cross, *Canaanite Myth and Hebrew Epic*, 113–20.

5. Holladay, *Jeremiah 2*, 166.

6. Moshe Greenberg, "The Design and Themes of Ezekiel's Program of Restoration," *Interpretation* 38 (1984), 181–208.

7. See Paul D. Hanson, *The Dawn of Apocalyptic* (Philadelphia: Fortress Press, 1975).

8. The whole matter is complex; see conveniently Raymond Abba, "Priests and Levites," *IDB* 3:876–89; Merlin D. Rehm, "Levites and Priests," *ABD* 4:297–310.

9. Hanson, *Dawn of Apocalyptic*, 94–95.

10. Bright, *History of Israel*, 369.

11. For a discussion of the possibility that the text of 6:12 was changed, see John Bright, *History of Israel*, 371 and references, and Bruce T. Dahlberg, "Zerubbabel," *IDB* 4:955. But compare the careful treatment in Carol L. Meyers and Eric M. Meyers, *Haggai, Zechariah 1–8* (AB 25B; Garden City, NY: Doubleday, 1987), 354–57, 366–75.

12. David L. Petersen, *Haggai and Zechariah 1–8* (OTL; Philadelphia: Westminster, 1984), 247.

13. *Ibid.*, 245–54.

14. *Id.*, 254–63.

15. See Hanson, *Dawn of Apocalyptic*, 209–79.

16. For my understanding of these six chapters, I have drawn heavily on Hanson, *Dawn of Apocalyptic*, 280–380.

17. *Ibid.*, 292–324.

18. *Id.*, 324–34.

19. *Id.*, 334–37.

20. *Id.*, 337–54.

21. *Id.*, 354–68.

22. Reinhold Niebuhr, *The Irony of American History* (New York: Scribner's, 1952), 63.

11

Beyond the Covenant: Wisdom

❦

The covenant between Yahweh and Israel is the metaphor we have taken to be the central organizing one for the Old Testament; nevertheless, there is important material in the Old Testament in which the covenant is not at all central—material that is not closely tied to the specificity of Israel, and that is of universal relevance and appeal. I refer specifically to the three so-called "wisdom" books: Proverbs, Job, and Ecclesiastes.

It is not a simple matter to define the biblical category of "wisdom." The search for wisdom was the effort to make sense out of the world, to understand and put into language the way the world works, particularly the way human affairs work; in Israel, it was specifically the effort to make sense out of God's world, to understand how God works, and especially how God works in human affairs. It was the effort to grasp the ways of God not in God's mighty acts such as the rescue from Egypt or some awesome earthquake but rather in the day-to-day events of ordinary people. If, among the Greeks, the attempt to make sense out of the world led to the pursuit of philosophy, to the pondering of first principles, and ultimately to the beginnings of science (compare my remarks in Chapter 7), then among the Israelites the corresponding attempt led to the pursuit of wisdom.

In the book of Proverbs, as we noted at the beginning of Chapter 4, one repeatedly finds an equation between the pursuit of wisdom and the "fear of Yahweh." The standard formulation is "The fear of Yahweh is the beginning of wisdom" (Prov. 9:10), but there are several variations, for example, Prov. 1:7, "The fear of Yahweh is the beginning of knowledge; fools despise wisdom and instruction," and Prov. 15:33, "The fear of Yahweh is instruction in wisdom, and humility goes before honor." A similar formulation is found once in the book of Job, though, as we shall see, it sounds an ironic note in the context of that book: "Truly, the fear of the Lord, that is wisdom" (Job 28:28). In the book of Ecclesiastes, a book still different from the first two, wisdom is mentioned repeatedly; for example, "To the one who pleases him God gives wisdom" (Eccl. 2:26), and the book ends with the familiar command to fear God:

"Fear God, and keep his commandments; for that is the whole duty of every-one" (Eccl. 12:13). At least superficially, then, these three Old Testament books appear to be united by the identification of the pursuit of wisdom and the "fear" of Yahweh, an attitude that, as we saw in Chapter 4, suggests "rever-ence" as much as "fear" in the narrower sense.

The "fear of Yahweh" might therefore seem to give a distinctively Israelite angle of vision of wisdom in the Old Testament; nevertheless, at important points, the Old Testament search for wisdom drew significantly from sources outside of Israel, and it is the international scope of wisdom that first takes our eye. Before we determine, then, how we might hear God in the material found in these books, we need to try to extend our knowledge of the origin and purpose of the material—that is, to use historical-critical tools, as we have done for other types of Old Testament literature. This will not be easy for material so little tied to time and place. And because wisdom literature is not centrally dependent on the metaphor of covenant, we will be moving out in fresh theological directions.

Wisdom Crosses Frontiers: Creation

Given the international scope of wisdom, let me raise what might at first ap-pear to be a side issue: Does there exist in the Old Testament any religious tes-timony, related to a particular time and circumstance, which the covenant people communicated beyond their frontiers with the expectation that the testimony would be heard and understood beyond those frontiers? Many pro-nouncements of the Old Testament prophets were, on the surface, directed at foreign nations; we discussed some of them in the course of Chapter 9. There are not only the collections of oracles against foreign nations within Amos, Isaiah, Jeremiah, and Ezekiel, but shorter sequences as well, like the word against Assyria in Isa. 10:6-11 and the charge to Cyrus, king of Persia, in Isa. 45:1-7. But, as we found out, these passages, while understood as Yahweh's word effective on other nations and ostensibly directed to them, were doubt-less in reality shaped for the ears of the Israelites: the Israelites were intended to be eavesdroppers, so to speak, on Yahweh's word to foreigners.

I can locate at least one passage of religious testimony, however, that ful-fills my description: Jer. 27:3-11. The time is 594 B.C. Rumors had reached Jerusalem of efforts in Babylon to unseat Nebuchadnezzar. Consequently, Zedekiah, the king of Judah, calls a kind of "summit conference" of repre-sentatives from the trans-Jordanian states of Edom, Moab, and the Am-monites, and from Tyre and Sidon north of Judah on the Mediterranean, to see whether they could not form a coalition to unite in rebelling against

Nebuchadnezzar. Into this conference comes the prophet Jeremiah, unbidden, carrying tokens of his own personal submission to Nebuchadnezzar: parts that fit into a yoke. He gives to the visiting ambassadors a word from Yahweh that they should submit to Nebuchadnezzar's will. Even though he introduces the word from God to them with "Thus says Yahweh of hosts, the God of Israel" (v. 4), it is not a word that argues from the covenant with Israel. Instead, it speaks of Yahweh as creator of the world: "It is I who by my great power and my outstretched arm have made the earth, with the people and animals that are on the earth, and I give it to whomever I please. Now I have given all these lands into the hand of King Nebuchadnezzar of Babylon, my servant, and I have given him even the wild animals of the field to serve him. All the nations shall serve him and his son and his grandson, until the time of his own land comes; then many nations and great kings shall make him their slave" (vv. 5-7). It was clear to Jeremiah that Yahweh's covenant with Israel might not be recognized past the boundary of Judah, but the claims of a creator God might well be so recognized.

The question then arises: How might the Moabite ambassador have heard this word, or his king, if indeed he passed the message on? The national god of the Moabites was Chemosh (Jer. 48:7, 13, 46), and the Moabites spoke about the involvement of Chemosh in their affairs much as the Israelites did about Yahweh, as we know from an inscription of Mesha, one of the Moabite kings.[1] But one wonders: Did the Moabites view Chemosh not only as a national god but also as a universal god of creation? In the inscription I have mentioned, the name Chemosh is compounded once with Athtar or Ashtar, the planet Venus; Chemosh was then understood at least as a manifestation of this astral deity.[2] If the Moabites understood Chemosh as a creator god, then could the Moabite ambassador have heard Jeremiah's word from Yahweh as a word from Chemosh? One wonders. In any event, Jeremiah at least glimpsed the problem of speaking out of his own tradition into an alien one, and he located common theological ground with the representatives of other nations outside Israel on the basis of creation rather than covenant.

If Jer. 27:3-11 offers us a sample of Israelite religious testimony that might be accepted as valid by foreigners, Psalm 104 is an example of the process in the other direction: foreign religious testimony adapted by Israel and accepted as valid. The origin of Psalm 104 is evidently to be found in an Egyptian hymn: the psalm bears a striking resemblance to the Hymn to the Sun of the Egyptian Pharaoh Akh-en-Aton (ca. 1364–47 B.C.).[3] In this instance, the Egyptian hymn was adapted, not simply borrowed directly. One recent authority, claiming that the Old Testament psalm offers traces of Phoenician linguistic usage, has suggested that the hymn came into Israel through

Phoenicia (present-day Lebanon), which had close commercial ties with Egypt.[4] Again, as with the word that Jeremiah proclaimed to the foreign ambassadors, this psalm centers on God's activity in creation. Creation, then, is a theological category that can cross frontiers. We can therefore link wisdom both with creation and with an international reach: if wisdom was the search for how God's world works, then there will be strong ties between wisdom and creation; and wisdom was the category of religious material in the Old Testament that was most open to international sharing.

We found it difficult to define apocalyptic literature in Chapter 10, and we find it equally difficult at this point to define "wisdom" in the Old Testament sense. In Prov. 1:2-6, one finds a whole series of synonyms for wisdom: "For learning about wisdom and instruction, for understanding words of insight, for gaining instruction in wise dealing, righteousness, justice and equity; to teach shrewdness to the simple, knowledge and prudence to the young—Let the wise also hear and gain in learning, and the discerning acquire skill, to understand a proverb and a figure, the words of the wise and their riddles." One has the impression that the Hebrew equivalent of an English thesaurus was scoured to locate enough synonyms, but this passage scarcely defines wisdom in any satisfactory sense.

The Social Location of Wisdom

Let us start with the social location of wisdom. Jer. 18:18a mentions, alongside the priests and prophets, a category of people in Israel called "the wise." In this verse, the enemies of the prophet Jeremiah are expressing a wish to defeat him. "Then they said, 'Come, let us make plots against Jeremiah—for instruction shall not perish from the priest, nor counsel from the wise, nor the word from the prophet.'" I have already cited this verse in Chapter 3 when I took note of the fact that "instruction" here translates the Hebrew *tôrâ*, normally understood as "law"; the priests were responsible in Israel for preserving and passing on the tradition of instruction in legal norms. Similarly, the prophets were responsible for hearing and declaring the fresh "word" of Yahweh in fresh circumstances (see Chapter 9).

One usually thinks of the priests and the prophets as making up the totality of the religious leadership of Israel; indeed, there are many passages that encourage this conclusion (for example, Isa. 28:7 and Jer. 5:31). One may note further that the words of both Israelite priests and Israelite prophets reflected the specificities of the covenant—the priests in their role of guarding the permanent legal norms of Israel, and the prophets in their task of proclaiming a new, fresh word from Yahweh. When we turn from Israel to examine the variety of cultures in the ancient Near East—those of the Philistines and the Syrians and all the rest—we realize that each of them maintained a religious leadership that was analogous to the priests and prophets of Israel and would offer its own teaching and revelation to its own society.

In Jer. 18:18, however, alongside the Israelite priests and prophets, a third group is mentioned, the "wise" with their "counsel." In contrast with the lore of the priests and prophets that was specific to the theology of covenant, the lore of the "wise," as I have already indicated, could be shared across national frontiers. Thus, the wise men in Egypt could offer counsel about how to be- have in order to live a successful life, and they did, and that counsel would not, after all, be too different from such counsel in Israel; advice that commit- ting adultery has dire consequences could be given by Egyptians as well as by Israelites, and it was. The result was that Israelites could borrow wisdom from other nations, and they did. Thus, most scholars agree that Prov. 22:17— 23:11 (indeed, perhaps an even longer sequence, 22:17—24:22) is dependent on a prior Egyptian source, the Instruction of Amen-em-ope.[5] To the extent that Israel had contact with other nations, in trade and in political and mili- tary relations, Israel was open to the traditions of wisdom that freely crossed borders.

Proverbs 10–31

The conventional, traditional wisdom of Israel is to be found in several collec- tions within Proverbs 10–31, so we turn first to the book of Proverbs. Though the book claims its origin to be with Solomon (Prov. 1:1; 10:1), this is doubt- less a late attribution. We will bypass for the moment chapters 1–9, dealing first with the traditional wisdom of chapters 10–31.

Most of the entries in these chapters are units only a single verse long, say- ings so universal in application that determining their origin is out of the question. We surmise that these pithy sayings guided conduct in families and clans and originated there: these are Israelite sayings that are the equivalent of "A stitch in time saves nine." One learns that it is important to respect one's parents: "A wise child makes a glad father, but a foolish child is a mother's grief" (10:1). "If you curse father or mother, your lamp will go out in utter darkness" (20:20). "The eye that mocks a father and scorns to obey a mother will be pecked out by the ravens of the valley and eaten by the vultures" (30:17). It is important to be diligent: "A child who gathers in summer is pru- dent, but a child who sleeps in harvest brings shame" (10:5).

Alongside the traditional clan sayings found within these chapters are other sayings that clearly have their setting in the royal court. They embody what we would call etiquette, and they obviously emerged after the advent of the monarchy. Here is one that is evidently adapted from Egyptian wisdom: "When you sit down to eat with a ruler, observe carefully what is before you, and put a knife to your throat if you have a big appetite" (23:1-2)—in other words, moderate your appetite when you dine with a king. We find not only guidance on how to behave in the presence of kings but guidance as well in how to behave as a king. "By justice a king gives stability to the land, but one who makes heavy exactions ruins it" (29:4).

One finds many sayings that deal with fairness in buying and selling, a trait linked to Yahweh's will: "A false balance is an abomination to Yahweh, but an accurate weight is his delight" (11:1). "The people curse those who hold back grain, but a blessing is on the head of those who sell it" (11:26). More generally, many sayings have to do with riches and poverty: "Better is a dry morsel with quiet than a house full of feasting with strife" (17:1). One might surmise that these sayings arose with the development of a merchant class during the monarchy, but, in fact, people had always been buying and selling.

A large number of proverbs describe fools and contrast them with the wise: the words "fool" and "folly" together occur over 50 times in the NRSV of Proverbs. "Doing wrong is like sport to a fool, but wise conduct is pleasure to a person of understanding" (10:23). "One who is clever conceals knowledge, but the mind of a fool broadcasts folly" (12:23). Indeed, "Better to meet a she-bear robbed of its cubs than to confront a fool immersed in folly" (17:12). Saying after saying deals with the destructive effects of strife, slander, and pride. "The beginning of strife is like letting out water; so stop before the quarrel breaks out" (17:14). "The words of a whisperer are like delicious morsels; they go down into the inner parts of the body" (18:8). "Before destruction one's heart is haughty, but humility goes before honor" (18:12). Here we begin to move closer to an understanding of the nature of wisdom and folly; one gains a sense of the character traits traditionally admired in Israel.

Our first reaction is that many of these sayings urge the development of character traits that are admirable in any age, but then one also finds expressions of the centrality of men and the subordination of women that will dismay most readers of the present generation. "A good wife is the crown of her husband, but she who brings shame is like rottenness in his bones" (12:4). "Like a gold ring in a pig's snout is a beautiful woman without good sense" (11:22).

Beyond sayings that deal with ideal conduct, there are more imaginative leaps. Thus, there are sayings that find analogies between disparate realms. Here are four phenomena manifesting uncanniness: "Three things are too wonderful for me; four I do not understand: the way of an eagle in the sky, the way of a snake on a rock, the way of a ship on the high seas, and the way of a man with a girl" (30:18-19). Here are four phenomena manifesting insatiability: "Three things are never satisfied; four never say, 'Enough': Sheol, the barren womb, the earth ever thirsty for water, and the fire that never says, 'Enough'" (30:15b-16). One can understand that Sheol is insatiable for the dead (Isa. 5:14), that the earth, at least in the experience of the Israelites, never gets enough water, and fire devours without limit; one assumes then that the reference to the barren womb is a depiction of a barren woman's steady craving for sexual relations that will produce offspring.[6] Such sayings as these point one away from the conventions of acceptable behavior and toward the mysteries of the world. Occasionally, one may affirm not only the mysteries of the world but the mystery of God. "It is the glory of God to conceal things, but the glory of kings is to search things out" (25:2). Kings may send out expeditions, and spies; but so much of God's activity is past our understanding.

Again and again we hear the changes rung on the preciousness of wisdom, the delights of wisdom, the value of wisdom. One saying must do for many: "Wisdom is a fountain of life to one who has it, but folly is the punishment of fools" (16:22).

Proverbs 1–9

Such sayings about the value of wisdom lead us to a consideration of chapters 1–9. Whereas chapters 10–31 offer individual sayings, the first nine chapters of Proverbs in general offer extended instruction, as if from a parent to a son (1:8; I say "son" in view of the references to a prostitute, which I shall discuss below). From a variety of directions, one may surmise that this material took shape in the early postexilic period.[7] Here are laid out in more extended fashion the agenda of the circles of the "wise": instruction of the young, discernment in human relations, success and satisfaction in living, delight in striking sayings.

The most noteworthy mark of these first nine chapters, however, is that the wisdom so often praised in chapters 10–31 is here *personified,* most notably at the beginning and the end of these chapters: Wisdom appears as a woman in 1:20-33 and in chapters 8–9. We hear her speak (8:4-36), and in her speech she proclaims herself of divine origin, created at the foundation of the world (8:22-31). In the last-cited speech, Wisdom offers a self-description, though unfortunately there is some uncertainty about the meaning of a key Hebrew term in 8:30: Is she a "master builder" beside Yahweh (so the NRSV) or Yahweh's darling child (compare the REB)? In any event, she proclaims her unique status with Yahweh. Beyond these passages, others refer to wisdom in terms that might imply a personification ("Say to wisdom, 'You are my sister,' and call insight your intimate friend," 7:4). One of the chief missions of personified Wisdom, it appears, is to keep the young man who is being instructed from consorting with a "loose woman" (2:16-19; 5:3-9; 7:5-20), an adulteress (6:24-35), or a "foolish woman" (9:13-18). All this material is striking enough for us to pause and ask: What is going on here?

The first, most obvious thing to say is that the word for "wisdom" in Hebrew, *ḥokmâ,* is feminine in gender; if, therefore, one is to speak metaphorically of seeking and getting wisdom, the phraseology in verses like 4:5-9 and 7:4 is not surprising.

Second, as I mentioned in Chapter 2, some in Israel in pre-exilic times evidently believed in the existence of a divine consort for Yahweh (she was named Asherah), a belief that waned after the fall of Jerusalem in 587 B.C. The fall of the city was interpreted as God's punishment for breaking covenant, and Second Isaiah preached eloquently the uniqueness of God (Isa. 44:6). It may be, then, that, among the "wise," the personification of Wisdom emerged as a partial compensation for the emphasis on a sole deity understood to carry masculine attributes (on this matter, see Chapter 12).

This process was doubtless reinforced by a development in Egypt: the Egyptian principle of *ma'at,* variously translated as "justice," "world order," and "truth," was personified as a goddess,[8] and, given the international nature of wisdom, this process in Egypt seems to have encouraged the personification of Wisdom in Israel.[9]

Third, the conventional view of God in the postexilic period emphasized God's height and remoteness; consequently, more and more elaborate schemes emerged to mediate between God and human beings (in Chapter 10 we took note of the place of angels in Zechariah's visions). Thus, in wisdom circles, the figure of personified Wisdom served as a plausible mediator with God.

In any event, this female figure is represented as wielding enormous power: she raises her voice in the streets and squares, locations in the city that are ordinarily the precinct of men (1:20-21), and, through her activity, kings and princes of the world get and keep their high positions (8:15-16).

The use of the language of sexuality particularly arouses our curiosity. This language functions in these chapters both metaphorically and concretely. Metaphorically, the young man is told to love and embrace wisdom (4:6, 8). Concretely, he is told to confine his enjoyment of sexual intercourse to that with his own wife (5:15-20) and is repeatedly instructed, as we have seen, to avoid the loose woman, the adulteress, and the foolish woman. Yet the description of the foolish woman (9:13-18) is clearly a counterfoil to personified Wisdom, so the description is metaphorical as well: as Wisdom has built her house and offers her invitation, "You who are simple, turn in here!" (9:1, 4), so the foolish woman sits at the door of *her* house and offers the same invitation, "You who are simple, turn in here!" (9:13, 16). There is justification in understanding the foolish woman as personified Folly.[10]

Beyond the obvious—that the young male who is being instructed has either entered puberty or is about to and will therefore struggle with the urges to which males are subject from adolescence onward—what we have here is an aggregation of sexual rhetoric that emerges out of a very specific set of social assumptions. First, it was a male-dominated society: to the young male who is being instructed, the female is presented as the *other,* split into both total virtue (personified Wisdom) and total vice (personified Folly), with the vice centered in sexual attraction. Second, in the postexilic period, there was a strong concern for ethnic purity as a means of preservation of the social group, and one suspects that behind the words against the "strange woman" is the urging that gave rise to the program of Ezra and Nehemiah, that Jews divorce their foreign wives (Ezra 9:1-15; 10:1-44; Neh. 13:23-30). Third, this male-dominated society projected overwhelmingly male characteristics onto the sole God, but at the same time had struggled for centuries against various forms of polytheism in which female deities were usually characterized by their sexuality; one senses that the descriptions of the strange woman share phraseology used elsewhere of fertility goddesses—for example, in the matter of the descent to the underworld (5:5; 7:27), an important theme in the myth of the fertility goddess in ancient Near Eastern mythology.[11] But since fertility worship in the pre-exilic period evidently involved sexual intercourse with the devotees (compare Hos. 4:12-14), it is easy to see how the theme of adultery functions both metaphorically and literally. Finally, to the pursuit of wisdom—a wisdom that promises to grant a kind of mastery in the art of living and—even to some kind of grasp of ultimate matters, one could bring a passion and devotion reminding one of sexual passion and at the same time partaking of the divine.[12]

As if to heal the split between total virtue and total vice represented by Dame Wisdom and Dame Folly, one finds, at the very end of the book of Proverbs, an acrostic poem on the capable wife (31:10-31) that is as down-to-earth and as appealing as anything in the Old Testament. It is still a reflection of a male-dominated society: she does her husband good all the days of her life (v. 12) and makes her husband known at the city gates (v. 23). Her milieu is clearly that of the upper class (she buys fields, v. 16). With this restriction, it is a lovely portrayal of a wife whose talents are genuinely appreciated: "Her children rise up and call her happy; her husband too, and he praises her: 'Many women have done excellently, but you surpass them all'" (vv. 28-29).

Proverbs, Summary

The book of Proverbs assumes that we may understand God not in the spectacular events of earthquake and battle, as the prophets proclaimed, nor in the specificities of Moses' law, as the priests taught, but in the daily activities and personal relationships in which every human being participates. Before we face the question whether we can hear God in its verses, however, we need to take account of the two other wisdom books that challenged that comfortable assumption.

Job

The first of these is the book of Job.[13] In contrast to the collections of sayings in the book of Proverbs, this book is a long, intricate poem bracketed by a prose prologue and prose epilogue. It voices the classic protest that God is not fair: it is the biblical exploration of the problem summarized in the title of Harold Kushner's recent book *When Bad Things Happen to Good People*.[14] The book of Job most probably was created during the exilic or early postexilic period. We have had occasion at several points in this work to discuss the Israelite explanations for suffering. The overwhelming assumption in the Old Testament is that any suffering that people undergo is punishment for sin (see especially Chapter 8); the suffering of an individual, if not easily associated with any sin on his or her part, may be associated with some sin within the family or the corporate group of which the individual is a part (see Chapter 5). If no sin is obvious in the corporate group, one can always explain suffering as a warning from God (Amos 4:6-11: see again Chapter 8).

But these traditional assumptions began to seem inadequate in the exilic period. Indeed, even before the fall of Jerusalem, the prophet Jeremiah became convinced that these explanations were inadequate in his own experience, and he poured out his dismay in a whole series of laments; I made reference to these at the end of Chapter 9. He accepted without question his calling as a prophet, but he could not understand why God would allow him to suffer persecution as a result of his prophetic activity. The words of Jer. 12:1-3 are a particularly clear example of the prophet's conviction that God has not been playing fair with him. Then the prophet Ezekiel, as we have seen in Chapter 10, called the whole notion of corporate personality into question, insisting that each individual is to be held responsible for his or her own conduct (Ezekiel 18). Deutero-Isaiah appears to have rejected any correspondence at all between suffering and what one deserves: in Isa. 52:13—53:12, he sets forth a vision of a vocation for suffering (see again Chapter 9). In short, several prophets declared in various ways that the old explanations about suffering were no longer altogether convincing. These prophets gave voice to what many people, battered by the miseries of the exile and the immediate postexilic period, suspected but hardly dared to say out loud: "God is not always fair, and we know it in our own experience."

Now the notion that one's treatment by one's deity is not fair is not confined to the community of the Old Testament—indeed, it is a rare human being who becomes convinced that his or her suffering is merited, and the thought that one has been treated unfairly is surely widespread. The literatures of both ancient Egypt and ancient Mesopotamia offer examples of works that struggle with the question of suffering that appears unmerited. In one work from Egypt, a man debates whether to commit suicide,[15] and in another a peasant is threatened with death when he insists on justice.[16] From Babylon there comes a text usually called "I will praise the Lord of Wisdom," a psalm of thanksgiving of a righteous sufferer who struggles with the issue of his own suffering until the god Marduk rescues him from death,[17] and still another in which a skeptic and a pious man debate the misfortunes of the pious and the success of the ungodly.[18] But the theological issue of unmerited suffering takes different forms in a polytheistic context: in such a context one could always assume that one had fallen afoul of particular demons, or that one was a victim in a dispute between two gods, or that the deity in control of one's own destiny has turned out to be less than just.[19] In the Old Testament context, however, in which one sole God is responsible for the world, the issue of unmerited suffering is keen. True, the immediate suffering of Job is attributed in the prologue (Job 1:6-12; 2:1-7) to "Satan," more literally "the Accuser" (see the footnote in the NRSV), who acts as a kind of prosecuting attorney in the divine realm, but Satan (or "the Accuser") in the book of Job is not acting against God's will but in accordance with it.

Curiously, however, for a book that struggles so keenly with the question of suffering from an Israelite viewpoint, its narrative is set outside of Israel. At the beginning, Job is said to be a blameless and upright man in the land of Uz (1:1), described as in "the east" (1:3). Where is Uz? In Lam. 4:21, the Edomites are described as living in the land of Uz, and Edom was centered to the southeast of the Dead Sea. Furthermore, the tribal affiliations of Job's three friends (Job 2:11) again suggest Edom or north Arabia. But the use of the name Uz here simply suggests a vague reference to "far away and long ago." True, the specific Israelite divine name "Yahweh" does occur in the book (1) in the passages in the prologue in which Satan appears, which I have already cited, (2) in the introductory words of God's and Job's speeches at the end of the book (38:1; 40:1, 3, 6; 42:1), and (3) in the epilogue (42:7-12). In the poetry in the body of the book, by contrast, God is usually referred to by the antique generic term *ʾĕlôah*, translated simply "God" in the NRSV (see, for example, 3:4). The overwhelming impression given by the book, then, is of a work that struggles with the issue of unmerited suffering (an urgent issue for the Jewish community in the exilic period) by reference to the experience not of Jeremiah or some other recent and well-known figure but of a generic righteous man from far away and long ago.

The prose prologue (chapters 1–2) sets the stage. With seven sons and three daughters, Job is rich in family. He is rich in cattle as well, and he is upright; he even offers burnt offerings to cover any sins his children may have committed (1:5). In heaven, the Accuser comes before God and argues that Job is upright only because he has not suffered. God then allows the Accuser to bring an awesome series of losses on Job—various raiders and storms deprive him of his cattle, and a great wind strikes the house where his children are feasting so that they are all crushed to death; still Job blesses God. In heaven, God appears vindicated: Job continues in his uprightness. But the Accuser counters that it is only because Job's own person has not been touched. God thereupon allows the Accuser to afflict Job with loathsome sores but commands that Job's life be spared. It is done. Then come three friends— Eliphaz, Bildad, and Zophar—to commiserate with Job; they sit in silence for seven days. Then the poetic dialogue begins—speeches of Job, out of the radical distress he endures in his loss of wealth and health, given his innocence; and speeches of the friends, expressing the traditional pieties regarding the meaning of suffering.

Job begins (chapter 3); then Eliphaz speaks (chapters 4–5) and Job answers (chapters 6–7); Bildad speaks (chapter 8) and Job answers (chapters 9–10); Zophar speaks (chapter 11) and Job answers (chapters 12–14). Then the cycle begins again: Eliphaz (chapter 15), Job (chapters 16–17), Bildad (chapter 18), Job (chapter 19), Zophar (chapter 20), and Job (chapter 21). A third cycle follows, though unfortunately it is somewhat mangled. Thus, Eliphaz speaks (chapter 22), then Job (chapter 23 at least). The text labels the short chapter 25 as a speech of Bildad's. But even though the text of chapters 24 and 26–27 is assumed to be speeches of Job, the rhetoric of 24:18-24 and 27:13-23 is typical of Job's friends, so that some scholars wonder whether one or both of these sequences do not embody all or part of the last speech of Zophar.

Suddenly, in chapter 28, comes something unexpected, an interlude in the voice of neither Job nor his friends, on the inaccessibility of wisdom: it is evidently a kind of summary by the poet of the arguments thus far. The next three chapters (29–31) embody Job's final defense—a soliloquy really, since he is not addressing his friends. Then, in the next six chapters, we have another sudden shift: four speeches from an altogether new speaker, Elihu, who in his frustration with Job and Job's three friends, attempts his own answers to the problem.

Then, again suddenly, God delivers two speeches (chapters 38–41), to which Job offers a short rejoinder (42:1-6). The book concludes with a prose epilogue (42:7-17) in which God gives instruction to Eliphaz, Bildad, and Zophar (Elihu is left unmentioned) and brings restoration to Job.

Job's first speech begins where Jeremiah had left off: line after line of 3:3-7 ring the changes on Jer. 20:14, "Cursed be the day on which I was born!" Indeed, the whole of chapter 3 offers variations on Jer. 20:14-18. Job curses the day he was born and the night when he was conceived (vv. 3-10) and then laments his fate in a series of "why?" questions; a hint of what is to come is afforded by v. 23: "Why is light given to one who cannot see the way, whom God has fenced in?" "The way" for a human being is normally understood to be laid out by God; one hears, for example, in Prov. 16:9, "The human mind plans the way, but Yahweh directs the steps." But in Job's instance the way of the sufferer is hidden, and hidden by God!

The first friend, Eliphaz, takes up the challenge: Job has counseled many, it seems, and now he needs counsel himself (4:2-4). He affirms the old orthodoxy: "Who that was innocent ever perished?" (4:7). The old rules must be right! He then testifies to a vision he has had (4:12-21), that inasmuch as even angels fall short of God's righteousness, human beings fall even shorter: here he offers an opportunity for Job to admit to his shortsightedness. His advice to Job: "As for me, I would seek God. . . . He does great things and unsearchable" (5:8-9). He waxes eloquent about the wonders God does in creation (5:10). Then, having suggested that Job is in some way culpable, he covers himself by suggesting that suffering is in any event disciplinary ("How happy is the one whom God reproves; therefore do not despise the discipline of the Almighty," 5:17) and should be welcomed by Job. Already at the beginning, then, many of the themes of the work are set out.

Job's reply is double. The first part (chapter 6) is directed to Eliphaz, not so much to his argumentation as to the tone of his words. What for Eliphaz was sincere piety is for Job the tasteless pap (6:7) of false friends (6:14-23) that amounts to cruelty (6:27); he challenges his friends to show him how he has erred (6:24, 30). The second part (chapter 7) of his reply is a renewed lament: his nights are onerous, his days fleeting (7:4-6). Eventually, he addresses God (7:12-21). Why, he asks, does God pay so much attention to him, as if he were the cosmic primeval Dragon himself? (7:12). He offers an ironic variation of Psalm 8, a psalm that praises God for care of human beings: "What are human beings, that you make so much of them . . . visit them every morning, test them every moment?" (7:17-18). Job could do with a little less care from God! At least God could let him catch his breath (7:19). Mockingly, he asks: Why not just pardon me and be done with it? Soon I shall be dead anyway (7:21).

Then it is the turn of the second friend, Bildad. Unlike Eliphaz, he has no personal vision to vouchsafe, only an insistence on the old answers: "Does God pervert justice?" (8:3). With unintended cruelty, he declares that Job's children were destroyed for their sins (8:4). Bildad then turns to a parallel from nature analogous to the similes in Psalm 1, but his parallel has an exotic, Egyptian sound, as if the poet is poking quiet fun at the presumed superiority of Egyptian wisdom. He seems to refer to two plants: one (the papyrus reeds) associated with the wicked, that withers into insubstantiality when water is gone (vv. 11-15), and one that thrives and spreads (vv. 16-19: the translation of the beginning of v. 16 in the NRSV is evidently in error—the Hebrew says, "He [evidently the second plant] thrives before the sun").[20] And Bildad ends with a confident assurance to Job that is no assurance at all, "See, God will not reject a blameless person. . . . He will yet fill your mouth with laughter" (8:20-21).

Job's reply is again double; he first addresses his human opponent (chapter 9) and then God (chapter 10). But the human opponent whom he answers is not so much Bildad as Eliphaz—the question in 9:2 ("How can a mortal be just before God?") is really a reflection on that in 4:17 ("Can mortals be righteous before God?"). The real implication of 9:2 is: "How can anyone be declared innocent in a legal battle with God?" The question suggests that Job suspects he has lost the legal battle before he starts. Job is now contemplating the initiation of a lawsuit against God, a theme that is once more an elaboration of one in Jeremiah's laments (Jer. 12:1-2). But how can one contend on equal terms with an opponent who is great enough to move mountains (9:5) and who is invisible at that (9:11)? What to Eliphaz were God's wonders in creation (5:10) are to Job the nightmare works of an overbearing God. Though legally Job might be innocent, God would doubtless find a way to condemn him (9:14-15). Indeed, he wonders how he might subpoena God (9:16). Job then explores his options. He could charge God with injustice, inasmuch as God brings the same fate to both the blameless and the wicked (9:22). Or he could drop his charge (9:27), though if he did so, God would doubtless take it as an admission of guilt (9:28). Or he could undergo an ordeal of self-purification (9:30) or find a mediator (9:33), though again these measures are clearly unavailing. Chapter 10 is addressed to God: here

Job throws caution to the wind and rehearses (10:2) what his argument will be against God in court: God oppresses his creatures (10:3), spurns his own creation (10:8-9), and spies on Job in particular (10:14), hunting him down like a lion (10:16). Job closes by repeating earlier expressions: he laments that he was ever born (10:18, compare 3:11) and asks only that he be granted a brief respite from his misery (10:20, compare 7:19).

Zophar, the third friend, then defends God's justice (chapter 11), and he does so even more immoderately than Bildad has done. He is scandalized that Job should insist on his purity and innocence (v. 4). God's wisdom is deep, and if Job only knew the depths of God's wisdom, he would understand the reason for his suffering: indeed God is compassionate enough to exact of Job less suffering than he deserves! (v. 6). Zophar then waxes eloquent about the depths of the secrets of God, broader than earth and heaven (vv. 7-11), and implies that Job is an empty-headed fool (v. 12). He concludes with a good old-fashioned appeal for repentance: if Job will only confess his sins, God will forgive him and he will live happily ever after (vv. 13-20).

To all this, Job offers a long response (three chapters). In the first section of his speech, he offers his own biting reflection on wisdom. Sarcastically, he proclaims his friends the experts on wisdom but then insists he has his share as well (12:2). He admits he is the laughingstock of his friends for contemplating the arraignment of God (12:4). He offers a scathing description of the omnipotent God: where many people praise the wonders of creation and the power of God to bring down the mighty, Job simply sees an exercise of amoral power: God's actions are all negative, destroying society by rendering its leaders powerless and disoriented, like drunks wandering in darkness (12:12-25). Job affirms this out of his own knowledge (13:1-3) and repeats his contempt for the worthless counsel of his friends (13:4-5). The remainder of the chapter consists of what one commentator calls Job's pretrial declaration.[21] In 13:6-12, he questions his friends as potential witnesses in his lawsuit. Will they be partial toward God (v. 8)? Can they withstand God's cross-examination (vv. 9-11)? Then (vv. 13-16) he declares he is going ahead with his lawsuit, though he risks all by doing so. He turns to challenge God directly (v. 19). He asks for a guarantee that the trial will be fair: God must remove the divine hand, the agent of his affliction, else he will be viewed as guilty, and God must remove the divine "terror" (v. 21). He taunts God by asking why the divine face is hidden (vv. 24-25). Then suddenly, in a climactic speech (chapter 14) in which Job continues to address God, he meditates on the subject of mortality. Human beings are mortal (vv. 1-6); yet what might life be if there were hope of new life (vv. 7-22)? This chapter uses analogies from nature, ranging from fragile flowers to enduring mountains (v. 2, 7-9, 11, 18-19), and it uses the theme of the lawsuit already set forth (vv. 3-4, 15-17) to offer a vision that there might be post-mortem litigation in which Job would be vindicated. "If mortals die, will they live again? All the days of my service I would wait until my release should come. You would call, and I would answer you; you would long for the work of your hands" (vv. 14-15). "But the mountain falls and crumbles away . . . so you destroy the hope of mortals" (vv. 18-19).

The second cycle of speeches continues and deepens these themes. Eliphaz challenges Job's wisdom (chapter 15), implying that Job claims to have been with personified Wisdom at the foundation of the world (v. 8). Job then complains that his friends are no friends at all and that God is his enemy (chapters 16–17). Bildad depicts the world of the wicked, implying that Job is to be included in the category (chapter 18). Job renews his plaint (chapter 19) against both friends and God and suddenly expresses the hope that his legal case can be permanently recorded on a rock to outlast his life (vv. 23-24) and that there might be a vindicator ("redeemer") who can rise up in court to testify on his behalf (v. 25): really he would like to be present in person, to be face to face with God in his innocence (vv. 26-27). For Christians, of course, this passage is a high point of the book of Job: one thinks of "I Know that my Redeemer Liveth" in Handel's *Messiah*. But we must make sure we read this passage in the light of the rest of Job's speeches, part of scenarios for the seeking of justice in which belief and unbelief are intricately intertwined. Zophar counters with a conventional speech on the sad fate of the wicked (chapter 20). Job replies that, to the contrary, the wicked remain happy and avoid calamity (chapter 21).

Eliphaz begins the third cycle of speeches (chapter 22) with an astonishing indictment of Job, going so far as to offer a list of the sins he must have committed; for example, "You have given no water to the weary to drink, and you have withheld bread from the hungry" (v. 7). All of this is out of Eliphaz's own imagination, almost as if he had consulted a little black book that matched punishment with sins—loathsome sores (2:7) = no food shared with the hungry, and the like; he must insist that the presumed divine judgment on Job is thus justified. Job expresses the wish that he might face God (chapter 23). Chapters 24–27 continue the argumentation, though, as I have already indicated, there may be some displacement and mislabeling of the speeches. In any event, familiar themes reappear: Job addresses his friends sarcastically (26:2-4); in his desperation, he is ready to go to court with his enemy, God (27:7-12).

Then suddenly, as we have seen, chapter 28 offers wording that cannot be matched with the outlook of any speaker we have heard; it is a lyrical poem that stands above all the ebb and flow of the argumentation up to this point in the book, evidently a reflection of the poet himself: wisdom, it affirms, is inaccessible. This poem employs the theme of the vistas of the created world in many ways. Thus, even though miners may dig into the depths of the earth for jewels and gold, making trails that birds and animals do not know (vv. 1-11), and even though wisdom is more precious than jewels and gold, nevertheless no mortal knows where wisdom may be found, nor do the birds, nor the sea, nor Death itself (vv. 12-22). But God knows the way to it: God sees and knows everything, and God has not only apportioned the wind and the water but above all has established wisdom (vv. 23-27). One wonders: Is the wisdom of this chapter to be understood as personified, like Wisdom in Proverbs 8–9? One can translate the pronouns in vv. 21-23 and 27 as "her" rather than "it" and "its" (the NJB has done so).

The poem reflects themes that have already been set forth in the book, but in such a way as to challenge the assumptions of both Job's friends and Job himself. Zophar, in 11:7-9, has already made the same point that God's secrets are far too remote for human beings to discern, but his implication in making that point is that Job's quest for understanding is futile. On the other hand, if, as the poem affirms, God sees everything (v. 24), then Job has every right to insist that God will see that he is not guilty (10:4-7). Furthermore, Job is as aware of the glories of creation as the poet of chapter 28 is. Job has rehearsed the spectacle of the sea, the constellations, and all the rest that God has laid out (9:8-10), but for him the mysteries of creation are not pointers to the greater mystery of wisdom but rather evidences of the oppressive power of God (compare 10:8-9; 12:12-25). On the other hand, the theme in the poem of God's power over creation prepares the way for Yahweh's speeches in chapters 38–41; I shall discuss these below.

Then, suddenly, the last verse of the chapter (v. 28) offers an ironic twist even on the poem of the first twenty-seven verses. The verse begins, "And he [God] said to humankind. . . ." Having in our minds soared far above the earth and seen how far God is above that, we suddenly have a word, a direct word from God! And what is that word? "The fear of the Lord, that is wisdom, and to depart from evil is understanding." It is simply the old watchword of the book of Proverbs. How are we to hear this verse? Are we to reckon it as of small account? Is it "And all that God has ever said to humankind is 'Fear the Lord'"? We who have struggled with Job in his plight must not forget that the book began with the declaration that Job "feared God and turned away from evil" (1:1), and we are well aware of what Job's exemplary conduct has gained him. So where does this verse leave Job—and us?

We return to Job: in chapters 29–31, he gives his final testimony. In chapter 29, he offers his remembrance of things past: the honor he received in the city square (v. 7), the poor and orphans on behalf of whom he administered justice (v. 12)—a rebuke to Eliphaz's imaginary listing of his sins against the needy (22:5-9). By contrast (chapter 30), he is assaulted by the rabble (vv. 9-11), by the terrors of death (vv. 12-15) and by God (vv. 16-19), and his cry for justice gets no answer (vv. 20-31). In chapter 31, Job swears an oath that he is pure by offering a long list of sins he has not committed (vv. 7-34), and he ends by expressing the wish for an arbiter and for a written indictment from God specifying his sins (v. 35).

There follow six chapters in which a new character, Elihu, steps forward and offers a set of speeches. Since, Elihu says, Job's three friends have been unable to refute Job, he will offer himself as an arbiter (32:12-17). He restates Job's case (33:8-11); to Job's complaint that God does not answer (33:13), he argues that God does answer—both by dreams (33:15-18) and by suffering—and that suffering is both an evidence of God's chastisement (33:19-22) and an occasion for God's restoration (33:23-28). Elihu then defends God's justice (chapter 34). How could one who hates justice govern (34:17)? God is not answerable to a human court (34:23), so Job has no case (35:13-16). God is the champion of the afflicted (36:2-7). God is, furthermore, the powerful Creator before whom we should be in awe (36:22-25), notably in the storms God sends (36:26—37:13): these are matters Job cannot possibly explain (37:14-22).

Immediately following these speeches, Yahweh addresses Job out of the whirlwind. Earlier, Job had stated that if God were to respond to him in court, God would crush him with a whirlwind (9:16-17): now here is the whirlwind! But Job had also expressed a wish for a face-to-face encounter with God (13:15, 20, 24; 19:26-27), and now the wish is granted. Yahweh offers two speeches in defense of the Creator's cosmic design. In the first speech, Yahweh challenges Job to demonstrate any mastery over the inanimate, physical world—the earth, the sea, the constellations, and all the rest (38:4-38), and over animals and birds, from lion to eagle (38:39—39:30). Job admits he is struck dumb by all this (40:3-5). Yahweh then goes to the heart of the matter: Does Job question Yahweh's justice (40:8), a justice of governing and universal control (40:9-14)? Yahweh offers awesome evidence of that control in describing two great beasts, Behemoth (40:15-24) and Leviathan (chapter 41). The description of Behemoth reflects the Egyptian understanding of the hippopotamus, but it functions here as a mythic creature for Job to ponder. God made Behemoth side by side with Job (40:15), and God is able to tame Behemoth. A recent scholar translates 40:24 as "[God] takes him by the mouth with rings, He pierces his nose with hooks."[22] Since, as we noted in Chapter 4, "nose" in Hebrew is used for "anger," and since Job has used his mouth for boasting, one has the impression that Yahweh suggests Job needs to be subjugated just as Behemoth is.[23] Leviathan, too, though modeled on the crocodile, is portrayed as the dragon of Canaanite mythology. Could Job tame it and make a pet of it (41:4-5)? Even the gods are overwhelmed at the sight of it (41:9, 25)! If Job were to quail at a confrontation with Leviathan (41:10-11), how, by implication, can he hope to survive a confrontation with Yahweh? But, it is implied (41:11), Yahweh has silenced the beast.

Job then offers a closing speech (42:1-6) in a tone that is not altogether easy to discern; I follow the cogent analysis of Habel,[24] who translates the difficult v. 6 as follows: "Therefore I retract, and repent of dust and ashes." He points out that Job's speech is divided in two by the two citations of Yahweh's words, in v. 3a (= 38:2) and v. 4 (= 38:3). As to the first citation, Yahweh had asked who challenges the divine design without knowledge, and Job acknowledges that he is the one, and that he does not have the knowledge to run the universe (v. 3). As to the second citation, Yahweh had demanded that the challenger listen and then declare an answer, and Job acknowledges that whereas he had heard of Yahweh before, he now sees him (v. 5), and the fact that Yahweh has taken Job's challenge seriously enough to put in an appearance at all is enough to vindicate Job's integrity. He does not force Yahweh to acknowledge Job's innocence; he withdraws his case (this seems to be the meaning of "retract" in v. 6). What of the "dust and ashes"? The preposition appears to mean "concerning" dust and ashes, not "in" dust and ashes. We recall that Job had been sitting among the "ashes" (2:8) and that his friends had expressed their dismay with his situation by throwing "dust" in the air upon their heads (2:12). The "dust and ashes," therefore, represent (among other things) Job's status as an isolated sufferer and litigant. This status he now retracts. Job has made no confession of sin, guilt, or pride. Both Yahweh and Job have thus preserved their integrity.

The prose epilogue rounds off the story: Yahweh judges the three friends for not having represented the deity rightly, prescribes a penalty, and directs Job to pray for them (vv. 7-9). His kith and kin console him for all the disaster he has undergone, and then Yahweh blesses Job once more: he has more cattle than before (v. 12), and once more seven sons and three daughters (v. 13). But there is a surprise even in this stylized restoration: we are specifically told the names of the three daughters (v. 14) and are not told the names of the sons. (We were not told the names of any of the children in his first family.) We are not only specifically told how beautiful they are, but we learn that, in contrast to normal Israelite procedure, they inherit along with Job's sons (v. 15). What is going on here? Is Job going the second mile in justice? Is this a subversive critique of Israelite patriarchy?

Let us see what we can do to isolate a few common threads in this awesome book. It offers a double debate: between Job and his friends on the one hand, and between Job and God on the other.

With regard to the debate between Job and his friends, his friends defend the traditional, static orthodoxy. They maintain that everything will turn out all right, and God will take care of Job (5:19-26); they suggest that Job is only being tested, that it is all for his own good (5:17); they insist that Job and his children must be great sinners to have deserved all this (8:4; 22:5-9), and that Job should repent (8:5). This line of argument meets neither Job's emotional desolation ("you are fair-weather friends," 6:14-21, 27, "worthless physicians," 13:4-5, "miserable comforters," 16:2, compare 26:2-4) nor his theological desolation ("teach me where I have gone wrong," 6:24). Yet the irony is that there is a profound sense in which Job's friends are right and he is wrong. God *is* great and powerful: indeed, Eliphaz anticipates Yahweh's words out of the whirlwind (15:7-8). But because the friends are so concerned to defend God's integrity and so judgmental toward Job, we instinctively sense the unreality of their arguments and side with Job. God does too, as the denouement indicates (42:7-9).

With regard to the debate between Job and God, it is clear that Job both loves and hates God. He says in effect, "God is most unjust, having so afflicted me, an innocent man; but God, being just, must surely see the light and come to my aid." Job insists on his innocence (9:15) and at the same time wonders why, if God has treated him as if a sinner, the sin is not simply forgiven so that the relation can return to normal (7:20-21). Job addresses God by such taunting terms as "watcher of humanity" (7:20), yet he is aware, at least ironically, of the care God has bestowed on his life (10:12). It is remarkable that Job never rejects God, as his wife suggests he might (2:9): in saying in effect, "I have been treated unjustly, and therefore God is unjust," he does not say, "therefore God is incompetent," or "God does not matter," or "God cannot be known," or "God does not exist." If God is unjust, then that injustice can be demonstrated in court.

In all this, Job cannot acknowledge his creatureliness. This is what is bizarre about the notion of his taking God to court. Job complains that it is not a fair fight (9:12-19), but at the same time he simply will not submit to God. Here is irony: at the very moment when Job is most certain of his uprightness before God, he is in deepest rebellion against God. Sin is ultimately rebellion.

At the beginning, neither Job nor his friends have any room in their system for God's grace: the friends know what is right and wrong and claim that people get their just deserts, and Job knows what is right and wrong and demands he get his just deserts. But something else is happening: Job senses from time to time the need for grace—not for groveling, but for grace. He daydreams that he is dead, and that God is reaching out after him (10:1-12); even amid cries of virtue, he knows how little these will turn God's head, and he frantically looks around for a mediator, someone to vouch for him (9:14-20, 32-33). He daydreams of an afterlife and of a loving God who will yearn after what he has created (14:13-17); he dreams of a vindicator after his death who will keep his case open before God (19:23-24), perhaps even of an occasion finally to look God straight in the eye (19:25-27). But, for all Job can see, these dreams are vain (14:18-19). When God appears out of the whirlwind, the confrontation is not marked by grace so much as by a kind of reality principle that at the same time leaves much unsaid, on both sides.

So we have this curiosity, a lawsuit without a prior covenant. It is true that the covenant with Israel is marginally implied (compare the discussion on 28:28 above), but the lawsuit does not draw on it overtly. If there is no covenant with mutual claims and mutual promises, on what can Job base his suit? Job's life has gone awry, but God has made no promises to him. What to do? This theological puzzle is the reason for the steady appeal in the book to the evidence from creation. God has made no promises to him, but in any event God has created him. Job's friends assume that the Creator of all things must of necessity be just (5:10), and this is the burden of the poem in chapter 28 and of Yahweh's speeches out of the whirlwind. Job acknowledges the care of God in creation (12:7-10) but uses this argument to extend his insistence that God is unjust (9:5; 12:14-25; 14:18-19).

On the edges of the argumentation are two other themes, death and wisdom. As for death: in the minds of Job's friends, God redeems the righteous from death (5:20) and sends the wicked to death (chapter 18); for Job, death puts an end to his hopes for vindication (14:10-22; 30:23), and indeed death is the fate for both the righteous and the wicked (9:22). As for wisdom: Job's friends claim the wisdom to know what is right and wrong and challenge Job's wisdom (11:6); Job for his part offers his own claims for the wisdom to understand justice (12:2-4). As for death and wisdom: death may be powerful, but wisdom is deeper still (11:8; compare 28:22). All these themes crowd our attention, challenging us to clarify our own understanding. I postpone how we hear God in all this until we have examined the third book in the wisdom literature of the Old Testament.

Ecclesiastes

This third book is different from either of the other two.[25] It is a loose-jointed series of observations, and in this respect it is like Proverbs rather than being a tightly organized work like Job; still, it is like Job in offering a message at odds with the assumptions of most of the Old Testament.

The name "Ecclesiastes" is a Greek rendering of the puzzling Hebrew word to designate the author—Koheleth. The NRSV translates the word as "Teacher" (1:1-2), but it is a word that perhaps designates a "collector" (of sayings) or the like.[26] The implication of 1:1 is that the author is Solomon, but this attribution, like that for Proverbs, is evidently unhistorical; though the author assumes the identity of a king in 1:12—2:26, he soon abandons the fiction. There is no indication, for example, that the author can put down the oppressors of the poor (4:1). When was the book written? Evidently late in the Old Testament period; a variety of indications, particularly late Hebrew vocabulary, suggest a date in the Ptolemaic period, perhaps 250–225 B.C. The book thus seems to have emerged some three centuries after the book of Job.

Our inquiry must begin with a discussion of the meaning of a motto that appears at the beginning of the book (1:2) and at the end (12:8): the NRSV translates 1:2, "Vanity of vanities! . . . All is vanity." Beyond 1:2 and 12:8, the word translated "vanity" appears 28 times in the book; clearly it is crucial for our understanding of the message of the book. But it is not easy to find an ideal English translation of the term. The Hebrew word, *hebel,* means a transitory hot "breath" or "vapor" (compare Isa. 57:13; Ps. 62:9). One commentator of Ecclesiastes translates 1:2, "A vapor of vapors! . . . Thinnest of vapors! All is vapor!"[27] The word evidently implies both transitoriness and meaninglessness; the NIV translates the verse, "Meaningless! Meaningless! . . . Utterly meaningless! Everything is meaningless." The New Jewish Version (*Tanakh*) translates the verse, "Utter futility! . . . Utter futility! All is futile!"[28] Ronald Knox, in his translation several decades ago, uses a different metaphor in English, "A shadow's shadow . . . a world of shadows!" and then in the body of the book he paraphrases the word with expressions like "frustration" (2:11).[29] Edwin Good discusses the use of the term in Ecclesiastes and concludes that it means "incongruity."[30] We shall have to feel our way in understanding how the author intends *hebel* to be understood.

Following the opening motto, the author poses a question that really sets the theme for the whole book: "What do people gain from all the toil at which they toil under the sun?" (1:3)—in the translation of Ronald Knox, "How is man the better for all this toiling of his, here under the sun?" This theme is followed by a poem (vv. 4-11) that affirms the essential meaninglessness of history. The generations of human beings are nothing but repetition: "Age succeeds age, and the world goes on unaltered" (1:4, Ronald Knox). Things only seem new because of the human tendency to forget the past.[31]

The author then offers descriptions, one after another, of activities that, in his estimation, are evaluated as *hebel*. Pleasure: with all the elaborate schemes for enjoyment that he sets up, he finds it is all *hebel* (2:1-11). Work: all the deeds his hand has done, and all his toil, are *hebel* (2:11). Why? Because he will leave his wealth to his heir, who may be wise or may be foolish (2:18-19, 21) but in any case has not worked for the wealth. Wealth: those who amass wealth are never satisfied; this is *hebel* (4:7; 5:10).

Wisdom: here our author hedges. At several points, he affirms that wisdom is better than folly (2:13; 7:5; 10:12), but he points out that the wise and the foolish ultimately suffer the same fate, and both will be forgotten, so this, too, is *hebel* (2:14-15); at another point, he wonders what advantage the wise really have over fools (6:8). He cannot see any essential difference between human beings and animals (3:18-21), "for the fate of humans and the fate of animals is the same; as one dies, so dies the other"; this too is *hebel* (3:19).

The author gestures in the direction of the eternal verities in Israel: "I said in my heart, God will judge the righteous and the wicked, for he has appointed a time for every matter, and for every work" (4:17); "Guard your steps when you go to the house of God; to draw near to listen is better than the sacrifice offered by fools" (5:1). Nevertheless, since the same fate awaits both the righteous and the wicked, the good and the evil, the clean and unclean, those who sacrifice and those who do not sacrifice (9:2), what good is it to affirm God's justice? Power belongs to the oppressors (4:1), and in the real world one finds wickedness where there should be justice (3:16). Indeed, "Do not be too righteous, and do not act too wise; why should you destroy yourself?" (7:16). One cannot be altogether sure what is implied by this advice: is it a reflection of the Greek "nothing in excess," or is it simply the author's conviction that inasmuch as the traditional conviction (that righteousness is rewarded and wickedness is punished) does not work out in practice, one should not attempt to be perfect because it is impossible? It is also worth noting that the author maintains not only that one should not try too hard to be righteous but also that one should not try too hard to be wise: he suspects that either achievement offers a temptation to boast. I shall return to this issue later when we discuss Paul's attitude on this matter in 1 Corinthians 1–2.

Yet the author of Ecclesiastes is not bitter. "There is nothing better for mortals than to eat and drink, and find enjoyment in their toil. This also, I saw, is from the hand of God" (2:24); and again, "Go, eat your bread with enjoyment, and drink your wine with a merry heart; for God has long ago approved what you do. . . . Enjoy life with the wife whom you love, all the days of your life of *hebel* that are given you under the sun, because that is your portion in life and in your toil at which you toil under the sun. Whatever your hand finds to do, do with your might; for there is no work or thought or knowledge or wisdom in Sheol, to which you are going" (9:7, 9-10; compare 3:13, 22; 5:17; 8:15; 11:9-10).

If the author is not bitter, what is the implication of *hebel?* Hardly "futility," one of the current translations, for "futility" suggests "uselessness." Indeed, what can one do with *hebel* in the passage just quoted? Since the author commends enjoyment, "your vain life" (NRSV) cannot be right, either in that passage or in 6:12 and 7:15, where the same phrase occurs. Nor is "your futile life" right.[32] True, the author maintains that it is futile to try to escape the grave, but the life one lives may not be futile, though it is certainly both "fleeting"[33] and "uncertain."[34] If the word refers both to transitoriness and meaninglessness, as I have already affirmed, then I would suggest that it refers to what has no lasting or ultimate significance. The author keeps his eye firmly on the present and on whatever modest gains and satisfactions the present can offer; we have already noted that he sees no meaning in history. In this connection, it would be useful to clarify the meaning of 3:11, a famous verse. What is it that God has planted in the human heart (or mind)? The Hebrew word ⁽ôlām does not really mean "eternity" (RSV) but may refer either to an extent of time to the indefinite past, or an extent of time to the indefinite future, or to both. Therefore the NRSV translation, "moreover, he [God] has put a sense of past and future into their minds,"[35] is likely to be right; and the verse concludes, "yet they cannot find out what God has done from the beginning to the end."[36] If this is a correct understanding, then God has put into our minds a hunger for a permanent place in history, which is specious, and a craving to know and control the future, which is not ours to have.

To sum up: we cannot know the future, nor can we know the total work of God. "I have scrutinized God's whole creation: you cannot get to the bottom of everything taking place under the sun; you may wear yourself out in the search, but you will never find it. Not even a sage can get to the bottom of it, even if he says that he has done so" (8:17, NJB).

We may conclude that we have here a modest and genial skeptic, a kind of ancient existentialist. But we need to take account also of what is not here, even within the limits of the author's skepticism. He does acknowledge the importance of family ties (4:7-12): someone with sons or brothers is better than someone with none. But he is not kind to women, and we lack any sense from him that children bring joy. As far as women are concerned, we hear of the delights of the flesh, and of concubines (2:8); but he repeats the notion we found in Proverbs 7 that women are a trap (7:26) and seems to say in 7:28 that one man out of a thousand may be better, but not one woman; his word about enjoying life with the wife you love (9:9) has to be heard in that context. Children are mentioned a couple of times: in 5:14 we hear of parents of children who lose their money in a bad business venture, and in 6:3 the author cites the hypothetical case of a man who begets a hundred children and lives a long life, but he maintains that neither feature guarantees a happy life. Alongside the word about sons in 4:7 we must place the wry word we have already mentioned, that one's property will be inherited by someone who did not work for it (2:21). The pride and the joy one may take in one's children (compare Psalms 127 and 128) are simply missing.

There is a final twist: this collection of words from the skeptic has received an editorial ending that brings it back within the orbit of traditional teaching: "The end of the matter; all has been heard. Fear God, and keep his commandments; for that is the whole duty of everyone. For God will bring every deed into judgment, including every secret thing, whether good or evil" (12:13-14).

The Wisdom Books, Summary

How can we sum up these three books? As we have seen at the beginning of this chapter, they are all products of wisdom circles in Israel, the early sequences of Proverbs from the pre-exilic period, the finished book from the postexilic period, and Job and Ecclesiastes from that period as well. They are united in that each of them attempts to understand the ways of God with humankind, seen through eyes sharpened by the traditions of Israel.

Yet these books are certainly disparate. Where Proverbs takes it for granted that wisdom is accessible, not only as a collection of maxims but even as a ideal to be pursued as passionately as a man pursues a woman, Job and Ecclesiastes in contrasting ways assert that wisdom is ultimately inaccessible—Job because the human experience of the injustice of God's world precludes any final sense that wisdom is accessible, Ecclesiastes because no human experience has ultimate significance. Proverbs offers confident reflections of Israel's value system; Job and Ecclesiastes level ironic critiques at that value system.[37] Proverbs is optimistic about human possibilities; Job and Ecclesiastes are pessimistic: for both the latter, human beings are, if not trapped, certainly impeded in crucial respects. For Job, human beings can never be sure that their moral status is significant in God's sight; for Ecclesiastes, no moral effort of human beings can be significant. Job asks how he can get God to notice; Ecclesiastes is convinced that any effort to get God to notice is quixotic. Job struggles; Ecclesiastes shrugs his shoulders, content to live life as it comes.

As I have stated several times in this chapter, these books move beyond the metaphor of the covenant with Israel to use the category of creation. But it is

curious that these books do not explore the possibility of a divine covenant
with creation. That possibility was proposed by the Priestly Source (see Chapter 5): the Priestly narrative understood God's word to Noah, after the flood,
to be a covenant sealed by the rainbow (Gen. 9:8-17), and it was therefore a
word to all humankind. But there is no evidence that the wisdom literature
used the metaphor of covenant with respect to creation.

Hearing God in the Wisdom Books

Given these disparities, in what way or ways might we expect to hear God in
these books? Because of the variety of points of view in these books, our answer will be complex. As we try to formulate an answer, we must resist two
urges: (1) given the mutual contradictions among these books, the urge to
minimize their importance; (2) the urge to flee too quickly to New Testament
affirmations.

With regard to the book of Proverbs, we have already anticipated an answer: in many of its maxims we can surely hear God, but other sayings, notably those that scorn women, we are impelled to pass by.

Relating the perspectives of the New Testament with Job and with Ecclesi-
astes is another matter: they not only challenge the traditional assumptions of
Israel, they are in contrast both with each other and with the New Testament.
Given this circumstance, I suggest that our first obligation is simply to pause
and ponder that fact that the Jewish community accepted Job and Ecclesiastes
as scriptural along with all the books that Job and Ecclesiastes challenge: the
Old Testament community was clearly able to live with an understanding of
Scripture that allowed internal challenge and even contradiction. Given the
fact that the Old Testament collection of Scripture was accepted as scripture
by Christians, it behooves us as Christians to emulate the earlier Jewish tolerance, to raise our own tolerance for internal challenge and contradiction
among books of Scripture. We are not obliged to run around nervously trying
to straighten everything out!

With regard to Job, a basic problem is the fact that it is dialogue: if we may
claim to hear God in God's own speeches and actions in the book, how at the
same time could we hear God in Job's speeches, which challenge God so profoundly? We recall one clue in the epilogue: God declared that Job had spoken
rightly and his friends had not (Job 42:7); God wants us therefore to listen to
Job even as he challenged God. Another clue might be found in the conviction
of traditional Christian theology that the nature of God is to be found in dialogue—this is one meaning at least of the Trinity. Job's words, accepted by
God, become part of the whole communication of God that is summed up in

Jesus Christ, the incarnate Word. Even if we are unwilling to struggle with the notion of the Trinity, we could start with Jesus' word on the cross, "My God, my God, why have you forsaken me?" (Mark 15:34). Jesus was citing the opening words of Psalm 22, but they were words that matched his situation. If Jesus is understood by Christians to be the incarnate Word of God, he may still perceive that he is abandoned by God. We might ponder likewise Jesus' prayer in the Garden of Gethsemane, "Father, for you all things are possible; remove this cup from me; yet, not what I want, but what you want" (Mark 14:36). It is noteworthy, that as early as Gregory the Great (ca. 540–604), Job is a prototype of Christ and the church.[38]

A different kind of puzzle is represented by Ecclesiastes: How might declarations that life has no meaning at the same time be words through which we hear God? Again we may find clues from Jesus' words. Jesus told a parable about two sons whose father told them to work in the vineyard: the first said, "I will not" but later changed his mind and went: the second said yes but did not go. Which son, Jesus asked, did the will of his father? The answer, of course, is "the first" (Matt. 21:28-31). The parable suggests that those who refuse the authority of God may still do the will of God. The story of the lost son (Luke 15:11-32) also suggests that Jesus understands God to be able to accept rebellious sons. A book like Ecclesiastes, rebellious though it is, might function as a means through which we might hear God.

Some years ago, at a retreat of college students, I had great success working through the book of Ecclesiastes with them. Most of this particular group of students were impelled to doubt everything they had been told in church, and Ecclesiastes spoke to their condition. That these chapters of skepticism are to be found within the covers of the Bible was a surprise to them, and it allowed them to work through a lot of their reactions to perceived hypocrisy within the Church that needed to be shared. We may agree that Ecclesiastes is not the last word in faith and still acknowledge that, for some people, it is a welcome invitation to conversation about the faith; indeed, we may be very grateful for its participation in Scripture.

We may be even more grateful for the book of Job. How many sufferers, bothered by well-meaning friends who imply or even say straight out that the suffering will cease when the sufferers give themselves to God, have taken solace in the book of Job, reveling in Job's insistence, in chapter after chapter, that it just isn't so? So many instances crowd into my mind: a colleague, living his last few weeks with inoperable cancer, rereading the book of Job; another colleague, enduring terrible pain through the years, declaring how wonderful a gift the book of Job is to us. The gift is that precious breath of reality that we breathe in the pages of the book.

But we would like to be a people who make the New Testament faith our own, and both Job and Ecclesiastes nourish a lack of faith! A clue in this circumstance may be found in Mark 9:22-24. The father of an epileptic boy had come to Jesus for a cure for the boy; he said, "If you are able to do anything, have pity on us and help us." Jesus said to him, "If you are able! All things can be done for the one who believes." The father answered, "I believe; help my unbelief!" Mark then describes Jesus' dramatic healing of the boy. I suggest that the father's word, "I believe; help my unbelief!" and Jesus' acceptance of that word, offer an opening for us in our inquiry. We also, poised between belief and unbelief, may ponder the New Testament for our belief and ponder Job or Ecclesiastes for our unbelief.

The most obvious contrast between the New Testament and these books is in regard to the question of death. To the Christian, the New Testament promises resurrection and eternal life. To Job's rhetorical question, "If mortals die, will they live again?" (Job 14:14), and to his answer in the negative (Job 14:18-19), and to the skepticism of Ecclesiastes (Eccl. 3:18-21), comes the affirmation of John 11:25, "Jesus said to her, 'I am the resurrection and the life. Those who believe in me, even though they die, will live." As we glory in that New Testament affirmation, it is important for us to remind ourselves, as we noted in Chapter 10, that there were Jewish circles in the two centuries before the time of the New Testament that likewise affirmed the resurrection; one striking example is found in one of the extra books in Roman Catholic Bibles (see Chapter 1), in 2 Maccabees 7. But the fact remains that the New Testament affirmation offers a new path to human beings who, in the expressions of both Job and Ecclesiastes, see themselves as impeded or even trapped in their destiny.

As New Testament Christians, how might we deal with the specific disparities between Job and Ecclesiastes, and between both of them and Proverbs? I suggest that, given the variety in theological approaches offered in the New Testament, it may be possible to some degree to match specific bodies of material in the New Testament with given wisdom material. A reader for whom the Letter to the Romans is central can find its partner in the book of Job: both books use the language of the law court, both struggle with the same array of questions centering around the problem of how one can ultimately be accepted and declared innocent by the all-powerful God. Job maintains that he has lived a good and moral life and it does not seem to have pleased God. Paul insists that there is no way to please God by however moral a life we may live, and that what bridges the chasm between God and ourselves is God's grace and our faith in Jesus Christ. Job looked for an umpire between himself and God (Job 9:33); Paul affirmed that Jesus Christ fulfilled that role

(Rom. 7:24-25). One cannot read that Elihu was angry at Job because he justified himself rather than God (Job 32:2) and Paul's words that we are justified by faith (Rom. 5:1) without pondering the resonance between these two books.

By the same token, those who center their understanding of Jesus in the Gospel of John may ponder, in the book of Proverbs, the figure of personified Wisdom with God from the foundation of the world (Prov. 8:22-23, compare John 1:1-2); the resemblance of these two figures has often been noted.[39] As Wisdom in Proverbs, a personified abstraction, is understood to be accessible to human beings, so now a real human being, Jesus, the very manifestation of God's glory (John 1:14), is accessible to human beings, and will continue to be so (John 20:29).

If we pursue this line of thinking, we find that this parallel of motifs in the Gospel of John between personified Wisdom and Jesus has become for Paul an identity: he affirms that Christ Jesus became for us wisdom from God (1 Cor. 1:30). Matthew seconds the motion: he evidently intends the saying of Jesus, "Yet Wisdom is vindicated by her deeds" (Matt. 11:19), to be understood as Jesus' own self-identification.

I would propose that those who listen hard to Jesus' teachings in the synoptic Gospels might well listen to the author of Ecclesiastes: though the differences between the two are profound, there are certainly likenesses as well. Both of them challenge the dogged concern for obedience to the Jewish law; both see through the pretensions of those who claim righteousness. One may lay Eccl. 7:20, "Surely there is no one on earth so righteous as to do good without sinning," alongside Jesus' word to the scribes and Pharisees, "So you also on the outside look righteous to others, but inside you are full of hypocrisy and lawlessness" (Matt. 23:28). Both Ecclesiastes and Jesus see the irony of the work of God in human life: one may usefully compare Eccl. 8:14, "There is a vanity that takes place on earth, that there are righteous people who are treated according to the conduct of the wicked, and there are wicked people who are treated according to the conduct of the righteous. I said that this also is vanity," with Matt. 5:45, "[Your Father] makes his sun rise on the evil and on the good, and sends rain on the righteous and on the unrighteous."

Jesus was himself a teacher of wisdom. In Chapter 9, we saw how the role of prophet was part of Jesus' self-understanding; now we see that the role of wisdom teacher was part of it as well. Therefore, we must look to the wisdom literature of the Old Testament, as well as to the prophets, to grasp Jesus' own self-understanding.

Let us turn now to the notion of "wisdom" in the narrower sense. The book of Proverbs, as we have noted repeatedly, assumes that the pursuit of wisdom is a good thing and is a realizable goal. But Paul reminds us in 1 Corinthians 1–2 that wisdom is not what it seems. There were some people in the Corinthian church who were tempted to boast of their superior knowledge (1 Cor. 8:1-6); this was surely a temptation not only for those coming from a Jewish background (compare my remarks above on Eccl. 7:16) but also for those coming from a Greek background (compare my remark at the beginning of this chapter on the parallel between Jewish wisdom and Greek philosophy). Paul insists that God has turned the wisdom of the world into foolishness and that the wisdom of God is the folly of the cross (1 Cor. 1:18-21). From this point of view, Job 28:20-21 is right after all: the wisdom of God has been secret and hidden (1 Cor. 2:7) until God determined to reveal it to us.

Finally, I return to the topic with which I began this chapter—the range of wisdom literature beyond the confines of the covenant people to the wide world, so that the category of creation becomes central. If the church is understood as the community of the new covenant (see the end of Chapter 2), and if the wisdom literature understands its scope to be all humankind, then the Church is the intersection of both covenant and wisdom perceptions. The creation of the Church is thus an event of world history, balancing the theological scope of the narrative in Genesis 1–11, a narrative that begins with creation and subsequent events that are understood to have taken place before God embarked on the solution to the problem presented by humankind. Indeed, there was a belief in Jewish circles, based on their interpretation of Gen. 3:17, that when sin came into the world it infected not only humankind but all the created world as well. This is the background for Paul's words in Rom. 8:18-25, especially vv. 22-23: "We know that the whole creation has been groaning in labor pains until now; and not only the creation, but we ourselves, who have the first fruits of the Spirit, groan inwardly while we wait for adoption, the redemption of our bodies." Paul can thus envision a time when everything, both human and nonhuman, which has suffered defects, will be transformed by the work of God that has begun in Christ. In this way the specific concerns of wisdom contribute to the theological streams of the New Testament that testify to the culminating act of God.

Notes

1. See *ANET,* 320–21.
2. John Gray, "Chemosh," *IDB* 1:556.
3. For a translation of the Egyptian hymn, see *ANET,* 369–71.
4. Mitchell Dahood, *Psalms III* (AB 17A; Garden City, NY: Doubleday, 1970), 33.

5. For a translation of the Egyptian text, see *ANET,* 421–25; for the relation of the Proverbs text to Amen-em-ope, see William McKane, *Proverbs* (OTL; Philadelphia: Westminster, 1970), 371–85.

6. McKane, *Proverbs,* 656.

7. Thomas P. McCreesh, "Proverbs," *New Jerome,* 453–54.

8. For the process in Egypt, see John A. Wilson, *The Burden of Egypt* (Chicago: University of Chicago, 1951), chapter 9.

9. Henri Frankfort and others, *Before Philosophy, The Intellectual Adventure of Ancient Man* (Harmondsworth: Penguin, 1949), 244; Gerhard von Rad, *Wisdom in Israel* (New York and Nashville: Abingdon, 1972), 152–53; Roland E. Murphy, "Introduction to Wisdom Literature," *New Jerome,* 450; McCreesh, "Proverbs," *New Jerome,* 454.

10. McCreesh, "Proverbs," 457.

11. For the Sumerian version, see *ANET,* 52–57; for the Assyrian, see *ANET,* 106-9.

12. Helpful here is Carole R. Fontaine, "Proverbs," in Carol A. Newsom and Sharon H. Ringe (eds.), *The Women's Bible Commentary* (Louisville: Westminster/John Knox, 1992), 147–48.

13. Especially helpful are Samuel Terrien, "Introduction and Exegesis, Job," *IB* 3:875–1198, and Norman C. Habel, *The Book of Job* (OTL; Philadelphia: Westminster, 1985).

14. Harold S. Kushner, *When Bad Things Happen to Good People* (New York: Schocken Books, 1981).

15. "A Dispute over Suicide," *ANET,* 405–7.

16. "The Protests of the Eloquent Peasant," *ANET,* 407–10.

17. "I will praise the Lord of Wisdom," *ANET,* 434–37.

18. "A Dialogue about Human Misery," *ANET,* 438–40.

19. For two thoughtful treatments of the Babylonian point of view on these matters, see Henri Frankfort and others, *Before Philosphy,* 227–31, and A. Leo Oppenheim, *Ancient Mesopotamia, Portrait of a Dead Civilization* (Chicago: University of Chicago, 1964), 272–75.

20. See Habel, *Job,* 171, 177.

21. *Ibid.,* 223–32.

22. *Id.,* 551.

23. *Id.,* 559.

24. *Id.,* 575–83.

25. Particularly useful is James L. Crenshaw, *Ecclesiastes* (OTL; Philadelphia: Westminster, 1987); see also Carole R. Fontaine, "Ecclesiastes," in *Women's Bible Commentary,* 153–56.

26. Crenshaw, *Ecclesiastes,* 32–34.

27. R. B. Y. Scott, *Proverbs, Ecclesiastes* (AB 18; Garden City, NY: Doubleday, 1965), 209.

28. Compare Crenshaw, *Ecclesiastes,* 57.

29. Ronald Knox (tr.), *The Holy Bible* (New York: Sheed & Ward, 1956).

30. Edwin M. Good, *Irony in the Old Testament* (London: Society for the Propagation of Christian Knowledge, 1965), 176–83.

31. Crenshaw, *Ecclesiastes,* 62.

32. Compare the NJB and the REB.

33. The translation of James Moffatt, *A New Translation of the Bible* (New York and London: Harper, 1935), and the New Jewish Version—*The Writings, Kethubim* (Philadelphia: New Publication Society, 1982).

34. The translation of Ronald Knox (see note 29).

35. So also the REB.

36. The matter is by no means assured: see the analysis of James L. Crenshaw, "The Eternal Gospel (Eccl. 3:11)," in James L. Crenshaw and John T. Willis (eds.), *Essays in Old Testament Ethics, J. Philip Hyatt in Memoriam* (New York: Ktav, 1974), 40–42.

37. Good, *Irony*, chapters 6 and 7.

38. M. G. Mara, "Job, In the Fathers," in Angelo Di Berardino (ed.), *Encyclopedia of the Early Church*, tr. Adrian Walford (New York: Oxford University, 1992), 1:437b. Compare also the balancing of Job and Paul on the fourth-century sarcophagus of Junius Bassus: see Elizabeth Struthers Malbon, *The Iconography of the Sarcophagus of Junius Bassus* (Princeton: Princeton University, 1990), 54–55. I owe these references to my colleague, Professor Robin M. Jensen.

39. A useful recent treatment of the matter is Raymond E. Brown, *The Gospel According to John, I–XII* (AB 29; Garden City, NY: Doubleday, 1966), CXXII–CXXV.

12

Female and Male[1]

∽

The issues with which this work has dealt up to this point have always been recognized by Christians, and Christians through the centuries have devised a variety of approaches to deal with them. But the topic of the present chapter has emerged with urgency only in the past few decades. It is so fresh that some Christians simply dismiss it as a fad of fanatics. It is not a fad, however, and the issue will not go away; it is poignant and particularly urgent for the Old Testament, though it strikes at the heart of the whole biblical message. I refer to gender bias.

I mentioned this issue in Chapter 1, but it is far more complex than that brief presentation indicated. There are separate questions here, though they are obviously closely related: the bias in favor of males in the Israelite understanding of the relative status of females and males in society, and the bias in favor of the masculine gender in the Israelite metaphors for God. Specifically, there is in the Old Testament a masculine bias in four interrelated matters: (1) the male-dominated structure of society in Old Testament times (and analogous structures in our own society as well); (2) the fact that the circles that produced the Old Testament were overwhelmingly male; (3) the routine use of masculine nouns and pronouns to refer generically to human beings in the Hebrew text, a use reflected until recently in English translations; and (4) the overwhelming use of masculine metaphors for God, and the unvarying use of masculine pronouns for God in the Hebrew text, a use that (at least until now) has been carried over into our English translations. I shall devote most of this chapter to a discussion of the status of women in the Old Testament, saving the matter of metaphors for God until the end.

THE STATUS OF WOMEN IN ISRAELITE SOCIETY

The Questions

Let us begin with an attempt to specify the status of women in ancient Israelite society. Unfortunately, we do not have enough data at our disposal to offer a full treatment of the matter. Furthermore, as we try to understand what we can of women's status, we face several questions. The text of the Old Testament depicts a society in key areas of which men are dominant over women and in which men fill roles denied to women. Since that text has shaped Jewish and Christian understandings of the status of women, most of our discussion will concern that text. But we must at least raise questions about the adequacy of the text to reflect the actual status of women in ancient Israel. As a sampling of those questions, I offer the following.

Since the Old Testament is the product of circles of literate people, almost all of whom were males in Jerusalem (see below), to what extent do its texts represent an accurate reflection of the relation between the sexes in cities and towns outside Jerusalem or in villages and rural areas?

The texts—especially the laws—portray males as holding power in crucial areas of society. So one wonders: Did females hold power in other areas of society that are not reflected in the texts? Only occasionally do we get a glimpse of wives who wield some kind of power or who maneuver affairs behind the scenes—Bathsheba working deviously to gain her son Solomon the throne instead of Adonijah (1 Kings 1); wives of the upper class giving orders to husbands for more drinks (Amos 4:1); Queen Vashti refusing to appear at the king's drunken party, and the consequent fear of the courtiers that this refusal could trigger more such refusals among the wives of other officials (Esth. 1:10-18). We have no way of knowing whether such glimpses are representative of women in general, or are representative simply of upper-class women, or are exceptional and aberrant vignettes.

One wonders about the nature of the laws that maintained men in power or were biased in favor of males. Did these laws reflect the actual practice in Israelite times, or were they an idealized portrayal of the social structure to which males aspired?

Physical Work and the Education of Children

Recent work of the scholar Carol Meyers offers the best available overview of the position of women in ancient Israelite society.[2] Meyers has extracted her data not only from the biblical text but also from the findings of archeology and, beyond these findings, from the conclusions of anthropologists working in analogous cultures of the present day as well. She has suggested that women in the ancient Near East at about 1500 B.C., two and a half centuries before Moses' time, enjoyed relatively more equality with men than they did in the next few centuries, when biblical Israel was taking shape; in the centuries after 1500 B.C., various wars, famines, and plagues brought on a population crisis that in Israel at least intensified the role of women in domestic affairs and childbearing and tended to restrict them to these roles. We must assume high mortality rates in early Israel both for infants and for women, particularly in childbearing. Women were highly valued, as is shown by the fact that the bride did not bring a dowry into marriage, but rather the groom paid a bride-price (Hebrew *mōhar*) to the bride's father (Exod. 22:16-17, compare 1 Sam. 18:25).[3] Meyers points out that the earliest Israelites settled in the Palestinian highlands, an area that had not been settled by the Canaanites; the soil there was poor and offered inadequate natural sources of water. The Israelites were therefore "pioneers" in clearing the forests, making the terrain suitable for farming by terracing the hillsides, and digging out cisterns to retain the runoff of rain for the water needed by each household. These pioneering settlements in new areas required an enormous outlay of work by both men and women and put a premium on a high birthrate: families needed all the children they could raise for potential labor.[4]

The early texts in the Old Testament record a society organized by tribes, by clans within each tribe, and by households within each clan. The data available from archeology indicate that, in the period before the monarchy, the Israelites lived in self-contained villages, and many of them continued that mode of existence thereafter. In these villages, the typical layout of a dwelling indicates that a household normally consisted of more members than our present-day nuclear families do; indeed, it has been suggested that the laws of forbidden sexual relations in Leviticus 18 and 20 are an attempt to enforce incest taboos for households consisting of an extended range of members beyond the unit of a married couple and their children.[5]

These households were almost completely self-sufficient economically. One can easily imagine the tasks performed exclusively or principally by men in these early settlements: the clearing of forests, the digging of cisterns, the heavy agricultural work such as plowing. But we must remind ourselves: it was the women who drew water and carried it into the house (1 Sam. 9:11-13), who ground the grain into flour, using a large flat stone (quern) and a small grindstone held in the hands,[6] who baked the bread (1 Sam. 8:13), boiled porridge and other dishes, and were responsible for the storage of food resources—grain, wine, oil, and condiments—and their allocation as well. They spun, wove, and sewed, and they may have shared in making pottery. They must also have expended much energy caring for gardens and for the domestic animals. As an analogy, it is useful to recall the hard work done by women in the pioneer settlements of the American colonial period and the early decades of the republic. Though the description of the good wife (Prov. 31:10-31), as we saw in Chapter 11, is doubtless from a late period and describes a woman of the elite class, the array of kinds of work she does is a reminder of the workload of most women in Israelite times.[7] It is important to remember that the commandment to honor parents mentions mother as well as father (Exod. 20:12).

Israelite women expended energy not only in the fetching of water, in cooking and in sewing, and in childbearing; they shared in the task of educating children in the skills and traditions necessary in their society; Prov. 1:8 comes to mind: "Hear, my child, your father's instruction, and do not reject your mother's teaching." The fact that in the book of Proverbs Wisdom could be personified as a woman (see again Chapter 11) in itself suggests the existence of the teaching role of women and its importance.

"Wise Women"

If "wise men" were a recognized feature of Israelite society (see once more Chapter 11), then one hears as well of "wise women," those who were evidently renowned for their discernment in human affairs. Thus, there was the wise woman of Tekoa whom Joab directed to approach King David, when the latter had exiled his son Absalom, to urge a reconciliation between them (2 Sam. 14:1-20); her approach to David was devious but effective. And there was the wise woman of Abel-beth-maacah, who confronted Joab and was able to save her city from destruction when the rebel Sheba was hiding there (2 Sam. 20:14-22). The plural, "wise women," was further used for those who led funeral lamentations (Jer. 9:17-18, 20: the NRSV translates the Hebrew "wise women" in v. 17 as "skillful women"). We conclude that there were women who offered leadership in specific matters in the villages and in specific neighborhoods.

The Power of Women in the Premonarchical Period

Given this division of labor, what might we say about the actual relation of power between men and women in this period? We can surmise some things with fair certainty. Meyers states, "Gender differentiation, particularly in a society living at subsistence level, implies complementarity and hence interdependence. . . . Even in societies with developed patterns of female subservience . . . the internal dynamics reveal functional equality and male awareness of dependence on female talents and labor."[8] She cites a study of a Palestinian village in the same highlands area today: the investigator found that, although the villagers in their external cultural forms maintained male dominance, there is much more actual parity in power between the sexes in the day-to-day relationships of the village. Despite official hierarchical arrangements, the primacy of the women's contributions to subsistence secured their positions "more effectively than could any verbal affirmation of equal rights."[9] In short, "When the household occupies the preeminent place in a society, women have a strong role in decision making and consequently exercise considerable power in the household."[10]

The main advantage that men held over women in Israelite society was in the continuity of land tenure: land passed down in the male line. Land was not only the incarnation of the family's identity from generation to generation, it was the very source of sustenance for the family.[11] Therefore, upon marriage, the wife inevitably moved from her own family's location to her husband's location. Meyers speculates that this structure was advantageous in the Palestinian highlands, where neighboring regions have contrasting climatic conditions: the men, who made the decisions on plowing, sowing, and harvesting, could learn and hand down the seasonal necessities of a particular region.[12]

The Power of Women in the Monarchical Period

With the coming of the monarchy, the balance of power shifted more toward males. This shift was the result of several interrelated factors. One was the emergence of an urbanized public world: military, royal, and religious bureaucracies developed that were both male and hierarchical—a standing army, schools to train scribes, an expanded priesthood in Jerusalem. These organizations helped to absorb from the villages younger sons who could not hope to inherit enough land to sustain a living. Furthermore, the traditional tribal institutions were largely broken by Solomon when he set up new administrative districts (1 Kings 4:7-19) for the purpose of tax gathering and when he instituted the forced labor of Israelites for his building projects (1 Kings 5:13-18; 11:18).[13] As both domestic and foreign trade developed and new goods came into the market, village households inevitably became less self-sufficient. Debt slavery became more common. There was a steady movement of population from the villages to the growing cities, and, with the fall of Samaria in 721 B.C., a movement of refugees southward, particularly into Jerusalem, enlarging its population. All these developments meant that the traditional rural values and folkways were overtaken by the new male-centered patterns of urban life.[14]

One development that evidently took place in the city, given its potential for the mixing of men and women, was a kind of functional and locational segregation of women. The gathering places for men were the streets and squares, where they conducted their activities of work, trade, and public discussion, and the city gate, the site for legal decisions. Women, when not within the home, came out by their own paths to draw water.[15] Only prostitutes broke this segregation.

Prostitutes

Prostitutes were always a separate category. It is difficult to define their precise status in Israel: one must distinguish the attitude of the rest of society toward them from their attitude toward themselves. The existence of prostitutes is taken for granted (1 Kings 3:16-28). Consorting freely with men, they could break with the custom of segregation of adults of the two sexes. Rahab, the prostitute in Jericho (Joshua 2), became a heroine in Israel's story (Josh. 6:17, 23-25). The narrative implies that she was head of her household (2:3; 6:23), which consisted at least of her parents and siblings and perhaps others as well; she certainly took the initiative in hiding Joshua's spies and in dealing with the city authorities. One detail in regard to prostitutes in the whole of the ancient Near East is that they were (understandably) associated with windows, a detail that suggests both a break with the normal seclusion of women and the vulnerability of prostitutes to public shame. A widespread artistic motif in the ancient Near East is that of the prostitute looking out her window.[16] Rahab's window figures prominently in her story (Josh. 2:15). Prostitutes painted their eyes (Jer. 4:30), so when we read that Queen Jezebel "painted her eyes, and adorned her head, and looked out the window" (2 Kings 9:30), we are led to wonder whether it does not imply that in the eyes of orthodox Yahwists she was no more than a prostitute. Prostitutes were understood to have lost the capacity for shame (Jer. 3:3). We may conclude that the prostitute broke with the conventions of women in a society dominated by men, but at the price of the contempt of those who shaped opinion (for expressions of this contempt, see Isa. 22:16 and Jer. 4:30). "To become a prostitute" was a traditional curse (Amos 7:17).[17] I shall return to this matter below when I discuss the prophets' metaphorical application of the term "prostitute" to the whole nation when accusing it of breaking the covenant with Yahweh.

Women in the Cult

I turn now to cultic matters. Only males could function as priests in the conducting of the sacrificial worship of Yahweh; the priesthood was originally drawn from the male descendants of Aaron, in the tribe of Levi, but later the priesthood in Jerusalem was confined to males descended from the priest Zadok. Any women who functioned as leaders in religious ritual were associated with fertility worship (compare 2 Kings 23:7; 2 Chron. 15:16) or with other heterodox practices (Ezek. 13:17-23). We may suspect the existence in the villages of religious customs led by women. What, for example, were the "teraphim"? They were evidently household gods, either miniature (Gen. 31:19, 34-35) or life-size (1 Sam. 19:13, 16); they seem to have been associated with practices of divination. Several narratives associate teraphim with women: Rachel (in Genesis 31, as we have just seen); the mother of the Ephraimite Micah (Judg. 17:1-6); Michal, the wife of David (1 Sam. 19:13, 16). Were the teraphim then particularly the province of women? Such images were still in existence in Hosea's day, in the eighth century B.C. (Hos. 3:4-5), but we know nothing about their function. Then there is the narrative of Saul's dealings with a woman in the village of Endor who was a medium, believed to be able to consult the dead (1 Samuel 28). Such practices were doubtless widespread.

TEXTS IN THE OLD TESTAMENT RELEVANT TO THE STATUS OF MALES AND FEMALES

We now turn to texts in the Old Testament that are relevant to this discussion. There are dozens of these texts, some of them crucial—the narratives of creation and of the "fall" of humankind in Genesis 1–3—but these chapters, along with Jer. 31:22 and the Song of Songs, I reserve for special treatment below.

Let us begin with some typical legal texts, and then turn to some passages in the historical narratives and in the prophets. Some of the texts assume that males and females are in parity, and some assume that males are in a privileged position in comparison with females. Indeed, one may note in passing that the contrast between parity in the sexes and the privilege of the male extends in the sacrificial laws to the animal world as well. The animal for an "offering of well-being" may be either male or female (Lev. 3:1), but the animal for a burnt offering must be a male (Lev. 1:3). The old Covenant Code specifies that the Passover lamb to be slain must be "a year-old male, without blemish" (Exod. 12:5).

Legal Texts

As we ponder the texts that set forth the relationship between men and women in ancient Israel, those that loom largest in our minds are the legal texts, so it is to these that we first turn. We have already discussed the maintenance of landholding in the male line. This practice lies behind many of the laws relating to the status of male and female. Normally, only sons were heirs; indeed, according to Deut. 21:17, the firstborn son received a double share of the inheritance. Though the institution of levirate marriage (Deut. 25:5-10) may not have been systematically practiced, the provision for it at least reminds us of the pressure to produce a son for inheritance. In this law, if a man died without a son, his younger brother was to marry the widow to produce a son for the dead older brother. This was the custom presupposed in the narrative of Tamar and Judah's sons (Genesis 38) and in the problem of the disposition of the property of Elimelech, Naomi's husband (Ruth 4:1-12). In another notable case, Zelophehad had five daughters but no sons, and they came to Moses to ask for inheritance rights; he granted these with the proviso that the daughters must marry within their father's tribe (Num. 26:33; 27:1-11; 36:1-12); again the effort was to keep land within the kinship-based group.

For similar reasons, as we saw in Chapter 8, genealogies normally list males only: among other purposes, a genealogy would legitimate one's right of inheritance and one's standing in the community. Further, because it was men who held property and had public status, widows and orphans were vulnerable—they not only had no secure economic support but they had no male head of family to defend them in legal matters. Indeed, the Hebrew word translated "orphan" (*yātôm*) strictly speaking means "fatherless" (compare Lam. 5:3). There is no instance of the use of the word in the Old Testament where it is clear that both parents are dead.[18]

The laws regarding marriage and divorce do not cover every situation but surely offer a picture of disparity between the sexes. A husband had the right to divorce his wife, but a wife seems not to have had the right to divorce her husband (Deut. 24:1-4). One wonders: What happened to the bride-price when a husband divorced his wife? The law allowed a father to sell his daughter into concubinage (Exod. 21:7: the word translated "slave" in this verse means "concubine"). But just at the point when we are appalled by this cruel detail, we read on and discover that the same law allowed instances in which the concubine was allowed to leave an unjust relationship with her master (Exod. 21:8-11).[19]

There are laws in which a female is explicitly less valued than a male. One of the most clear-cut instances is the set of laws for the redemption of a person who had been vowed to God's service (Lev. 27:1-9). In these laws, the money value is given, and a female is valued at half to two-thirds of the value of a male, depending on age. One may view this valuation as simply economic rather than pejorative to women; it is evidently based on the comparative amounts of physical work females and males could be expected to do at given ages. Mature women have less strength than mature men, and one must reckon that females between fifteen and forty-five years of age normally devote periods of time to childbearing.[20]

What is one to do with Lev. 12:1-5, where a law states that a woman is rendered unclean twice as long after the birth of a girl as after the birth of a boy? This law implies a devaluation of females that has no economic justification. It is doubtless based on taboos regarding the potential of females for what was understood to be ritual impurity during menstruation and childbirth (compare Lev. 15:19-30). In these taboos, we may glimpse a basis far removed from rationality for the Israelite devaluation of women.

It is often held that the Old Testament regards women as property; is this a valid conclusion? Let us examine three passages from the legal material that could be so taken. One that comes easily to mind is the last of the Ten Commandments: "You shall not covet your neighbor's house; you shall not covet your neighbor's wife, or male or female slave, or ox, or donkey, or anything that belongs to your neighbor" (Exod. 20:17). At first reading, we are offended to find "wife" after "house" and before slaves and animals. But we may be reading the verse in an oversimplified fashion. Some scholars have suggested that the original form of the commandment was simply, "You shall not covet your neighbor's house," with the implication "you shall not covet (and conspire to take over) anyone or anything in your neighbor's household," and that the rest of the verse is a later addition that specifies what the law covers: "your neighbor's wife, or slaves, or domestic animals, or anything else in the household."[21] The first item in the expansion is the neighbor's wife, followed by persons of lesser importance, followed by animals. But neither the assumption that the neighbor is male nor the listing of "wife" alongside servants and animals is to our taste, and we are left only with the modest comfort that the neighbor's "wife" comes first.

Our suspicion grows when we read a description of curses in Deuteronomy 28 that was evidently added after the fall of Jerusalem to reflect the events at the beginning of the exile. It is said that the hearer will lose his eyesight and be abused and robbed, with no one to help (v. 29); then it is said, "You shall become engaged to a woman, but another man shall lie with her. You shall build a house, but not live in it. You shall plant a vineyard, but not enjoy its fruit" (v. 30). (It should be noted that the association of these may go back to Deut. 20:5-7: the three activities that exempt an Israelite man from participating in holy war are to have built a house but not dedicated it, or planted a vineyard and not eaten its fruit, or become engaged to a women and not married her.)[22] The next verse predicts that the hearer will see his ox butchered but will not eat of it, and his donkey and his sheep stolen (v. 31). Then, in v. 32, "Your sons and daughters shall be given to another people, while you look on; you will strain your eyes looking for them all day but be powerless to do anything" (v. 32). This sequence lists helter-skelter the items in a man's life of which he will be deprived—wife, house, vineyard, animals, children. The list does begin with his wife, but, as with Exod. 20:17, it is a list centered specifically on the satisfactions of a male head of household.

Beyond these passages, there is ample evidence that women were indeed treated as a kind of property. In the Covenant Code, the law that provides for restitution to a father when his daughter is seduced by someone directly follows the law providing restitution to the owner of an animal that is injured or dies when a neighbor borrows it (Exod. 22:16-17). We must conclude that a woman was indeed treated as a kind of property of her father or husband, and only occasionally were there limits to the husband's authority over his wife.[23]

Narrative Texts

When we turn to the historical narratives in the Old Testament that reflect the relation of power between men and women, we note the forthrightness of some of the women who are portrayed in the narratives of Genesis 12–50: the scheming of Rebekah to make sure Jacob received his father's blessing instead of Esau (Genesis 27), Rachel's stealing her father's household gods (Genesis 31), Tamar's bold act to ensure offspring for herself (Genesis 38). We cannot help but wonder how these stories reflected (and shaped) how men perceived women (and how women perceived themselves) during the centuries when the stories were being handed down in oral tradition. We ponder other strong female characters in the narratives of the beginning of Israel's story: the midwives in the birth story of Moses, who offered a brazen response to Pharaoh (Exod. 1:15-20), and Moses' sister Miriam, who was remembered as a prophet (Exod. 15:20-21). We have already mentioned Rahab, the prostitute (Joshua 2). And there was Deborah, a prophet and judge (Judges 4), whose name is attached to a memorable piece of war poetry (Judges 5), a song celebrating the heroism of Jael, the woman who killed the Canaanite general Sisera. We note that it was a woman (whose name was subsequently forgotten) who dropped a millstone from the top of a tower onto the head of the would-be king Abimelech and crushed his skull (Judg. 9:50-57).

One could continue the roll call of notable Israelite women: Abigail and Bathsheba, who became wives of David (for Abigail, see 1 Samuel 25; for Bathsheba, see 2 Samuel 11–12 and 1 Kings 1–2); Athaliah, a devotee of Baal who ruled temporarily over Judah (2 Kings 11); Huldah the prophet, whom Josiah's officials consulted on the validity of the Deuteronomic scroll discovered in the temple (2 Kings 22:14-20).

But the historical narratives also portray a devaluation of women. Returning to the narrative of Abimelech, whose skull was crushed by a woman, we must also note that after he was wounded, he begged his armor-bearer to kill him so that people would not be able to say, "A woman killed him" (Judg. 9:50-54). We ponder Samson's fate. After he was blinded, "he ground at the mill in the prison" at Gaza (Judg. 16:21). Grinding grain was onerous women's work (compare Isa. 47:2)—although her millstone was a handy weapon for the woman who killed Abimelech—and to be put to grinding grain was a humiliating punishment for a proud man remembered for his physical exploits.

Staying within the book of Judges, one comes across other instances of the mistreatment of women. Jephthah sacrificed his own daughter in fulfillment of a vow (Judg. 11:29-40). A Levite traveling through the territory of Benjamin, to forestall his own rape by the men of Gibeah, offered them his concubine, who died after being gang-raped through the night. The Levite thereupon dismembered her body, sending one part to each of the tribes of Israel, to summon them to avenge this atrocity (Judg. 19:22-30). One still recoils in horror from these accounts.[24]

Perhaps the narrative in 1 Samuel 1 of Hannah, the mother of Samuel, is emblematic of the status of Israelite women. Hannah was one of two wives of Elkanah, and though she was his favorite (v. 5), her co-wife, who had children, constantly taunted her because of her barrenness. She went to the sanctuary at Shiloh to pray—not simply for a child but for a son (v. 11). As we know, her prayer was granted and Samuel was born. The narrative is a vivid reminder of an Israelite woman's self-image: her social value lay in her bearing sons.

Most of the Old Testament narratives then only reinforce our general conclusion: though women played a crucial role in Israel, it was in almost every instance a subservient one. Only occasionally did they rise to independent notice.

Prophetic Texts

This picture is not greatly modified by texts in the prophets, to which we now turn. I begin with the portrayal of women as victims of social injustice. As we have seen, the law attempted to inculcate a concern for widows and orphans, and the prophets condemned the community's neglect of them (Isa. 1:17, 23; 10:2; Ezek. 22:7, compare Jer. 7:6; Zech. 7:10). In Amos 2:7b, we hear God condemn "Father and son sleeping with the same girl and thus profaning my holy name" (NJB). The word "same" is not in the Hebrew text, and the judgment here is evidently not so much of incest as of taking sexual advantage of a defenseless girl.[25] One finds an occasional mention of a war atrocity committed on women: Amos 1:13 mentions the mutilation of the pregnant women of Gilead by the Ammonites. But these are only scattered references.

When the prophets depict Yahweh's judgment on Israel by the horror of defeat in war, women are sometimes mentioned as suffering alongside men. Jer. 6:11b reads, "Pour it out on the children in the street, and on the gatherings of young men as well; both husband and wife shall be taken, the old folk and the very aged." But only rarely is the focus on the suffering that women (and children) undergo in the defeat of war apart from the corresponding mention of the sufferings of men: "The women of my people you drive out from their pleasant houses; from their young children you take away my glory forever" (Mic. 2:9).

Isa. 32:9-14 is a warning directed to the complacent women of Judah; the passage is difficult to date but perhaps stems from the time of the fall of Jerusalem in 587 B.C.[26]

There are passages that depict the specific sins of women. Amos 4:1-3 indicts the women of Samaria, contemptuously called "cows of Bashan," for their oppression of the poor; the passage embodied in Isa. 3:16-17, 24-26; 4:1 similarly indicts the women of Jerusalem ("daughters of Zion") for their flirtatious ways. But beyond such indictments is the rare text of Hos. 4:13b-14, a passage declaring that the wrongs committed by women may have been instigated by men.

Readers of the book of Isaiah in the RSV and the NRSV will find a verse suggesting that the prophet is contemptuous of women; the NRSV of Isa. 3:12a reads, "My people—children are their oppressors, and women rule over them." It needs to be said, however, that the word translated "children" is of uncertain meaning, and the word "women" (*nāšîm*) is perhaps a misreading of *nōšîm* "extortioners," as the ancient Greek translation (the Septuagint, see Chapter 1) has it. The NJB translates, "O my people, their oppressors pillage them and extortioners rule over them!" (and the REB has a similar rendering),[27] so that this verse is not a dependable indication of Isaiah's perception of gender roles.

I now pay particular attention to three conventional modes of reference to women in prophetic texts from the pre-exilic and early exilic period: (1) the curse of warriors turned to women, (2) the use of the metaphor of harlotry for Israel's infidelity to Yahweh, and (3) the personification "daughter Zion."

Curses were a stock-in-trade of speech in Old Testament times; we have already noted that "become a prostitute" was a traditional curse. Curses were leveled against one's personal enemies and, in time of war, against national enemies: for an impressive list, read Ps. 109:6-14—typical is v. 9 there, "May his children be orphans, and his wife a widow." These traditional curses appear frequently in the pronouncements of the prophets.[28] Among these curses, one seems particularly offensive to us: "Your warriors shall become women." This curse is leveled against the Assyrians in Nah. 3:13 and against the Babylonians in Jer. 50:37 and 51:30.

Yet this curse also appears, surprisingly, in a word against the defenders of Jerusalem, in Jer. 30:6: "Ask now, and see, can a man bear a child? Why then do I see every man with his hands on his loins like a woman in labor?" Here is another instance of a theme discussed in Chapter 6—that Yahweh the divine warrior is perceived to have turned against his covenant people.

This conventional curse reminds us that the Old Testament reflects a world in which the men who fought the battles took pride in their prowess and were cut to the quick by any challenge to their maleness; the same attitude is reflected in the details of the stories of Abimelech and Samson, which we have already examined.

If the curse of warriors turned to women reflects the conventional view of the disparity of power between women and men, the repeated use by the prophets of the metaphor of Israel as harlot reflects the dishonor in which prostitutes were held. The theme of Israel's infidelity to Yahweh was one of the major themes of the pre-exilic prophets, as we saw in Chapter 9: Israel forsook Yahweh to worship the fertility god Baal instead.

Hosea, in the eighth century, perceived Yahweh to be calling him to dramatize the religious situation of Israel by marrying a prostitute: "Go, take for yourself a wife of whoredom and have children of whoredom, for the land commits great whoredom by forsaking the Lord" (Hos. 1:2). Thus, Hosea married the prostitute Gomer, by whom he had three children (Hos. 1:3-9). At some point, she appears to have deserted Hosea for a lover; eventually, Hosea bought her back (this is the most plausible interpretation of Hosea 3). Behind Hosea's symbolic action were four interrelated factors: (1) the perception that there is an analogy between Yahweh's covenant with Israel and the covenant between husband and wife; (2) the perception that, in the divine covenant, Yahweh takes the initiative with Israel and holds power over Israel, just as in the disparity of power between husband and wife in Israel the husband took the initiative with his wife; (3) the correlation between the human sexual relation and the relation between fertility deities that was assumed by their devotees to be sexual; and (4) the sexual relations between the worshiper and the cult prostitute that was acted out in the fertility cult. Hosea reasoned: As my wife has broken her marital obligation to me and gone off after a lover, so Israel has broken fidelity with

Israel and has gone off after Baal. In this way, Hosea used the vocabulary of fertility worship against the validity of that worship.

Jeremiah continued the same metaphor: much of Jeremiah 2–3 offers such imagery, and it occurs elsewhere in the book as well. Thus, in Jer. 2:2, Yahweh speaks of Israel's pristine faithfulness: "I remember the devotion of your youth, your love as a bride, how you followed me in the wilderness, in a land not sown"—"follow" translates a verb in Hebrew that suggests worship. But then Yahweh continues in v. 5, "What wrong did your ancestors find in me that they went far from me, and went after worthless things, and became worthless themselves?" "Worthless things" is Jeremiah's contemptuous reference to Baal. "You said, 'It is hopeless, for I have loved strangers, and after them I will go'" (v. 25). The result, according to Jeremiah, is that the nation has become one vast whorehouse (Jer. 5:7-8).

Ezekiel used the metaphor, not with the tender emotion we find in Jeremiah, but crudely, when he set forth allegories of Israel and Judah (Ezekiel 16; 23). In his words, Jerusalem was worse than a prostitute, who would be paid for her services; instead, she herself paid her lovers (Ezek. 16:30-34).

Even though we may accept the reality of prostitution in Israel (see above), we may take offense at the use of the term "prostitute" as a metaphor. We often perceive prostitutes to be exploited and abused, trapped in a situation not of their own making, and so we judge the prophets to be using language that hits women when they are down. This kind of discourse, we think, is demeaning to women and to the common humanity of women and men. But we must bear in mind that Israelite law held marriage bonds inviolate, and a woman who was unfaithful in marriage was held responsible for her actions. Above all, from our discussion of the wrath of God in Chapter 4, we must bear in mind that the metaphor of sexual relations in marriage and of the breaking of marriage bonds is a powerful one to portray the seriousness of Israel's infidelity to Yahweh.

"Daughter of Zion," another expression in the prophets, needs particular discussion; it occurs particularly in Isaiah and Jeremiah (see, for example, Isa. 1:8 and Jer. 4:31). One needs to understand that, in Hebrew, the names of cities like "Jerusalem" are construed as feminine in gender, and that "Zion" was the name of the elevation in Jerusalem on which the temple stood; it is natural then that a personification of the temple area was feminine. The phrase "daughter Zion" is an expression of endearment and as such suggests helplessness and vulnerability; occasionally, that impression is reinforced by the expansion "virgin daughter Zion" (Isa. 37:22).

If the term "daughter Zion" offers a positive feminine image, by turns tender and strong, we may take note of other prophetic passages that likewise offer positive images of women and empathize with the distinctive experiences of women. This is particularly the case in Jeremiah, in Isaiah 40–66, and in prophetic material from still later times.

My own understanding of Jer. 4:30-31 is that Yahweh speaks in v. 30, addressing Jerusalem as a prostitute, and that Jeremiah speaks in v. 31, preferring instead to understand Jerusalem as an innocent young woman gasping as she bears her first child; in this way, Jeremiah appears to counter Yahweh's image.[29] It is Jeremiah who portrays Rachel weeping for her lost children (Jer. 31:15), and who offers a picture of the people's return from exile, among them the handicapped—not only the blind and the lame, but pregnant women and those in labor (31:8). Above all, it is Jeremiah who foresees a reversal of the curse of the soldiers of Judah turned to women (we recall the expression in 30:6): God will recreate the very pattern of sexual relations between female and male, so that the female will take the initiative and embrace the male (this is the evident meaning of 31:22). This startling verse needs special attention; I shall return to it below when I discuss Genesis 1–3 and the Song of Songs.

Within Isaiah 40–66, chapters that stem from the exilic period, there is an abundance of positive female imagery. There are passages of good news in which women are mentioned alongside men: for example, "Thus says the Lord God: 'I will soon lift up my hand to the nations, and raise my signal to the peoples; and they shall bring your sons in their bosom, and your daughters shall be carried on your shoulders. Kings shall be your foster fathers, and their queens your nursing mothers" (Isa. 49:22-23a; similar are 43:6; 60:4).

As we have just noted, "Jerusalem" and "Zion" are construed as feminine, and it is noteworthy that, in these same chapters (Isaiah 40–66), Jerusalem and Zion are repeatedly addressed, beginning in 40:9: "Get you up to a high mountain, O Zion, herald of good tidings; lift up your voice with strength, O Jerusalem, herald of good tidings, lift it up, do not fear; say to the cities of Judah, 'Here is your God!'" In these passages, the rhetoric is positive, tender, and reassuring. Isa. 51:17—52:2 is a particularly striking example; 52:1-2 reads, "Awake, awake, put on your strength, O Zion! Put on your beautiful garments, O Jerusalem, the holy city; for the uncircumcised and the unclean shall enter you no more. Shake yourself from the dust, rise up, O captive Jerusalem; loose the bonds from your neck, O captive daughter Zion!" As we examine these passages in which Jerusalem is addressed, it is important to note that Hebrew distinguishes gender in the second-person forms of verbs and pronouns, so that the feminine singular forms in the Hebrew text of these passages strike the ear with surprise (it is, unfortunately, a distinction impossible to make in English).

There are apocalyptic passages that mention women alongside men, portraying them either as destined for suffering and destruction (Zech. 14:2) or for new life. A particular prediction in the book of Joel (Joel 2:28-29) is familiar to us because it figured in Peter's sermon at Pentecost (Acts 2:17-21): in the time to come, God's spirit will be poured out on all: "your sons and your daughters shall prophesy," and "even on the male and female slaves, in those days, I will pour out my spirit."

Thus, prophetic texts, like narrative texts, run the gamut from those accepting the subordination of women to those assuming the equality of women. The question then arises in our minds: Why did the prophets not level any criticism against the institutional subordination of women in Israelite society? I shall return to this question below.

OLD TESTAMENT TEXTS AS THE WORK OF URBAN MEN

Let us now back away from these texts themselves to ponder for a moment the implications of the obvious: by and large, the Old Testament was the product of urban men. It was urban men who were literate, who were capable of compiling literary works; priests, scribes, teachers, and disciples of the prophets brought together the material that became the Old Testament. Almost all of them were men, and most of the work of compilation of all the scattered traditions was done either in Jerusalem or, while in exile, in the company of other exiles from Jerusalem. Inevitably, then, these texts reflect the norms and values of Jerusalemite men. Even when such works contain material attributed to women—one thinks of the Song of Deborah in Judges 5 and the Song of Hannah in 1 Samuel 2—those of us who read the Bible with an eye alert to these matters may say, yes, but these women's songs are works that were acceptable to male editors. Such considerations must be raised before we may frame an adequate answer to how we might hear God in these texts.

Are there any books or portions of the Old Testament that with fair certainty can be attributed to women? The author Harold Bloom has recently raised the question of whether the author of the so-called Yahwistic Source in the early books of the Old Testament (see Chapters 1 and 5) was not a woman,[30] but he offers this notion as a discussion point rather than as a seriously urged proposal, and scholars think it unlikely. However, a German scholar has recently argued that the first two verses of Psalm 131 were originally deposited in the Jerusalem temple by a woman as a thank-offering, and that the text was taken up and extended by the last verse before its incorporation into the collection of Psalms. This suggestion is to me convincing.[31]

More substantially, the question has been raised whether the Book of Ruth was not written by a woman, or at least whether it does not come out of circles of women's storytelling.[32] Whatever its origin, we can at least draw two conclusions: (1) the tale reflects a world in which village women have little power and are marginal to men, and (2) the tale brings to our hearing the voices of such women themselves, whether or not the narrator of the tale was female.

In the same way, the possibility has been raised that the story of Queen Vashti in the first chapter of Esther might originally have been an apocryphal harem story,[33] but, in the book of Esther, one hears her words through a male narrator, and the story reflects the world of an Oriental court in which the women of the harem are again foils within the world of men. Of a quite different sort is the voice of women one hears in the Song of Songs, a work so distinctive as to need a careful examination after we deal with Genesis 1–3. We turn, then, to discuss these two bodies of material, sandwiching between them a consideration of Jer. 31:22.

THREE CRUCIAL TEXTS: GENESIS 1–3; JEREMIAH 31:22; THE SONG OF SONGS

Genesis 1–3

The narrative of the first three chapters of the Bible, or rather the traditional Christian interpretation of them, has deeply shaped our understanding of male and female. It is not necessary here to explore the matter in depth; 1 Tim. 2:11-14 sets the tone: "Let a woman learn in silence with full submission. I permit no woman to teach or to have authority over a man; she is to keep silent. For Adam was formed first, then Eve; and Adam was not deceived, but the woman was deceived and became a transgressor." This passage thus presses more specifically what is implied in 1 Cor. 11:8-9, "Indeed, man was not made from woman, but woman from man. Neither was man created for the sake of woman, but woman for the sake of man." Inasmuch as recent scholarship has brought forth fresh insights about the original intention of Genesis 1–3, we need to expose ourselves to these insights rather than beginning with the assumptions of the author of 1 Timothy or with Paul's assumptions, or with Augustine's or Milton's.

It is clear that these chapters offer two separate creation narratives: Gen. 1:1—2:4a is a narrative of creation according to the Priestly Source, and Gen. 2:4b—3:24 offers a narrative of creation according to the Yahwistic

Source (these building blocks of narrative are described in Chapters 1 and 5). The two narratives offer contrasting sequences of events: in the Priestly Source, the animals were created first (Gen. 1:20-25) and then human beings, both male and female (Gen. 1:26-27); in the Yahwistic Source, the male human being was created first (Gen. 2:7), followed by the animals (Gen. 2:19-20), and finally the female human being (Gen. 2:21-22).

In the narrative of the Priestly Source not only are the male and female created side by side, but the structure of Gen. 1:27 (whether that verse is taken as prose, as the NRSV does, or as poetry, as the NJB and the REB do) suggests the conclusion that since "male and female" parallel "image of God," the image of God that is reflected in human beings is their joint maleness-and-femaleness.[34] This conclusion is reinforced by the wording of a later portion of the Priestly Source, Gen. 5:1-2. (I shall return to this matter of God's image at the end of this chapter.) At the very least, we may conclude that this narrative implies the simultaneous creation of both female and male and that it implies no subordination of the female to the male.

What may be said about the narrative in the Yahwistic Source? In some respects, it is a narrative parallel to that in the Priestly Source, but in other respects it contrasts with the Priestly narrative. The Yahwistic narrative says that the female is created as a partner to the male, being built from the rib of the male. But what we are not likely to notice is the wonder of having a narrative devoted to the specific creation of the female at all: one authority notes that "Gen 2 is unique among the creation myths of the whole of the Ancient Near East in its appreciation of the meaning of woman, i.e., that human existence is a partnership of man and woman."[35] As we have seen, this narrative states that the male was created first and the woman last, but that does not give us the warrant to assume that the narrative implies that the male takes priority over the female: to the contrary, just as in the Priestly narrative the creation of human beings is God's last and culminating act of creation, so here one might argue from the shape of the narrative that the female is God's final and culminating act of creation. God withdraws, the male offers a jubilant poem about the female (v. 23), and the last two verses of the chapter suggest that the way is open to sexual union.[36]

As for Genesis 3, we are accustomed to reading this chapter as an account of "original sin," following Paul's understanding in Rom. 5:14 and 1 Cor. 15:22, but we must notice that the word "sin" does not appear in Genesis 3—it first appears in Gen. 4:7 in God's word to Cain after Cain displayed anger at God's preference for Abel's offering. Genesis 3 assuredly describes the disobedience of the man and the woman, a disobedience in which they jointly participate. One the other hand, one might conclude that the narrator wishes in his way to portray the woman's exploration of theology and ethics, and that in her testing of limits it is she who is the curious one, the seeker of knowledge, far more than her passive husband is: in a way, it is she who establishes what it is to be human.[37] If the woman blames the snake for the outcome of events (3:13), the man blames the woman whom God had given him (3:12). What indeed is the man saying here—that it is the woman's fault, or that it is God's fault? Neither the woman nor the man is taking responsibility! The close of the chapter indicates that it is an etiological narrative (see Chapter 5), an attempt to offer an explanation for why snakes crawl on the ground, why women experience pain in childbirth, and why men must sweat to bring forth food from the earth. All these come, it is said, because of the disobedience of the first woman and the first man. Ultimately, this chapter holds a mirror up to human beings, both male and female, by displaying the human capacity for avoiding responsibility.

We must now look specifically at Gen. 3:16, the verse traditionally taken as a justification for the domination of females by males. The scholar Carol Meyers, in a careful analysis, translates the verse as follows: "I will greatly increase your toil and your pregnancies; (Along) with travail shall you beget[38] children. For to your man is your desire, And he shall predominate over you."[39] Meyers suggests that this pronouncement to the woman, like the corresponding pronouncement to the man in vv. 17-19, comes out of the Israelite village culture of the pre-monarchical period, a period, as we have seen, in which a high birthrate was a necessity; in this situation, the male's will in sexuality is to be imposed on the will of the female, but this specific imposition by no means signifies a general institutional domination by males over females.[40]

Much more might be said about the narratives of the first three chapters of Genesis, but one may conclude that they portray three realities that are in tension with each other: (1) the primal intention of equality between males and females, and at the same time contrasting gender roles that point in contrary directions toward (2) the possibility that females might take the lead with males and (3) the reality that the necessities of childbirth and the care of small children create a functional subordination of females. In these respects, the first three chapters of Genesis do not portray a different reality than do the legal, narrative, and prophetic texts that we have already surveyed.

Jeremiah 31:22

Very different indeed is Jer. 31:22. I have already mentioned this verse in the course of my discussion of various passages in Jeremiah that offer strong and positive images of women. The prophet, we recall, having had in mind the old curse of warriors turned to women, had applied the curse to the soldiers of

Judah (Jer. 30:6) evidently in the midst of a very specific emergency, namely the siege of Jerusalem. At a later point, he foresaw a startling reversal of this curse, a reversal accomplished by a fresh act of creation on God's part. In this reversal, the female will take the initiative and embrace the male in sexual relations.[41] Jeremiah, faced with the fall of Jerusalem, was convinced that nothing is too hard for God (compare our discussion of this matter in Chapter 7). Yahweh will have created a "new thing": God will be able to change the pattern of creation in such a way that the warriors turned to women will be a blessing rather than a curse.

One must conclude that Jeremiah took it for granted that the reality of his world, in which sexual initiative is taken by the male with the female, was part of God's original act of creation. We may further conclude that at least the pre-exilic prophets lived in a culture in which the parity of male and female implied in Gen. 1:26-27 was not assumed, a world in which the priority of male over female (whether derived from Genesis 2 or not) was considered part of the created order.

Now we may have a clue to answer the question already raised: why the pre-exilic prophets, who stood out so sturdily against the prevailing assumptions of their culture in matters of social justice, seem never to have questioned a society in which there was male domination. If these prophets lived in a culture in which the priority of male over female was understood to be part of the created order, then their acceptance of the priority of male over female is not surprising. After all, they lived under a set of laws that reinforced the priority of male over female, laws that both they and their fellow-citizens understood to be a reflection of the covenant. Given the fact that the prophetic critique of society was based on Israel's perceived disobedience of Yahweh's will in covenant—and thus, certainly, in creation—the prophets' acceptance of the priority of male over female is not surprising.

What is surprising is the ability of Jeremiah, in this curious verse, to envision what had not theretofore been envisioned.

The Song of Songs

This body of material challenges the idea that the domination of male over female is part of the order of creation. It would not be useful here to set forth an account of the origin of this book or of the range of interpretations it has occasioned.[42] In general, scholars today reject the attribution of the book to Solomon; the notice in 1:1 is probably a late title, in which case the references in 3:7-11 to Solomon are fictional: if a wedding procession is intended in that passage, then the bridegroom is "king" for the day. Most scholars would agree that the book contains a collection of love poems, some or all of which may have had their origin in wedding celebrations. These love poems are unified by the identity of the speakers: one hears both a female speaker and a male one, each of them wooing the other; occasionally, one hears the "daughters of Jerusalem," who serve as a kind of chorus. (One can almost always identify which of the lovers is speaking because of the contrast in Hebrew, as I have already noted, between masculine and feminine pronouns and verbs in the second person as well as in the third person.)

The book offers two striking features. The first is that not only does God not speak in the book, God is not even referred to. How then did the book come to be included in the Old Testament? The answer is that, late in the period of compilation of the Old Testament, the book was perceived to be a metaphorical expression of God's love for Israel. We recall the prophets' use of the metaphor of the relation of husband and wife as a depiction of Yahweh's covenant with Israel (Chapter 9); this metaphor, so prominent in Hosea, Jeremiah, and Ezekiel, became the key for hearing the Song of Songs. God loves Israel, and Israel is to love God, with the passion that the Song of Songs sets forth. That understanding carried over into the Christian church—Christians have traditionally read the book as a metaphor of Christ's love for the Church. I shall return to this interpretation in a moment.

The second striking feature of the book may be related to the first: it offers the only opportunity we have in the Old Testament to hear women's voices unmediated by men. Here, in contrast to the books of Ruth and Esther, there is no mediating narrator who might have been male. How might this circumstance have come about? If the book had a secular origin in the context of village life, then the female voices within it might not have been subject to male control; and when the book was brought into the Old Testament as a metaphor for God's love of Israel, then its words of mutual devotion might not have been perceived to need male editing.

In any event, both lovers in the book speak purely out of love, indeed out of sexual passion, without any regard for the world of obligations, laws, or the institutions of society; only in 3:11 is there even a hint of marriage. Not only is the voice of the female lover unrestrained by the world of men; we hear her voice more often than we do the male lover: a rough tally totals 62 verses spoken by the woman and 46 by the man. The speeches of both the woman and the man offer descriptions of the physical beauty of the other, invitations to love, and the like; the female thus takes the initiative in these invitations more often than the male does. She begins the book, and she ends it.

Phyllis Trible suggests[43] that the Song of Songs picks up where Genesis 2 ends, offering a scenario contrasting with that set forth in Genesis 3. At the end of Genesis 2, we recall, God has created the female as the final act of creation and then withdraws as the way is open for sexual union between the female and the male; then, in the narrative of Genesis 3, the female takes the initiative in a fashion that leads to her being dominated sexually by the male (3:16).

In the Song of Songs, however, the female takes the initiative in a fashion that expresses the mutuality of sexual relations without any mention of the constraints of either childbirth or agricultural toil. If Genesis 2 takes place in the Garden of Eden, the Song of Songs refers repeatedly to the gardens that belong to the lovers (*e.g.,* 4:16; 6:2); indeed, the male affirms that the female is his garden (4:12; 5:1). If the scenario of Genesis 3 involves touching and tasting the fruit (v. 2), the whole Song of Songs is filled with sensory vocabulary—one notices 4:10, 11, 16 within a single chapter. If in Genesis 3 the serpent bruises the heel of male and female (v. 15), in the Song of Songs animals and birds figure in the descriptions of the partners as similes and metaphors for human joy (2:8-15; 4:1-5; 6:4-10). If in Genesis 3 childbirth is marked with pain (v. 16), in the Song of Songs references to the mother who bore the beloved underline the beauty of motherhood (6:9) and of birth (8:5)—strikingly, nowhere is there any reference to the father of the beloved. Most significantly, in the Song of Songs not only does the female twice say, "I am my beloved's and my beloved is mine" (2:16; 6:3), she expands once on that expression and says, "I am my beloved's and his desire is for me" (7:10), where the word "desire" (Hebrew *tĕšûqâ*) is the same word that appears in Gen. 3:16; that is to say, if in Genesis 3 the woman's desire for the man is made subject to his domination of her, then in the Song of Songs, by contrast, the man's desire is for the woman, and neither dominates the other.

What are we to make of this striking scenario, this alternative to Genesis 3? If the narrative in Genesis 3 was intended to be heard as a description of events in primeval times that have shaped reality ever since, then there is no hint in the Song of Songs that it is intended to be heard as a description of primeval times. On the other hand, there is no hint either that it is a description of the relation of female and male in an eschatological future, when the miseries of this life are overcome. Instead, it appears to depict what human beings can know now, though perhaps fleetingly, in present history.[44] So, are we to understand from this alternative scenario that we are to gaze with frustrated longing on an ideal world of male and female without worries, tears, or tragedy, a world far from any actuality? That female and male can know each other in parity during courtship, wedding, and honeymoon, only to have the male become dominant thereafter? That God intends male and female to maximize in this life the experiences of parity and to minimize the experiences of male domination?

Before we try to answer, we must remind ourselves once more of the interpretation of the book as God's love for Israel. If, on the one hand, the Song of
Songs originated as a collection of love poems, perhaps wedding poems,
poems exalting sexual love without any overt reference to God, and if, on the
other hand, the book functions in the Old Testament as a depiction of God's
love for Israel (or Christ's love for the Church), then are we not mishearing
God when we propose to hear in the Song of Songs God's intention of love
between female and male? My answer is a double one. First, I would maintain
that if the Song of Songs is the elaboration of the relationship between female
and male that God is understood to have intended at the end of Genesis 2,
then we are to hear it so. Second, I would maintain that the passion of human
love and the passion of divine love are not to be sundered: ultimately, the Old
Testament seems to say, they are one and the same. My answer, then, is that we
are not mishearing God when we hear God's intention for female and male in
the Song of Songs; it is simply that we must struggle to realize that intention
in the life we live.

THE OLD TESTAMENT TEXTS, SUMMARY

How may we summarize what we have seen in these Old Testament texts?
They appear to arrange themselves on a broad spectrum, from those at one
end that suggest a parity of female and male (Gen. 1:27; 2:24) or even a coun-
terbalancing initiative of the female with the male (Jer. 31:22; the Song of
Songs) to those at the other end that suggest the submission of the female to
the male (Gen. 3:16; most of the specific laws, narratives, and prophetic pronouncements).

How might we hear God in these Old Testament texts? For guidance, we
need to look at least briefly at analogous texts in the New Testament.

GUIDANCE FROM THE NEW TESTAMENT

Many people today are familiar with the resources in the New Testament on
the question of gender. If one turns to Paul's letters, one can find contrasting
perspectives. There are passages that appear to give women a subordinate position—the husband is the head of the wife (1 Cor. 11:3), women should keep
silent in church (1 Cor. 14:34-35)—and those passages regarding the subordination of women are reinforced in the (later) pastoral letters, for example, 1
Tim. 2:8-15. On the other hand, there is the proclamation of absolute equality
between the sexes in Gal. 3:28: "There is no longer Jew or Greek, there is no
longer slave or free, there is no longer male and female; for all of you are one

in Christ Jesus." Here, it is altogether possible Paul is citing a traditional baptismal formula (compare v. 27).[45]

When one turns to Jesus, one again finds contrasting texts. Let us deal first with the tradition of Jesus' recorded actions. He is remembered as having healed both men and women without favoritism: one can read in Mark 6 narratives both of his healing the Gerasene demoniac and of the raising of Jairus's daughter, and the healing of the woman with a hemorrhage along the way. He is remembered as having compassion on both tax collectors and prostitutes (Matt. 21:31-32)—the outcasts of both sexes. The Gospels retained a special memory of Mary Magdalene's devotion to Jesus: he had healed her, she followed him in his itinerant ministry in Galilee, and contributed financially to his movement (Luke 8:1-3); she followed him to Jerusalem, was present at the Crucifixion (Mark 15:40-41), and, after his death, visited his tomb to anoint his body (Mark 16:1). On the other hand, it could be maintained that crucial to the discussion is the fact that Jesus chose only men to be his disciples.

When we turn to Jesus' teaching, we note that Luke recorded two of Jesus' parables side by side, one about a (male) shepherd who sought and found a lost sheep and the other about a housewife who sought and found a lost coin (Luke 15:3-10). Is this an example of Jesus' notion of the parity of the sexes, or of Luke's editorial artistry, or both?

Jesus' recorded teaching about divorce is certainly germane to the topic, but the Gospels offer a whole array of versions, forcing us to sort out what appears to be the form that is earliest and likely to be closest to Jesus' own intention. Though it is generally accepted that Mark is the earliest Gospel to be written, scholars have concluded that the material in Mark 10:1-12 is already an adaptation of Jesus' original teaching. In vv. 2-9 of Mark 10, we have the narrative in which the Pharisees challenge Jesus: there he defends his teaching, "no divorce," on the basis of Gen. 1:27 and 2:24, passages that certainly suggest the parity of male and female.[46] Then, in vv. 10-12, we hear Jesus' clarification for the disciples, and there the parity is clear—husbands should not divorce wives, and wives should not divorce husbands. But scholars suggest that v. 12 (wives should not divorce husbands) is *Mark's own extension* of Jesus' teaching, reshaped for the larger Greco-Roman world, where such a thing was possible: in Jewish law, with rare exceptions, it was only husbands who took the initiative in divorce, and Jesus was undoubtedly speaking to the immediate Jewish situation. We note further that the wording that stands behind another recording of the teaching, Matt. 5:32 and Luke 16:18, speaks of divorce completely from the husband's point of view.[47] We have, then, a mixed record: Jesus appears not to have offered parity in the divorce saying itself but to have based his prohibition of divorce nevertheless on texts in Genesis that do suggest parity.

As to the tradition that Jesus chose only males to be his disciples, it is not appropriate to deal here with the matter in detail, but it begs for some kind of treatment. The tradition of "the twelve" was an early one—Paul mentions them in 1 Cor. 15:5, a letter written in the early 50s A.D., as part of the tradition about the resurrection he himself had received, and they are mentioned repeatedly in Mark, the earliest gospel. One wonders: Did the group that Jesus gathered around him in reality consist of both male disciples and women like Mary Magdalene? If the tradition is trustworthy that he sent out the twelve to preach and heal in his name (Mark 6:7), one could not imagine Mary Magdalene having requisite authority in that culture. The tradition remembers some of the twelve trying to gain authority for themselves (Mark 10:37), so the tendency was there from the beginning to exalt male at the expense of female leadership.[48]

One may conclude that the question of the New Testament outlook in the matter of male and female cannot be resolved simply by counting up texts on one side or the other. Four things are clear about the New Testament as a whole. (1) The status of women was severely restricted in the first century in both Jewish society and the wider Greco-Roman culture. (2) Both Jesus' teachings that have implications for women and his actions toward women gave women a status and a dignity that they had not otherwise known in their time and that persisted in the life of the Christian church in the decades after Jesus' earthly ministry. (3) There are traces in the New Testament of women in leadership roles in the earliest decades of the church: for example, in Rom. 16:7, Paul lists Junia as among the apostles (Junia is a woman's name). (4) Men soon assumed the leadership roles in the church, beginning with the twelve disciples, and later texts in the New Testament reflect the growing subordination of women (see again the teachings in 1 Timothy, not only 2:8-15 but chapters 3 and 5 of that book).[49]

If the New Testament does not speak with a single voice, then what guidance can we gain from it on the matter of female and male? Some people today would conclude that the affirmation "there is no longer male and female; for all of you are one in Christ Jesus" is a statement not about what the human situation may be now but about what it was in Genesis 1–2 and what it will be when creation is finally transformed.[50] Others would see it as the will of God for the present, both in the churches and in society at large. If Jesus broke with the conventions of his society in his treatment of women, then at least we may agree that the affirmation "there is no longer male and female" suggests that the perceptions and experiences of women must be taken as seriously as the perceptions and experiences of men in the mutual working out of gender roles. Thus, even though the texts of the New Testament pull in different directions on the matter of female and male, it is nevertheless difficult to avoid the conclusion that Jesus in some fashion assumed the equality of the sexes, an equality he took to be a given of creation, an equality that is reflected in Gal. 3:28 as well.

HEARING GOD IN PASSAGES ABOUT FEMALE AND MALE IN THE OLD TESTAMENT

If this conclusion regarding the New Testament is valid, then we are driven back to hear the parity of female and male in Genesis 1 and to ponder the possibility that the narrative in Genesis 2 may portray the advent of the female as the climax of creation. We are driven also, through the Song of Songs, to ponder what it might mean to live in a world in which there is gender parity, even a world in which the female might be more assertive than the male, might offer leadership more than the male.

Given this perspective, we shall have to conclude that much of the Old Testament offers material in which the will of God for parity of female and male was never glimpsed, let alone expressed. Having heard God's voice for the parity of female and male, we will read chapter after chapter both aware of what is not said and saddened by what is said. We will be saddened that we so rarely hear the voices of women, even the voices of women distorted by the perception of male narrators. We will be gladdened that occasionally men preserved narratives of the deeds of women, and we will rejoice to hear of those deeds; but we will also mourn the fact that the very names of many of the women in these narratives have been forgotten—one thinks again of such passages as Judg. 9:53; 11:34-40; 2 Sam. 14:1-20 and 20:16-22—and we will mourn, too, the almost complete lack of women's names in the genealogies and chronicles (we discussed this matter in Chapter 8). Ecclus. 44:9, a verse in the book of Eccesiasticus (Sirach), one of the extra books in Roman Catholic Bibles (see Chapter 1), is appropriate here. The author was far from being a believer in the parity of female and male, and the verse is part of his celebration of noteworthy men in the past, but by extension it may apply to the forgotten mothers in Israel: "But of others there is no memory; they have perished as though they had never existed; they have become as though they had never been born, they and their children after them."

We may hear God in many wonderful and surprising ways in the Old Testament, but in the crucial matter of relations between the sexes the Old Testament does not in general offer God's direct voice.

ISSUES OF TRANSLATION

Having raised the question of the extent to which we may hear God in texts that to a large degree are biased in favor of males, we must face questions of the way the Hebrew text is to be translated into English. We have said little about translation in this work, but the way Hebrew is translated into English is crucial here because of the masculine bias built into the Hebrew language. We need to consider two related matters: (1) the masculine bias in various modes of expression in Hebrew for human beings, and (2) the masculine bias in various modes of expression in Hebrew to refer to God.

Masculine Bias in Various Modes of Expression in Hebrew for Human Beings

When we consider Hebrew expressions for human beings, we must discuss two related usages. The first is the use of plurals of masculine nouns ("sons," "men," and "fathers") and masculine pronouns, not only to denote a plurality of males but also to denote a mixed group of males and females. The second is the use of the singular of a masculine noun (like "the man") to express a typical case that really implies a plurality of either males only or of a mixed group of males and females. Until recently, such modes of expression in Hebrew were often carried over into English without question, as we shall see.

Let us first consider masculine plurals. The masculine plural expression *běnê yiśrā'ēl* literally means "the sons of Israel"; in Gen. 46:5, it refers only to sons and is correctly so translated in the NRSV. But the identical Hebrew expression is used in the Old Testament again and again to refer to males and females together. In Exod. 1:7, for example, the matter is quite clear; here the KJV translates "the children of Israel," the RSV "the descendants of Israel," and the NRSV "the Israelites." Such a usage in biblical Hebrew suggests that females tended to become invisible behind males in both the text and in society at large. But a translation that is alert to this usage is surely obligated to find terms in English that are not gender-specific.

The problem is similar but perhaps more difficult to solve with the word *'ābôt*, literally "fathers." Sometimes it is appropriate to translate "ancestors." In Gen. 48:21, the RSV translates Jacob's word to Joseph, "Behold, I am about to die, but God will be with you, and will bring you again to the land of your fathers." But women lived in the land and belonged there too, so it is appropriate for the NRSV to translate the last phrase as "the land of your ancestors." One may make a similar judgment in Deut. 1:35, where the

NRSV translates, "Not one of these . . . shall see the good land that I swore to give to your ancestors." But what do we do with a variation of this phraseology in Deut. 7:8? The translation in the RSV renders the Hebrew literally, "The Lord loves you, and is keeping the oath which he swore to your fathers"; the NRSV translates the last phrase "to your ancestors." Did God swear the oath to Sarah, Rebekah, Rachel, and Leah as well as to Abraham, Isaac, and Jacob? Or did God not rather swear specifically to the male ancestors with reference to the whole people? Here are puzzles that reach to the heart of what a translation should be, so that we may hear God most directly.

I now turn to the other problematic Hebrew usage in reference to human beings, the use of the singular of a masculine noun to express a typical case implying a plurality either of males only or of a mixed group of males and females. I will illustrate the problem with Psalm 1. The RSV gives a translation close enough to the literal Hebrew to exemplify the issue. "Blessed is the man [Hebrew *hāʾîš*, the adult male] who walks not in the counsel of the wicked," and so on; there are third-person singular masculine references through v. 3. Verse 4 begins, "The wicked [Hebrew *hārĕšāʿîm*, masculine plural] are not so," and so on; there are masculine plural references to "the wicked" and the synonymous "the sinners" through v. 5, and to the opposite, "the righteous" [Hebrew *ṣaddîqîm*, masculine plural], as well. Verse 6 sums up the psalm: "For the Lord knows the way of the righteous [masculine plural], but the way of the wicked [masculine plural] will perish." The first three verses might well give the impression that one righteous male is being described, in contrast to vv. 4-6, which describe a plurality of wicked males. This is not so, however; the use of the masculine plural of "righteous" in vv. 5 and 6 makes it plain that "the man" in v. 1 is simply a stylistic variation of the masculine plural in vv. 5-6. But now comes the crucial question: Are females as well as males to be understood behind the masculine references? How can we formulate an answer?

Before attempting an answer, I must pause to discuss the philosophy of translation. Not every reader of this book may fully realize both how arbitrary every language system is and how inexactly two different language systems can be made to fit together. Let me speak first of the inexactness of the fit between two languages. Every translation is to some degree a compromise. We have already noticed that, in Hebrew, second-person references are gender-specific, and when the Hebrew text shifts from masculine to feminine references, there is no easy way to signal the shift in English. By the same token, English verbs are much more specific for modal nuances than Hebrew verbs are, leaving translators with many choices: Is an event described in the Old Testament going to happen? or should it happen? or could it happen? or might it happen? There are few clues in the Hebrew text by which to make the choice.

Now let me speak of the arbitrariness of a language system. I maintain that every speaker of English at the moment speaks either of two dialects—Dialect A and Dialect B. In Dialect A, the word "man" refers to both sexes: this is the traditional dialect of English. In Dialect B, the word "man" refers to males only; this is a new dialect that has emerged in the past few decades precisely because women and men have begun to be aware how much one's assumptions are shaped by patterns of language. My point is this: one cannot refer to a dictionary and insist that one meaning is right and the other is wrong. There are two dialects, with different ranges of usage. Further, more and more speakers are shifting from Dialect A to Dialect B.

So the questions regarding Psalm 1 (and, by extension, any Old Testament text) number at least three: (1) Who were the original reciters of Psalm 1 and to what extent did they assume females to be neglected by the masculine language, or contrariwise to be included under the masculine language? (2) Who uses a current translation to recite the psalm and to what degree is there congruence in gender between the original reciters and present-day reciters—indeed, to what extent is the intention of the original reciters binding on present-day reciters? (3) Into what dialect of English shall the psalm be translated?

One might answer these questions as follows. (1) The original reciters of the psalm might well have been men in the Jerusalem temple who assumed that as heads of families they had the privilege and responsibility to take their obligations to Yahweh seriously not only on their own behalf but on behalf of their families. One could well imagine that few if any females recited the psalm in its original context. (2) By contrast, there are both sisters and brothers of the faith among present-day reciters, and in this respect the intention of the original reciters is not binding on us. (3) A translation into Dialect A will satisfy some sisters and brothers—in churches, one may often hear the remark from both women and men, "To me 'man' means both sexes." At the other extreme, there are women and men who are angry enough with the gender bias of the Old Testament to accept a translation into Dialect A simply in order to demonstrate how irrelevant and even harmful these voices from the past are. But most folk, I daresay, will welcome a translation into Dialect B, so that women and men can own the psalm equally. This is the reason for the pluralization in the NRSV: "Happy are those who do not follow the advice of the wicked . . . . They are like trees planted by streams of water . . . ." This is the reason for other such efforts in translating the Psalms and similar material into language that is not gender-specific for human beings.

Sometimes the right solution is not so clear. This is particularly the case in the laws. Exod. 21:22 (RSV) says, "When men strive together, and hurt a woman with child, so that there is a miscarriage . . . ." Is the NRSV justified in translating, "When people who are fighting injure a pregnant woman so that there is a miscarriage . . . ."? Would this law have been invoked in Israel if two women were brawling and a third, pregnant woman was hurt? I doubt it, but there is really no way to know.

Masculine Bias in Various Modes of Expression in Hebrew to Refer to God

If we turn now to deal with modes of expression to refer to God, we are dealing with a different though related matter. Human beings are both female and male, and it is appropriate therefore that our discourse about human beings signal that fact; but, as I pointed out in Chapter 1, inasmuch as no one has ever seen God (1 John 4:12), all language that refers to God is metaphorical. God has no sexual parts (compare Deut. 4:16). On the other hand, one cannot in English use neuter pronouns like "it" for God—not if the metaphor of covenant is central, because a covenant implies that each party is personal and is under obligation.

Given the origin of the metaphor of covenant in the political institution of suzerain with vassal (see Chapter 2), it was almost inevitable that the vast majority of the metaphors for God in the Old Testament would be masculine: "lord," "king," "judge," "father," "shepherd." Indeed, many of these metaphors are carried over into the New Testament; one notes particularly the use of "Father" in the Lord's Prayer, and in Jesus' general use of that metaphor for God. And one may add that the masculine metaphors for God are indirectly but powerfully reinforced in the New Testament by the male identity of Jesus. Yet, in passing, it is noteworthy that at least once Jesus is remembered as having compared himself to a hen (Matt. 23:37; Luke 13:34).

To return to the Old Testament: scholars are now generally agreed that the name of God in the Old Testament, "Yahweh," was originally a masculine verb meaning "he brings into existence, he creates."[51] The Old Testament in Hebrew consistently refers to God with masculine pronouns and verbs, a practice carried over into English translations in the use of masculine pronouns like "he" to refer to God.

Israel had had experience with goddesses. The Canaanites, among whom the Israelites lived, had goddesses as well as gods; these goddesses were largely fertility deities, and, as we have already seen (Chapter 9), the Old Testament turned its back on the goddess option. There is not even a specific word for "goddess" in Hebrew: the English word "goddess" in 1 Kings 11:5, 33 simply translates the ordinary word for "god" in Hebrew.

On the other hand, theologians have always recognized that God cannot be visualized as exclusively male. To take only a single example, the Lutheran theologian Johann Arndt, in his work *True Christianity* (1606), describes God this way: "In his word God addresses us in more friendly a fashion than the fashion by which any father, any mother can address her crying children. . . . As a mother surrounds her child with love, so the goodness of the Lord surrounds us."[52]

Yet few questions were raised about the matter until recently, and most Christians, both women and men, have been content in referring to God as "he."

But it has become clear that, though it is a metaphor, the masculine identity of God works profoundly on our sensibilities. I cite two examples. Judith Plaskow, a professor of religious studies, notes that a student of hers (in an "Introduction to Religion" class at Wichita State University) reported that when she asked her boss why there were no female executives in the company she worked for, he replied, "Because God is a man."[53] And the front-page headline in the *New York Post* for June 17, 1991, referring to a homily on the subject of feminism preached the previous day (Father's Day) by Cardinal John O'Connor of New York, repeated the same words: "God is a Man."[54]

If, however, God is not sexually defined in the same way male human beings are, then it should certainly be possible to use female images to refer to God and to describe God, difficult though it may be for many people to accept the idea. It is important to realize that, in spite of the male bias in Israelite society and in the Hebrew language, there are occasional passages in the Old Testament that do just that. Let us look at a few.

The first is precisely Gen. 1:27, a verse we have already examined. If, according to this verse, God created male and female human beings in parity, then at the same time the pattern of parallelism in the verse suggests that the image of God is reflected in both male and female.

In the course of the old poem found in Deuteronomy 32, God is referred to as "the Rock" (the grammatical gender of this noun is masculine); though the metaphor is impersonal, v. 4 makes it personal, so that the pronoun references in English must be "his" ("his work," "his ways"), and the reference to God as "the Rock" recurs in v. 15. Then in v. 18 comes a surprise; one reads, "You [Israel] were unmindful of the Rock that bore you; you forgot the God who gave you birth." Here, though the verbs are grammatically masculine to match "the

Rock," the metaphors are specifically female ones, "bore," "gave you birth"; indeed, the latter in Hebrew is literally "was in birth-pangs with you."

Hos. 11:1-4 appears to offer a picture of God's maternal care for Israel: in
the NRSV, God teaches the infant Israel to walk (v. 3) and feeds him (v. 4)—
but the Hebrew text is difficult and to some degree uncertain, and the linguistic evidence may not support such a conclusion.[55] Hos. 13:8 offers a
comparison of God to a she-bear, though it is an angry she-bear robbed of
her cubs!

However, just as Isaiah 40–66 offers many texts that speak positively of
women, so at the same time there are in these chapters several passages that
offer female images for God. Thus, in Isa. 42:14, the prophet uses the simile of
birth-pangs for God. God speaks: "For a long time I have held my peace, I
have kept still and restrained myself; now I will cry out like a woman in labor,
I will gasp and pant." Again, in 45:9-10, God is compared successively to a
potter, to a father, and to a mother. In 49:14-15 and 66:13, God is again compared to a mother; the former passage reads, "But Zion said, 'The Lord has
forsaken me, my Lord has forgotten me.' Can a woman forget her nursing
child, or show no compassion for the child of her womb? Even these may forget, yet I will not forget you."[56]

It may also be pointed out that the female personification of Wisdom as an
expression of God from the foundation of the world (Prov. 8:22-31: see Chapter 11) mitigates at least to some degree the overwhelming domination of the
deity by masculine imagery.

I pointed out at the beginning of this chapter that men gained dominance
over women in the monarchical period in the context of urbanization and
the elaboration of male-dominated royal, military, and religious institutions.
One wonders, then, whether both the increased number of passages in Jeremiah and particularly in Isaiah 40–66 that touch on women's concerns and
that use feminine similes and metaphors for God is not at least indirectly a
reflection of the collapse of the monarchy and of the army of Judah and the
destruction of the Temple. One could argue that metaphors for God were
sought in the one institution that survived, namely the family.[57]

What may we conclude with regard to the preponderance of male imagery
for God in the Old Testament? Let me offer three general considerations. My
first is a reinforcement of an observation I have already made: given the fact
that monarchs in the ancient Near East were almost without exception male,
then if the central metaphor of the Old Testament was to be the covenant, a
metaphor based on the political model of suzerainty treaties, it was inevitable
that male imagery for God would be dominant. If God is understood to have
covenanted with Israel, to have held Israel responsible for adhering to the

stipulations of the covenant, to have taken Israel to court for any breach of the covenant, and to bring about a remedy when appropriate, then, given the social structures of the time, masculine images for God, those of lord and king, were inevitable.

On the other hand—and this is my second consideration—the Old Testament at the same time offers occasional feminine images of God, images scattered across many centuries of texts. God was in birth pangs to bring Israel into existence (Deut. 32:18) and will pant like a woman in labor to bring forth new possibilities (Isa. 42:14-15); it is hardly conceivable that a mother could ever forget her child, but even if that were possible, God will never forget Israel (Isa. 49:14-15). Jesus, as we have seen, was remembered as telling a story about a housewife looking for a lost coin as well as a story about a shepherd looking for a lost sheep. More profoundly, if women have been victimized by men, then Jesus' own willingness himself to be a victim shapes profoundly the Christian understanding of the character of God, an understanding that Christians can then seek within the texts of the Old Testament.

My third consideration is that we who are shaped by our experience with human beings, who are either male or female, find it extraordinarily difficult to form an image of a personal God who is other than *either* male *or* female. That difficulty is powerfully reinforced in an English translation by the linguistic difficulty that we have no pronoun by which to refer to God that is not either "he" or "she." I sometimes think that our task might be easier (not much easier, but a little easier) if we spoke and wrote Armenian, or Turkish, or Hungarian, or some other language that has third-person singular pronouns that are not gender-specific. These languages have a "he/she" pronoun. It is important to think about how a translation might be made from the Old Testament into English that avoids gender-specific pronouns for God. People sometimes try, simply by repeating "God," but what results is often awkward in the extreme (Gen. 2:2: "And on the seventh day God finished the work that God had done, and God rested on the seventh day from all the work that God had done"). A language can hardly dispense with pronouns, and it does not simply innovate new pronouns easily. I myself do not know how to solve this problem, but whether an appropriate answer is forthcoming or not, it is certainly crucial to raise the question.

We need specific images of God; still, as we noted in our examination of Ezek. 1:28 in Chapter 1, every image of God is four steps removed from reality. Inasmuch as the Old Testament offers scattered images of women who are not subordinate to men, and scattered female images of God, we may muster the courage to gather images of God that no longer reinforce a male bias.

Notes

1. There is an extended literature on the questions raised in this chapter. Beyond the works cited here, one should note that a useful survey for the general reader is Cullen Murphy, "Women and the Bible," *Atlantic* 272, no. 2 (August 1993), 39–64.

2. Carol L. Meyers, *Discovering Eve: Ancient Israelite Women in Context* (New York and Oxford: Oxford University, 1988); and see conveniently her "Everyday Life: Women in the Period of the Hebrew Bible," *Women's Bible Commentary,* 244–51.

3. Meyers, *Eve,* 64–71; and see in more detail her "The Roots of Restriction: Women in Early Israel," *Biblical Archeologist* 41 (1978), 91–102.

4. Meyers, *Eve,* 47–121.

5. *Ibid.,* 122–38.

6. See the illustration in *IDB* 3:380b.

7. Meyers, *Eve,* 139–64.

8. *Ibid.,* 172.

9. *Id.,* 172–73. The citation is from Nancy Datan, "Ecological Antecedents and Sex-Role Consequences in Traditional and Modern Israeli Subcultures," in Alice Schlegel (ed.), *Sexual Stratification: A Cross-Cultural View* (New York: Columbia University, 1977), 330.

10. Meyers, *Eve,* 174.

11. Walter Brueggemann, *The Land* (Philadelphia: Fortress Press, 1977), 192–93.

12. Meyers, *Eve,* 185–86.

13. These fiscal measures are discussed in Bright, *History of Israel,* 221–23.

14. Meyers, *Eve,* 189–96.

15. C. H. J. de Geus, "City of Women, Women's Places in the Ancient Israel Cities," in John A. Emerton (ed.), *Congress Volume, Paris, 1992* (VTSup; Leiden: Brill, forthcoming).

16. William L. Holladay, *Jeremiah 1* (Hermeneia; Philadelphia: Fortress Press, 1986), 170.

17. Delbert R. Hillers, *Treaty-Curses and the Old Testament Prophets* (Biblica et Orientalia 16; Rome: Pontifical Biblical Institute, 1964), 58.

18. Otto J. Baab, "Fatherless," *IDB* 2:245–46.

19. Childs, *Exodus,* 469.

20. Meyers, *Eve,* 170–71.

21. J. Philip Hyatt, *Exodus* (The New Century Bible Commentary; Grand Rapids, Mich.: Eerdmans, 1971), 215–16.

22. Mayes, *Deuteronomy,* 355.

23. For a careful assessment of the matter, see Anthony Phillips, "Some Aspects of Family Law in Pre-Exilic Israel," *Vetus Testamentum* 23 (1973), 349–61.

24. See Phyllis Trible, *Texts of Terror: Literary-Feminist Readings of Biblical Narratives* (Philadelphia: Fortress Press, 1984).

25. Shalom M. Paul, *Amos* (Hermeneia; Minneapolis: Fortress Press, 1991), 81–83.

26. Hans Wildberger, *Jesaja 28–39* (BKAT 10; Neukirchen: Neukirchener, 1972–82), 1265–67.

27. See the discussion in Hans Wildberger, *Isaiah 1–12* (Minneapolis: Fortress Press, 1991), 137–39.

28. Hillers, *Treaty-Curses.*

29. Holladay, *Jeremiah 1,* 148–49.

30. *The Book of J, Translated from the Hebrew by David Rosenberg, Interpreted by Harold Bloom* (New York: Grove Weidenfield, 1990), 24–35.

31. Gottfried Quell, "Struktur und Sinn des Psalms 131," in Fritz Maass (ed.), *Das Ferne und Nahe Wort: Festschrift Leonard Rost* (BZAW 105; Berlin: Töpelmann, 1967), 173–85.

32. Edward F. Campbell, Jr., *Ruth* (AB 7; Garden City, NY: Doubleday, 1975), 21–23, offers two suggestions for the origin of the book of Ruth, either (male) Levites or wise women.

33. Hans Bardtke, *Das Buch Esther* (KAT; Gütersloh: Mohn, 1963), 249-50; see also Carey A. Moore, *Esther* (AB 7B; Garden City, NY: Doubleday, 1971), LI.

34. Phyllis Trible, *God and the Rhetoric of Sexuality* (Philadelphia: Fortress Press, 1978), 15–18.

35. Claus Westermann, *Genesis 1–11* (Minneapolis: Augsburg, 1984), 232.

36. Trible, *God and the Rhetoric of Sexuality,* 102.

37. *Ibid.,* 110; Susan Niditch, "Genesis," *Women's Bible Commentary,* 13.

38. *Sic;* a better rendering would be "bear."

39. Meyers, *Eve,* 118; for the whole analysis, see 95–121.

40. *Ibid.,* 116.

41. For this interpretation, see Holladay, *Jeremiah 2,* 195.

42. Most helpful here is Roland E. Murphy, *The Song of Songs* (Hermeneia; Minneapolis: Fortress Press, 1990), 3–105.

43. Trible, *God and the Rhetoric of Sexuality,* 144–65.

44. *Ibid.,* 158 and note 17 there.

45. Hans Dieter Betz, *Galatians* (Hermeneia; Philadelphia: Fortress Press, 1979), 181–85.

46. Daniel J. Harrington, "The Gospel According to Mark," *New Jerome,* 617.

47. John P. Meier, *A Marginal Jew, Rethinking the Historical Jesus,* I (New York: Doubleday, 1991), 132.

48. Elizabeth Schüssler Fiorenza, *In Memory of Her, A Feminist Theological Reconstruction of Christian Origins* (New York: Crossroad, 1983), esp. 48–53.

49. There is a large bibliography on the topic. For a short older survey, see Robin Scroggs, "Woman in the NT," *IDBSup* 966–68; for a thorough recent treatment from a feminist perspective, see Elizabeth Schüssler Fiorenza, *In Memory of Her;* for her discussion of Junia, see there 47–48.

50. Carolyn Osiek, "Galatians," *Women's Bible Commentary,* 335.

51. David Noel Freedman, "YHWH," *TDOT* 5:513–16.

52. Johann Arndt, *True Christianity,* 2.42; I have consulted *Vier Bücher von wahren Christenthume* (Nurnberg: Heinrich Haubenstricker, 1826), 468. For this quotation see William L. Holladay, *The Psalms through Three Thousand Years* (Minneapolis: Fortress Press, 1993), 339.

53. Judith Plaskow, *Standing Again at Sinai, Judaism from a Feminist Perspective* (San Francisco: Harper & Row, 1990), 156, n. 10.

54. Holladay, *Psalms through Three Thousand Years,* 339.

55. Francis Andersen and David Noel Freedman, *Hosea* (AB 24; Garden City, NY: Doubleday, 1980), 579–83.

56. Susan Ackerman, "Isaiah," *Women's Bible Commentary,* 167–68.

57. *Ibid.,* 168: the suggestion is that of Leah Bronner.

13

Face to Face with God: Worship[1]

~

It is taken for granted in both the Old Testament and the New that we have an obligation to worship God, both as individuals and as communities of the covenant. Religious faith assumes the practice of prayer; that is, faith implies more than simply a set of beliefs about God or the acting out of ethical principles. Faith implies an ongoing interactive relationship between believers and God. The Bible assumes, moreover, that members of its covenantal communities will relate to God not only in spontaneous and immediate prayer in the context of the needs and moods of the moment but also in more coherent and regular worship, and it is that worship that I stress in the present chapter.

I shall not undertake to offer any theological justification for worship. Having heard God, we are moved to respond to God. God does not "need" our worship in the way human beings need encouragement from each other. But worship is normal in just the way that it is normal for lovers, having sworn loyalty to each other, to affirm and to refresh their love for each other by continuing to say "I love you." Furthermore, though God does not "need" worship, we stand in need of worshiping God to keep fresh our awareness of God. Indeed, if we go back to the covenant as our central metaphor, and if the biblical understanding of covenant is based on the model of suzerainty treaties (see Chapter 2), then we realize that the covenant people cannot keep themselves from responding directly to God any more than a vassal can hold himself aloof from his suzerain. The vassal responds regularly, so that suzerain and vassal have intimate acquaintance with each other, and so that the vassal continues to be alert to the will of the suzerain.

The Old Testament offers many indications of how the Israelites carried out their worship. Central to that worship was the offering of sacrifices, particularly animal sacrifices. In Chapter 3, we examined the laws regulating such sacrifices and concluded that, for Christians, these laws are irrelevant except as pointers to our obligation to give our entire selves to God. We also took note in that chapter of the commandment to keep the sabbath, and we saw how that commandment has been transmuted by most Christians into the honoring of Sunday.

But there is one great body of material coming out of Israelite worship that Christians have taken over without modification as vehicles for their own worship, a poetic collection of hymns and prayers that we know as the book of Psalms. In this chapter, we shall examine the Psalms and ponder the extent to which we can come face to face with God through them.[2]

Through most of Jewish and Christian history, the assumption has been that King David wrote all the Psalms. Indeed, many of the *superscriptions* (notes at the beginning of most psalms that are printed in italics in many recent translations), though not all of them, reinforce that assumption. Thus, the superscription of Psalm 3 attributes that psalm to David, as do several dozen similar superscriptions thereafter. On the other hand, there are psalms that are attributed to writers about whom we know little or nothing—the Korahites (see, for example, Psalm 42) or Asaph (see, for example, Psalm 50). But a close analysis of the style and content of the individual one hundred fifty psalms suggests that the psalms were collected from a whole variety of authors, most of whom are of necessity anonymous, over a very long period of time.

Scholars do find it plausible to assume that a few of the psalms carrying an attribution to David may indeed have been written by him. One example is Psalm 18, a close variant of which is found also in 2 Samuel 22: v. 1, which specifically states that David "spoke the words of this song." But the superscription "of David" is hardly to be trusted for many of the psalms that carry it. For example, Psalm 29 carries this attribution, but in that psalm Yahweh is described in terms that had been used for the fertility god Baal in Canaanite mythical material, and indeed the poetic patterns of the psalm strongly suggest that someone took an archaic hymn to Baal and simply substituted the name "Yahweh" for "Baal." If this is the case, then the form of this psalm with "Baal" is likely to have been sung long before David's day. On the other hand, Psalm 51, which likewise carries the superscription "of David," ends with a plea to God to rebuild the walls of Jerusalem (v. 18); this psalm therefore is likely to have originated in the early postexilic period, four centuries after David's time.

One might say it this way: given the seeming variety of sources for the Psalms, the book of Psalms appears to owe its origin to King David in much the way a modern Lutheran hymnal owes its origin to Martin Luther: just as without Martin Luther there would be no Lutheran hymnal, so without King David there would have been no book of Psalms. But it is safer not to depend on the wording of the superscriptions for authorship, understanding them instead to mean something like "from the Davidic collection" or the like: they seem to represent late efforts (perhaps in the fourth century B.C. or thereabouts) to establish an origin for various psalms. We shall then take the Psalms as anonymous songs of worship written at various times in Old Testament history in response to various needs, songs that became permanently useful for the Old Testament people.

Variety of Form in the Psalms

One sees variety in the one hundred fifty psalms not only in their origin but also in their format, approach, and content. Thus, sometimes God is addressed in the second person, "you," as in Psalm 5; sometimes, by contrast, God is referred to in the third person, as in Psalm 1 ("the Lord," vv. 2 and 6). Sometimes there is a shift back and forth between second-person address to God and third-person reference to God, as in Psalm 23, where we find "the Lord" and "he" in vv. 1-3 and 6, but "you" and "your" in vv. 4-5. When God is referred to in the third person, there is variety in the identity of the one who is addressed (or the ones who are addressed), that is, the identity of the "you," the audience: in Pss. 42:5, 11 and 43:5 the psalmist directly addresses his own "soul," that is, his "self," though in those psalms the addresses to the soul alternate with addresses to God (42:1; 43:1-3, 4b). Sometimes the audience is clearly fellow Israelites (Psalm 150), but sometimes it is the elements of the whole created world (Psalm 148). In the unique Psalm 45, a courtier addresses first the king (vv. 1-9) and then the queen (vv. 10-17), evidently on their wedding day.

There is likewise variety in the speaker, in those psalms that give a clue to the speaker. Most often it is "I," and one must discern from the context whether the speaker is the king (Psalm 89), or whether it is someone in the royal circle who is calling God's blessing on the king for long life (Psalm 72) or success in battle (Psalm 20), or whether, by contrast, the speaker is simply a pilgrim from outside Jerusalem (Psalm 84) or someone who is gravely ill (Psalm 88). Occasionally, the speakers are plural, "we" (Psalm 12, see v. 7 there). Sometimes the diction shifts between "we" and "I": Psalm 44 is almost entirely "we," but v. 4 momentarily slips to "I." The tragic song of the exiles in Babylon, Psalm 137, begins in vv. 1-4 with "we" but then shifts to "I" in vv. 5-6.

But the greatest variety in the psalms is what scholars call their "type" or "form." Most of the psalms fall into three main "types" or categories. First there are "hymns" to God that celebrate the wonders of creation (such as Psalm 104) or celebrate the kingship of God over the world (such as Psalm 93), or call upon the elements of creation to praise God (such as Psalm 148).

Then there are "laments" that describe difficult circumstances in the individual life of the speaker, such as illness or persecution or the like, or in the common life of the whole people, such as military defeat, and then call upon God for deliverance. There are "thanksgivings" for the deliverance God has brought to the speaker or to the people as a whole out of such difficult circumstances. Beyond these three categories are other types, like Psalm 45, the wedding song for the king, to which I have just referred, or the long meditation on the law, Psalm 119. This great variety, touching on so many human circumstances, has helped make the Psalms steadily useful to both Jews and Christians through the centuries.

How Do We Hear God in Words to God?

Given the variety of categories of psalms, I shall confine my suggestions in this chapter to the hymns, laments, and thanksgivings among the Psalms. When we pose our question—Do we hear God in these psalms, and if so, how?—we are confronted by a simple but unexpected problem: the words of the psalms originate with speakers who *address* God or who *testify about* God, so how are we to hear God in such material? (It is true, there are words spoken by God in the Psalms, but they are couched as citations within psalms spoken by the worshiper: see for example Ps. 2:6-9, or 81:6-16.) The traditional assumption has been that the Psalms, being part of Scripture, are inspired in the same way as the rest of Scripture is understood to be, or at the very least that the Psalms, the words of various Israelite worshipers, having been collected and used over so many centuries, have proved their validity as trustworthy means for the worship of God. But still, the question needs an answer.

Difficulties in the Psalms of Lament

Are the Psalms trustworthy for Christians? The easy answer is to say yes, but we must take care here. Many of the psalms *are* trustworthy—the hymns, for example; it is always appropriate to praise God, and the hymns are good guides for our praise. Or the thanksgivings: the Letter to the Ephesians reminds us that we are to give "thanks to God the Father at all times and for everything in the name of our Lord Jesus Christ" (Eph. 5:20). But with the laments we encounter trouble—we are made uncomfortable by the expressions of self-righteousness and of hatred for enemies that we frequently find there. For example, Psalm 101 is heavy with self-righteousness: "I will walk with integrity of heart within my house" (v. 2); "no one who practices deceit shall remain in my house" (v. 7). Again and again, the psalmist assumes his innocence, or explicitly affirms it—see 7:3-5; 18:20-24; 26:6. And there are repeated expression of hatred of enemies. Psalm 137, for example, is a poignant lament of those from Jerusalem who have been exiled to Babylon, but its last three verses express terrible hatred, in v. 7 for the Edomites, who took advantage of the desolation of Jerusalem to raid the area (compare Obad. 8-14), and in vv. 8 and 9 for their Babylonian captors, pronouncing felicitations on those who could bash Babylonian babies' brains out: these verses are invariably omitted when Christians recite the psalm, for example in a responsive reading. There is also Psalm 139, a beloved expression of the omniscience and thorough care of God for the worshiper: but vv. 19-22 are usually excised from the psalm when it is recited ("Do I not hate those who hate you, O Lord? . . . I hate them with perfect hatred," vv. 21, 22).

The New Testament set forth a very different spirit. Both Jesus and Paul teach us to bless and pray for our persecutors (Matt. 5:44; Rom. 12:14), and the New Testament reminds us that we all stand under the judgment of God and that all of us are baffling mixtures of good and evil (Matt. 7:11a; Rom. 3:23). Paul tells us in humility to regard others as better than ourselves (Phil. 2:3). How, then, can we turn and recite these psalms? We may be daunted by Jesus' command to love our enemies, but at the same time we are made uncomfortable reciting psalm verses that express hatred for our enemies. I once knew a spiritual director who was so distressed by this problem that he used to say, "The Psalms are sub-Christian. We need a Christian Psalter." If this is so, then on the face of it we cannot dependably hear God's will for our worship in the Psalms. What resources can we marshal in these difficulties?

The Old Testament Understanding of the Undivided Self

I begin by exploring the Old Testament assumptions about the unitary nature of the human being, assumptions that help to explain these expressions of self-righteousness and of hatred of enemies. In Chapter 1, we noted that in Hebrew the word meaning "word" (*dābār*) implies more than a vocable with a meaning—it implies "self-expression in action"; therefore, in the mind of an Israelite, what a person thinks, says, and does is understood to be all of a piece. The human being is viewed as a totality, a combination of inner impulses and outer activity.

This totality is expressed by a key Hebrew term that is hard to translate into English, the term *nepeš* (pronounced "nefesh"). Traditionally, this term has been translated by "soul," but that translation is really misleading—in English, the word "soul" suggests both something ethereal, something in contrast to the body, as when we say, "She doesn't eat enough to keep body and soul to-gether," and at the same time it suggests that essence of a person that is un-derstood to survive death and is involved with God, as in "John Brown's body lies a-mouldering in the grave, but his soul goes marching on." But the He-brew *nepeš* is not in contrast to the body, it is rather expressed by the body; and it is not understood to survive death. Let me cite a few examples of the use of *nepeš* in the Old Testament so that we can gain an impression of its range of meanings.

It refers to the human being in both physical and psychological manifesta-tions. Sometimes it refers to one's cravings: so in Prov. 23:1-2, verses I cited in Chapter 10, the phrase "a lord of *nepeš*" simply means someone with a large appetite. When we read in 1 Sam. 18:1 that the *nepeš* of Jonathan was bound to the *nepeš* of David, and Jonathan loved him as his own *nepeš*, we must infer that the *nepeš* here means the affections of each man that lead to the joining of their destinies. Sometimes the word means one's "will," and it is so trans-lated in the NRSV in Ps. 27:12: "Do not give me up to the *will* of my enemies." In Chapter 5, we pondered the Israelite conception of corporate personality, so we are not surprised that *nepeš* may refer not only to the will, the outlook, and the mood of an individual but also to that of the larger community. In Ps. 33:20 we read, "Our *nepeš* waits for Yahweh; he is our help and shield." Often, the word indicates an individual human life: "those who are seeking after my *nepeš*" (Ps. 35:4 and often) are "seeking after my *life*." Again, "my *nepeš*" may mean little more than "I myself." For example, in Ps. 3:2, one finds the phrase, "many are saying to my *nepeš*," but the NRSV simply translates "many are saying to me." To sum up: the *nepeš* is the total self, a self typified by all the physical and psychological characteristics that make up the self—the cravings, the moods, and the ambitions; it is the identity that makes one self distinctive from other selves; furthermore, that distinctive identity may be that of an individual but may as well be that of a family, a clan, a tribe, or a nation that is perceived to act and react in a distinctive way.

When we read in Ps. 42:1-2, "As a deer longs for flowing streams, so my soul longs for you, O God. My soul thirsts for God, for the living God," it is the psalmist's *nepeš* that longs for God, and we must therefore understand the lines to mean that just as the deer is completely absorbed by her thirst for cool streams, so the psalmist is completely absorbed by his thirst for God: his *nepeš* is totally characterized by that craving. Indeed, the psalmist goes on to address his own *nepeš* in vv. 5 and 11 of that psalm (and in Ps. 43:5, Psalm 43 being originally a continuation of Psalm 42). I have already cited these verses to illus-trate the variety of addressees in the psalms, but we see now how misleading the NRSV is in continuing the traditional translation "soul." By the same token, when we hear the psalmist of Psalm 23 affirm that God restores his *nepeš* (v. 3), we may be misled by the conventional translation "soul": we are not to think that God restores some holy or religious part of him but rather that God restores his mood, his courage, his integrity, all that makes up his total being.

In contrast to this unitive view of the self in the Old Testament, the New Testament assumes that selves are divided, that people act out of mixed motives, that there are cross purposes in the lives of each of us. In Matt. 7:11, a verse I cited in Chapter 4, Jesus takes it for granted that his audience knows they are evil—nevertheless they still know how to give good gifts to their children. The hypocrites, whose pious practices are insincere, are stock characters in Jesus' sayings (see, for example, Matt. 6:1-18; 23:13-36); one thinks particularly of his comparison of hypocrites with tombs whose exterior is whitewashed but which are filled with the bones of the dead and all kinds of filth (Matt. 23:27). Paul, for his part, devotes a half a chapter (Rom. 7:15-25) to the divided self: "For I do not do the good I want, but the evil I do not want is what I do" (v. 19); I shall return to this passage below. The New Testament affirmed long ago the truth of the remark made by the cartoon character Pogo, "We have met the enemy, and it is us."

The Psalmist's Conviction of Innocence

Now let us return to the Old Testament. There are, it is true, a few passages there that admit of the divided self—people who say one thing and do another. One thinks of Isaiah's word, "These people draw near with their mouths and honor me with their lips, while their hearts are far from me" (Isa. 29:13, a passage cited by Jesus, according to Mark 7:6), and Jeremiah's reflection of that word, "You are near in their mouths yet far from their hearts" (Jer. 12:2b)—but such expressions are not common. It follows then that when the psalmist utters a psalm, he (and it must have been almost universally "he" at the beginning—see Chapter 12) takes it for granted, by virtue of uttering the psalm, that he is wholeheartedly on God's side, and he is altogether unaware that he may harbor any opposition to God, any wrongdoing or blemish. The psalmist's conscience is clear, at least while he is uttering the psalm. When he refers to the evil in the world, which, we all agree, is real, then he locates that evil entirely *out there,* external to himself. He is, in short, self-righteous.

There is a further factor to consider, a factor of English translation. The Hebrew word *ṣaddîq* is consistently translated "righteous" in the NRSV, and its opposite, *rāšāʿ,* is consistently translated "wicked," but these words mean "innocent" and "guilty" in the legal sense as much as they mean "righteous" and "wicked" in the moral sense. Indeed, the discussions in Chapters 2 and 3 make clear how consistently the relationship between Yahweh and Israel was conceived in legal terms, so that in matters of conduct and attitude the Old Testament felt most comfortable with legal terminology. Thus, it is helpful not only to read Psalm 1 as a contrast between "righteous" and "wicked" but as a contrast between the "innocent" and the "guilty" as well. In the psalms of lament, in which the psalmist is laying out his grievous situation before God, he assumes not so much his righteousness, an assumption that is problematic for us, as his innocence in his particular situation, and in that situation he is asking God to come to his aid.

The Psalmist's Enemies; Honor and Shame

Let us turn now from the seeming self-righteousness of the psalmist to his expressions of hatred and contempt for enemies. What, we may ask, are his enemies doing to him, if we can believe his complaints? There are, first of all, national enemies. The kings of the earth plot again Yahweh's anointed (that is, the king, Ps. 2:2-3) or against Jerusalem (48:4); the nations do battle with Israel (18:31-42). In these references to the nations there is the sense of the distinctiveness of Israel, given the covenant with Yahweh, and of the consequent vulnerability of Israel to outside forces: if it were not for Yahweh's help, the nation would soon be defeated.

Beyond the national enemies loom personal enemies—again and again we hear of these. "[My eyes] grow weak because of all my foes" (6:7). These enemies are often referred to as "neighbors" (89:41; 101:5) or "friends" (38:11). They plot against him (64:2, 6) and pursue him (7:1); occasionally, it is implied that they want to murder him (7:1-2; 22:20-21). But most often the enemies offend by their talk (10:7; 64:3). They mock him (22:7; 35:21), scorn (89:41) and slander him (101:5); they curse him and utter lies against him (7:14). They are false witnesses (35:11). We must remind ourselves of the Israelite notion that words imply actions as well; words then have power.

The psalmist is baffled: they render him evil for good (38:20). He is devastated; he weeps in the night (6:6), he grows weak and ill (22:14-15) and is in danger of entering Sheol, the realm of the dead (6:4-5; 9:13; 18:4-5). Indeed, he assumes such a close association between illness and the work of enemies (Psalm 6), that one wonders whether the psalmist does not believe that the enemies have put a curse upon him.

One central concern of the psalmist is striking to us when we begin to notice it: he seeks at all costs to avoid being shamed (31:17). His enemies have shamed him (69:8) or seek to shame him (4:2), and he in turn hopes to see his enemies shamed (6:10, 35:4, 26; 83:16-17). It was taken for granted that one should be able to maintain one's name with honor and hold one's head high in the midst of one's neighbors in the public square. And it was not just the psalmists who were concerned to preserve honor and avoid shame: we recall the discussion in Chapter 12 of the narratives of Abimelech, who begged his armor-bearer to kill him rather than to suffer the shame of having been killed by a woman, and of Samson, who was condemned to be shamed by doing women's work, grinding grain. This concern to shame one's enemies lies behind an important phrase in Psalm 23, a phrase we usually ignore: "You prepare a table before me in the presence of my enemies" (v. 5a): the psalmist affirms that God offers him a full meal while his enemies look on hungrily. Though it is a note that seems petty to us in the midst of the sublime faith of the psalmist, it is typical of Israelite mentality. There is an unforgettable narrative in 2 Sam. 10:1-5 of the shame experienced by the ambassadors whom King David sent to the king of the Ammonites: taking them to be spies, the Ammonite king shaved off half the beard of each, cut their garments off at the hips, and sent them away.

And this is the world of the New Testament as well: one thinks of Jesus' teaching about not seeking places of honor at a banquet, so as to avoid the disgrace of having to give way to someone of higher rank (Luke 14:7-11); one thinks of the attempt of the sons of Zebedee to guarantee themselves places of honor in the kingdom of God (Mark 10:35-40). Paul was laughed at for his preaching (compare Acts 17:32; 1 Cor. 1:18-25), yet he was not ashamed of the gospel (Rom. 1:16). It is said that Jesus, "for the sake of the joy that was set before him endured the cross, disregarding [not its pain, as we might think, but] its shame" (Heb. 12:2). The biblical world, then, is a world of people who are concerned for honor and positive recognition, who bristle at the hint of insult, the kind of world we can become acquainted with today through the novel *Prizzi's Honor*,[3] or the film made from it (1985).

We return to the psalmist's hatred for his enemies (one thinks once more of Ps. 139:21-22). What fate does he envisage for them? He prays that they might cease their oppression (7:9) or that God would take away their power to oppress (59:11). He rejoices over the possibility of gloating over the enemies' downfall (52:6-7); he even wishes death on them (55:15; 58:10; 137:9).

We wonder: Did these psalmists really have so many enemies? Were there really all those people out there laughing and plotting against them, or were these psalmists the victims of some kind of paranoid tendency? Let us begin with the king, since, as we have determined, some of the psalms were first uttered by kings. Among the kings' enemies, one thinks first of foreign nations: Israel and Judah, in their special covenant relation with Yahweh, could easily know themselves to be threatened by the policies of neighboring peoples. So

we can understand the testimony of the psalmist that Yahweh held various nations in contempt: "Moab is my washbasin; on Edom I hurl my shoe; over
Philistia I shout in triumph" (60:8; 108:9). But the king had domestic enemies
as well. In Chapter 5, we noted some of the twists and turns in David's career.
He did not lack enemies! One thinks of Absalom's revolt against his father
David (2 Samuel 15), and of the claim of his son Adonijah, when David was
on his deathbed, to be king against his father's wishes (1 Kings 1). Beyond the
king himself, the royal court was filled with intrigue for centuries: to take
only one example, about 842 B.C. the priest Jehoiada, loyal to Yahweh, revolted
against Athaliah, queen of Judah, who was a daughter of King Ahab of Israel
and who was a devotee of the god Baal (2 Kings 8:26; 11:1-20). There would
be countless occasions in which a loyal Yahwist would have been embattled.
Beyond court circles, various prophets suffered opposition: the prophet
Amos was opposed by the priest at Bethel (Amos 7:10-17), Jeremiah was ar-
rested and tried after his temple sermon (Jer. 26:1-19); indeed, Jeremiah mentioned repeated plots of enemies against him (Jer. 11:18—12:6; 15:10, 15-18;
17:18; 18:18-23; 20:7-12). We may suspect power struggles between the country gentry and the court in Jerusalem (compare 2 Kings 23:30 and 34), and
one can assume that there would be factions within towns and villages, where
disputes can fester for years. So we do not lack for circumstances in which the
psalmist's perception of the work of enemies might be expressed. At countless
points, those who sang these psalms would be right: they had enemies. And
beyond court intrigues and village vendettas there were struggles for religious
loyalty: if one considered oneself loyal to Yahweh, one would be aware of
devotees of Baal in the land, devotees who could not be considered as anything but Yahweh's enemies.

Three more matters need to be stressed here. The first is that Israelite culture was almost completely an oral one. In times nearer our own, situations of
social conflict have called forth pamphlet wars, anonymous manifestos on
public walls, and the like—one thinks of the period of the Reformation, or
the period just before the French Revolution. But in pre-exilic Israel the
medium of social conflict was word of mouth. If the psalmist was aware that
people were plotting against him, then those plots would surely be expressed
in spoken words.

The second matter is related to illness: in many of the lament psalms that
are preoccupied with enemies, the psalmist describes the symptoms of illness—this is notably the case with Psalm 22. Illness was understood to be
punishment for sin (see, for example, Ps. 38:3-4, 18). Therefore when someone fell ill, though his own conscience might be clear (again those protesta-
tions of innocence), there would be other people who would ask, "What did

he do to deserve this?" (As we saw in Chapter 11, this was the reaction of Job's friends.) To someone who was ill, it must have been maddening to be half-aware of such speculation among people who were part of one's own community. Further, to be ill is by definition to feel particularly helpless and vulnerable; if a person was sleepless with fever, then feverish notions and nightmares would be bound to contribute to that sense of being surrounded by enemies ready to take advantage of one's weakness, particularly when one is concerned to maintain one's honor.

Finally, many of those who recited these psalms with clear conscience and with the sense of being beset by enemies must have been projecting their own unacknowledged faults onto their friends and neighbors. We all know folk who hide their own sense of inadequacy by lashing out against those around them.

Self-righteousness and Hatred of Enemies: Our Own Assumptions

Given all this background, what are Christians to do with these expressions of self-righteousness and hatred of enemies? We begin by affirming that there is indeed evil in the world. In a way, this hardly needs to be said; it is a matter taken for granted in the biblical understanding. But it needs to be said in this context: the psalmist may have been wrong about the location of evil, but he is certainly right about its existence. Much that goes on in this world is opposed to God's will. There are people who really are malevolent. There are social structures that conspire to keep people down. There are impulses within all of us that pull away from God's rule. The existence of evil in our midst is not something we like to be reminded about; we would all rather think of ourselves and of our corner of the world as relatively benevolent. But even though the psalmist may need to be corrected on the question of the location of evil, at least we can benefit from his reminders to us of its reality.

Our First Approach: Identification with Victims

To these problematic psalms, I propose three approaches that supplement each other rather than being mutually exclusive. The first approach is what one might call "sharing the plight of the victims of this world." There are plenty of people in this world who are victims of evil. Doubtless many of those who read this book need to be reminded not only that they participate in structures that victimize, but also that they should be sensitive to the plight of the victims, who might find a voice in these psalms of lament. We must ponder the matter: there are people who may feel shame, who may feel that whatever is wrong in their lives is their own fault, when as a matter of fact they are being victimized by others. For example, a battered woman may find her voice through a psalm like Psalm 41. She is reminded through v. 1 that there are those who care about her fate. She finds the energy to call upon God to be gracious to her (v. 4). She affirms that her batterer and those like him want her dead (v. 5). His promises to reform are empty (v. 6). Her batterer thinks she will not rise to assert herself (v. 8). And the worst of it is that her batterer is one she trusted, one who shared her bread (v. 9). But she has come to the point of knowing that God upholds her in her integrity. A recent newspaper item described the plight of a Vietnamese woman in Boston who was being mistreated by the man she was dating. When a translator finally helped her to get a restraining order, she said, "I felt very ashamed. I still feel maybe it is my fault for what, do not know."[4]

There are (alas) countless other categories of people in our world who are victims—children who are denied an adequate education; ethnic minorities who are discriminated against in our land and others; refugees from political oppression and torture. For all these and more, the psalms of lament may be recited by all of us as a powerful means of identification with those folk who are denied what God wills for them. Paul bids us to weep with those who weep as well as to rejoice with those who rejoice (Rom. 12:15).

Our Second Approach: Perceiving the Demons within Us

The second approach I propose for reading these problematic psalms is what we might call "perceiving the enemies within us," an approach derived from the theological perspectives of the New Testament. If we wish to read these psalms as Christians, it becomes appropriate to recall our discussion of the identity of Jesus' enemies in Chapter 6, namely Satan and the demons. It is they who are his steady enemies, and it was they whom he was called to cast out (Matt. 10:8), so that demon-possessed men and women might be restored to health. Not only do we hear that Satan tempted Jesus in the wilderness, but when Peter protested at Jesus' prediction of his death, Jesus said, "Get behind me, Satan!" (Mark 8:33 and parallels), and when Judas undertook to betray Jesus it is said that Satan entered into him (Luke 22:3). For Jesus and his followers, then, the world is a battleground between God and the angels on the one hand and Satan and the demons on the other.

My proposal, then, is simple: that in our recitation of these psalms we hear the references to enemies as references to Jesus' enemies, namely Satan and the demons, whom God wishes to defeat. This proposal may at first appear bizarre for two contrasting reasons: (1) because it is an imposition on the Old

Testament, whose writers, so far as we know, did not maintain any lively belief in demons at all but instead were referring to flesh-and-blood people, and (2) already suggested in Chapter 6, because it is an imposition on most of those who will read this book, inasmuch as few of these readers will hold a lively belief in the reality of Satan and the demons either. Nevertheless, I would like to pursue the proposal.

Let us bear in mind what we have already established. The psalmist is theologically realistic (one really does witness extensive activity against God in this world) but at the same time he is psychologically naive (he is convinced that he himself takes no part in any such activity). But if we equip ourselves with the realistic psychology of the New Testament, we can put these psalms to work.

We need then to ponder two matters: first, the testimony of the New Testament on the nature and location of evil and good within both the self and the community, and second, what our own stance might be toward the New Testament belief in Satan and the demons.

As we examine the New Testament, we turn first to two texts. The first is Rom. 7:14-25, where Paul is describing the divided self. From our point of view, his vocabulary is awkward, but the experience he describes has become central in the Christian understanding of the self. He refers to the entity within the self that is against God simply as "I" (vv. 15-16), but at the same time it is no longer "I"—rather it is "sin that dwells within me" (vv. 17, 20), enslaving him (vv. 14, 25). This entity is also called "the flesh" (vv. 14, 18), a term that refers not so much, as we might assume, to one's physical nature as to the whole self in its enslavement to sin. On the other hand, he also testifies to the existence of his "inmost self" (v. 22), which he also calls his "mind" (vv. 23, 25); this entity "delights in the law of God"—it is a part of the self that is on God's side. Given the existence of the divided self, he finds that he does not do what he wants to do but instead does what he does not want to do (vv. 15, 20, 21): there is, in fact, warfare going on within him (v. 23). This divided self, which he refers to as "this body of death," renders him wretched (v. 24), and it is not a situation that can be overcome from his own resources—it is overcome only by God's action of rescue through Jesus Christ (v. 25).

The same teacher of the spiritual life to whom I have already referred, who maintained that we need a Christian psalter, taught his students this prayer: "O Lord, all that I have, and the little that I am, I give to you, for I am with you, against myself." To become a Christian then is to invite a civil war to be fought within the self.

The second text is Eph. 6:12, a verse that I cited in Chapter 6. Here I propose it as a key to understanding the enemies in the Psalms. "For our struggle is not against enemies of blood and flesh, but against the rulers, against the authorities, against the cosmic powers of this present darkness, against the spiritual forces of evil in the heavenly places." Ultimately, then, the enemies of God are not specific people but spiritual forces. This passage hints at the vast organization of evil beyond the limits of the self.

Paul uses similar vocabulary elsewhere when he speaks of our being enslaved not to sin but to "the elemental spirits of the world" (Gal. 4:3), "beings that by nature are not gods" (Gal. 4:8). In Rom. 8:38-39, he refers vaguely to various cosmic powers, both good and evil: "For I am convinced that neither death, nor life, nor angels, nor rulers, nor things present, nor things to come, nor powers, nor height, nor depth, nor anything else in all creation, will be able to separate us from the love of God in Christ Jesus our Lord." Whatever the nature of these cosmic powers, God's grace surpasses them all.

Strikingly, the book of Revelation equates the existing Roman empire with the demonic forces of which we have been speaking: even though, as we saw in Chapter 8, God's enemy is called "Babylon" (17:5; 18:2), the reference is clearly to Rome, built on seven hills (17:9). One may begin with that evil that is within the self, but one ends with the institutional organization of evil in the world.

Jesus for his part did not offer any such thoroughgoing description of evil, but the comments he is remembered as making point in the same direction. At times, he seems to imply, as the Psalms do, that some people are good and some are bad ("[God] makes his sun rise on the evil and on the good, and sends rain on the righteous and on the unrighteous," Matt. 5:45); at other times, as we have already noted, he takes it for granted that people are uniformly evil ("if you then, who are evil, know how to give good gifts to your children . . . ," Matt. 7:11). According to Matthew, at the time when Simon confessed Jesus as Messiah and Son of God, Jesus changed Simon's name to Peter, the "rock" on which the church would be built, but then in the very next moment Jesus called him "Satan" for questioning Jesus' destiny to undergo suffering and death (Matt. 16:13-23). Peter, then, could be both the vehicle for God's will and the agent of Satan.

Jesus is remembered as telling a wry story about a demon, expelled from a person, who went through the desert looking for a resting place, but finding none, determined to return and inhabit his former house, that is, the person whom he had possessed; he returned and found it swept and open, so he brought with him seven demons worse than himself, so that the person ended in worse condition than at first (Matt. 12:43-45).

There is no way to draw up a summary of all this: the Christian communities of the first century found various ways to testify to their understanding of what it is within individuals and communities that pulls them toward God, and what it is within individuals and communities that pulls them away from God. In spite of this variety of expression, the voices within the New Testament are keenly aware of the power of evil as well as the power of good within our lives.

When we turn from the New Testament to our own outlook, we find a curious thing. On the one hand, most of us are all too keenly aware of the existence of evil in our world. Our newspapers, radios, and televisions offer a steady catalog of bad news: domestic violence, drug-related murders in our city streets, the threat of terrorism, ethnic and ideological conflicts across the world. Given this barrage of bad news, it is a brave and optimistic person who can argue for human progress, at least within the span of a single human lifetime. On the other hand, most of us, hearing the narratives of Jesus' casting out of demons, tend to "tune them out," relegating them to the far away and long ago, and, hearing in Ephesians of the cosmic powers of this present darkness, find it equally difficult to relate this testimony to our own lives. It is true that the traditional seven deadly sins of the Middle Ages still claim the attention of a few—occasionally, one hears of a pastor who preaches a series of sermons on them; but by and large we do not apply the labels of pride, covetousness, lust, envy, gluttony, anger, and sloth to the behavior of people we witness inside or outside our churches.

The place to begin, I suggest, is with the question of addiction: in our day we are very much preoccupied with the problem of compulsive dependence on some habit-forming substance or behavior. As we recognize, the central problem for addicts is their inability to end the dependence by willpower alone. This is the whole effectiveness of twelve-step programs: the affirmation that the potential to give in to one's addiction is permanent, the need for a community of understanding people with whom to be honest in one's struggle against the addiction, the confession of one's need for a higher power. Here is a link with the New Testament belief in demons: the conviction that a person is possessed by a demon is the conviction that the person is "not himself," is "not herself," is not in control, manifesting instead a destructive personality pattern. Drug addicts have been known to say that "there is a monkey on my back," and that monkey, of course, is not benign but malign. In a recent interview, a recovered alcoholic who is an Episcopal priest stated, "Addiction is a hole in the soul. Addicts are the walking dead. My alcoholism was sick, depraved, like being possessed by the devil. I know what demon possession means." Again, "recovering from alcohol addition . . . is a spiritual journey, learning to worship the right God and not one in a bottle."[5]

I am not insisting here on the real existence of demons (however one defines "real") but simply that discourse about demons may be pointing to experiences that are central to our own lives. In Chapter 1, we examined the metaphoric nature of religious language; in Chapter 2, we analyzed covenant as a metaphor. Similarly, demons may be understood as a metaphor for the destructive personality patterns in our lives. When we pray to God that the demons that possess us be expelled from our lives, we can always say "the demons, *so to say.*" I suggest that we not be too fascinated by the power of Satan and the demons, that we maintain a sense of humor and irony, but take the struggle against them seriously. The tone adopted by C. S. Lewis in his book *The Screwtape Letters,*[6] the purported letters of a senior devil to a junior one, is exactly what I have in mind.

We can enlarge the metaphor of demons to encompass destructive patterns beyond what we understand to be addictions in the narrower sense: we can include our patterns of verbal abuse to those around us, and patterns of neglect within families; we can include culturally shaped patterns of sexism and racism, institutionally shaped patterns of economic exploitation, juridically sanctioned practices of torture, and the drives that lead to militarism. These too inhibit the will of folk who desire to do the will of God; these too can be seen as expressions of "the cosmic powers of this present darkness."

Let us now return to the psalms that speak of enemies and read Psalm 139 with the approach I propose. The psalmist expresses his wonder that God knows him through and through; the psalm therefore explores the life of the psalmist from God's point of view—not only the psalmist's actions of sitting and standing but even of his thoughts before he puts them into words (vv. 2-3). There is no realm into which the psalmist can escape from God, for God is everywhere (vv. 7-12). He expresses his awe that God has cared for him from the time even before his birth (vv. 13-16). This introspection appears to come to a sudden end with vv. 19-22, verses that, as we have noted, are usually omitted from our recitation of the psalm. But suppose we continue the introspection. Suppose we understand the enemies, called here "the wicked," "the bloodthirsty," "those who speak [of God] maliciously," "those who hate and rise up against [God]," to be the demonic forces in our personalities: what then? Suppose we take these verses to be an occasion to affirm our stand with God against everything within us that would tear down God's work: against the impulse to get ahead of a troublesome driver on the highway, against the impulse to low self-esteem that leads us to say, "I'm just a housewife," against the impulse to tell an ethnic joke that betrays our distancing ourselves from other human beings. With this approach, the troublesome verses are not only integrated into the psalm, they become the climax of the psalm, leading to the closing verse, "See if there is any wicked way in me, and lead me in the way everlasting."

Psalms that deal with national enemies can be dealt with in a similar fashion. The first six verses of Psalm 137 voice the sad homesickness of Jews from Jerusalem as they find themselves exiled in Babylon; but in the last three verses of the psalm they express their hatred of the Edomites, who took advantage of the fall of Jerusalem to raid and harry, and of the Babylonians themselves, who are the cause of their present humiliation.

Is there any way present-day Christians can use this psalm, which carries all the specificities of the Jewish circumstance of 580 B.C.? This psalm, unlike Psalm 139, does not deal with the inner life of the individual. Every individual has an inner life, beyond all historical specificities. But Psalm 137 is organized around its specificities, and if we concentrate on them the psalm will be unusable to us. On the other hand, if we understand the Christian Church to be covenanted with God in such a way that the covenantal perspectives of the Old Testament apply to the Church (see Chapters 5 and 9), then the question comes up again, as it did in the discussion at the end of Chapter 9: Is the metaphor of exile appropriate to the Church? My answer in Chapter 9 suggested that "Babylon" could serve as a symbol of the present-day secular nation-state; now I should like to press the matter in a different direction and suggest that "Babylon" is a symbol of organized, demonic evil. If the Church is exiled by the kingdom of evil from its former state, then where should we locate that former state?

Tastes and judgments will differ, but let me suggest, as a possibility for discussion, the description of the early Church in Acts 2:43-47. That description is no doubt idealized to some degree, but it gives us a point of departure. "Awe came upon everyone, because many wonders and signs were being done by the apostles. All who believed were together and had all things in common; they would sell their possessions and goods and distribute the proceeds to all, as any had need. Day by day, as they spent much time together in the temple, they broke bread at home and ate their food with glad and generous hearts, praising God and having the goodwill of all the people. And day by day the Lord added to their number those who were being saved."

When we think of our own congregations, where wonders and signs may be few, where it is hard to imagine how we might hold all possessions in common, where glad and generous hearts are often missing, where the Lord may be adding to our number a less-than-gratifying number of those who are being saved, it might become plausible to see ourselves in exile from a former glorious state. It must be said, however, that the contrast between then and now may not be cogent for all of us: there may be many folk in our congregations who see no reason at all to weep that our common life does not conform to the description in Acts 2. But let us persevere: it may be that we have had little idea how far into exile we have traveled, it may be that we need to be reminded by this psalm to weep for what we have lost, it may be that this psalm can stretch us into regaining the communal memory of what our former Jerusalem was like—and, one may add, what our future Jerusalem will be like (compare Revelation 21).

Now let us return to the mention of Babylon in vv. 8 and 9 in the psalm. There is a Christian tradition that goes back to the Old Testament itself. As we noticed in Chapter 5, the first six chapters of the book of Daniel use the figure of Nebuchadnezzar to represent the current tyrant of the second century B.C., and as we noticed, "Babylon" was used as a figure for Rome in the Book of Revelation. The Babylonian exile thus becomes a symbol for Christian existence in the "exile" of this world before Christians gain the future Jerusalem in the consummation of all things. A stanza of a hymn written by Peter Abelard in the Middle Ages, translated into English in the nineteenth century, says it well: "Now, in the meanwhile, with hearts raised on high, we for that country must yearn and must sigh, seeking Jerusalem, dear native land, through our long exile on Babylon's strand."[7] We can thus be led to take "Babylon" to represent all the forces in this world that lead us away from God—in short, the forces of Satan and the demons. Can we hear the forces of Satan mocking us as we sing our hymns (v. 3)? Can we, in the words of v. 9, express triumph at the destruction of every demon, no matter how small?

But what might we do with Edom in v. 7? I made the suggestion at the end of Chapter 9 that nations like Edom might be identified as other benevolent institutions in our society. Now, as with Babylon, let us turn the discussion in another direction. Historically, as we have seen, the Edomites took advantage of the Babylonian capture of Jerusalem to harry and raid. In the memory of Israel, Edom had a very special place, because Israel and Edom were remembered as descending from the twins Jacob and Esau respectively (compare Gen. 25:23; 36:1). There is thus a fraternal hatred in the words of v. 7. The question then becomes: Can we identify a spirit intimate in our churches that seeks to destroy them? I have a suggestion: we might see in "Edom" the spirit of complacency, the false sense of security, the sense of business-as-usual that is always our temptation. (One has the impression from Mark 14:36 and parallels that it was a temptation even for Jesus in the Garden of Gethsemane.) In a recent novel, the leading character maintains that "the important thing is *not to act*—to be blameless, to be safe, to be passive and untroubled, not to have to choose."[8] Can v. 7 of the psalm remind us how such a spirit really wants to tear down a church that is obedient to God?

I do not insist that we be too specific in finding fresh identities for the national enemies named in the psalms (Psalms 60:8 and 108:9 come to mind
once more) but simply that there is always the possibility that the Church is
beset by organized spirits that are working against it.[9]

Our Third Approach:
Listening to Jesus Christ Recite the Psalms

The third approach I propose for dealing with these problematic psalms is
what we might call "listening to Jesus Christ's recitation of them." Christian
testimony has been that Jesus Christ was obedient to God (Phil. 2:8), that he
was tested as we are, yet was without sin (Heb. 4:15). From this testimony,
we may conclude that only for Jesus Christ was evil completely external:
from a theological point of view, Jesus Christ is the only person who may
safely pray these psalms that maintain the innocence of the speaker and locate all the evil in enemies. He is remembered as having struggled with external evil, personified as the devil, in the temptations in the wilderness
(Matt. 4:1-11; Luke 4:1-13). I propose, then, that we watch and listen as Jesus
Christ prays the psalms.

The Christian church has understood many psalms this way; this is notably
the case with Psalm 22, given the memory that Jesus was heard to recite the
first verse of that psalm on the cross (Mark 15:34 and parallels)—indeed,
Heb. 2:12 cites Ps. 22:22 as spoken by Jesus. Jesus' feelings, then, of abandon-
ment and pain can be open to us as we hear him reciting this psalm.

Other psalms are open to this approach as well—Psalm 3, for example. As
we recite this psalm, can we hear Jesus' citation of the tempters who say to
him, "There is no help for you in God"? Can we hear his affirmation of faith
in God, his conviction that God will destroy his tempters?

We may observe that this approach is analogous to our paradoxical conclusion in Chapter 10 regarding the dialogues in the book of Job, that God's
word may be manifested in *dialogue with* God. I propose that we understand
the meaning of these laments to God as the word of Jesus Christ to God. We
may observe also that these three approaches are not mutually exclusive. Jesus
himself is remembered as identifying himself with the "little ones," those who
suffer in this world: "Truly I tell you, just as you did it to one of the least of
these who are members of my family, you did it to me" (Matt. 25:40). By this
understanding, then, to hear a psalm of lament spoken by a victim of violence
or abuse is not different from hearing it spoken by Jesus himself, who identified with those who suffer. Thus does the contemporary theologian Rosemary

Radford Ruether use the sections of Psalm 22 in a "Rite of Healing for Wife Battering."[10]

We can use these psalms of lament to stretch our faith and to identify both with our Lord and with the victims of this world.

Hearing God in the Psalms

Given the fact that the Psalms are Israel's words of approach to God rather than God's words to Israel, we may conclude that we do not hear God speaking to us directly in the Psalms, but that, by God's grace, we nevertheless may hear the ideal conversation between ourselves and the God whom we worship, the conversation in which we are invited to participate. It is a conversation that ranges from adoration to lament, from complaint to thanksgiving. John Calvin called the book of Psalms "an anatomy of all the parts of the soul," for, he said, "there is not an emotion of which any one can be conscious that is not here represented as in a mirror. . . . Here the prophets themselves, seeing they are exhibited to us as speaking to God, and laying open all their inmost thoughts and affections, call, or rather draw, each of us to the examination of himself in particular, in order that none of the many infirmities to which we are subject, and of the many vices with which we abound, may remain concealed."[11]

Notes

1. Some of the approaches and suggestions in this chapter have appeared in a different form in various chapters of William L. Holladay, *The Psalms through Three Thousand Years* (Minneapolis: Fortress Press, 1993).

2. The literature on the Psalms is immense. A useful reference for the origin of the Psalms and their life situation is Leopold Sabourin, *The Psalms, Their Origin and Meaning* (New York: Alba House, 1974). On the question of the Christian use of the Psalms, see the work cited in note 1.

3. Richard Condon, *Prizzi's Honor* (New York: Coward, McCann & Geoghegan, 1982).

4. Bella English, *The Boston Globe*, 21 June 1993, 13.

5. Interview with the Rev. Monte Pearse, *The Boston Globe*, 3 September 1991, 28, 31. See further, Gerald G. May, *Addiction and Grace* (San Francisco: Harper & Row, 1988), and Patrick McCormick, *Sin as Addiction* (New York: Paulist, 1989).

6. C. S. Lewis, *The Screwtape Letters* (New York: Macmillan, 1943).

7. *The Hymnal 1982* (New York: The [Episcopal] Church Hymnal Corporation, 1982), no. 623, fourth stanza.

8. Jonathan Dee, *The Liberty Campaign* (Garden City, NY: Doubleday, 1993), 216.

9. For this whole approach, see particularly the three works of Walter Wink, *Naming the Powers: The Language of Power in the New Testament* (Philadelphia: Fortress Press, 1984); *Unmasking the Powers: The Invisible Forces that Determine Human Existence* (Philadelphia: Fortress Press, 1986); *Engaging the Powers: Discernment and Resistance in a World of Domination* (Minneapolis: Fortress Press, 1992).

10. Rosemary Radford Ruether, *Women-Church: Theology and Practice of Feminist Liturgical Communities* (San Francisco: Harper & Row, 1985), 153–59.

11. James Anderson (tr.), *Calvin's Commentaries: Psalms* (Edinburgh: Calvin Translation society, 1843–45; repr. Grand Rapids, Mich.: Eerdmans, 1948–49), 1:xxxvii.

14

Afterword:
Hearing God in the Old Testament

~

We have come a long way. We have crossed and recrossed much of the territory of the Old Testament, searching for ways to hear God that offer theological integrity. It is time to sum up and to offer some general considerations in our enterprise.

Reading Each Testament through the Other

For Christians, the New Testament holds pride of place. In the New Testament, we hear the witnesses of the first century to the tradition about Jesus. Given the centrality of the New Testament, then, questions regarding the necessity and relevance of the Old Testament will not go away. Why should we take time for any material from the time before Jesus? There are many possible answers to this question, but two come immediately to mind. One is that the Old Testament was Scripture for Jesus and therefore brings us into his mental world. The second, more substantial one is that the first-century church interpreted the events they had witnessed to be in continuity with the events set forth in the Old Testament. For such reasons, we take the road the Church at its best has always taken, and we become more and more acquainted with the Old Testament, listening expectantly for God's voice within it.

Again and again in this book we have sought to gain our bearings in the Old Testament by the norms of the New. Again and again we have tried to understand the law, or genealogies, or wisdom by examining what the New Testament has done with such bodies of material. I want to make a contrary suggestion now: there is a sense in which we must read the New Testament by the norms of the Old Testament.

Let me spell out what I have in mind. At several points in this work, I have had occasion to point out contrasts between the Old Testament and the

Greek thought-world—for example, Greek thinking tended to move toward abstractions, toward philosophy, toward science. The New Testament is written in Greek, and as soon as the Christian church began to explain the meaning of the New Testament, those who did the explaining were writing in Greek, or in Latin that was shaped by Greek thinking. As a result, the Church fell into the habit of understanding the New Testament in philosophical terms. And, as I pointed in Chapter 7, all of us in our modes of thinking are children of the Greeks.

For example, the Gospel of John begins with the well-known statement, "In the beginning was the Word." People shaped by the outlook of the Old Testament would see in that statement an understanding of God's steady self-communication throughout the ages (compare Chapter 1); people shaped by Greek philosophy, however, would understand the "Word" to be the rational principle that governs all things,[1] and the latter understanding became more and more the norm for the Church.

The Gospel of John in particular is open to an understanding of God's action in Jesus Christ that is seen apart from the ups and downs of history, and Christians who are particularly nourished by that Gospel tend to understand the good news as something that touches the individual soul in a spiritual realm apart from the world of buying and selling, of wars and rumors of wars, of marrying and giving in marriage. By now my point is clear: the Old Testament offers the specificities of history, of politics and economics, and the fact that it is part of the Bible is a powerful guarantee that the good news of the New Testament will be heard as part of that world of the specificities of the headlines.

But knowing as I do the way in which the Christian gospel, in the early centuries of the Church, was steadily shaped by Hellenistic thinking, I have often wondered what our understanding of the New Testament might be if it had not been so shaped. As a matter of fact, we have at least one clue what it might be: that clue is the hymns of Ephrem (or Ephraem) the Syrian.

Ephrem was born about 306 in Nisibis (near the present-day city of Al-Qāmishli in northeast Syria); eventually, he was ordained a deacon. In the year 363, the Romans lost a battle with Persia and Ephrem was forced to move west to Edessa (the present-day Urfa in southeastern Turkey). He died there in 373 while nursing victims of the plague. Edessa was the earliest center of Syriac-speaking Christianity, and Syriac was the language Ephrem used. It was a dialect of Aramaic and thus a sister-language to Hebrew. Though he did not write in Greek, Christian leaders who did write in Greek or Latin acknowledged his poetic gifts, and Ephrem is honored as saint in both the Eastern and Western Churches.

Ephrem's hymns are heavy with allusions to the Old Testament. His *First Hymn on the Nativity*, which contains ninety-nine verses, is a virtual catalog of Old Testament narratives. For example, since Jesus was a descendant of David, v. 13 reads, "Ruth lay down with Boaz because she saw hidden in him the medicine of life; today her vow is fulfilled since from her seed arose the Giver of all life." And v. 27 is a recollection of Exod. 7:12: "Aaron anticipated Him—he who saw that if his staff swallowed reptiles, His cross would swallow the Reptile that swallowed Adam and Eve."[2]

Ephrem sees the taking of the Eucharistic (communion) elements as the reversal of the Old Testament theme of death: "Today let Eve rejoice in Sheol, for behold the Son of her daughter as the Medicine of Life came down to save the mother of His mother."[3] And one more image of the Eucharist: "Your bread killed insatiable death which had made us its bread. Your cup put an end to death which gulped us down. Lord, we have eaten and drunk you, not to exhaust you, but to have life in you."[4]

Ephrem, then, in his proclamation of the New Testament gospel, not only draws on the material of the Old Testament but employs the kind of imagery and specificity which is so typical of the Old Testament. In short, he reads the New Testament through the Old. And that is as necessary, I maintain, as to read the Old Testament through the New.[5]

Ignoring the Variety within the Old Testament, and Taking Account of It

For centuries, Christians have read the Old Testament flatly, guided by the selectivity of church tradition to make sense of the material, most notably hearing in it anticipations of the New Testament. But the Old Testament has always offered more material than could be compassed under the shelter of New Testament anticipations, so that Protestants, in particular, have been moved to read the Old Testament from cover to cover in the conviction that God's word would come clear in this total reading. These readers took in everything that came along, trusting the Holy Spirit to guide their understanding. In this way, the material of the Old Testament was understood to do its work on its readers directly. These readers would often be aware of the variety within the material, but all of it was understood to offer God's communication equally.

By contrast, this present book, reflecting scholarly efforts of the past century or two, has underlined the variety within the Old Testament. There is first of all the variety of ways in which God is presented. One finds narratives in which God is the only actor (Genesis 1), narratives in which God is a major actor alongside human beings, and occasional narratives in which God plays no part at all (Esther). One finds God's instructions to Moses, or to Joshua, and there are whole chapters of laws understood as the direct utterances of God; there are oracles delivered by the prophets, again understood as the direct utterances of God. But one also finds words directed by human beings *to* God (Psalms). Such variety immediately raises questions about how we are to hear God within it.

Beyond such obvious variety, the present work has indicated still more variety by setting forth the historical contexts in which specific material took shape, historical contexts spread across a thousand years of the experience of the covenant people. Thus, the optimism of the decades of David's monarchy called forth a different sort of material than did the desolation of the decades of Babylonian exile.

In the course of this exploration, I have encouraged readers to bring to the material of the Old Testament the same kind of sensitivity they would to any other great literature. For example, we notice from time to time the existence of irony. It is ironic that Jeremiah should understand God to level the curse of warriors turned to women upon the soldiers of his own covenant people (Jer. 30:5-7). It is ironic that the prophet Jonah should be portrayed as more concerned about a bush that had given him shade from the sun than he was about the fate of innocent children of the city of Nineveh, which he had hoped to see destroyed (Jon. 4:10-11).

I have likewise offered suggestions about how oral tradition is shaped and conserved, given the fact that much of the Old Testament evidently began as oral tradition. I have suggested how many of the Old Testament books consist of original layers that were expanded by later additions in subsequent centuries. I have set forth some cultural assumptions held by the Old Testament people that are not necessarily self-evident to current readers, such as that of corporate personality (see Chapter 5) and matters of honor and shame (see Chapter 13).

Christians who hear these approaches typically respond in either of two contrary ways. One response, a positive one, is that these considerations can help to make the material "come alive." The other response, a negative one, is a rejection of the whole enterprise, a rejection that reflects the fear that the more one views the material in the Old Testament as a human work, the less one will hear of God in it. I trust that my suggestion in Chapter 1, that we see Scripture as both fully human and at the same time as material in which God has been heard to speak—an approach of both/and rather than of either/or— will help to overcome that fear. In any event, it has been the steady approach in the chapters of this work.

Scripture Explaining Scripture

I trust also that the approaches developed in this work can encourage the readers to move out into material in the Old Testament that I have not touched on directly. For example, one can read the narrative of Balaam (Numbers 22–24) by the guidance of some of the suggestions in this book. Balak, the Moabite king, is trying to prevent the passage of the Israelites through his kingdom. He hires Balaam, a Mesopotamian diviner, to put a curse on them. Balaam, alas, turns out to have less sensitivity to God than does the female donkey on which he rides. Having learned that lesson, Balaam finds he is unable to curse Israel but only to bless them. Here is narrative mocking the enemy of a sort similar to the narrative in Exodus in which Pharaoh is mocked (compare Chapter 6). We see, then, that the more we read, the more we are able to read with understanding: we are able to use Scripture to explain Scripture.

When Variety Baffles Our Efforts to Hear God, and Some Practical Considerations

There is yet more variety within the Old Testament, variety that brings with it real problems for our discernment of God's will. I refer to passages in which we do seem to understand God's word but which are to be grouped into contrary messages. To take a simple example, the prophetic books offer us both oracles of judgment and oracles of reassuring hope. Presumable, one message is destined for one set of hearers in one set of circumstances and the other for another set of hearers in other circumstances, as we affirmed in Chapter 9; but to which are we to listen? It is all very well to say that the prophets comforted the afflicted and afflicted the comfortable, and therefore that by extension God may do the same for us, but how can we be sure whether we are afflicted or comfortable?

Even more urgently, what are we to do when passages that appear to be meant for us flatly contradict each other? Are we to listen to Proverbs, in which we learn that we can find and embrace wisdom, or to Job and Proverbs, that affirm we cannot (see Chapter 11)? Are we to take as our own what we like, or what we think we need, and leave the rest, or what?

Let us back away from questions about the variety of material and ponder the various modes by which we read the Old Testament, or listen to it. A few folk may start out to read it from beginning to end (see Chapter 1). More, I suspect, may read in it at random or may read a particular selection. Some may read out of curiosity, or to expand their horizons, or may read to reacquaint

themselves with material read years ago. Some may read with urgency, pro-
pelled by a sense of their own needs. Some may read with a commentary or
help of some sort; others on the contrary may read without any help, letting
the words fall where they may. Some may study the material in a group; others may proceed on their own. Some may hear a passage in church, where it
may be the text for the day or one text in a lectionary selection alongside New
Testament texts. All these modes of reading and listening will shape the extent
to which God is heard in the material, and how.

We cannot set any limits to the ways God may be heard: God is God, and
God's communication to us may come in surprising and unexpected ways as
well as in ways sanctioned by our traditions and our learning. Nevertheless,
let me make some unsystematic suggestions of ways God is more likely to be
heard. Let me start with one's reading or hearing of the Old Testament outside the weekly church service. My own conviction is that it is better done in
the context of a group committed to sensitivity to God—a segment of the
church or the like. I say "or the like" because it must be admitted that, in the
matter of Bible study, particularly of the Old Testament, churches sometimes
hinder more than they help. Sometimes lay members or pastors are frightened of the Old Testament, like the pastor whom I mentioned in the Introduction; sometimes they have fixed ideas about the material that work
against one's sensitivity to the hearing of God. In such situations, it is better
to form an ad hoc group of people committed to the process of discernment
as they read the text together. But whether one is in a group sponsored by the
church or alongside it, one would hope that some of the rich resources from
the larger Church, both theological and biblical, might be at hand.

I can think of three reasons why, in Bible reading, I am more likely to hear
God in a group than alone. First, other folk in the group may well be able to
sensitize me to aspects of God's word of which I might be unaware. Each
member of a group brings questions, experiences, and sensitivities that I may
need. The risk, of course, is that the group may include one or more individuals who dominate unhelpfully; how one deals with such folk is an issue in
group dynamics that I fear is beyond the purview of this book. But still, I may
benefit from the resources that others in the group may make available to me.

The second is related: the group can help me overcome my own tendencies
to deceive myself, my tendencies to fight against hearing what God means me
to hear. I have my favorite passages to read; everybody does. But the word God
wishes to speak to me is not always the word I hope to hear or want to hear.
Therefore, I need to hear passages that I do not want to hear, and I need to
hear God's word to me that I do not want to hear. The discipline of a group
helps me away from my own private notions of what God's word to me might be.

The third reason a group is useful is that it can remind me of the reach of the Church's concern across the world. For example, I may not perceive myself to be oppressed or in any need of liberation, but by group study of some Old Testament passage I could well be led to listen to the cry of the oppressed of this world, or to the prayers of those in need of liberation, and thereby deepen an awareness of my own place in God's economy.

Where should we begin? There is nothing wrong with starting with Genesis, and indeed a study of Genesis can bring great rewards, from meditations on creation and sin to hearing the narratives of the covenantal forebears of our faith. Nevertheless, because the Old Testament is a library of books, there is no necessity to begin at the beginning. There is much to be said, for example, for beginning with a book like Amos. It contains only nine chapters, it has few problems involving literary additions, and the meaning of most of it is plain enough. It plunges its readers into questions of social justice and of the nature of God's will for the covenant people that are always appropriate.

The Old Testament readings in the lectionary that is followed by many churches are likewise useful to us in hearing God. One does not hear the whole of the Old Testament in these readings, far from it; but, chosen as they usually are for their appropriateness to corresponding readings from the New Testament, they at least lead one into corners of the Old Testament that one might not necessarily come to on one's own. These readings also help to overcome the trap of staying only with what one likes. Beyond the fact that these readings do not cover the entire Old Testament, however, one encounters another difficulty when trying to hear God in them, and that is that the preacher or homilist rarely does much with the Old Testament reading, usually preferring to stay with one or both New Testament passages.

The text for the sermon may well be an Old Testament text, and the preacher may well unfold the text so that God's word may be heard. Nevertheless, the use of such a text, and the preaching derived from it, cannot be a substitute for earnest, sequential grappling with material from the Old Testament.

None of these practical considerations can solve the riddle of the variety that the Old Testament presents. One can only affirm that God's word can never be specified in the abstract but only be heard and responded to in our specific situations. In our own specific situations, then, God invites us to listen, and as a channel to that process the Old Testament stands ready.

Notes

1. Otto Proksch, "The Word of God in the Old Testament," *TDNT* 4:91-100; Hermann Kleinknecht, "The Logos in the Greek and Hellenistic World," *TDNT* 4:77–91.

2. Kathleen E. McVey (tr.), *Ephrem the Syrian, Hymns* (New York and Mahwah, NJ: Paulist, 1989), 65, 67.

3. *Hymns of the Nativity* 13.2; see McVey, *Ephrem,* 137.

4. Ephrem, *Hymns on Faith,* 10, 18: see Joseph P. Amar, "Perspectives on the Eucharist in Ephrem the Syrian," *Worship* 61/5 (September, 1987), 445.

5. This is also the burden of Brevard S. Childs, *Biblical Theology of the Old and New Testaments, Theological Reflection on the Christian Bible* (Minneapolis: Fortress Press, 1993); see esp. 91–94.

Index of Scripture and Other Early Writings

It is to be noted that this index does not record any references to whole books of the Bible. It is also to be noted that references to partial verses are recorded as the full verses in question: thus "v. 3b" is recorded as "v. 3."

OLD TESTAMENT

APOCRYPHA/DEUTEROCANONICAL BOOKS

NEW TESTAMENT

Index of Authors and
Other Post-biblical Persons

It is to be noted that this index does not include the names of editors or translators.